FOOD • WINE • ROME

FOOD WINE ROME

BY

DAVID DOWNIE

PHOTOGRAPHS BY ALISON HARRIS

A Terroir Guide

THE LITTLE BOOKROOM

Book Design:
Jessica Hische and Andy Evans/Louise Fili Ltd
Map: Adrian Kitzinger

Library of Congress Cataloging-in-Publication Data

Downie, David.
Food wine Rome: a terroir guide / by David Downie;
photographs by Alison Harris.
p. cm.
ISBN 978-1-892145-71-0 (alk. paper)
1. Restaurants—Italy—Rome—Guidebooks.
2. Grocery trade—Italy—Rome—Guidebooks.
3. Wine and wine making—Italy—Rome—Guidebooks.
I. Title.
TX907.5.I82R652 2009
647.9545'632—dc22
2008041454

Published by The Little Bookroom
435 Hudson Street, 3rd Floor
New York, NY 10014
editorial@littlebookroom.com
www.littlebookroom.com

Printed in China.

ACKNOWLEDGEMENTS
The author and photographer would like to thank Shirley Caracciolo for her generous hospitality, and Antonio Paolini for his insight and expertise.

TABLE OF CONTENTS

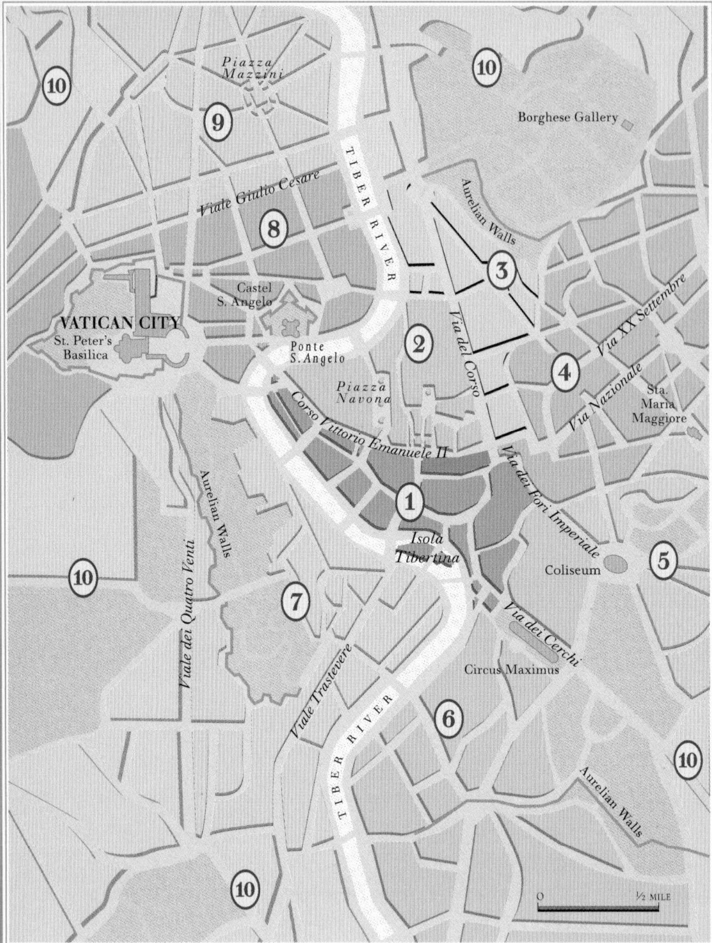

1. Campo de' Fiori, Ghetto, Capitoline/Forum
2. Campo Marzio, Pantheon, Piazza Navona
3. Piazza del Popolo/Pincio, Piazza di Spagna, Fontana di Trevi
4. Monti, Quirinale, Salaria, Sallustiano, Via Veneto
5. Esquilino, Celio, Termini, San Lorenzo, San Giovanni
6. Testaccio, Ostiense, Garbatella
7. Gianicolo, Monteverde, Trastevere
8. Castel Sant'Angelo, Prati, Vaticano
9. Piazza Mazzini, Trionfale
10. Outlying Areas (Appia Antica, Appio and Via Appia Nuova, Salaria-Tagliamento-Nemorense, Monte Mario-Prisciano-Balduina, San Giovanni di Dio-Donna Olimpia, Ponte Milvio, Flaminio, Piazza Bologna)

INTRODUCING ROME, ITS WINES AND FOOD

THE CITY-STATES OF RENAISSANCE ITALY EXPRESSED THEIR INDIVIDUALITY THROUGH constant warfare. Today, each Italian region and province claims culinary supremacy over others and does battle with knife and fork. Rome, capital of Italy, the province of Rome, and the region of Lazio, is no exception. It may very well be the country's supreme food city. Rome certainly believes itself to be, and is at least on par with the other great Italian culinary centers Florence, Genoa, Naples, and Venice. Visitors may complain about the mediocre meals they've eaten, in the company of busloads on Piazza Navona or near the Vatican, but can they really be surprised? Mass tourism brings in its wake food for the itinerant masses. Tens of millions of pilgrims, bureaucrats, and vacationers besiege the Eternal City each year. The lives of Rome's residents run in parallel, with a degree of overlap at shops and eating places in the historic center of town.

This guidebook is unabashedly about eating and drinking the Roman way. The selection of food artisans, specialty food and wine shops, and places to eat and drink, reflects native sensibilities, and reaches beyond the touristed areas into many outlying neighborhoods, where the concentration of culinary delights, and their degree of authenticity, are high.

The reasons Rome ranks among Italy's great food cities are many, but the three most convincing are: first, because Rome is wealthy and has the means to spend on quality; second, because its gastronomic traditions are ancient; and, third, because it has some of the most demanding food consumers in Italy, who will not buy mediocre ingredients or eat mediocre meals for long. Rome is a culinary talent magnet. Many of the best cooks and the best products from all over the country are here.

Admittedly, Rome is not immune to global trends. Agribusiness is gradually taking over the age-old peasant traditions of rural Italy, fundamentally changing the way

food is grown and animals are raised. Unquestionably, supermarkets are more popular than ever, and nowadays seem to be cropping up in every neighborhood in the city; the municipality of Rome puts their current number at nearly 400. Certainly, globalization is profoundly transforming the country and its foodways, and fast food and junk food are also taking hold, especially among adolescents. Roman commentators call junk food adepts *il popolo della pizza*—pizza people (a play on *il popolo della piazza*—the rebellious students of 1968). If only they stuck to good, wholesome pizza, all would be well.

Happily, the combined worldwide phenomena of factory farming, discount hyper-markets, and processed or fast food have not yet killed off Rome's dozens of vibrant, small, often family-run, traditional food and wine specialists, one-of-a-kind retail food shops, *caffès*, trattorias, *hosterias*, *osterias*, pizzerias, and restaurants. In fact, while the onslaught of standardization continues, increasing numbers of Italians, including many belonging to *il popolo della pizza*, are turning back to the traditions of their forebears. There are sound reasons to believe the marked excellence of the Italian eating experience in general and that of Rome in particular will survive into the foreseeable future.

Not only are ice cream, chocolate, pizza, and pasta outstanding in Rome. Take, instead, the case of Rome's unsung fruit and vegetables. No scientific evidence proves Italian produce is superior to that of other nations, but many connoisseurs agree it is. The most important factor keeping up the quality of the country's produce is Italy's millennial attachment to the soil and the traditional diet of the Mediterranean poor, which is rich in fruit, vegetables, and olive oil. The districts around Rome, thanks to the climate, volcanic soil, and proximity to the coast, are among Italy's prime farm areas. Near Rome, market gardeners—called *coltivatori diretti*—grow fabulously good tomatoes, eggplant, zucchini and other squash, and what might just be the best mild globe artichokes anywhere, the specialty of the farm towns Sezze and Ladispoli. The region's lettuces and herbs, both wild and cultivated, are remarkable. Peaches, apricots, pears, and strawberries from Lazio and abutting regions can also be

extraordinarily good, and, in season, arrive in the city's municipal outdoor or covered markets within hours of being picked. To distinguish this perfectly fresh produce, growers sometimes sell it marked with the words *non di frigo*—meaning, it's never been in a refrigerator or cold storage. This is *terroir* at its best.

Like the city's name and history, much of Rome's cooking is familiar to people across the globe. Many classic Italian dishes come from Rome and Lazio, or other adjoining central Italian regions within the orbit of the capital: Campania, Abruzzo, Tuscany, and Umbria. Experts wrangle over where certain dishes were invented and when, but, like it or not, Romans make claims on *bruschetta*, braised artichokes *alla romana*, *fettuccine Alfredo*, *penne all'arrabbiata*, *spaghetti alla carbonara*, *bucatini all'amatriciana*, *spaghetti alla puttanesca*, *stracciatella* (egg-drop soup), *saltimbocca alla romana*, grilled *abbacchio* (suckling lamb), spit-roasted stuffed *porchetta* (suckling pig), *crostata* jam tarts, *tartufo* chocolate ice cream, *tiramisù*, *zabaglione*, and *zuppa inglese*.

The city's food has also been influenced by Rome's Jewish heritage. Over the last 2,000 years, Roman-Jewish food has developed a distinct character, contributing many dishes to the mainstream Roman repertoire: fried artichokes *alla giudia*, sautéed spinach with pine nuts and raisins, sweet-and-sour salt cod, slow-cooked beef pot roast, and Roman-Jewish ricotta cheesecake, to name only a few of several dozen.

In all, the traditional Roman repertoire includes over 200 recipes, making Rome one of the only cities anywhere to have its own long-established, codified cuisine.

ITALIAN TERROIR TERMINOLOGY

Where the French say *terroir* to designate authentic, unadulterated foods and wines tied to a region's soil and seasons, the Italians use several terms. *Tipico* identifies something as coming from a specific area; *prodotti tipici* and *piatti tipici* are what we would call local or regional specialty foods and dishes.

Tipicità is a buzz word among wine lovers, especially those who favor native or heirloom grape varieties (*vitigni autoctoni*) and highly typified, old-fashioned wines made with native yeasts, using large, seasoned oak barrels and cement-lined vats, or stainless steel. The spreading use of selected, high-performance yeasts and new-oak casks results in what Italians call *vini tecnici*—technical wines, the opposite of *terroir* wines.

Genuino means both genuine and authentic, and is often used to describe cooking, wines, and foodways. *Naturale* is a buzz word in the ice cream world, designating ice creams that are handmade from scratch using only fresh, wholesome ingredients (i.e. no concentrates, colorings, artificial flavorings, preservatives, thickeners, emulsifiers, or other industrial or semi-industrial products).

Cucina casalinga means home cooking. Its opposite is *cucina creativa* or *cucina innovativa*, what we would call nouvelle cuisine, *cuisine d'auteur*, or fusion cooking.

NOTA BENE

Business hours and closing days often change seasonally, and sometimes at the whim of owners, particularly when the business is small and family run. Annual vacation closings can slide. What is printed on a business card or posted on a website might not correspond to reality. In Rome, the sense of time may be more elastic than what American or English visitors are used to.

The Internet is still in its infancy among many small businesses in Rome, so do not be surprised if emails go unanswered, and if information on websites is not updated or accurate.

The telephone numbers in Rome and the Rome area are currently changing from six, seven, eight, or nine digits to a standard ten digits. For the time being, all land-line numbers begin with "06," but the number of digits following varies widely. Often, an old telephone number will continue to work for a year or more while a neighborhood is moving to ten digits; many businesses now have two, three, or even four functioning telephone and fax numbers, which will eventually be narrowed to one or two land-line numbers with ten digits.

Many businesses in Rome go by a variety of names and nicknames, and the use of articles associated with these names—Il, Al, Da, Dal, Dar, Der, and others—is not consistent. Romans refer to the celebrated ice cream shop Al Settimo Gelo as Settimo Gelo, dropping the Al, but the business is usually listed under Al Settimo Gelo. Il Pompiere, the famous Ghetto-area restaurant, is often given as Al Pompiere or Dal Pompiere. Ask for Pizzeria Ai Marmi—the official name—and Romans will shrug. That's because locals refer to this cult pizzeria as either "Panattoni" or "L'Obitorio." The first reference is to the name of the family that owns it, the second means "the morgue." The list of such variations on names appears to be endless. The names used in this guidebook are the official names and, where helpful, reference to a variation is duly noted.

PRACTICALITIES

ROME IS BOTH A CITY AND A PROVINCE, AND IS ALSO THE REGIONAL CAPITAL OF LAZIO and the capital of Italy. Lazio comprises five provinces: Frosinone, Latina, Rieti, Roma, and Viterbo. With the exception of wineries, the listings in this guide are for establishments within the city limits of Rome. The Rome municipal area officially has a population of about 2.6 million. The central city has seven hills: the Aventine, Caelian, Capitoline, Esquiline, Palatine, Quirinal, and Viminal (in Italian: Aventino, Celio, Capitolino, Esquilino, Palatino, Quirinale, and Viminale). It is crossed by the meandering Tiber River. Rome is about ten miles upriver from the Tiber's mouth at Ostia, on the Mediterranean coast. Greater Rome is encircled by the A80-A90 beltway or ring road, which Romans call GRA (Grande Raccordo Annulare).

The province of Rome, designated by the letters RM, reaches far beyond the city limits and GRA and has a population variously estimated at between 4 and 5.2 million. North past Ponte Milvio, Tor di Quinto, and GRA are Saxa Rubra and Prima Porta, both within the orbit of Greater Rome and firmly within the province of RM (it was at Saxa Rubra that, according to Christian legend, in the fourth century AD, Constantine the Great, the first Christian Emperor of Rome, saw the sign of the cross above the setting sun, with words spelled out in stars). To the west and northwest, RM includes the main airport and coast at Fiumicino and the municipality of Allumiere; to the east, the older airport at Ciampino and the abutting Alban Hills (also referred to generically as the Castelli Romani). The province also stretches south by southeast beyond the Via Appia Antica and Via Appia Nuova as far as Carpineto, due south on Via Cristoforo Colombo to EUR, and southwest on Via Ostiense or Via del Mare to the coast at Ostia, and then all the way south to Nettuno.

Normal retail business hours are Monday through Saturday 8/8:30am to 12:30/1pm and 3:30/4pm to 7/7:30pm; few retail businesses stay open during lunchtime.

Opening hours for bakeries and fish shops vary widely, sometimes starting early in the morning (6/6:30am). Wine shops and wine bars often open late (10/11am) and close late (8/9pm). Coffee shops (*caffè*) open early (7am), and remain open through lunchtime, closing at 7/8pm. It's worth noting that Romans eat later than many Italians: most restaurants seat guests for lunch from 1/1:30pm to 2:30/3pm; dinner is from 8pm to 10/10:30pm. Early service is noted in guidebook entries.

Important: Nine in ten food- and wine-related businesses are closed Sundays and a half day or full day once a week, often Thursday afternoon. Most businesses close for vacation for several weeks or a month, usually in August. Summer hours are often shorter than fall/winter/spring hours. Unusual opening or closing hours of businesses are noted in guidebook entries.

Addresses

In Rome, finding an address can be a challenge. On many of the older streets of the historical center of the city, the street numbers run in what Rome's municipal police force calls "an inverted horseshoe pattern." That means the numbers begin at 1, "at the first nail of the inverted horseshoe, on the bottom left." They run to the end of the street—the top of the inverted U—cross the street, and run back to the last "nail" on the lower right of the horseshoe. Cardinal points are not part of this arcane equation: the horseshoe falls randomly, with no regard for east, west, north, or south. This system, if such it may be called, is not used everywhere in Rome's old neighborhoods. Only a few dozen streets still have horseshoe numbering, but many are in the heart of the city. The numbering on one such street, Via Giulia, defeats all logic. Via Giulia runs parallel to the Tiber River, starting (or ending) behind Palazzo Farnese. However, the numbering begins halfway down the west (Tiber) side of the street. There, the buildings segue from #262 to #1. The simple rule is, if you can't find an address, ask a policeman or shopkeeper.

Telephone numbers

Rome land-line telephone numbers begin with 06 and are followed by from five to eight digits, depending on the neighborhood where the address is found, and the age of the subscription. Always dial all of the numbers, including the 06. To reach any of the numbers in this guidebook from the United States, dial 011 39 and then the subscriber's number.

Etiquette

In busy *caffè*, and in some snack bars and bakeries, make sure to stand in line, pay, and get a receipt for your order at the cash register before lining up at the bar or counter to ask for your coffee and breakfast roll. If you don't, you'll lose your place and will have to start over again. In busy food or wine retail shops, check when you step inside whether you need to take a number from a dispenser. Sometimes, in worst-case scenarios, you must take a number, wait, and then place your order, and then stand in line again to pay at the cash desk before battling your way back again to the counter to pick up your order. This arcane system is one of the reasons many Romans now shop in supermarkets.

How to use this guidebook

Officially, the city is divided into twenty Rioni—neighborhoods—each with its own Municipio—town hall. In reality, the Rioni are often small and centered around church parishes or monuments, streets or squares, and do not correspond to wider, contemporary conceptions of the city. The divisions in this guidebook reflect the street layout and topography of Rome, and each division includes several Rioni. For ease of use, the divisions are listed from the center of the city outwards, the first nine divisions spiraling clockwise and covering all of central Rome. Division ten includes areas lying outside central Rome. The ten divisions are:

1. Campo de' Fiori, Ghetto, Capitoline/Forum
2. Campo Marzio, Pantheon, Piazza Navona
3. Piazza del Popolo/Pincio, Piazza di Spagna, Fontana di Trevi
4. Monti, Quirinale, Salaria, Sallustiano, Via Veneto
5. Esquilino, Celio, Termini, San Lorenzo, San Giovanni
6. Testaccio, Ostiense, Garbatella
7. Gianicolo, Monteverde, Trastevere
8. Castel Sant'Angelo, Prati, Vaticano
9. Piazza Mazzini, Trionfale
10. Outlying Areas (Appia Antica, Appio and Via Appia Nuova, Salaria-Tagliamento-Nemorense, Monte Mario-Prisciano-Balduina, San Giovanni di Dio-Donna Olimpia, Ponte Milvio, Flaminio, Piazza Bologna)

Listings

Listings within each of the first nine divisions are alphabetical; because they are scattered widely, entries in division ten are not alphabetical, but rather are listed by their location, as you might encounter them if exploring the area on foot. An alphabetical index of place names, as well as thematic indexes, are found at the back of the book.

Prices

Prices for a three-course meal, per person, without beverages: Inexpensive = under 30 euros; Moderate = 30 to 40 euros; Expensive = 40 to 50 euros; Very Expensive = over 50 euros; Extremely Expensive = 70 to 90 euros; Astronomically Expensive = over 90 euros.

FOOD

ROMAN GASTRONOMY TODAY ARISES FROM MULTIPLE SOURCES, STARTING WITH THE FOOD OF THE Etruscan shepherds and swineherds who roamed the region 3,000 years ago. Like several other central-southern Italian and Mediterranean island cuisines, many Roman lamb and pork recipes popular today derive from this tradition, among them grilled or roasted lamb with wild rosemary or fennel, and spit-roasted, herb-stuffed *porchetta* (whole pig).

Not many traces are left in Roman home and trattoria cooking of the complicated cuisine of Imperial Rome. If you dine at one of the city's trendy or international style restaurants, where postmodern-fusion is fashionable, you may get a sense of how Apicius and other gourmands ate.

The excesses of Rome's emperors were swept away by the so-called Barbarian hordes, and the elaborate, pan-European cuisine of the papal court that followed never took root among Romans, changing with culinary fashions and the succession of countless cardinals and popes. The Vatican's main culinary legacy is the so-called Canonical calendar of dishes (see below), and the division of each week and various periods of the year into lean days and feast days. For centuries, on Fridays, Christmas Eve, and throughout the 46 days of Lent, strict Roman Catholics ate (and continue to eat) fish or other "lean" foods, while during Carnival everything was (and is) permitted (*carne vale* means "meat is allowed").

The prime source of contemporary Roman cooking, however, is *cucina povera*, the food of impoverished peasants and city dwellers. Rome's version is sui generis, descending in part from the city's paradoxical isolation. After the decline of the Roman Empire and right up to the mid-1800s, Rome was ruled by the Vatican, and Romans lived behind the Vatican's imposing city walls, which were connected to the ancient city walls of Marcus Aurelius. By and large, Romans ate what they grew, raised, gathered, or fished within the walls: chicory and field greens, wild herbs, capers, figs, plums, almonds and cherries, poultry and rabbit, Tiber perch, sturgeon, and eels. Goats, sheep, and cattle were pastured until the late nineteenth century in the Forum, then nicknamed Campo Vaccino, "cow pasture." With full Italian unification in 1870, Rome was freed from the shackles of the Vatican and became the nation's capital. Industrialization led to large-scale meat processing, and in the 1880s and '90s the slaughterhouse workers of the Testaccio neighborhood on the south side of town created their own cryptically named cooking style, Quinto Quarto—the fifth quarter. Workers were paid partly in kind with oxtails, organs, nerves, and heads—parts that other classes rejected and which total about a quarter of an animal's weight, the often undesired, difficult-to-sell fifth quarter.

In food, particularly when it is eaten at home, Romans cling to what's tried and true. Many homes and family-run trattorias—which are an extension into the public arena of the Roman dining room—follow an informal, unscientific weekly recipe calendar. It was established centuries ago and is based partly on religious tenets—eating fish or other lean foods on Fridays, for instance—or simply on long-forgotten practicalities such as the limited availability of certain ingredients. Romans call the foods served following this calendar *piatti canonici*—Canonical dishes. Monday is the day for *riso e indivia in brodo* (rice and curly endive in chicken broth) or *bollito* (boiled beef or chicken); Tuesday is *pasta e ceci* (pasta and chickpeas), *pasta e fagioli* (pasta and beans), oxtail stew, or fish; on Wednesday, anything goes; Thursday is *gnocchi di patate* (potato gnocchi); Friday is either *pasta e ceci*, *pasta e broccoli*, or *minestra di arzilla* (skate soup) and/or *baccalà*; Saturday is *trippa alla romana* (tripe with mint and pecorino romano); and on Sunday *fettuccine alla romana* precede *abbacchio* (fettuccine with a hearty meat, chicken liver, and tomato sauce, and oven-roasted suckling lamb).

Respecting traditions doesn't mean Romans are retrograde provincials obsessed with the past: the city's most highly touted chef, Heinz Beck, is a Germanic import who specializes in fanciful *cuisine d'auteur*, playing variations on Lazio and other Italian themes. Rather, respect for traditions suggests Romans strive to transmit from generation to generation the best foods and eating habits, and a way of life clearly worth preserving.

The test of a new or improved recipe in Rome has long been: is it *da non rimpiangere il vecchio*? That means, is it good enough so that you don't miss the original version? Usually,

THE BIG NAMES OF OLD

A SHORT-LIST OF THE MAIN SOURCES OF WRITTEN RECIPES AND DESCRIPTIONS OF ANCIENT Roman food and lifestyle should include, in approximate chronological order:

Cato: also known as Cato the Censor. He wrote the farming treatise *De agricultura* in circa 180 BC.

Apicius: his full name was either Apicius Caelius, who lived in the reign of emperors Augustus and Tiberius (27 BC to 37 AD) or, more likely, Marcus Gavius Apicius, the first-century AD author of the widely quoted *De re coquinaria* (sometimes erroneously given as *De arte coquinaria*). In reality, the book is a ninth-century copy of a fourth- or fifth-century compilation of the original two-part, ten-volume work, which was lost. The title in English is usually *The Art of Cooking*. A mine of culinary information, the writings of Apicius influenced umpteen generations of cooks throughout Europe, and appear to live on in Paris, New York, San Francisco, Sydney, and Rome to this day.

Columella: his full name was Lucius Junius Moderatus Columella, and he wrote *De re rustica*, with many recipes, between 35 and 45 AD (it was published in 60 AD).

Petronius: his full name was Gaius Petronius Arbiter, his birth date is unknown, and he committed suicide in 66 AD. He wrote *Satyricon*, with its famous banquet scene, the *Cena Trimalchionis* (*Trimalchio's Feast*), set during the reign of Emperor Nero (54 to 68 AD). It inspired Federico Fellini's film *Satyricon*.

Pliny the Elder: his real name was Gaius Plinius Secundus, and he lived from 23 to 79 AD, and wrote *Naturalis historia*. Among other remarkable things, Pliny credited Apicius with the invention of foie gras, a fact the French still find hard to swallow.

Martial: his real name was Marcus Valerius Martialis, and he lived circa 40 AD to circa 104 AD. A poet, he authored epigrams describing, among other things, the Saturnalia festival and many banquets.

Juvenal: his real name was Decimus Junius Juvenalis, a poet and masterful jokester, who lived circa 60 to 130 AD. His *Satires* poke fun at imperial excesses, above all gluttony. Were he alive today, he would have a field day with Rome's many play-with-your-food neo-chefs, who brandish their toques, bow ties, snails, stars, and other guidebook distinctions like the wands and amulets of ancient soothsayers.

FOIE GRAS, ROMAN STYLE

IF PLINY THE ELDER IS RIGHT, APICIUS INVENTED FOIE GRAS BY FORCE-FEEDING GEESE WITH FIGS (*ficatum* in Latin, which gives the modern Italian *fegato* and the French *foie*). Cultivated Romans know that their forebears invented foie gras and a myriad of other dishes which have survived, much changed, into the current day, from *garum* and *liquamen* fish sauce, now represented by salted anchovies and anchovy *colatura*, to *millefoglie* layer cake (described by Cato), called *millefeuille* by the French. But it's a stretch to suggest that foie gras is a "Roman" specialty today. Some restaurateurs do just that, and one of them happens to be among the city's most talented: Arcangelo Dandini, of Ristorante L'Arcangelo (area 8, see page 290).

the answer is no, and the old version eventually wins out. How about trying zucchini, clams, and/or saffron in your *carbonara*? Or why not transform oxtail stew into a beautiful French-style *terrine*? What about a tri-colored risotto, to resemble the Italian flag, made with tomatoes, arugula, and tuna tartare mixed with pecorino romano? Sure. Maybe. They're worth a try. Dozens of neo-trattorias and a few gourmet restaurants offer one, both, or all three of these nouvelle dishes. However, if you have a sensitive palate and are not wowed by novelty for its own sake, the second time you eat your clams with pecorino, zucchini, egg, and saffron, you'll probably understand why classic *carbonara* is infinitely more satisfying: the ingredients work together, not against each other. They become something wonderful precisely because of the recipe's straightforward simplicity. The same goes for the chilled oxtail terrine, held together by aspic, *à la française*. The flavors, texture, and cold temperature simply do not work: oxtail stew is luscious when hot, not cold, and what could be more satisfying than picking the tender meat off the tailbones? As to the need to depict the Italian flag with risotto, and mix delicate raw tuna with salty, piquant pecorino romano, the less said the better.

Food-loving seniors sometimes tell a parable to make a point about the eternal return of Rome's eternal favorites. They cite *A Martian in Rome*, the controversial play by Ennio Flaiano, Federico Fellini's celebrated scriptwriter. "Foreigners always make a great first impression," says one of the characters in the play, "because they're novel. Then you discover they're idiots." The parallel between the Martian and Rome's food is clear: at first the city's tastemakers, intellectuals, and journalists fawn over the new recipe, new chef, exotic restaurant, or innovative cooking style. But soon they tire of it, ignore it, and eventually wish it would go away, like the Martian in the play. It usually does.

But not always. So-called *cucina creativa*, *nuova cucina*, or *alta cucina* (creative, nouvelle, or haute cuisine) is nonetheless practiced by many budding and some established Roman chefs today. Most cater to tourists, bureaucrats, and trendy young out-of-towners. Many creative chefs have spent at least several days or weeks in the kitchens of a Michelin-starred colleague, usually a French chef, though going to England or America for a pedigree is equally fashionable these days. The results are sometimes felicitous, more often of the play-with-your-food variety, the kind of fusion-confusion that has transmogrified French haute cuisine into Late Imperial entertainment, and made a mockery of honest kitchens from San Francisco to Sydney. To be fair, Rome's novel cooking is not merely an imitation of international *cuisine d'auteur*, but rather reaches back to the days of Imperial Roman decadence, when roast flamingo tongues, and the eating of live fish and animals, or cooked dishes made to look like living animals, were the rage. With few exceptions, Rome's novel cooking holds limited appeal for food lovers passionate about *terroir*, in Rome to experience only-in-Rome, Roman food.

It's worth noting that a recent change in Rome's city ordinance has made it possible for scores of new, informal businesses to serve food and drinks. These range from improvised wine bars to snack bars, cafeterias, and food-in-shop eateries. At the same time, Rome is experiencing a boom in nightclubbing and party life unseen since the Dolce Vita of 50 years ago. Romans have dubbed this food-and-clubbing phenomenon "La Movida," because it has led to the kind of bloom witnessed in the post-Franco era in Barcelona. Rome's apolitical, unapologetically hedonistic version has certainly increased revenue for Roman tax collectors. It has also created a culinary free-for-all.

There are still family-style trattorias in every Rome neighborhood serving classic recipes, but for the reasons mentioned above, and others, the restaurant scene is no longer predictable. One example is seafood, which has gone from being a cheap source of protein featured on many menus, to a food for the privileged. Seafood is often extremely expensive; many Romans drive to the coast at Anzio, Fiumicino, Ostia, or Nettuno to eat fish at less than astronomical prices. Almost without exception, Rome's seafood restaurants are luxurious, international style or trendy places such as Hosteria del Pesce, near Piazza Farnese, or Alceste al Buon Gusto, near Piazza Navona; each has its own fishing boat to ensure highest-quality supply. Fish features prominently on the menus of the big hotel restaurants, such as Michelin three-star La Pergola del Hotel Hilton Cavalieri, on Monte Mario, presided over by the aforementioned celebrity chef, Heinz Beck.

As the capital of Italy, inhabited by thousands of homesick Italian provincials, Rome is naturally home to many excellent non-Lazio regional restaurants. They are listed separately in these pages, at the end of each area.

The restaurants, trattorias, *osterias*, and pizzerias included in this guidebook are tried and true, serve Roman *terroir* food, and could only be found in Rome. Trendy or international-style restaurants, and establishments serving food that may be very good and skilfully prepared but which has little or nothing to do with Roman tradition, are similarly listed at the end of each area, under the rubric Trendy or Top Non-*Terroir* Tables.

ANCHOVY *(acciuga, alice, aliciotto)*

The scientific name for this fish is *Engraulis encrasicholus*. The Mediterranean anchovy is not a sardine, contrary to common belief. It's often confused with Atlantic sprat (*Clupea harengus*) or a similar Mediterranean fish, the true sardine or pilchard (*Sardinia pilchardus*). All are distant cousins and all are consumed fresh or, when preserved, usually packed in salt or oil, in cans or jars. When eaten fresh, Romans call certain anchovies *aliciotti*, indicating they're slightly larger than the standard tiny three-to-five-inch canning anchovy. Fresh or preserved, the anchovy has been the cult fish in Rome since antiquity. Fermented in brine, it was the prime ingredient of the prized, fishy *garum* and *liquamen* sauces that constituted not only the Romans' prime salt substitute but also their favorite condiment or flavoring for innumerable recipes. The Italian anchovy catch has fallen drastically because of pollution and over-fishing. In Rome, most of the anchovies salt-packed in cans or barrels (*acciughe sotto sale* or *acciughe in barile*) come from Spain. Anchovy paste, sold in tubes, is called *pasta d'acciughe*. A favorite fresh-anchovy recipe is the Roman-Jewish *aliciotti con l'indivia*—baked anchovies with endives.

ARTICHOKES *(carciofi)*

Romans consume several types of artichoke, their favorite vegetable. The prized local artichoke is a large but tender globe variety that usually has no fluffy, hairy choke in the middle and is thorn-free. It's called *carciofo romanesco* and is protected by IGT (Indicazione Geografica Tipica) status. The scientific name is *Cynara scolymus*. Romanesco artichokes are derived specifically from the so-called *castellammare* and *campagnano* cultivars. The best of these come from Ladispoli north of Rome and Sezze to the south. *Cimaroli* are the largest specimens (about four inches in diameter) that grow at the uppermost tip of the plant's main stalk; those beneath are called *braccioli* (meaning arms, from *braccio*). Romans whittle their artichokes down almost to the heart, with an average waste volume of 65 percent, meaning they eat only 35 percent of what they buy. The scaly leaves, technically called "bracts," are part of an immature inflorescence (flower bud) and, unlike the French, Romans rarely eat them. The *carciofo romanesco* was developed in the last 500 years by selective breeding. Most botanists believe artichokes are derived directly from wild artichokes or cardoons. The ancient Romans also grew them outside of Rome, in a variety of Mediterranean places, particularly in what's now Tunisia. Marcus Gavius Apicius in *De re coquinaria* refers repeatedly to artichoke or possibly cardoon bottoms as *sfondilos*. What he probably meant was what we call artichoke hearts, as anyone who's tried to carve out the bottom of a tiny, tough cardoon flower would know. Iconographic evidence—bas-relief sculptures and mosaics—also show artichokes in antiquity. However, some scholars insist that only cardoons, which Apicius (recipes #112, #113, and elsewhere) calls *carduos*, were available.

BREAD *(pane)*

Exit the monumental Porta Maggiore city gate southeast of Termini train station and take a look at the Sepulcrum Eurysacis, known in English as the Baker's Tomb, built in the first century BC. The low-relief sculptures on the frieze show the main steps in breadmaking as well as the finished breads of the time. Step into any Roman bakery and you'll see a round *ciambella* loaf seemingly lifted off the tomb. Today's version of *ciambella*, made with white bread flour, is light and porous. Rome's other traditional breads are *ciriola* (a short, white bread often used for making panini); *fila* and *filone* (a long, thin loaf resembling a baguette); *pagnotta* (a thick, oval, or round loaf

ARTICHOKES AND HEALTH

THE ANCIENT ROMANS BELIEVED ARTICHOKES WERE APHRODISIACS. CONTEMPORARY ROMANS merely think them miraculous. A poster at Giggetto, the Ghetto trattoria celebrated for its artichoke dishes, makes the following claims. "Liver functions and bile: artichokes fight toxins and stimulate the liver, reducing cholesterol and triglyceride levels in the blood. They have diuretic effects and are mildly laxative. They have anti-diabetic effects: the artichoke's inflorescence, when eaten fully cooked, is healthful and since it contains no sugar, may be enjoyed by diabetics."

sometimes made with whole wheat); *pizza bianca* (Roman flatbread topped with salt and olive oil, but thinner and crisper than focaccia); *rosette* (*michette* in northern Italy; hollow rolls the size and shape of a hydrangea blossom); and *tartarughe* (small, turtle-shaped rolls similar to *rosette*). Romans also bake or truck in huge quantities of whole wheat and white sourdough loaves such as *pane di Terni* (large round or oblong loaves, originally from the village of Terni in Umbria) and *pane di Genzano* (large sourdough *filoni* and *pagnotte* baked in the wood-burning ovens of Genzano di Roma in the nearby Alban Hills). Romans are big eaters of *pane sciapo* (unsalted oblong loaves with a hard, shell-like exterior), much of it brought in from Umbria, Le Marche, and Tuscany. *Forno*, literally "oven," and *panificio* (occasionally *panetteria*) are interchangeable words for "bread bakery." Most but not all bread bakeries also make pastries, cakes, pies, tarts, and cookies.

CHEESE *(formaggio, cacio)*

Romans often call cheese *cacio*, an older name for it than *formaggio* (which derives from *forma*—the form of cheese). The two standard-bearing cheeses of Rome are pecorino romano and ricotta di pecora. Other Lazio and Central Italian regional cheeses found widely in Rome include mozzarella (and treccia, which is braided mozzarella), and fior di latte (cow's milk mozzarella), provola, and caciocavallo, the latter two semi-soft, medium-sized cheeses made from water buffalo or cow's milk, plus ricotta di bufala (buffalo's milk ricotta). Provola is usually shaped like a melon or a pear and is in essence a small provolone. Caciocavallo, which is often sold in pairs linked by twine like saddlebags, is sometimes aged with red wine grapes from the Lake Bolsena area in northern Lazio. Despite its name, which literally means "horse cheese," and derives from the saddlebag shape, there's nothing equine about it. Caciotta romana is a semi-fresh ewe's milk cheese that comes in ten-inch-diameter rounds; pecorino del pastore is a similar cheese in smaller rounds aged for about one month; scacione, a fresh cow's milk cheese, is sold in small pats; marzolina is a small, quarter-pound round which can be made with either ewe's, goat's, or cow's milk, and is usually stored in glass jars with olive oil and vinegar for several months before being eaten. In another category is giugata, the first curds from ewe's milk that float to the surface, are skimmed off, shaped into pats, and presented on fig leaves for immediate consumption; giugata is difficult to find in Rome nowadays.

BREAD

TO SALT OR NOT TO SALT?

OVER THE LAST TWO DECADES, ROME HAS BECOME ITALY'S BREAD CAPITAL, HOME TO A WIDE variety of loaves both salted and unsalted. The newfound variety of breads is a reaction; the city long produced just two local specialties: *ciriola* (a baguette-shaped white bread one to two feet in length, the ancestor of the miniature pale loaf used worldwide for *panino* sandwiches) and the broader, shorter, crusty classic white bread *fila* or *filone* (a jumbo *fila*). Both come in salted and unsalted versions. The city's other baked specialty since at least the 1940s, *pizza bianca*, is a flatbread akin to focaccia incorporating olive oil and coarse sea salt.

Romans are notorious for their love of salty food, unsurprisingly since Rome is the historic hub of Europe's salt routes, which spread outwards from the city through Italy and into neighboring countries. The Via Salaria, a radial artery running east from central Rome, lies atop the main Bronze Age salt highway. Not much unsalted bread is made in Rome nowadays. Most is "imported" from Umbria. Both the ancient Greeks and Romans considered bread and salt "gifts of the gods." The English "salt" (and Italian *sale*) comes from the name of the Roman god of health, Salus, giving us positive words such as salubrious, salutary, salute, salve, and salvation. In Roman times salt was extremely valuable and often used in lieu of coinage. When salt rations ran out, soldiers were given *salarium*—their salary—to buy salt. In Italy today, *un prezzo salato* (a salty price) indicates something expensive.

Guanciale, *pancetta*, pecorino romano, and salted anchovies are very salty. That's the main reason unsalted bread is so popular. As top baker Pierluigi Roscioli of Antico Forno Marco Roscioli puts it, "There's plenty of salt in the food, so why put it in the bread? Bread should be neutral. With saltless bread, you taste the wheat and that's all, with an aftertaste of grain." Roscioli's "proof" of unsalted bread is the fine texture, neutrality, and whether it "melts" in the mouth. Taste a really good unsalted bread from Roscioli or another Rome bakery and a popular Italian expression might spring to mind: *buono come il pane*—as good as bread. Ironically, in English, that saying is usually translated as "the salt of the earth."

CHICORY *(puntarella)*

One of Rome's favorite salads, dressed with garlicky anchovy dressing, is made with the carefully shaved tips of *puntarella* spears. A variety of *catalonia* (also spelled *catalogna), puntarella* is classed as both a head chicory and a shooting chicory. Its scientific name is *Chichorium intybus Puntarella. Puntarella* has up to 20 shoots, each called a *punta*, in its center. They look like pale asparagus spears, which is why in America and England this unusual vegetable often goes by the name of asparagus chicory. It matures in early spring or late winter and is at its best in April. The shoots must be harvested when young and tender or they become weedy, hollow seed-bearing stalks. When buying *puntarella* at a Roman market, check that the stalks are slender, firm, and about two to four inches long. If thick and tough they're past their prime. You can buy a special tool for slicing the spears, called a *taglia puntarella*, at some of Rome's kitchen tools stores and greengrocers' stands (including Claudio Zampa at Campo de' Fiori, see area 1 page 82).

CHOCOLATE *(cioccolato)*

Shortly after chocolate reached Spain from the New World in 1527, it found its way to Rome, where the Vatican unwittingly popularized it by allowing unsugared chocolate to be eaten during Lent and on days of fasting. The austere Vatican traditions of old help to explain the comparative simplicity of Roman chocolate today. Simple preparations using unsweetened or lightly sugared semisweet dark chocolate in the sixteenth-century style, though without the cinnamon often used during that period, were and remain the norm.

The Roman style of chocolates, and dipped or molded chocolate candies, was also influenced starting in the late 1800s by France. Today in Rome, solid or filled *cioccolatini* and filled French-style pralines are favorites. Dark chocolate, semisweet or bitter, is far more popular than milk or white chocolate; the creamy, fatty, sweet chocolates often associated with Belgium are rarely found. Largely because of the hot Roman climate, fresh dairy products are used sparingly in Roman confectionery and cooking in general. All the best Roman *cioccolaterie* use fresh raw materials, not ready-made concentrates, to flavor their chocolates.

COFFEE, CAFÉ, AND CAFFÈ

In standard, modern Italian, "*caffè*" means coffee, the substance, while "bar" means café, as in coffee shop or espresso bar. However, many cafés have "*caffè*" in the name, such as Caffè Sant'Eustachio or Gran Caffè Esperia. To avoid confusion, the cafés/espresso bars in this guide are referred to as "*caffè*;" so, too, is coffee. In Rome, *caffè* is often outstanding. Coffee roasters based in or near the city produce blends you will find here and nowhere else.

Coffee has a long and proud history in Rome. For much of the eighteenth and nineteenth centuries, the city's roasters were forced to group themselves around the base of the Marcus Aurelius column in Piazza Colonna, which gives onto Via del Corso, central Rome's main street. At the time, citizens and municipal authorities reportedly objected to the smell of roasting coffee. When the law was changed, roasters and *caffè* did not move far, and three of the best are still within a few hundred yards of the piazza. They also happen to be on the route of the ancient Aqua Virgo aqueduct (resuscitated in 1453 as the Acqua Vergine Antica and still in use), whose water was long held to be the best for coffee brewing. Since the 1970s, however, Rome's tap water has been a cocktail of spring waters from various sources—extremely pure, low in chlorine, high in minerals, refreshing, and excellent for brewing coffee.

Some coffee connoisseurs propagate the myth that the best coffee in Italy is roasted and served in the southern half of the country, which may have been true once. Now all but the very best southern Italian coffees are composed of 80- to 100-percent valley-grown, full-sun Robusta of dubious quality, roasted very dark, and served *ristretto* (short) because the beans are too strong, bitter, and thin, and they have too little aroma and aftertaste, for the coffee made from them to be served *normale* or *lungo*. By contrast, in Italy's center and north, especially in the cities of Trieste, Bologna, Turin, Genoa, and Rome, the coffee is mostly and often entirely Arabica, roasted medium or dark, and mild, flavorful, and satisfying. Certainly, good Robusta is better than bad Arabica, but in a world market flooded by an overproduction, there's no reason apart from greed, or a peculiar passion for the flavor, the foamy head, or extremely high caffeine content of Robusta, to use anything but good Arabica.

As with many things Roman, with coffee nothing is particularly new. The less novelty, the better the results. At Roman *caffè* frequented by Romans, you find no flavored coffees and usually no choices beyond one or two blends. As is true elsewhere in Italy, Roman coffee is often better when consumed at a *caffè* than brewed at home, even when the beans are exactly the same. The reason is that at a *caffè*, you're getting coffee roasted and blended specifically for making espresso using a professional machine, operated by a professional *barista* (barman). Italians have an expression to explain this, the "four M's": *la miscela, la macchina, il macinino, e la mano del banchista.* In other words, the blend of coffees, the espresso machine, the grinder, and the skilled hand of the barman.

Until the 1960s, scores of mom-and-pop roasting businesses—*torrefazioni*—could be found in the city, practically one on every shopping street. Of the 20 or so artisanal or family-run roasters that remain, many are excellent and four rank among the most accomplished in the country. One, Giovanni De Sanctis (near the Quartiere Coppedè and Via Salaria in eastern-central Rome, area 10), unfortunately does not brew coffee on site, although Romans go out of their way to buy coffee there. Another, Teichner (Piazza di San Lorenzo in Lucina, area 2), sells an excellent 100-percent Arabica blend at its specialty food shop but brews mediocre coffee at its bar. The two other world-class *caffè-torrefazioni*, Caffè Sant'Eustachio and La Tazza d'Oro (Pantheon outlet only), make peerless espresso and other coffees: precisely balanced in acidity and mildness, fragrant, and powerful.

DESSERTS *(dolci)*

Roman pastries range from the simple, homey dry biscuits such as *tozzetti*, of centuries past, to lusciously elaborate *zuccotto* (pudding cake) or *zuppa inglese* (trifle) and *tiramisù* (in Italian, spelled with an accent). By and large, the pastries of Rome are less showy, buttery, and sweet than their French or northern European counterparts. One classic Roman drop-cookie is a gloss on the city's pastry as a whole: *brutti ma buoni*, a name which means "ugly but good." Many bread bakeries and most *pasticcerie* (pastry shops) bake classic *biscottini* ("butter" cookies that are usually made with a blend of butter and vegetable shortening); *castagnole* (sweet, aniseed-flavored fritters fried in olive oil and eaten around Carnival); *ciambelline* (sugar-dusted wine-dipping cookies), *ciambelloni* (sugar-crusted coffee cakes in rings the size of dinner plates); *crostata* (a tart with a short crust topped with jam, the favorite variety being sour cherry

THIRTY-THREE WAYS TO ORDER COFFEE

AND THEN SOME

ROMANS ARE COFFEE MAD. LUIGI SANTORO, THE AFFABLE OWNER OF BAR DEL CAPPUCCINO (area 1), has catalogued the 33 ways to order coffee commonly used by his clients: *amaro* (bitter), *ristretto*, *lungo*, *corto* (*ristretto*), *alto* (*lungo*), *macchiato*, *molto caldo* (very hot), *molto freddo* (very cold), *decaffeinato*, *corretto* (with a drop of *eau de vie*), *doppio*, *doppio in tazza grande* (in a big cup), *in tazza piccola* (in a small cup), *Americano* (watery), *cappuccino*, *cappuccino senza schiuma* (with no foam), *cappuccino tiepido*, *cappuccino decaffeinato*, *cappuccino con cacao*, *caffèlatte*, *latte macchiato*, *latte macchiato con decaffeinato*, *marocchino* (espresso with a drop of hot, foamy milk and chocolate powder), *in tazza fredda* (in a cold cup), *con latte freddo* (with cold milk), *con latte a parte* (with milk on the side), *freddo* (cold), *freddo shakerato* (cold and shaken like a cocktail), Irish, *frappé*, *caffè crème* (French style). Three new appellations should be added to update his list: *monachella* (espresso, hot chocolate, and whipped cream), *moretto* (another way to say *marocchino*), and *genovese* (a *moretto* or *marocchino* without chocolate powder). And there's one old-timer Santoro appears to have forgotten: *in vetro* (in a glass).

jam); *maritozzi* (puffy sweet buns, sometimes studded with raisins and candied fruit or, when plain, filled with whipped cream); *millefoglie* (similar to French *mille-feuille*, made of pastry cream layered between crisp, translucent leaves of dough); and *torta di ricotta* (Jewish ricotta cheesecake).

FISH, SHELLFISH, MOLLUSKS
(pesce, frutti di mare, molluschi)

In its original form, Marcus Gavius Apicius' first-century recipe collection filled ten separate books, two of them entirely on fish, proof if any was needed that the Romans have been eating a wide variety of fish, shellfish, and mollusks for a long time. Emperor Domitian (81 to 96 AD) is famous among other things for having called the Senate to special session to decide how best to cook a giant turbot he'd received as a gift. Since contemporary Rome's cooking is derived from the last few centuries' *cucina povera*—poor folks' cooking—many Roman recipes call for types of fish or seafood that were formerly cheap. That's why the most popular fish in Rome are still anchovies either

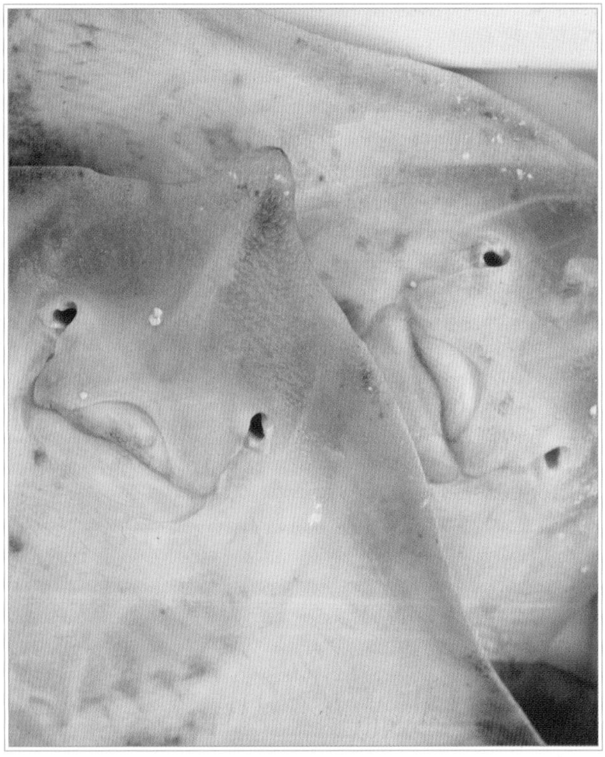

WHERE TO EAT FLIPPING-FRESH FISH IN ROME

ALBERTO CIARLA

PIAZZA DI SAN COSIMATO 40

TEL: 06 581 8668 ✦ WWW.ALBERTOCIARLA.COM

DINNER ONLY, CLOSED SUNDAY NIGHT

VERY EXPENSIVE *to* EXTREMELY EXPENSIVE

TRASTEVERE, AREA 7

ALCESTE AL BUON GUSTO

CORSO RINASCIMENTO 70 ✦ TEL: 06 686 1312

CLOSED SUNDAY *and* AUGUST ✦ VERY EXPENSIVE

PIAZZA NAVONA, AREA 2

ARCHEOLOGIA

VIA APPIA ANTICA 139

TEL: 06 788 0494 ✦ WWW.LARCHEOLOGIA.IT

CLOSED TUESDAY ✦ EXPENSIVE *to* VERY EXPENSIVE

APPIA ANTICA, AREA 10

CANTINA CANTARINI

PIAZZA SALLUSTIO 12 ✦ TEL: 06 474 3341

CLOSED SUNDAY *and* AUGUST ✦ MODERATE

SALLUSTIANO, AREA 4

DA BENITO E GILBERTO

VIA DEL FALCO 19

TEL: 06 686 7769 ✦ WWW.DABENITOEGILBERTO.COM

CLOSED SUNDAY, MONDAY, CHRISTMAS

HOLIDAYS *and* AUGUST ✦ EXPENSIVE *to* VERY EXPENSIVE

VATICAN, AREA 8

DA CESARE

VIA CRESCENZIO 13

TEL: 06 686 1227 ✦ WWW.RISTORANTECESARE.COM

CLOSED SUNDAY DINNER *and* AUGUST

MODERATE *to* EXPENSIVE ✦ VATICAN, AREA 8

DA DANTE

VIA MONTE SANTO 36/38

TEL: 06 375 15537 ✦ CLOSED SUNDAY *and* AUGUST

MODERATE ✦ PIAZZA MAZZINI, AREA 9

ENOTECA CAPRANICA

PIAZZA CAPRANICA 99/100

TEL: 06 699 40992 ✦ WWW.ENOTECACAPRANICA.IT

CLOSED SATURDAY LUNCH *and* SUNDAY

EXTREMELY EXPENSIVE *to* ASTRONOMICALLY EXPENSIVE

PANTHEON, AREA 2

F.I.S.H.

VIA DEI SERPENTI 16 ✦ TEL: 06 478 24962 ✦ WWW.F-I-S-H.IT

CLOSED MONDAY *and the* SECOND HALF *of* AUGUST

VERY EXPENSIVE *to* EXTREMELY EXPENSIVE

MONTI, AREA 4

GIUDA BALLERINO!

LARGO APPIO CLAUDIO 344

TEL: 06 715 84807 ✦ WWW.GIUDABALLERINO.IT

DINNER ONLY, *plus* LUNCH *on* SUNDAY, CLOSED WEDNESDAY

EXPENSIVE *to* VERY EXPENSIVE

APPIO/TUSCOLANO/CINECITTÀ, AREA 10

HOSTERIA DEL PESCE

VIA DI MONSERRATO 32 ✦ TEL: 06 686 5617

DINNER ONLY, CLOSED SUNDAY ✦ EXTREMELY EXPENSIVE

PIAZZA FARNESE, AREA 1

IL DRAPPO

VICOLO DEL MALPASSO 9

TEL: 06 687 7365 ✦ WWW.ILDRAPPO.IT

CLOSED SUNDAY *and* AUGUST, MODERATE *to* EXPENSIVE)

PIAZZA FARNESE, AREA 1

LA PERGOLA DEL HOTEL HILTON CAVALIERI

VIA A. CADLOLO 101

TEL: 06 350 92152 ✦ WWW.CAVALIERI-HILTON.IT

DINNER ONLY ✦ CLOSED SUNDAY *and* MONDAY,

AUGUST 10 *through* 25, *and* JANUARY 1 *through* 26

ASTRONOMICALLY EXPENSIVE ✦ MONTE MARIO, AREA 10

LA ROSETTA

VIA DELLA ROSETTA 8

TEL: 06 686 1002 ✦ WWW.LAROSETTA.COM

EXTREMELY EXPENSIVE ✦ PANTHEON, AREA 2

MAMMA ANGELINA

VIALE ARRIGO BOITO 65 ✦ TEL: 06 860 8928

CLOSED WEDNESDAY *and* AUGUST

MODERATE *to* EXPENSIVE ✦ QUARTIERE AFRICANO, AREA 10

MICCI

VIA ANDREA DORIA 55A

TEL: 06 397 33208 ✦ WWW.FRATELLIMICCI.IT

CLOSED MONDAY ✦ MODERATE

TRIONFALE MARKET, AREA 9

PIAZZA CAPRERA

PIAZZA CAPRERA 5 ✦ TEL: 06 853 53807

CLOSED SUNDAY, FIRST HALF *of* JANUARY *and* SECOND HALF *of* AUGUST ✦ EXPENSIVE

NOMENTANA/VILLA PAGANINI, AREA 10

QUINZI E GABRIELI

VIA DELLE COPPELLE 5

TEL: 06 687 9389 ✦ WWW.QUINZIEGABRIELI.IT

CLOSED SUNDAY, MONDAY, 2 WEEKS *in the* SECOND HALF *of* AUGUST, *and* MOST *of* JANUARY

EXPENSIVE *to* EXTREMELY EXPENSIVE

PANTHEON, AREA 2

RICCIOLI CAFÉ

VIA DELLE COPPELLE 13

TEL: 06 682 10313 ✦ WWW.RICCIOLICAFE.COM

OPEN DAILY *except* SUNDAY 9AM *to* 1AM ✦ MODERATE

PANTHEON, AREA 2

ROSCIOLI

VIA DEI GIUBBONARI 21/23

TEL: 06 687 5287 ✦ WWW.ANTICOFORNOROSCIOLI.COM

CLOSED SUNDAY ✦ MODERATE *to* EXPENSIVE

CAMPO DE' FIORI, AREA 1

TRATTORIA

VIA DEL POZZO DELLE CORNACCHIE 25, TEL: 06 683 01427 WWW.RISTORANTETRATTORIA.IT ✦ CLOSED SATURDAY LUNCH, SUNDAY ✦ EXPENSIVE ✦ PANTHEON, AREA 2 fresh or preserved, salt cod, mollusks of all kinds, red mullet, shark or dogfish, eel, skate, monkfish, scorpion fish, squid, octopus, mussels, clams, and, to a lesser degree, river or lake fish like perch, pike, and trout. A special case is *lattarini*—tiny freshwater fingerlings eaten whole, usually after frying and pickling. Seafood of all kinds is a costly delicacy nowadays yet Romans consume great quantities of it, including "new" species such as farmed sea bass, popularized in the last 50 years or so, sole, and flounder.

GELATO—"ARTISANAL" ICE CREAM

(cremolato, granita, grattachecca)

The Roman emperors did not eat what we call "ice cream." Frozen dairy products, other than goat's milk mixed with snow or ice, were unknown in Antiquity. The ancients enjoyed fruit sherbets and juices frozen or, as with goat's milk, mixed with snow or ice. Sherbet, in the form of *sorbetto* from Sicily or Naples, is the true ancestor of Rome's centuries-old indigenous frozen dessert *cremolato*, which is made by crushing or blending fresh, ripe fruit and freezing it, stirring often to break up the ice crystals. It is different from sherbet because no water is added and the fruit is never cooked; small amounts of sugar are allowed. Few artisans make *cremolato* these days, because the process is time-consuming.

Granita di caffè is made in a similar way using freshly brewed coffee instead of fruit or juice. Other ices made with frozen, flavored water or juice, sold from sidewalk stands and called *grattachecca*, are, like *cremolato*, an endangered species; the quality of the ices the handful of remaining stands offer is uneven. Artificial colorings and flavorings are sometimes used.

Ice cream made with milk or cream is relatively recent to Rome, having made its appearance yesterday—meaning about 450 years ago—via southern Italy and Florence. Like other small-scale Italian ice cream makers, many Roman *gelatai* call their product *gelato artigianale*, meaning artisanal ice cream. Often the only artisanal or craft element lies in the dexterity with which the ice cream makers open the packages of the powdered, freeze-dried, or concentrated ingredients which they use to save time and money. The resultant ice creams are unnaturally showy and colorful, stiffly whipped, and cloyingly sweet; they often contain colorings, preservatives, and chemical stabilizers.

To distance themselves from unscrupulous *artigiani*, some honest artisans now describe their product as *gelato artigianale*

naturale. Until Italian or European legislation defines exactly what "artisanal" and "natural" mean, the ancient Latin motto applies: Caveat Emptor. Let the buyer beware.

Unless otherwise noted, the ice cream makers in this guide make authentic, "natural" ice creams, *semifreddi*, ices, and sorbets. Some use ready-made, semi-processed pastes for non-fruit flavors: crushed pistachios, hazelnuts, and almonds, or liquified chocolate and Nutela. For fruit flavors, only fresh fruit is used. It's worth noting that "ice cream" is a misnomer for *gelato*; milk, not cream, is used to make nearly all Italian non-fruit *gelati*; fruit flavors are made from water, sugar, and fruit, with no dairy products. That's the main reason why Italian *gelati* are lighter and less caloric than their northern European or American counterparts.

GOURMET FOOD EMPORIUMS
(Gastronomie)

In Rome, the old shop designations of *generi alimentari*, *latteria*, *norcineria*, *oli e vini*, *pizzicagnolo*, *pizziccheria*, *salsamenteria*, and *salumeria* have gradually disappeared in favor of the more generic name *gastronomia*, which, as applied to a specialty food emporium, dates from only the 1980s. That's when grocers, butchers, salami makers, and cheesemongers began to scent the danger from supermarkets; in response, they increased their range of foods, whether fresh, preserved, canned, baked, or cooked. Nowadays most Roman *gastronomie* are high-end food boutiques or mini-markets selling Italian and foreign delicacies at premium prices. Often included is a deli section, *tavola calda* (cafeteria), wine bar, or an actual restaurant on or near the premises. For example, the remarkable selection of cheeses at La Tradizione (page 324), Roscioli (page 99), and Emilio Volpetti & C. (page 251) is as good as or better than that of most cheese-only shops (*formaggi*).

LAMB *(abbacchio)*

Lamb (along with pork) is Rome's favorite meat. Roman suckling lambs are among the most delicious in the world, and are unlike those eaten elsewhere. They're slaughtered when less than two months old and weigh about 15 to 20 pounds. In line with a tradition ridiculed by the satirical poet Juvenal nearly 2,000 years ago, *abbacchio* must be entirely milk-fed. Juvenal's jibes about lamb were aimed at extravagant entertainers—the foodies of his day—but even he recognized that suckling lamb is enormously different in flavor and texture—sweeter, milder, meltingly tender—from very young lamb that has fed on grass. Favorite Roman recipes for lamb are *abbacchio scottadito* (grilled chops), whose name derives from burn (*scottare*) and finger (*dito*); *abbacchio al forno con patate* (roasted, with garlic and rosemary, and potatoes); *abbacchio brodettato* (braised in broth with white wine and beaten egg yolks); *coratella con carciofi* (sautéed offal, with slivered artichoke hearts); *pajata d'abbacchio* (tiny, milk-filled lamb intestines cooked with tomato sauce and served with rigatoni, or simply grilled); *cervelli fritti* (battered, deep-fried lamb's brain, sometimes served with sliced fried artichokes); *testarelle d'abbacchio* (whole lamb's head split open, sprinkled with salt, pepper, and rosemary, and oven roasted). The (originally) non-kosher Jewish-Roman dish *abbacchio in bianco alla cacciatora* (with white wine vinegar, chili, and a pinch of anchovy) is popular throughout the city and nearby Alban Hills.

MARKETS *(mercati)*

Business hours at markets are elastic. Rome's municipal outdoor and covered markets are officially open from about 7am to 2pm in spring and summer, 7:30 or 8am to 1 or 1:30pm in fall and winter (weather and mood permitting), and closed Sundays all day. Fish is best on Tuesdays and Fridays, and in many markets fish stands are only open on those days.

Supermarkets have appeared all over Rome in the last 20 years, changing the way Romans shop. However, most central neighborhoods still have a covered *mercato rionale.* Sprinkled between are often minuscule open markets. With few exceptions, when shopping for meat, cheese, pasta, wine, and desserts consumers are better served at specialty food shops. Rome's outdoor and covered markets are outstanding for fish and farm produce.

MINT

(menta, menta romana, mentuccia)

Unlike most Italian regional cuisines, that of Rome and Lazio makes lavish use of mint, always fresh. The favorite local variety is called *menta romana*, a mild variety of spearmint either cultivated or picked wild. Another variety Romans call *mentuccia* looks like wiry oregano and grows wild in the Alban Hills south of town (and elsewhere). Because of its powerful, almost medicinal flavor, *mentuccia* goes into only a handful of recipes, usually in combination with garlic and artichokes. Its scientific name is *Nepitella.*

OLIVES

The preferred table olive of Rome is the Gaeta black olive, from the coastal region near Gaeta and the celebrated seaside resort Sperlonga, about 75 miles south of the capital. The most-prized specimens actually come from groves at the village of Itri a few miles inland from Sperlonga. The variety's official name is Itrano, named after the village. Round to slightly oval, about one inch long and ranging in color from greenish-brown to black depending upon ripeness when harvested, these exquisite salt-cured olives have been protected for years by the Italian government DOC (*d'origine controllata,* controlled or guaranteed origin) quality label guaranteeing their provenance; the

DOC was elevated to DOP status—the European Union quality label—in 2008.

OLIVE OIL

Without olive oil, Italian cooking in general and Roman cooking in particular wouldn't exist. It's the fundamental kitchen fat, used in everything from *antipasti* to desserts (yes, desserts: *ciambelline* wine-dipping cookies are made with olive oil, not butter). Lazio olive oils are similar to those of abutting Tuscany: medium- to full-bodied, vibrant green or emerald when young with yellowish hues developing during maturation, piquant and bursting with floral and herbal essences, flavors, and scents. The main oil production areas are in the province of Viterbo near Lake Bolsena, bordering Tuscany and Umbria, where Canino DOP and the new Tuscia DOP originate; and in Sabina, northeast of Rome, where Sabina DOP originates.

The olive varieties used to make Canino DOP are Caninese, Leccino, Pendolino, Maurino, and Frantoio. The olive varieties used to make Tuscia DOP are similar: Caninese, Frantoio, and Leccino (minimum 90-percent), plus other varieties found in the Tuscia olive groves.

The olive varieties used for Sabina DOP are Carboncella, Leccino, Raja, Frantoio, Moraiolo, Olivastrone, Salviana, Olivago, and Rosciola.

In the Latina area south of Rome, and specifically the Monti Lepini, the main olive oil and table olive variety is Leccio (or Leccino), with some Frantoio and Moraiolo. Very little oil is produced with Gaeta (Itrano) table olives.

If you buy Lazio oil to take home, always prefer cold-pressed, pure, untreated extra virgin olive oil, preferably from a DOP production area. Nearly all olive oils not bearing the "extra virgin" label are extracted with heat and sometimes with chemical treatments that denature them.

PASTA FRESCA AND PASTASCIUTTA

Pasta fresca shops are a disappearing breed, because the profit margins on fresh pasta are slim, and supermarkets and *gastronomie* stock high-quality *pasta fresca*, much of it made by small-scale factories without shopfronts (and, therefore, with lower overhead). The traditional fresh pasta types of Rome are fettuccine, potato gnocchi, semolina gnocchi, maltagliati (roughly cut strips, like pappardelle), quadrucci (tiny squares, for soup), ravioli (filled with ricotta and spinach, or meat), tagliatelle, and tonnarelli (thick, square spaghetti).

Dry pasta types—*pastasciutta*—include all the Italian standards plus spaghettoni (large spaghetti), ricce (wavy-edged fettuccine), and bavette (alias trenette or linguine). Especially popular in Rome are bucatini, which are thick, hollow spaghetti. Central Italian and Roman short pasta favorites are strozzapreti ("priest stranglers," roughly shaped pasta tatters), exhaust pipe–sized tubular sections of pasta called paccheri, maniche di frate (elbows), and mezze maniche (also elbows, but usually smaller than full maniche). Penne or rigatoni are often used with *amatriciana* and *carbonara*, though, in theory, bucatini go with the former, spaghetti with the latter. (*Rigatoni con la pajata* is a cult dish featuring milk-fed lamb intestine in tomato sauce.) Short pasta is widely served in trattorias and restaurants not because cooks and eaters prefer it, but rather to avoid the Jackson Pollock effect: tomato and other sauces spattered, splashed or flung by whirled ribbon pasta onto shirts, ties, blouses, and skirts.

PECORINO ROMANO

Made exclusively of whole, fresh ewe's milk, pecorino romano is a salty, hard cheese produced between the months of October and July only. Mostly considered a grating cheese and aged 8–12 months, it's also eaten semi-aged at about five months as an accompaniment to a variety of fruits and vegetables (especially fresh favas and pears). Most pecorino romano is actually made in Sardinia and referred to as pecorino romano sardo; it can also come from the province of Grosseto, in Tuscany. High-quality pecorino romano from Lazio is made by R. Brunelli (and the sub-brand Tiberio). Authentic pecorino romano comes in large, keg-like rounds with a 10- to 14-inch diameter, weighing about 55 to 75 pounds, and is usually coated with black, waxy plastic and always marked with the words "Pecorino Romano DOC" (controlled origin) or "Pecorino Romano DOP" (*d'origine protetta*, protected origin). Pecorino romano is an effective salt substitute, and is best when melted into hot food, so Romans rarely present it in a bowl for sprinkling atop pasta (parmigiano reggiano is the table cheese used for sprinkling on pasta, as in the rest of Italy). The chef takes care of dosing it. The cheese's semi-sharp, muttony taste is very different from that of creamy, smooth cow's-milk parmigiano reggiano. Pecorino sardo, a similar ewe's milk cheese also made in Sardinia, comes in smaller rounds, is aged 2–12 months, has less salt if intended to be eaten fresh, and is found in many Roman cheese shops.

PASTA

A PASTA FAMILY TREE

The following pasta dishes are close relatives, with many shared ingredients:

Cacio e pepe: pecorino romano and black pepper

Alla gricia: cacio e pepe plus *guanciale* or pancetta

All'amatriciana: cacio, *guanciale* or pancetta, chili, canned tomatoes, red or white wine

Arrabbiata: cacio, guanciale or pancetta, chili, fresh tomatoes

Carbonara: cacio e pepe plus *guanciale* or pancetta, parmigiano reggiano, eggs

Alla papalina: cacio e pepe plus prosciutto *crudo*, parmigiano reggiano, eggs

Alfredo: parmigiano reggiano and butter

THE QUEEN'S ONIONS: AN AMATRICIANA SAUCE CONTROVERSY

LITTLE DOES QUEEN ELIZABETH II OF ENGLAND KNOW THAT HER ROYAL NAME IS SOMETIMES invoked in Rome to justify the presence of onions in that famous spicy tomato-and-cured-hog's-jowl sauce known the world round as *amatriciana*, the sole claim to fame of an otherwise sleepy Apennine hill town on the eastern edge of Lazio called Amatrice. The town has long supplied Rome with many of its professional cooks, and a high percentage of the capital's trattorias are in the hands of transplanted Amatriciani. Since Amatrice historically belonged to the Kingdom of Naples and came into Rome's orbit only 150 years ago or so—recent by Eternal City standards—many traditionalist Romans are uncomfortable with the town's culinary influence over authentic Roman cuisine. Some view it as hayseed hegemony. The fact is, alongside *carbonara*, *amatriciana* is possibly

Rome's most popular pasta sauce. Poets pen poems about it. Thousands of traveling gourmets make a pilgrimage to the hill town to eat the "real" *amatriciana.* Anyone who's passionate about Roman food—meaning 99-percent of the city's residents—has something to say about Amatrice and *amatriciana.* For instance, celebrated restaurateur Alberto Ciarla (in Trastevere, area 7) claims he has found 40 variations on the sauce, which is no mean achievement for a recipe with only a handful of ingredients. The juiciest bone picked by *amatriciana* sauce lovers involves the use or not of onions. The actor, wit, cookbook writer, and restaurateur Aldo Fabrizi (1903–1990), celebrated for his role of the fearless priest in *Rome, Open City*, famously asked everyone he met: "Do you use onions in your *amatriciana*?" Those who answered "yes" got a tongue-lashing. Another colorful restaurateur, originally from Amatrice, is Giovanni Coletti, owner of *osteria* Ar Galletto on Piazza Farnese (area 1). Giovanni feels anyone using onions in the sauce "should get a life sentence." Apparently Queen Elizabeth II of England feels differently. During an October 16, 2000, Jubilee visit, she reportedly approved of onions in *amatriciana*, and that caused many in Rome to pontificate. The background is as follows: in 1961, the then-young queen dined with the president of Italy Giovanni Gronchi at the Quirinal Palace. Gronchi's chef was Ettore Nibbi, from Amatrice, and on the sly, Nibbi daringly served his native town's pasta, with onions in the sauce. The royal guest pronounced it delicious. Ever since, it's been all right to add onions to *amatriciana*, and to anyone who disagrees you can always say, "If it's good enough for the Queen of England, it's good enough for me." The press secretary at Rome's British Embassy, however, has found no indication that Elizabeth ate *amatriciana*, and the tale might well be apocryphal. No matter, say foodies with a sense of history: in Ancient Rome, the pre-tomato, pre-pasta forebear of *amatriciana* was a *farro* (hulled wheat) porridge sauced with suet, wine or vinegar, cured pig's jowl (*guanciale*), and lots of onions. Several top Roman chefs today use onions in their *amatriciana* and, frankly, if you like the sweetness they impart to the dish, why not approve of them?

CHILI PEPPER *(peperoncino)*

Chili pepper (*Capsicum annuum Linné*) is widely used in Roman cooking, so if you don't like spicy food, beware whenever you see the words *peperoncino* or *piccante*. Though chili pepper (like sweet or bell peppers) is from the New World, *peperoncino* was actually created in Italy, probably in the 1600s, and in Rome crops up in recipes with vegetables, poultry, lamb, cured pork, and anchovies. About one to one-and-a-half inches long, *peperoncino* is curved like a sickle and bright cherry red when it's fresh. However, it's usually sold and used dried, when it has shrunk and straightened to about half an inch to one inch, and faded several shades to ox blood red.

PEPPER *(pepe)*

Two ingredients recur in almost every entry in Apicius's first-century *De re coquinaria* recipe book: *garum* fish sauce and black pepper. Pepper saved Rome from total destruction twice: in 408 AD Alaric the Visigoth lifted his siege after receiving a tribute of 1.5 tons of peppercorns, and in 452 AD Attila the Hun largely spared Rome after accepting payment of an unspecified quantity of cinnamon and pepper. Spices were literally worth their weight in gold and pepper was the spice to end all spices. *Pepe nero*, black pepper—never white or pink—is still extremely popular in Rome, featuring strongly in all kinds of recipes, the most famous of which is *cacio e pepe* (spaghetti, tonnarelli, or other pasta with freshly ground black pepper and pecorino romano).

PIZZA BIANCA ET AL

In Rome, pizza does not only mean pizza as it is known to the rest of the world. It can also be *pizza dolce*, a.k.a *pizza di Civitavecchia* (a porous, airy, lightly sweetened cake, flavored with Marsala, vanilla, cocoa, and aniseed), *pizza dolce ebraica* (a Roman-Jewish coffee cake with raisins, candied fruit, and dry fruit), *pizza pasquale* (also called *torta salata* and made with cheese, ham, mortadella, and olives) and, most popular of all, *pizza bianca*. *Pizza bianca* is an olive-oil based flatbread that's a cross between focaccia, bread, and normal pizza, but is crispier, more porous, and thinner than focaccia, and more like a bread than a pizza. It is unique to Rome. It's usually eaten plain, as a snack or at breakfast, and is sometimes brushed with olive oil at the last minute by the baker, if so requested by the customer.

Many *caffè* and snack bars serve *pizza bianca* plain or split it open and use it to make sandwiches of all kinds. Some bakeries, notably Antico Forno Marco Roscioli (see page 99), make fancy *pizza bianca* with a variety of toppings. They range from zucchini flowers with mozzarella and anchovies, to peeled split figs with translucent strips of Parma ham, or cherry tomatoes and arugula. It's worth noting that in Rome, most "normal" pizza is baked in pizzerias only in the evening.

PORK *(maiale)*

Long before the she-wolf of Rome, la Lupa, symbol of the city, there was the sow, la Scrofa. The sow showed the mythical founder of the Romans, Aeneas, and his fellow Trojans, where to find fresh water and build their settlement at Lavinio, south of the Tiber's mouth, after they fled the fall of Troy. In thanks, the Trojans slaughtered the sow and her 30 piglets, roasted them, and feasted in thanksgiving. This may have been the first recorded example of *porchetta*—spit-roasted pig stuffed with wild herbs, usually rosemary, or fennel. The Scrofa was really a boar, as ancient sculptures attest, and Romans still eat boar in the form of stews (sweet-and-sour *cinghiale in agrodolce*, for instance). Pliny the Elder claimed to be able to find 50 different flavors in pork, which was long judged the most versatile of meats. The Roman's favorite cut of pork for braising in milk (for the cult dish *maiale in tegame al latte*) is the neck and shoulder, *il collo*, which is marbled and especially flavorful. Other preferred cuts are the loin and saddle, which are commonly long-stewed or roasted.

PORK (FRESH), SALAMI, JOWL BACON, AND SPECIALTY FOODS
(norcinerie, salumerie, salsamenterie)

Once upon a time, a *norcineria* was a pork butcher shop, named for Norcia, a small city in the central, mountainous Umbria region of Italy known for its range-raised porkers, pork butchers, and ham. Today the term designates not just a place to buy fresh pork or ham. It is used interchangeably in Rome with *salumeria* (salami shop) and *salsamenteria* (salted pork products) and, occasionally, the catch-all *gastronomia*, which is a specialty food shop and, at times, also a deli or *tavola calda*. Most of the *norcineria* shops listed in this guide also sell a wide selection of foods, from dried mushrooms to *farro* (emmer), mozzarella, spices, salami, grappa, *sapa* (reduced grape must), and pasta made by small, traditional producers. However, Romans seek out *norcinerie* specifically to buy ham, salami, and *guanciale*. A dozen or so *norcinerie*, *salumerie*, and *salsamenterie* in Rome still make their own cured hog products.

PORK JOWL *(guanciale)*

Guanciale is the object of a food cult in Rome and much of central Italy. Guancia means "cheek" or "jowl" in Italian, and *guanciale* means both "hog jowl" and "pillow" (because you lay your cheek on it). Romans are mad for jowls, consuming colossal quantities of them both at home and in traditional trattorias. Purists insist that without *guanciale* it's impossible to make the true versions of the pasta sauces *carbonara* (eggs, black pepper, pork jowl, and pecorino romano), *gricia* (subtract

PIGGING OUT ON PORCHETTA

PORCHETTA IS THE FAVORITE STREET FOOD AT ROME-AREA FAIRS, BLOCK PARTIES, POLITICAL rallies, folksy arts exhibitions, and *festas* honoring the heroics of war heroes and patron saints. The city of Viterbo in northern Lazio lays claim to the best *porchetta*, but many Alban Hills communities such as Ariccia, Grottaferrata, and Marino hotly contest this claim. Near Viterbo, wild fennel is the stuffing-herb; the Alban Hills prefer *porchetta* stuffed with rosemary. Because whole pigs can no longer be roasted in most Rome delis and restaurants, making *porchetta* is a specialized job nowadays, carried out by *porchettari* equipped with giant rotisseries, almost all of them in the Alban Hills. A few *norcinerie*, *gastronomie*, snack bars, market stalls, and even a bakery or two in central Rome sell ready-to-eat *porchetta*. They include Antico Forno Marco Roscioli near Campo de' Fiori (area 1 see page 99), Iacozzilli near Piazza di San Cosimato in Trastevere (area 7 see page 280), and Dal Norcino at the Testaccio covered market (area 6 see page 242). Why is *porchetta* so good? The pork cooks slowly in its own juices, which are trapped by the pig's skin, making *porchetta* mouthwateringly moist.

the eggs and black pepper, and add hot chili and white wine), or *amatriciana* (add tomatoes to *gricia*). But *guanciale* also finds its way onto *bruschetta* and into soups as well as myriad other pasta sauces, vegetable medleys, *frittatas*, poultry, beef, and pork. The only course of a Roman meal in which *guanciale* does not appear is dessert. About 50 years ago, when Italian peasants still raised and slaughtered their own pigs and made their own pork products, *guanciale* and most other parts of the pig destined for preservation were dried in the home chimney and therefore inevitably smoked. They are rarely smoked now. Instead, the process is like the one used to make *prosciutto* and the most common *guanciale* substitute, which is *pancetta*, Italian bacon, made from the *pancia* or belly of the pig. Compared with *pancetta*, *guanciale* is more gelatinous and sweet, imparting a buttery, almost gamey depth to whatever it's cooked with.

RICOTTA

Rome's ricotta di pecora (also called ricotta romana) is famous throughout Italy and much of it is exported to the internal Italian market, and abroad. Some of it isn't from Lazio at all, and large-scale producers sometimes mix cow's milk into it. The authentic item is made exclusively from the re-cooked liquid whey of ewe's milk, a byproduct of making pecorino romano. When the whole ewe's milk is heated or cooked the first time and coagulated with rennet, it separates into curds and whey. The curds are worked into pecorino romano. The whey is reheated at a higher temperature (95°C) and the proteins cause it to coagulate again into tiny clots. When drained, cooled and stirred they form ricotta. The leftover whey is fed to pigs, which explains in part the excellence of the fresh pork and pork products of Lazio, Umbria, and other central Italian regions. A small quantity of water buffalo-milk ricotta comes from the Sperlonga and Anzio areas south of Rome, a byproduct of mozzarella making. It's primarily consumed locally. Ricotta salata, literally salted ricotta, is an aged, crumbly, salty ricotta from Campania and shows up on some Roman tables.

SALT-PRESERVED FISH *(baccalà)*

Salt-preserved fish was a specialty of the Gauls long before the Roman conquest of Gaul in 52 BC. A wide variety of fish, from sardines and anchovies to herring, haddock, and cod, were preserved in this way in the days before refrigeration. The technique survives despite depleted fish stocks. The cod eaten

THE STRAWBERRIES OF NEMI

NEMI IS A SMALL ALBAN HILLS TOWN SOUTH OF ROME POISED OVER A LAKE IN A VOLCANIC crater. It's home to Italy's most prized "wild" strawberries, *fragoline di Nemi*, which are in fact cultivated here. Emperor Caligula, whose hands were often soaked in blood (at least metaphorically) would travel to the village regularly from late May through June, the height of strawberry season, and, presumably, gorge on *fragoline*. To fully indulge his imperial fancy Caligula had two luxury ships fitted out for entertaining and launched onto the lake's placid waters. The slopes of volcanic Lake Nemi were cloaked in those days in wild strawberry plants. On board, Caligula and his sycophants feasted and, again presumably, the lake ran red with berries, wine, and blood, a reminder, perhaps, of the even older tradition associated with the cult of Diana established at Nemi long before the rise of Imperial Rome. There are many variations on the tale. One holds that a temple to the hunting goddess Diana sat amid strawberry fields and trees with golden branches. At regular intervals, the head priest of the temple had to fight challengers to the death to hold his job. Pretenders signaled their candidacy by breaking off a golden bough in Diana's woods (the tale inspired James G. Frazer's classic *The Golden Bough*). When Caligula's fortunes waned in 41 AD, his ships were sent to the bottom of the lake, where they were rediscovered in 1929, restored, and displayed in a lakeside museum. Retreating Nazis burned the museum and its ships in 1944 but could not destroy Nemi's true claim to fame: strawberries. The first Sunday in June sees the local *sagra della fragolina* strawberry festival, during which guests are treated gratis to tons of the thimble-sized delicacies. Though people continue to call them "wild," they're actually grown in high-tech hothouses stacked on lakeside terraces. *Fragoline di Nemi* do not travel well and in any case rarely have a chance to try. Alban Hill and Roman connoisseurs snap up most of them raw in desserts such as *tiramisù con le fragole*, or as jams, juices, and liqueurs.

in Rome (and elsewhere in Italy) comes primarily from Iceland and the Scandinavian countries, Newfoundland, Greenland, and Canada (New Brunswick). It has almost disappeared from the northeastern United States, where salting cod was a major industry right into the twentieth century. Romans probably discovered salt cod, which they and most other Italians call *baccalà*, around the eighth century AD. It was once a cheap, abundant, transportable fast food: soak it in water anywhere and you have fish. There are about a dozen *baccalà* recipes in the Roman repertoire, ranging from simple pan-fried filets (one venerable Rome fry shop near Campo de' Fiori is named Filetti di Baccalà) to more complex preparations involving sweet peppers, tomatoes, raisins, pine nuts, and a variety of other ingredients. Among favorites is sweet-and-sour *baccalà in agrodolce*, originally a Roman-Jewish recipe. *Baccalà* is one of Rome's cult foods: when you want to convey the idea that someone is tense you say "*rigido come un baccalà*"—stiff as salt cod. That's because once upon a time *baccalà* was sold flat, dry and hard, and strung up that way in the kitchen. These days, nearly all Roman fishmongers de-salt *baccalà* for their clients.

TOMATOES *(pomodori)*

Romans are tomato-mad. Local tomatoes come in all shapes, sizes, and shades of green and red, and go into just about everything but dessert. Rome and Lazio are blessed with some of the best tomato-growing areas in the world, specifically around the farm town of Fondi. Rome also gets the pick of the crop from Campania and Sicily. As a general rule, Romans peel and seed the tomatoes they cook. However, because of their size and tenderness, cherry tomatoes are spared this treatment; they're usually reserved for delicate dishes, including seafood and fish, or used raw in salads. Plum tomatoes (called *perini*, meaning little pears, because of their shape) are generally considered sauce tomatoes. Large round red or greenish types are usually sliced and eaten raw. The favorite Roman varieties include: *verdone romano*, a large, irregular and greenish heirloom tomato eaten raw in salads; *colonna romana*, an egg-shaped, green-and-red variety with a sharpness and crispness that makes it a fine salad tomato; *casalino*, an old-fashioned ribbed, dark-red tomato favored for sauces; *campagnolo*, oval and red, is another local sauce-tomato. In Rome as elsewhere in Italy, the *pachino* is very popular; about two inches long, oval, deep red and plump, it appears to be a cross between a plum

tomato and a small round tomato (and is named for the village of Pachino, in southeastern Sicily).

TRAMEZZINI

Tramezzini are triangular white-bread sandwiches. The name derives from terms used in the construction industry. A *tramezzo* is a thin dividing wall and *tramezzare* means to place something in between, i.e. to sandwich. The origin of *tramezzini* sandwiches is hotly contested. The English say Lord Sandwich invented the prototype about 200 years ago. However, if you wander across the Forum or Palatine, you'll see thousands of ancient triangular foundation bricks that look surprisingly like *tramezzini*. Lord Sandwich and the Ancients apart, Rome's white bread *tramezzini* descend directly from World War II American GI rations and the sliced white bread sandwiches the Occupation troops ate from 1944 onwards. Originally, the bread came from the commissary: Italians didn't know how to make it. Then in the early 1950s a baker named Umberto Roscioli went to work in Kenosha, Wisconsin, and brought home the bread-making equipment that allowed him to turn out American white bread in the Eternal City. Oddly, given the number of good homegrown breads, *tramezzini* remain as popular as they were 50 years ago.

LAZIO WINES

FOLLOWING NATIONWIDE TRENDS IN THE ITALIAN WINE INDUSTRY, LAZIO WINEMAKERS ARE COMING to terms with a new paradigm: the international boutique wine phenomenon. The quality of wines is increasing overall, but a desire to reach New World markets is putting at risk many Italian wines' *tipicità*—their typicity or *terroir*.

In Lazio as elsewhere, at the top of the traditional scale are wines labelled DOC (*d'Origine controllata*—made with a "controlled" quantity of grapes of specific origin); currently there is only one Lazio wine with the more prestigious DOCG label, *d'Origine controllata e garantita*—controlled and guaranteed origin, quantity, and winemaking processes. That wine is Cesanese del Piglio DOCG. When *riserva* (reserve) follows DOC or DOCG, it means the wine has met additional aging requirements (usually 18 months beyond DOC or DOCG norms). When *superiore* is added, it means the grapes used are of superior quality. The lesser IGT label guarantees geographical provenance and ensures a degree of typicity, without the stringent rules of a DOC/DOCG appellation. Dozens of Lazio table wines—*vini da tavola*, labelled V.d.t.—rarely leave the region; they're often served in *osterie* and *trattorie*, and sold in local wine shops.

Seventy percent of the wines made in Lazio are white wines. Many wine drinkers associate Rome with Frascati and its quaffable whites. Frascati is a suburban town in the Alban Hills a few miles southeast of Rome. The area is also, though inaccurately, known as the Castelli Romani. The vineyards of Frascati and nearby winegrowing villages stipple hillsides visible from central Rome. A pale, light wine made almost entirely from the two innocuous, productive grape varieties Malvasia di Candia and Trebbiano Toscano, with small amounts of the slightly more flavorful Malvasia del Lazio and Greco varieties, Frascati and its Castelli Romani brethren range from anemic to zippy. Like all of the area's wines, Frascati is easy to match to many Roman recipes and is a reliable, unexciting, but not unpleasant wine for sipping on hot summer days. A fraction of Frascati's harvest is left on the vine to make Frascati Cannellino, a late-harvest, peachy dessert wine derived from grapes with noble rot.

But Frascati is only one of the scores of winemaking villages in the Lazio, which is a major producer and exporter of wines.

The proximity of the Alban Hills and other Lazio vineyards to Rome is both blessing and curse. As Italy's capital, Rome is the destination for every bureaucrat, functionary, and private contractor in the country, swelling the clientele of lesser trattorias, where bulk wine is served on tap. Countless church officials and pilgrims visit the Vatican, and the restaurants in or near Vatican City are known for their supplies of such wine. Millions of tourists want plentiful, cheap wine on their Roman holidays. For a long time, the winemakers who supply the city from its suburbs and region believed they could rely indefinitely on undemanding customers in a seller's market.

They were wrong. In the 1980s, winemakers from Tuscany, Umbria, the Veneto and Friuli, Piedmont, Campania, Sardinia, and Sicily opted for quality over quantity. A decade later, their wines became popular in the capital, often displacing Lazio bottlings. At the same time, across Italy per capita wine consumption slipped from 90 liters to 50. The response from some Lazio producers has been heartening. Paola di Mauro/Colle Picchioni, Conte Zandotti, Villa Simone, Castel de Paolis, L'Olivella, and Fontana Candida were the first to make changes, and among many others now make very good DOC Frascati and other excellent wines from other growing areas.

If a gold rush with Baroque curlicues can be called a renaissance, then Lazio winemaking is in the throes of one. It has spread from DOC to IGT vineyards and beyond. IGT is in theory a less stringent identifier than DOC; also in theory, it is associated with a regional or communal origin including, though not exclusively, its typical grapes. In many parts of Italy, IGT wines are mediocre. In Lazio, some are, some are not. Several dozen winemakers in the region are capsizing trends by using forgotten local grapes or foreign varieties (or both) to make tantalizing IGTs, some of which are respectful of Lazio *terroir*, and are equals of better-known DOCs. Many winemakers have forgone the bewildering restrictions of the dozens of DOC or IGT appellations, some of which overlap, and for certain of their wines have opted to create name-brand or single-vineyard appellations instead, in the French or New World style. These wines tend to be muscular mavericks: fruit in your face, high alcohol, lots of wood. It's worth noting that most Lazio appellations also produce sparkling wines in white, rosé, and red, some of which are pleasant, none of which is remarkable.

When it comes to buying and tasting wines, Rome has several of the country's best-stocked bottle shops and wine bars. What they call themselves, as elsewhere in Italy, can be confusing. A *bottiglieria*, *bottega del vino*, *vini e olii*, or *vineria* usually does not offer tastings; an *enoteca* is often a retail wine shop offering wine tasting and a limited selection of food; in some cases it's a full-service restaurant, often but not always owned by a wine shop. *Gastronomie* also often sell quality wines. Note that most businesses that use the English term "wine bar" (or winebar, in one word) are actually restaurants, sometimes though not always with a strong wine list or a wine theme. The wine bar bloom began in 1997 with Uno e Bino, a restaurant with innovative food and many fine wines, in the San Lorenzo neighborhood (area 5 see page 237). Since then it has spread to every corner of the city. Fashionable Al Bric (area 1 see page 114) and Enoteca Ferrara (area 7 see page 285) are typical of the genre: thousands of wines on the wine list, and regional food so "updated" as to be almost unrecognizably Roman or even Italian.

STILL WINES OF LAZIO

DOCS AND IGTS AND THEIR GRAPE VARIETIES, BY PROVINCE

Province of Frosinone, red wines

APPELLATION	GRAPE VARIETIES
Castelli Romani Rosso Novello	*Cesanese, Merlot, Montepulciano, Nero Buono, Sangiovese*
Cesanese del Piglio	*Cesanese di Affile, Montepulciano, Sangiovese, Trebbiano Bianco, Bombino, Barbera*
Cesanese del Piglio, Cesanese di Affile and/or Superiore and Riserva DOCG	*Cesanese Comune (minimum 90%), plus 10% other red wine grapes from the DOC*

Province of Latina, red and rosé wines

APPELLATION	GRAPE VARIETIES
Aprilia Merlot	*Merlot (minimum 95%)*
Aprilia Sangiovese	*Sangiovese (minimum 95%)*
Circeo Rosso	*Merlot (minimum 85%)*
Circeo Rosso Novello	*Trebbiano Toscano*
Circeo Sangiovese and Sangiovese Rosato	*Sangiovese (minimum 85%)*
Cori Rosso	*Montepulciano (40 to 60%), Nero Buono di Cori (20 to 40%, Cesanese 10 to 30%)*

Note: Castelli Romani red, rosé and white are also produced in some growing areas in the Province of Latina.

Province of Latina, white wines

APPELLATION	GRAPE VARIETIES
Aprilia Trebbiano	*Trebbiano Toscano (minimum 95%)*
Circeo Bianco	*Malvasia di Candia (maximum 30%), Trebbiano Toscano (maximum 60%), other white grape varieties (maximum 15%)*
Circeo Trebbiano	*Trebbiano Toscano (minimum 85%)*

Province of Rieti, red and rosé wines

APPELLATION	GRAPE VARIETIES
Colli della Sabina Rosso, Rosso Novello and Rosato	*Sangiovese (40 to 70%), Montepulciano (15 to 40%), other varieties up to 30%*

Province of Rieti, white wine

APPELLATION	GRAPE VARIETIES
Colli della Sabina Bianco	*Trebbiano Toscano and Trebbiano giallo (40 to 60%), Malvasia di Candia and Malvasia del Lazio (40 to 60%), other varieties 20% maximum*

Province of Rome, red wines

APPELLATION	GRAPE VARIETIES
Aprilia Merlot	*Merlot (minimum 95%)*
Aprilia Sangiovese	*Sangiovese (minimum 95%)*
Castelli Romani Rosso, Rosso Novello and Rosato	*Sangiovese, Cesanese, Merlot, Montepulciano, Nero Buono, plus up to 15% other varieties*
Cesanese del Piglio, Cesanese di Affile, Cesanese di Olevano Romano	*Cesanese di Affile, Montepulciano, Sangiovese, Trebbiano bianco, Bombino, Barbera*
Colli della Sabina Rosso, Rosso Novello and Rosato	*Sangiovese (40 to 70%), Montepulciano (15 to 40%), other varieties up to 30%*
Velletri Rosso and Velletri Rosso Riserva	*Sangiovese (35 to 40%), Montepulciano (30 to 40%), Cesanese di Affile, Bombino Nero, Merlot, Ciliegiolo (up to 10%)*

Province of Rome, white wines

APPELLATION	GRAPE VARIETIES
Aprilia Trebbiano	*Trebbiano Toscano (minimum 95%)*
Bianco Capena, Bianco Capena Superiore, Bianco Capena Asciutto and Bianco Capena Abboccato	*Malvasia di Candia, Malvasia del Lazio, Malvasia Toscana, Trebbiano Toscano, Trebbiano Giallo, Bellone, Bombino*
Castelli Romani Bianco	*Malvasia di Candia and Malvasia Puntinata, Trebbiano Toscano, Trebbiano Romagnolo, Trebbiano di Soave, Trebbiano Verde, plus up to 30% other varieties*
Colli Albani Bianco and Novello	*Malvasia di Candia, Malvasia Puntinata, Malvasia Rossa, Trebbiano Toscano, Trebbiano Romagnolo, Trebbiano di Soave, Trebbiano Verde, plus up to 30% other varieties*
Colli Albani Bianco Superiore	*same, but no "other varieties" are allowed*

Colli della Sabina Bianco	*Malvasia di Candia, Malvasia del Lazio, Trebbiano Toscano, Trebbiano Giallo, plus up to 20% other varieties*
Colli Lanuvini	*Malvasia di Candia, Malvasia Puntinata, Trebbiano Toscano, Trebbiano Giallo, Trebbiano Verde, plus up to 10% other varieties*
Frascati and Frascati Superiore	*Malvasia di Candia, Malvasia del Lazio, Trebbiano Toscano, Greco*
Genazzano Bianco and Bianco Novello	*Malvasia di Candia, Bellone, Bombino, Trebbiano Toscano, Pinot Bianco*
Marino and Marino Superiore	*Malvasia di Candia, Malvasia del Lazio, Trebbiano Toscano, Trebbiano Romagnolo, Trebbiano di Soave*
Montecompatri Colonna and Montecompatri Colonna Superiore	*Malvasia di Candia, Trebbiano Giallo, Trebbiano Verde, Bellone, Bombino*
Tarquinia Bianco	*Malvasia di Candia, Malvasia del Lazio, Trebbiano Toscano, Trebbiano Giallo*
Velletri Bianco	*Malvasia di Candia, Malvasia Puntinata, Trebbiano Toscano, Trebbiano Giallo, Trebbiano Verde, Bellone*
Zagarolo and Zagarolo Superiore	*Malvasia di Candia, Malvasia Puntinata, Trebbiano Toscano, Trebbiano Giallo, Trebbiano Verde, Bellone, Bombino*

Province of Viterbo, red wines

APPELLATION	GRAPE VARIETIES
Aleatico di Gradoli, Aleatico di Gradoli Liquoroso and Liquoroso Riserva	*Aleatico*
Cerveteri Rosso, Rosso Novello and Rosato	*Cesanese (maximum 25%), Montepulciano, Sangiovese*
Colli Etruschi Viterbesi Rosso and Rosso Novello	*Montepulciano, Sangiovese*

Colli Etruschi Viterbesi Grecchetto Rosso	*Grecchetto Rosso (minimum 85%)*
Colli Etruschi Viterbesi Canaiolo Rosso	*Canaiolo Rosso (minimum 85%)*
Colli Etruschi Viterbesi Merlot	*Merlot (minimum 85%)*
Colli Etruschi Viterbesi Sangiovese Rosato	*Cesanese, Montepulciano, Sangiovese*
Colli Etruschi Viterbesi Violone	*Montepulciano (minimum 85%)*
Tarquinia Rosso, Rosso Novello and Rosato	*Cesanese (maximum 25%), Montepulciano, Sangiovese, and other varieties (maximum 30%)*
Vignanello Rosso Novello and Rosato	*Sangiovese (40 to 60%), Ciliegiolo (40 to 50%) and other varieties (maximum 20%)*

Province of Viterbo, white wines

APPELLATION	GRAPE VARIETIES
Bianco Capena, Bianco Capena Superiore, Bianco Capena Asciutto and Bianco Capena Abboccato	*Malvasia di Candia, Malvasia del Lazio, Malvasia Toscana, Trebbiano Toscano, Trebbiano Giallo, Bellone, Bombino*
Cerveteri Bianco	*Malvasia di Candia, Malvasia del Lazio, Trebbiano Toscano, Trebbiano Giallo, and other varieties (maximum 20%)*
Colli Etruschi Viterbesi Bianco	*Malvasia di Candia, Malvasia del Lazio, Trebbiano Toscano, Procanico, and other varieties (maximum 30%)*
Colli Etruschi Viterbesi Grecchetto Bianco	*Grecchetto Bianco (minimum 85%)*
Colli Etruschi Viterbesi Moscadello Bianco and Moscadello Bianco Passito	*Moscato Bianco (minimum 85%)*
Colli Etruschi Viterbesi Procanico and Procanico Bianco	*Trebbiano Toscano (minimum 85 %)*
Colli Etruschi Viterbesi Rossetto	*Trebbiano Giallo (minimum 85%)*

Est! Est!! Est!!! di Montefiascone	*Trebbiano Giallo, Malvasia Toscana, Trebbiano Toscano*
Tarquinia Bianco	*Malvasia di Candia, Malvasia del Lazio, Trebbiano Toscano, Trebbiano Giallo*
Vignanello Bianco	*Malvasia di Candia, Malvasia del Chianti, Trebbiano Toscano, Trebbiano Giallo and other varieties (maximum 10%)*
Vignanello Greco	*Greco*

Adding confusion to this already formidable list, seemingly assembled by Sorcerer's Apprentices under the influence of Bacchus, some grape varieties have two or three different names. They are used at random in different growing areas. Trebbiano Toscano is Procanico to certain growers, and vice-versa; Trebbiano Giallo is Rossetto (or Roscetto) to others, and vice-versa; Grecchetto and Greco appear to be the same variety to some, but not to other growers. Passerina, also spelled Passerana, is sometimes called Trebbiano Bianco. Moscato di Terracina is sometimes called Moscato Apiana or Uva Apiana. One man's Malvasia del Lazio is another man's Malvasia Puntinata. And so on.

As can be seen, most grape varieties found in Lazio are also found elsewhere in Italy, or they come from France. Chardonnay, Syrah, and Petit Verdot are novelty varieties. However, some French grapes such as Merlot and Cabernet Sauvignon di Atina have been grown in Lazio for a century or more, and growers no longer consider them foreign.

A short-list of successful Lazio wineries and their sometimes maverick wines, in alphabetical order:

AZIENDA VITIVINICOLA CHRISTINE VASELLI

PIAZZA DEL POGGETTO 12

CASTIGLIONE IN TEVERINA, PROVINCE OF VITERBO

TEL: 0761 947008 ✦ WWW.CHRISTINEVASELLI.IT

Noteworthy wines: Le Poggere (Cabernet Sauvignon 70-percent, Merlot 30-percent), Appunto (a blend of Canaiolo and Ciliegiolo), Accenno (Bombino and Malvasia). All are bigger than strictly necessary, and Le Poggere has little to do with Lazio, but it's well made.

AZIENDA VITIVINICOLA CONTE ZANDOTTI

VIA VIGNE COLLE MATTIA 8, ROME

TEL: 06 206 09000 ✦ WWW.CANTINECONTEZANDOTTI.IT

Noteworthy wines: Frascati (classic), Malvasia Rumon (pure Malvasia del Lazio, subtle, with a pleasantly bittersweet quality), La Petrosa (Sangiovese, Cabernet Sauvignon, Merlot, Ottonese Nero, aged in large, old barrels). One of the first wineries to make high-quality Frascati and other fine wines, Conte Zandotti is respectful of *terroir*, shunning new oak.

AZIENDA VITIVINICOLA GIOVANNI PALOMBO

CORSO MUNANZIO PLANCO 21

ATINA, PROVINCE OF FROSINONE ✦ TEL: 0776 610 200

WWW.CASSINO2000.COM/TERRITORIO/PALOMBO

Noteworthy wines: Duca Cantelmi IGT Rosso (Cabernet Sauvignon, Cabernet Franc, Syrah), Cabernet di Atina. These are big, oaky wines made primarily with French and imported varietals.

AZIENDA VITIVINICOLA PAOLO E NOEMIA D'AMICO

LOCALITÀ PALOMBARO, VAIANO, PROVINCE OF VITERBO

TEL: 0761 948 868, CELLAR: 0761 948034

WWW.PAOLOENOEMIADAMICO.IT

Noteworthy wines: Falesia, Calanchi di Vaiano. Both are Chardonnay del Lazio and both are huge and have little to do with the region, but are crowd pleasers.

CANTINA CERVETERI

CANTINA SOCIALE COOPERATIVA DI CERVETERI

VIA AURELIA KM 42,700, CERVETERI, PROVINCE OF ROME

TEL: 06 990 5697 ✦ WWW.CANTINACERVETERI.COM

Noteworthy wines: Tertium IGT Rosso (Montepulciano 60-percent, Sangiovese 40-percent, 13-percent alcohol), Cerveteri Rosso DOC Viniae Grande (Sangiovese 35-percent, Montepulciano 35-percent, Merlot 30-percent, 13-percent alcohol). Both are well-balanced wines, with oak but not a forest of it. This is a co-op winery, but, against expectations, it makes excellent wines.

CANTINA COLACICCHI

VIA ROMAGNANO 2, ANAGNI, PROVINCE OF FROSINONE

TEL: 06 446 9661

Noteworthy wine: Torre Ercolana (Cabernet Sauvignon, Merlot, Cesanese di Affile in more or less equal amounts). Colacicchi is now owned by Francesco Trimani, one of Rome's top winesellers. The wines are meticulously crafted but fit for the most part into the Baroque renaissance style.

CANTINA SANT'ANDREA

STRADA DEL RENIBBIO 1720
BORGO VODICE, PROVINCE OF LATINA
TEL: 0773 755 028 ✦ WWW.CANTINASANTANDREA.IT

Noteworthy wines: Moscato Capitolium (Moscato di Terracina, 13.5-percent alcohol, a delicious sweet wine), Circeo Rosso Preludio alla Notte (Merlot 85-percent, Sangiovese 15-percent, a giant). Despite the pretentious pseudo-Latin and romantic names, this upcoming winery also sells second wines direct from the tank, and, though not memorable, they're less bruising and more like real Italian wines than the premium bottlings.

CANTINE SAN MARCO

VIA DI MOLA CAVONA 26, FRASCATI, PROVINCE OF ROME
TEL: 06 940 9403 ✦ WWW.SANMARCOFRASCATI.IT

Noteworthy wines: Frascati Superiore DOC Meraco (a classic Frascati with the usual varieties), SoloShirza (pure Syrah, 14-percent alcohol, a killer), SoloMerlot (ditto).

CARPINETI

VIA DELLE COLONNE 25, CORI, PROVINCE OF LATINA
TEL: 06 9679462 ✦ WWW.MARCOCARPINETI.IT

Noteworthy wines: Dithyrambus IGT Lazio Rosso (Montepulciano 60-percent, Nero Buono 40-percent), Collesanti (pure Arciprete Bianco Peloso), Moro (pure Greco). All three wines are organic, fully respectful of the *terroir*, are subtle and flavorful, without a hint of oak, fat, or overripe fruit. Ludum, made from Arciprete grapes with noble rot, is a magnificent, Sauternes-like dessert wine. Marco Carpineti is an outstanding winemaker.

CASALE DEL GIGLIO

STRADA CISTERNA-NETTUNO KM 13
LE FERRIERE, PROVINCE OF LATINA
TEL: 06 929 02530 ✦ WWW.CASALEDELGIGLIO.IT

Noteworthy wines: Mater Matuta (Syrah 85-percent, Petit Verdot 15-percent, 13.5-percent alcohol), Satrico (Chardonnay, Sauvignon, and Trebbiano Giallo in equal amounts). The red Mater Matuta is a New World colossus, the white Satrico is not oaked and though it's made primarily with French grapes, it's a pleasant, quaffable wine that feels in the mouth almost like an Italian wine.

CASALE DELLA IORIA

PIAZZA REGINA MARGHERITA 1, ACUTO, PROVINCE OF FROSINONE TEL: 0775 560 31 ✦ WWW.CASALEDELLAIORIA.COM

Noteworthy wines: Torre del Piano, Cesanese. Both are made with Cesanese di Affile grapes, are very good and have plenty of ripe fruit but are not oaky.

CASTEL DE PAOLIS

VIA VAL DE PAOLIS 41, GROTTAFERRATA, PROVINCE OF ROME
TEL: 06 941 3648 ✦ WWW.CASTELDEPAOLIS.IT

Noteworthy wines: I Quattro Mori (Syrah 65-percent, Merlot 20-percent, Cabernet Sauvignon 10-percent, Petit Verdot 5-percent, spends 18 months on oak and is a New World bruiser), Frascati Superiore Campo Vecchio (Malvasia del Lazio, Bellone, Romanesca, Bonvino, Passerina, Grechetto, Trebbiano Giallo, a pleasant classic), Campo Vecchio Rosso (50-percent Syrah, 20-percent Cesanese di Affile, 20-percent Montepulciano d'Abruzzo, 10-percent Sangiovese, also spends 18 months on oak and is overbuilt), Frascati Superiore Vigna Adriana (Malvasia puntinata bianca, Viogner, Sauvignon in equal amounts, a dizzying 14.5-percent alcohol, eight months on new oak but well balanced). This is one of Lazio's premier wineries.

COLETTI CONTI

CORSO VITTORIO EMANUELE 116, ANAGNI
PROVINCE OF FROSINONE
TEL: 0775 728 610 ✦ WWW.COLETTICONTI.IT

Noteworthy wines: Cesanese del Piglio Romanico (Cesanese di Affile, an unbelievable 15-percent alcohol, and far too big for its roots), Cesanese del Piglio Haernicus (Cesanese di Affile, only slightly less head-thumping at 14-percent alcohol). Coletti Conti wines are sunny and well made but overly alcoholic.

COLLE PICCHIONI

VIA DI COLLE PICCHIONE 46, MARINO, PROVINCE OF ROME
TEL: 06 935 46329 WWW.COLLEPICCHIONI.IT

Noteworthy wines: Vigna del Vassallo Lazio Rosso IGT (Merlot, Cabernet Sauvignon, and Cabernet Franc, spends 18 months on oak, comes in at a mere 12.5-percent alcohol and is well balanced and pleasantly spicy), Marino Colle Picchioni Selezione d'Oro (Malvasia del Lazio, Malvasia di Candia, Trebbiano giallo, Semillon, and others), Le Vignole (Trebbiano, Malvasia, Sauvignon blanc), Marino Donna Paola (Trebbiano, Malvasia, with trace quantities of Semillon). All the wines made by Paola di Mauro and her family are outstanding. They own the trendy Rome restaurant Sanpietrino, in the Ghetto (area 1, see page 115).

FALESCO

LOCALITÀ LE GUARDIE, MONTEFIASCONE,
PROVINCE OF VITERBO ✦ TEL: 0761 825 803 ✦ WWW.FALESCO.IT

Noteworthy wines: Montiano (Merlot, spends 12 months in oak casks, has nothing to do with the region but is a fine wine), Vitiano (Sangiovese, Merlot, Cabernet Sauvignon in equal amounts, from the winery's vineyards in Umbria, well balanced), Marciliano (Cabernet Sauvignon 70-percent, Cabernet Franc 30-percent, also from Umbria, also French in spirit and also well made), Est! Est!! Est!!! di Montefiascone Poggio dei Gelsi (Trebbiano 30-percent, Roscetto 30-percent, Malvasia 20-percent, others 20-percent, a fine classic white from the area), Vendemmia Tardiva Est! Est!! Est!!! (Trebbiano 50-percent, Roscetto 20-percent, Malvasia 30-percent; late-harvested grapes and no oak make this a remarkable white wine), Ferentano (Roscetto, an indigenous variety exuding honeysuckle). Falesco wines are all extremely well made.

FONTANA CANDIDA

VIA FONTANA CANDIDA 11
MONTEPORZIO CATONE, PROVINCE OF ROME
TEL: 06 942 0066 ✦ WWW.FONTANACANDIDA.IT

Noteworthy wines: Frascati Superiore Santa Teresa (Trebbiano Toscano, Malvasia di Candia, Malvasia del Lazio, Greco, a classic Frascati). Fontana Candida is a huge winery making everything from jug wines on up. This is their best, and it's very good.

MOTTURA

LOCALITÀ POGGIO DELLA COSTA 1
CIVITELLA D'AGLIANO, PROVINCE OF VITERBO
TEL: 0761 914 533 ✦ WWW.MOTTURASERGIO.IT

Noteworthy wines: Muffo (Grechetto 50-percent, Procanico 50-percent, a nectarious late-harvest dessert wine, the Sauternes of Lazio), Nenfro Lazio Rosso IGT (Merlot 60-percent, Montepulciano 40-percent, spends 12 months on oak and is 14-percent alcohol but well balanced), Latour a Civitella (Grechetto, a 14-percent alcohol wine that spends nine months in oak). Sergio Mottura makes outstanding dessert wines.

L'OLIVELLA

VIA DI COLLE PISANO, FRASCATI, PROVINCE OF ROME

TEL: 06 942 4527 ✦ WWW.RACEMO.IT

Noteworthy wines: Tre Grome IGT Lazio Bianco (Malvasia Puntinata, Malvasia Rossa, Bellone, a 13-percent white that's lush, fatty, and oaky). Cesanese (Cesanese, a classic, with tobacco, red and black berries, but little oak), Frascati Superiore DOC Racemo (Malvasia del Lazio 50-percent, Malvasia di Candia 20-percent, Trebbiano Giallo 10-percent, Trebbiano Toscano 10-percent, Bellone 10-percent, a well-balanced, pleasantly light wine with only 12-percent alcohol).

PIETRA PINTA

VIA GRAMSCI 53, CORI, PROVINCE OF LATINA

TEL: 06 967 8001 ✦ WWW.PIETRAPINTA.COM

Noteworthy wine: Colle Amato (Cabernet Sauvignon, Syrah), a New World–style *vino da tavola* that's well made and easy to drink.

POGGIO LE VOLPI

VIA FONTANA CANDIDA 3C

MONTEPORZIO CATONE, PROVINCE OF ROME

TEL: 06 941 9491 ✦ WWW.POGGIOLEVOLPI.IT

Noteworthy wines: Frascati Superiore People (Malvasia di Candia 70-percent and late harvested, Trebbiano 20-percent, Sauvignon 10-percent, a round, big wine that's full of fruit but not overly oaky), Baccarossa (Nero Buono, spends 12 months in oak, a weightlifter at 13.5-percent alcohol).

PRINCIPE PALLAVICINI

VIA CASILINA KM 25,500, COLONNA, PROVINCE OF ROME

TEL: 06 943 8816 ✦ WWW.VINIPALLAVICINI.COM

Noteworthy wines: Amarasco (Cesanese, 14-percent alcohol, 12 months in oak and thick enough to slice), Rubillo (Cesanese, made from old vines, aged in stainless steel only, full of spicy fruit, a winner), Frascati Superiore Poggio Verde (Malvasia di Candia 50-percent, Malvasia del Lazio 20-percent, Trebbiano Toscano 10-percent, Grechetto and Greco 20-percent; aged on its lees for five months and therefore atypical, but successful because well made).

TENUTA LE QUINTE

VIA DELLE MARMORELLE 91
MONTECOMPATRI, PROVINCE OF ROME
TEL: 06 943 8756 ✦ WWW.LEQUINTE.IT

Noteworthy wines: Montecompatri Superiore Virtù Romane (Malvasia del Lazio 60-percent, Bellone, Bombino and Trebbiano Giallo 40-percent, a 14-percent alcohol wine that's big and fat and yet very well made).

TENUTA PIETRA PORZIA

VIA DI PIETRA PORZIA 60, FRASCATI, PROVINCE OF ROME
TEL: 06 946 4392 ✦ WWW.TENUTADIPIETRAPORZIA.IT

Noteworthy wines: Frascati Superiore Regillo Etichetta Nera (Trebbiano, Malvasia del Lazio, Malvasia di Candia, Bombino, Greco, a wine that officially reaches 13.8-percent alcohol but is probably closer to 14.5-percent; 10-percent of it is fermented in new oak casks, but the oak doesn't overwhelm this remarkable wine).

TENUTA SANT'ISIDORO

LOCALITÀ PORTACCIA, TARQUINIA, PROVINCE OF VITERBO
TEL: 0766 869 716 ✦ WWW.SANTISIDORO.NET

Noteworthy wines: Soremidio (Montepulciano, an overly alcoholic wine at 13.5-percent, but tons of berries and ripe fruit), Corithus (Sangiovese 50-percent, Montepulciano 30-percent, Merlot 20-percent, spends six months on new oak, is also a bruiser at 13.5-percent alcohol, but is also well made).

TRAPPOLINI

VIA DEL RIVELLINO 65, CASTIGLIONE IN TEVERINA
PROVINCE OF VITERBO ✦ TEL: 0761 948 381

Noteworthy wine: Paterno (Sangiovese, 13.5-percent alcohol, and lots of blackberry and red fruit components, plus bitter chocolate and violets).

VILLA SIMONE

VIA FRASCATI-COLONNA 29
MONTEPORZIO CATONE, PROVINCE OF ROME
TEL: 06 944 9717 ✦ WWW.PIEROCOSTANTINI.IT

Noteworthy wine: Vigneto Filonardi (primarily Malvasia di Candia and Trebbiano Toscano, plus Greco and Malvasia del Lazio; a classic, dry Frascati with hints of honey). Villa Simone is owned by Enoteca Costantini, among Rome's top wine shops.

CHAPTER 1

CAMPO DE'FIORI, GHETTO, CAPITOLINE/ FORUM

LOOK AT A SATELLITE PHOTO OF THE HISTORIC CENTER OF ROME, SPECIFICALLY, THE AREA FILLING the wavy "C" that the Tiber River forms between the Ara Pacis and the Theater of Marcellus. If you're hungry, or a lover of Arcimboldo or *guanciale* jowl bacon, you might recognize the silhouette of a pig's head. Corso Vittorio Emanuele II, a wide thoroughfare, bisects the area, forming the pig's grinning lips. The roughly triangular jaw of this imaginary beast would run from the snout-end at the riverbank east past Campo de' Fiori and the Ghetto to the base of the Capitoline Hill. Along with the Pantheon area, which is north of the pig's lips, and the Palatine, one hill east of the Capitoline, this mandible-shaped neighborhood is Rome's oldest. It's also the most densely packed with cultural and culinary treasures (the Palatine and Forum and most of the Capitoline are short on places to eat, however, unless you graze on dandelions among the ruins). As is true of most of antique Rome, the only way to explore the Campo de' Fiori-Ghetto-Capitoline area is on foot, with a detailed map at the ready.

Most guidebooks will not tell you that Monte dei Cenci, a hummock in the Ghetto, is built atop the still-buried ruins of the third-century BC circus of censor Caius Flaminius; for the last 150 years the mound's crown has been home to the outdoor terrace of Ristorante Piperno, owned by the self-styled "kings of artichokes." Nor do many visitors realize that in the cellar of Antico Forno Marco Roscioli, in Via dei Chiavari, lie remnants of the Theater of Pompey, where Julius Caesar was murdered. The subterranean dining areas of several nearby restaurants favored by tourists (and not listed in this guidebook) are claimed by each of their savvy owners to be the very spot upon which Brutus wielded his dagger. Medieval relics in the pig's jowl district are too numerous to mention, while the Renaissance and Baroque periods have littered it with mementos, some food-related. Among them are Il Pompiere restaurant, housed in the palace where Beatrice Cenci lived, and whence she was dragged to the Ponte di Sant'Angelo to be executed. Campo de' Fiori has been a market square since the fifteenth century, and Ar Galletto, nearby on Piazza Farnese, has been serving earthy food and wine to all comers for just as long. In fact many of the family-run businesses dotted around the neighborhood have been around for a century or more, and some are into their third, fourth, or fifth generations.

This is all the more surprising because few other neighborhoods in Rome have been as radically changed as this one by the combined phenomena of gentrification, mass tourism, night clubbing, and modern food distribution—meaning supermarkets. The demographics have shifted, with working-class and middle-class Romans moving out, and short-term, out-of-town renters moving in. The eat-and-run tourism crowds and the heavy-drinking pub-crawlers who throng Campo de' Fiori are dismaying to many, particularly lovers of authentic old Rome. But the authenticity remains, sometimes buried like Pompey's theater, sometimes hidden down an alleyway, in a courtyard, or within the walls of a restaurant.

By its labyrinthine nature, much of the area is free of car traffic, and several streets have been pedestrianized of late, including Via del Portico d'Ottavia, the Ghetto's spinal column. Bounding the Ghetto as it is defined today are: Largo Arenula (with its streetcar terminus), the Tiber, Theater of Marcellus, and Piazza di Campitelli. Though Jews have lived in the Ghetto for centuries, Rome's first Jewish neighborhood was not here but rather in Trastevere, on the Tiber River's unincorporated west side (area 7, see page 261). During the Middle Ages, many Jewish *trasteverini* crossed the river to central Rome seeking safety within the fortified east-bank walls. Only in 1556, under Pope Paul IV, did that area become known as the infamous walled Ghetto. Rome's Jews suffered persecution and lived in poverty in the Ghetto, but also enjoyed many decades of religious tolerance and prosperity.

The Ghetto was abolished several times in the 1800s, after Napoleon Bonaparte first occupied the city. In 1848 the walls were partly removed; following Italian Unification, the remaining walls were destroyed and the synagogue was built. The twentieth century's legacy is mixed. The 1938 "racial laws" adopted during Fascism restricted Jewish business activities, and many Italian Jews were forced to leave the country. The Ghetto's Jewish population shrank during and after World War Two, when hundreds of residents died at the hands of Fascists and Nazis. Many middle-class survivors moved to attractive, modern housing in the Monteverde Vecchio or Marconi districts on the west side of the river, abutting Trastevere. In 1967, an estimated 5,000 Jews fled Libya, fearing persecution, and congregated in Rome, not in the Ghetto, but rather in the Nomentana neighborhood, around Piazza Bologna, in the eastern-central part of the city.

Though many of its members no longer live in the Ghetto, Rome's estimated 17,000-strong Jewish community still gravitates toward the neighborhood to worship, socialize, shop, and eat. Hulking old *palazzi* line alleys and courtyards. Ghetto streets are scented by olive oil and roasting lamb. A visitor might chance upon elderly residents draping thin strips of meat over sticks to dry in the sun; these are *coppiette secche*—beef or horse jerky. Because of European Union health laws, jerky is no longer officially available in shops, but if you're intrepid, you'll eventually find some.

Most of the neighborhood's Jewish butcher shops, bakeries, restaurants, and *caffè* are on or near the Via del Portico d'Ottavia, which is about 300 yards long. On its southeast end stands the eighth-century church of Sant'Angelo in Pescheria, built into the ruins of a second-century BC portico that Augustus Caesar rebuilt and dedicated to his sister, Octavia. The portico housed Rome's main fish market (la Pescheria) from the twelfth to the late nineteenth century, a market largely operated by Jews. On the archway near the entrance to the church, a stone plaque recalls the curious privilege of Rome's so-called Conservatori Capitolini (elected magistrates): they were to be given the heads of all fish over a certain length. Clearly, fish cheeks and fish stock were even more prized in the past than they are today.

With gentrification underway, the Ghetto is also witnessing an influx of non-Roman Jews, many from Eastern Europe, Russia, and Israel. Some long-established businesses are moving out, while a more international style of business, often kosher, moves in. Three new kosher eateries stand in a row on Via Santa Maria del Pianto, which is the continuation of Via del Portico d'Ottavia. They are: Kosher Bistrot (which isn't a bistro, but rather a deli); Chagat's Shabbat Kit Kosher Take Away (with filet-o-fish, schwarma, and schnitzle); and Fast Kosher (with MkFalafel and MkHotdog and other improbable MkKnock-offs).

Mercato di Campo de' Fiori is central Rome's celebrated, chaotic, parasol-dotted outdoor market in the square of the same name. It's about midway between Piazza Navona and the Tiber River, and only 100 yards east of Piazza Farnese. Before dawn, stand-holders trundle their sawhorses, planks, canvas umbrellas, and merchandise across the cobbled square and laboriously set up shop, a ritual going back to the late 1400s. The scene appears to be timeless. However, upon closer inspection, you will notice that the Campo is undergoing a socio-cultural tsunami. It has more tourists and fewer local customers these days than any of Rome's outlying

E.2.00 KG
CARCIOFI
E. 1.00
CARCIOFI
E.0.70
E.1.50 KG
E.230 KG
PUNTARELLE
E.1.50 KG
CARCIOFI
E.1.30

CORANG

neighborhood markets, including the bigger markets at Trionfale, Testaccio, and Esquilino-Termini. Clothing, souvenirs, and gadgets are gradually replacing food at the Campo's stands. Still, it's charming, the market most visitors to Rome will see and enjoy. In its center on a tall pedestal is the statue of Giordano Bruno, burned alive at the stake here in 1600.

Three of the market's merchants deserve special mention. The foremost and longest-established greengrocer here is stocky, black-haired, volatile **Claudio Zampa**, whose family has worked the Campo for the better part of a century. Zampa's sprawling stands face the flower sellers on the north end of the square, near the drinking water tap and ornamental fountain, and are covered by half a dozen umbrellas. He supplies many exacting customers, among them the Vatican, the French embassy, and the office of Italy's prime minister. Even in winter, Zampa displays mounds of top-quality artichokes from the Salentino south of Naples, and hothouse-grown ripe tomatoes from the slopes of Vesuvius and Etna, plus broccoli, spinach, dewy baby lettuce, zucchini, and zucchini flowers from Rome's suburbs. In spring, summer, and fall the choice is vast and peerless. Locals call Zampa "Cartier" but once you've gotten used to his produce, it's hard to shop elsewhere despite the high prices. Zampa also sells the hard-to-find kitchen tool used by Romans to slice *puntarella* chicory (ask for the *taglia puntarelle*).

About 40 yards south of Zampa, on the west (Tiber River) side of the square, friendly, white-haired **Marcella Banco**, a Campo de' Fiori fixture since the 1960s, sells excellent produce, and is known to insiders as among the fastest, most skilled trimmers of artichokes in the city. Her *carciofi romaneschi*, ready to be transformed into *carciofi alla romana* or *carciofi alla giudia*, are always excellent. About 50 yards south of Marcella's stand, in the center rank of the market's stands, near the drinking water tap and fishmongers, is **Mauro Berardi**, the herb-and-spice man. Mauro is now in his forties and has worked here since he was five years old. He mixes and matches seasonings for pasta, meat, and tomato sauce. One blend popular among vegetarians is called *carbonara*. It's roughly five-percent finely ground black pepper, 15-percent minced chives, and 80-percent onion. Sautéed in olive oil, it substitutes for *guanciale*, *pancetta*, or bacon in a classic *carbonara* recipe.

On the square's north side is **Il Forno Campo de' Fiori** (a bakery) and **Ristorante La Carbonara**; on its east side is

Antica Norcineria Viola (see page 97); on its west side is **Vito Ruggeri** (grocery/deli).

At the Campo there's always a lull in the afternoon, but at night, when the stands have been packed up and hauled away, the square is again crowded and animated, this time filling with a raucous party crowd. Restaurant and bar terraces overflow. Pub-crawlers and night clubbers congregate around the statue of Giordano Bruno until the early hours, moving on only when the city clean-up crews or police squads force them out of the way. By dawn, the greengrocers and other merchants have begun making their slow, eternal return to the square, setting up their stands, often in darkness.

RESTAURANTS AND TRATTORIAS

AR GALLETTO

UNLESS YOU EAT HERE IN WINTER—OR IN VERY BAD WEATHER—YOU PROBABLY WON'T ENTER THE HANDsome, cozy old dining room, with its sky-high ceilings held up by painted timbers, or the cavernous wine cellar with bottlings from about 500 different wineries. That's because Ar Galletto, an *osteria* since at least 1484, and once owned by the notorious Borgia family, has one of the city's most pleasant outdoor terraces, with tables on Piazza Farnese, facing a Renaissance fountain (with a recycled ancient Roman basin) and the lozenge-patterned façade of Palazzo Farnese (so embellished by Michelangelo). In this setting it's easy to forget the interior, not to mention the food. Luckily, owner Giovanni Coletti, his wife Luisa, and their family, do a good job with everything from the *carciofi alla romana* or *puntarella* salad to the *amatriciana* and oxtail stew, not to mention roast or grilled lamb and the house specialty, *galletto alla diavola*—spicy game hen flattened and grilled with lemon and chili. Giovanni twists his lavish moustache and quips or puns lustily with fellow Italian-speakers (he's polite to foreigners). Luisa runs the kitchen, and has been doing so since the 1960s. She still makes the pasta by hand; her fettuccine with *porcini* are excellent. The desserts are classic and homey—*tiramisù* and ricotta cake, for instance. Giovanni, his son, and waiters provide professional yet friendly service.

Be warned that the house antipasto—a huge platter of grilled vegetables, cold cuts, and mini mozzarella balls—is filling in the extreme. Reserve a terrace table ahead.

PIAZZA FARNESE 102/VICOLO DEL GALLO 1
TEL: 06 686 1714 ✦ CLOSED SUNDAY *and in* AUGUST ✦ MODERATE
Near: on northwest edge of Piazza Farnese, corner of alley, behind the fountain

BAR BENITO

DOORMEN, MAIL CARRIERS, COMMUTERS, OTHER LOCAL REGULARS, AND STRAY TOURISTS USE THIS family-run *caffè* and *tavola calda* for breakfast, snacks, and lunch. The dining room is cool, airy, and clean, with high, coffered ceilings, overhead fans, and linoleum-topped old wooden tables. The classic, tasty Roman food is made in the morning and kept warm—or reheated—when early-rising customers start showing up around noon. Expect to find *carciofi alla romana*, lasagna, *picchiapò* beef stew, *saltimbocca*, tripe, and other trattoria standards on the menu, which changes daily. The *torta di ricotta* is house-made and delicious, a true Roman cheesecake in the Jewish style. The service is casual, the atmosphere relaxed, and the prices impossible to beat. It's worth noting that the delicious *pizza bianca* comes from Antico Forno del Ghetto, which is about 200 yards away.

VIA DEI FALEGNAMI 14 ✦ TEL: 06 686 1508
CLOSED SUNDAY *and* AUGUST ✦ VERY INEXPENSIVE
Near: halfway between Via Arenula and Piazza Mattei, facing Vicolo dei Falegnami

DA SERGIO

WITH ITS RANK OF TABLES WRAPPED AROUND THE CORNER OF NARROW VICOLO DELLE GROTTE AND Via Capo di Ferro, this typical Roman neighborhood trattoria has been owned and run by the Mariotti family since the late 1970s. Sergio is in the background these days, but his three children run the show, cooking up the weekly, rotating wheel of Canonical classics. The gnocchi are comforting, the tripe gutsy and authentic, and the *carbonara* and *amatriciana* better than merely competent. The restaurant's interior is dark-ish, simply decorated and homey, a good place to chill out in hot weather, in the best trattoria style. Note that Da Sergio attracts both local regulars and tourists; it opens for lunch at 12:30pm and for dinner at 7pm.

VICOLO DELLE GROTTE 27 ✦ TEL: 06 686 4293
CLOSED SUNDAY *and* AUGUST ✦ INEXPENSIVE *to* MODERATE
Near: 150 yards southeast of Piazza Farnese

DAR FILETTARO A SANTA BARBARA

IF ROME WERE LONDON, THIS WOULD BE THE CITY'S FAVORITE FISH 'N' CHIPS JOINT. THE LOCALS WHO'VE BEEN flocking for decades to this cult fry shop, lionized by the late, great food historian Livio Jannattoni, call it either Filetti di Baccalà or Dar Filettaro, though you won't find either name posted outside, on the pocketsized square where booksellers and bookbinders—*i librari*—once plied their trade. The fry shop's interior is the size of several telephone booths clapped together, and if you choose to sit there in unparalleled coziness and savor the simple, delicious fried codfish; the platters of ham, salami, and cheese; the salads and cooked vegetable dishes; or salted anchovies served with a curl of butter, you will exit with the scent of essential Rome on your clothes. Outside, in warm weather, at one of the small tables in front of the spotlit façade of tiny Santa Barbara, a snack or a full meal becomes more than a mere eating experience, and allows you to avoid being mistaken later for a codfish. Note that no credit cards are accepted; the prices are startlingly reasonable.

LARGO DEI LIBRARI 88 ✦ TEL: 06 686 4018
OPEN *from* 5PM *to* 10:40PM ✦ CLOSED SUNDAY
VERY INEXPENSIVE ✦ *Near: 150 yards southeast of Campo de' Fiori, across from church of Santa Barbara*

DER PALLARO

ASK FOR A TABLE ON THE ENCLOSED TERRACE OUT FRONT, UNLESS YOU ENJOY DINING AMONG FELL-OFF-the-back-of-a-truck-style clutter. If there were an Eternal Trattoria award Der Pallaro would surely be on the short list. It has been run, since the 1950s, by Paola (and her husband, Mario). No need to worry about what to order. The menu is set. There is something reassuringly Nietzchean about the Eternal Return of the platter of abundant and tasty *antipasti* (olives, lentil salad, *prosciutto crudo*, mini mozzarella balls, meatballs, and fried potato dumplings); the rigatoni with red meat sauce and mountains of grated cheese (or another pasta with a simple sauce); the stews or cutlets or roast breast of veal; the seasonal vegetables (broccoli rabe sautéed with garlic and chili, or hand-sliced, fresh french fries); and the equally eternal dessert: a *crostata* with pastry cream and jam (usually peach) accompanied by a glass of freshly squeezed fruit juice (orange, strawberry, or other). The choice of wine is equally easy: house red, house white. Der Pallaro is also one of the few eateries left in Rome where the coffee is brewed in a stovetop Moka (it could be a little less bitter and bursting with caffeine). The price is right, the crowd a mix of local regulars and tourists.

LARGO DEL PALLARO 15 ✦ TEL: 06 688 01488
CLOSED MONDAY ✦ INEXPENSIVE
Near: 150 yards east of Campo de' Fiori, off Via dei Chiavari

GIGGETTO AL PORTICO D'OTTAVIA

GIGGETTO IS A CLASSIC AMONG MID-SCALE FAMILY-RUN ROMAN TRATTORIAS. IT COMES COMPLETE WITH sun umbrellas outside, white tablecloths, waiters in white jackets and black ties, and a white-washed interior with wine bottles on shelves, not to mention platters of appetizers temptingly displayed on service-area tables. Oil paintings and prints showing old Roman scenes hang on the walls, and the heavy wooden chairs with caned seats are comfortable. Luigi Ceccarelli, alias Giggetto, and his wife Ines, alias Sora Ines, founded Giggetto in 1923. The trattoria is now run by the second generation, Franco Ceccarelli, and the third generation, Franco's son Claudio. Pastry chef Stefano Ceccarelli (Claudio's brother) owns La Dolceroma (see page 108) pastry shop next door, and makes some of the delicious desserts served at the trattoria, including the exceptional *torta di ricotta* cheesecake. The Ceccarelli family is Roman Catholic, but like many non-Jewish Roman restaurateurs, their house specialties come straight out of the Roman-Jewish tradition. Giggetto serves excellent *carciofi alla giudia*, other fried vegetables, and the full range of traditional Roman trattoria favorites, from *amatriciana* or *carbonara* to offal and roast lamb. Atmosphere and setting are a big part of the trattoria's allure: the front sidewalk terrace runs up to the church of Sant'Angelo in Pescheria, and the tables sit between the ruined half-columns of the Portico of Octavia; the cellar is built into the ruins of the portico (and may be visited). Around the back of the sprawling restaurant, which fills half a dozen cavernous rooms, is another pleasant, quieter, shady outdoor dining area.

VIA DEL PORTICO D'OTTAVIA 21A/22
TEL: 06 686 1105 ✦ WWW.GIGGETTO.IT ✦ CLOSED TUESDAY
MODERATE *to* EXPENSIVE
Near: on the east end of the Ghetto's main street

GRAPPOLO D'ORO—ZAMPANÒ

ANYONE WHO REMEMBERS THE *NEW YORKER* WRITER WILLIAM MURRAY'S DISPATCHES FROM ROME IN THE 1960s and '70s will be familiar with the name Grappolo d'Oro. Were he alive today, Murray would no longer recognize the place. Like Ditirambo (the perpetually thronged pan-Italian, neo-trattoria across the street with which Grappolo d'Oro is now affiliated), this popular spot is difficult to classify. It has been around for decades in a variety of incarnations, some good, others less so. In recent years, after the arrival of Antonello Magliari, Grappolo d'Oro–Zampanò has morphed into a hip, designer property favored by trendy Romans and upscale tourists, many of whom have tried but failed to get into Ditirambo. The service here is casual-hip, and much of the food waltzes liberally, sometimes dizzily, with regional themes (a flan of pecorino with a sauce of *guanciale* and pepper, or *baccalà* drizzled with chickpea and rosemary coulis; lamb chops with pearl onions or Argentine Angus *tagliata* drizzled with olive oil). However, also on the menu are authentic Roman *puntarelle* with a perfect anchovy dressing, pan-fried chicory, an excellent, classic *amatriciana*, and a remarkable *carbonara* made with peerless *guanciale* from Norcia. Main courses are overly complicated and have little or nothing to do with Roman tradition; again like Ditirambo and other faux-traditional eateries, Grappolo d'Oro offers a selection of Italian cheeses, presented and sold in the French style. For dessert, spoon sweets only—nothing as vulgar as a good Roman *crostata*. The *zabaglione* with shaved almonds is very good, nonetheless. As might be expected, the wine list reflects a pan-Italian spirit.

The small outdoor terrace is pleasant in warm weather, and the luminous, modern interior is air-conditioned.

PIAZZA DELLA CANCELLERIA 80 ✦ TEL: 06 689 7080, WWW.GRAPPOLODOROZAMPANO.IT ✦ CLOSED TUESDAY
MODERATE *to* EXPENSIVE ✦ *Near: one block east of Campo de' Fiori*

IL POMPIERE

BEATRICE CENCI—THE TRAGIC RENAISSANCE FIGURE EXECUTED IN 1599 FOR ALLEGEDLY MURDERING HER father—lived in the hulking palazzo which houses this venerable, handsome, atmospheric restaurant, whose dining rooms are one story up from street level. Ghosts are not on the menu, however, despite the creaking floors and towering ceilings with massive exposed timbers. Rather, you'll find the full range of well-made, traditional Roman and Jewish-Roman cooking, from fried artichokes to battered and fried lamb or veal brains, oxtails and codfish to *puntarella* salad and more. The "more" means *carbonara* and *amatriciana* made with pork products, a hint that the association with Jewish cooking is tenuous. The Monteferri family has been at the helm since the early 1960s, in these premises, but is actually into the third generation in the neighborhood. They had a restaurant in nearby Piazza Mattei for about 40 years. The business is in their blood, which explains the professionalism: smooth service, a wine list designed to please all palates, and efficient air conditioning to lure in crowds in Rome's steamy summer weather.

VIA DI SANTA MARIA DE' CALDERARI 38 ✦ TEL: 06 686 8377
CLOSED SUNDAY *and* AUGUST ✦ MODERATE *to* EXPENSIVE
Near: on corner of Piazza Cinque Scole

LA CARBONARA

AN "EASY" ADDRESS, FOUNDED DECADES AGO AND VISIBLE TO ALL PASSERSBY ON CAMPO DE' FIORI, La Carbonara is shunned by snooty Romans. That is at once a mistake for them and a blessing for others, because it means that your chances of getting a good table are at least fair to middling. Reserve one on the terrace, which spills its tables behind the flower sellers and fountain on the market square's north end, or upstairs, by a window, with a view (the air conditioning makes indoor dining pleasant in hot summer weather). The menu offers all the Roman classics, well-prepared and served by professionals. Lovers of *carbonara* will want to pay homage to this restaurant, which Roman food historian Livio Jannattoni called the cradle of the first "modern" version of the dish, made with penne and not spaghetti or tonnarelli—to avoid stains. Many Romans insist that *carbonara* is named not for charcoal-burning woodsmen, but rather for the abundant black pepper in it. The pepper lends it the appearance of being powdered with carbon (*carbone* in Italian). Federico Salomone founded not this restaurant but its predecessor, on Via di Montevecchio, in 1912; he was a coal deliveryman, an urban *carbonaro*, and the trattoria's original name was Trattoria del Carbonaro. Salomone served not spaghetti, but penne, for the simple reason that when forked up, penne do not sling sauce onto the clothing of customers. Federico's daughter is Andreina Salomone, the owner, since Federico died, of La Carbonara on Campo de' Fiori. In her eighties today, the formidable Andreina is flanked by her family, and the *penne alla carbonara* served in her historic restaurant are still remarkably good.

CAMPO DE' FIORI 23 ✦ TEL: 06 686 4783
WWW.LA-CARBONARA.IT ✦ CLOSED TUESDAY
MODERATE *to* EXPENSIVE
Near: the flower stands on the north side of the square

PIPERNO

IF YOU DON'T MIND BREAKING THE PIGGY-BANK, AND WANT SOME OF THE HIGHEST-QUALITY TRADITIONAL Roman food in town, served in old-fashioned, slightly dowdy but very comfortable surroundings, consider Piperno, which has been owned by the same family since the mid 1800s, and seems to attract the same conservative, well-heeled crowd of Romans and foreigners decade after decade. The pasta—including remarkable gnocchi—is still made in-house by a little old Roman lady, and the artichokes every way they're served—fried, braised, or sliced thin and presented raw in a salad—are outstanding. The Piperno clan rather presumptuously call themselves "the kings of artichokes," and they may not be far wrong, though the title, since 1962, should really be attributed to the people who run the restaurant, the Boni and Mazzarella families. This is one of the few places that still serve labor-intensive *vignarola* (in spring only) and broccoli soup with skate. The *coda alla vaccinara* is luscious, the lamb exquisite. Even the jam that goes into the jam tarts is house-made and not overly sweet. Piperno's wine list currently boasts precisely 140 different bottlings from around Italy, including 11 from Lazio, and several hideously expensive Super-style wines from Tuscany and Piedmont. The cavernous interior, with four separate dining rooms, has touches of scarlet, which go with the late-1800s naïf murals. Though the carbon footprint is large, you will be happy to know Piperno is air-conditioned. The terrace, in a tiny *piazzetta* atop a knoll (behind the palace once owned by the luckless Cenci family), is a magical spot for fine-weather dining.

MONTE DE' CENCI 9 ✦ TEL: 06 688 06629, 06 683 3606
WWW.RISTORANTEPIPERNO.IT ✦ CLOSED SUNDAY DINNER
and MONDAY ✦ EXPENSIVE *to* VERY EXPENSIVE
Near: between Via Arenula and Piazza Cinque Scole

ROSCIOLI

ROSCIOLI IS AN ODDBALL, A CROSSOVER FOOD AND WINE BOUTIQUE, RESTAURANT, AND LATE-NIGHT HANGOUT for Roman hipsters. An astonishing success story, it belongs to the same hard-working family behind Antico Forno Marco Roscioli (see page 99). Under the guidance of brothers Alessandro and Pierluigi Roscioli, the family's former salami shop and grocery store was transformed into a boutique property with delicacies displayed like books on shelves, or jewels in cases. Long and narrow, with small black-topped tables and spotlighting, it has become one of the city's most innovative places to eat a mix of traditional and updated Roman food, and taste or buy excellent wine (600 different bottlings are sold, 40 from Lazio), olive oil, balsamic vinegar, cheese, and ham. All are made by small, high-quality producers. The luscious ewe's-milk ricotta arrives daily from Caseificio Giuseppe Lopez, one of the Lazio region's premier cheesemakers. The pecorino fiore sardo, an ewe's-milk cheese aged 18 months, is handmade by shepherd Giuseppe Cuguzi in Sardinia; he "washes" the rounds with olive oil and rubs them with juniper ash, which gives them a tobacco hue and an exquisite, smoked flavor. The amazingly flavorful salamis, *culatello*, and *fiocco* are handmade by Fulvio Pier Angelini from the meat of free-range, heirloom *cinta senese* pigs (and air-dried in Polesine Parmense, near Parma). The *pizza bianca* served

here is baked by Pierluigi Roscioli himself at the family bakery up the street, and is unquestionably Rome's best: crisp yet tender and redolent of olive oil. The cakes and many of the desserts also come from the bakery. You can eat any of the deli or bakery delights at table, but you can also order from the menu, which includes several outstanding dishes. The *amatriciana* is a classic. Roscioli's *carbonara* is often cited as Rome's best; it is certainly among the most luscious, flavorful, and elegantly presented in town, and the ingredients are peerless, from the aged *guanciale* to the organic eggs (only the yolks are used) to the pecorino di fossa, excellent parmigiano, and pepper from Sarawak. Chef Hadj Hussen Nabil is no Rome native: he moved at age 17 to Rome from Tunisia and worked at the luxurious restaurant of

the four-star Parco dei Principi hotel before joining Roscioli. His skill is apparent in everything from the simplest starters and pasta dishes—which are always beautifully plated—to the impeccably fresh grilled wild sea bass. At Roscioli, fish dishes are offered only once the daily catch gets to the restaurant from the fish markets of Anzio or Civitavecchia. Reserve ahead, or get to the restaurant before 12:30pm for lunch and 8pm for dinner, or be prepared to wait for a table.

VIA DEI GIUBBONARI 21/23 ✦ TEL: 06 687 5287
WWW.ANTICOFORNOROSCIOLI.COM
OPEN *for* LUNCH *and* DINNER MONDAY *through* SATURDAY
DELI OPEN 7:30AM *to* 8PM, CLOSED SUNDAY
MODERATE *to* EXPENSIVE ✦ *Near: equidistant—about 250 yards—from the Ghetto and Campo de' Fiori*

SETTIMIO AL PELLEGRINO

BE WARNED: IF YOU MANAGE TO GET A TABLE AT THIS OLD CULT TRATTORIA YOU WON'T DINE IN THE COMPANY of foreigners, but rather cheek-by-jowl with Roman insiders. The food is strictly traditional—the weekly rotation of classics such as *pasta e fagioli*, fettuccine, gnocchi, *baccalà*, lamb, beef rolls, and more. All are well-made, with good ingredients, and the short wine list is adequate and not overpriced. Owned and operated by the Zazza family, Settimio is a place of contrasts: the frosted glass panes on the street are there to keep unwelcome eyes out; the tiny entrance area has a second door with a doorbell. You must ring it to be admitted. There's no menu to study before entering. The contrasts continue inside: stone-clad walls but trattoria-style coat hooks, and the kind of hard, wooden chairs used in the bad old days in primary schools. The hours, like the entrance and lack of a menu on display, are in part devised to keep tourists at bay: lunch service starts at 1:30pm and ends at 3pm; dinner begins at 8:30pm and ends at 11pm. The hours also reflect the reality of a small, overworked, studiously insouciant staff. Settimio couldn't start serving earlier even if the Zazzas wanted to, and they don't. And don't be surprised if you're greeted with the words "who sent you here?" If you attempt to reserve by telephone, you might well be told "we don't take reservations by telephone unless we already know you." Is it worth the trouble? Maybe. Few places are more authentically Roman. For a similar dining experience but without the persnickety attitude, try Felice in the Testaccio neighborhood (area 6, see page 247). For similar surroundings, equally good (or better) food, and helpful, friendly service, plus reasonable opening hours, go to Gino, north of the Pantheon (area 2, see page 128).

VIA DEL PELLEGRINO 117 ✦ TEL: 06 688 01978
CLOSED WEDNESDAY *and for several weeks*
in JULY *and/or* AUGUST ✦ MODERATE
Near: about 200 yards north of Campo de' Fiori

SORA LELLA

THE CELEBRATED COOK AND 1950s–'60s ACTRESS SORA LELLA (ELENA FABRIZI) IS NO LONGER AMONG the living. However, her son, Aldo Trabalzi, and his heavyset sons, Mauro, Renato, and Simone, along with their sister Elena, continue to run Sora Lella with aplomb. This is a high-end, traditional gourmet restaurant, not a trattoria, and happens to be the only place to dine on the atmospheric Tiber Island. The prices are high, the servings smallish, the clientele demanding and often animated by self-love, and the tables a little too close by luxury restaurant standards. But there are few addresses in Rome that compare to Sora Lella when it comes to the quality of ingredients, the lightness of touch, and the authenticity of the food. You will not go wrong with any of the perfectly prepared classics, from the skate soup with broccoli to the *carbonara* or *abbacchio brodettato*—a kind of heavenly *carbonara* of lamb. Sora Lella also prides itself on resuscitating heirloom recipes. The fettuccine, for instance, come with a startlingly rich sauce made with sweetbreads, and the *ravioli alla tiberina* are a succulent variation on age-old Lenten *ravioli quaresimali* (stuffed with spinach, ricotta, parmigiano, and a pinch of nutmeg), sauced with tomatoes perfumed by fresh spearmint. The stuffed squid are simmered in white wine. The wonderful house-made ice creams include ricotta, and, on the same theme, the ricotta and sour cherry tart is exquisite. Wine lovers are well served, with over 200 bottlings to choose from. Reserve ahead and request a table with a view over the river.

VIA DI PONTE QUATTRO CAPI 16
TEL: 06 686 1601 ✦ WWW.SORALELLA.COM
CLOSED SUNDAY *and* TUESDAY LUNCH
EXPENSIVE *to* VERY EXPENSIVE ✦ *Near: on Tiber Island*

SORA MARGHERITA

SORA MARGHERITA IS A CULT HOLE-IN-THE-WALL TRATTORIA WITH A RED BEADED CURTAIN ACROSS THE DOOR and no sign identifying the premises. You'll recognize it by the line of people waiting; they haven't reserved a table. Don't make that mistake. Sora Margherita was run for decades by Margherita "Sora" Tomassini (in Rome, "Sora" means Signora). It is now in the hands of Sora Lucia, who prefers to keep a low profile. Officially Sora Margherita is a "social club" and not a trattoria, because it doesn't meet European Union norms regarding security and sanitation. First-time customers are asked to fill in a form and "join" the social club (free of charge). In this way the trattoria has been able to continue operating out of its cramped, narrow rooms and inadequate kitchen (flanked by a Third World restroom). Tomassini retired in the early 2000s, and none of the current staff here is Jewish, though Lucia and others worked alongside Tomassini and learned her tricks. Happily, the atmosphere and décor are unchanged—lively, noisy, cheek-by-jowl, and pre-modern. Thick white paper covers the wooden tables. The quality of the ingredients and the cooking are good enough, never excellent, and the key word is "homey." Margherita's menu has not changed, either, from anchovy to zucchini, literally. The delicious fresh pasta is made daily, and the *cacio e pepe* is particularly good and generously served. Everything is generously served, in fact; only the biggest of eaters will want to attempt tackling a meal from antipasto through dessert. The fried stuffed squash flowers, the marinated, pan-fried zucchini with vinegar and herbs, and the baked anchovy and endive casserole are sure to please anyone familiar with these Jewish-Roman dishes. Desserts are limited; the chunky *ciambelline* wine-dipping cookies and homey *crostata* jam tart are the best way to round off a meal. The choice of wines is also limited. Stick to the inoffensive house red and white from the Alban Hills, served by the carafe. Unless you enjoy waiting for a table, reserve ahead.

PIAZZA DELLE CINQUE SCOLE 30 ✦ TEL: 06 687 4216
OPEN *for* LUNCH MONDAY *through* SATURDAY, *for* DINNER FRIDAY *and* SATURDAY ONLY ✦ CLOSED SUNDAY ✦ INEXPENSIVE
Near: 50 yards west of the Ghetto's main street, on a parking lot

LA TAVERNA DEL GHETTO

THE SMALL SIDEWALK TABLES SHADED BY SUN UMBRELLAS OF THIS, ROME'S ONLY KOSHER RESTAURANT serving exclusively Roman-Jewish food, are a fine standpoint from which to watch life playing itself out on the Ghetto's main street. The street was recently pedestrianized in part, and traffic throughout the Ghetto has diminished, making for relaxed dining. At La Taverna you can savor remarkably good fried artichokes scattered with kosher salt, and braised lamb as good as you will find in any Roman trattoria. Worthy of note is the fact that La Taverna's marinated sautéed zucchini and anchovy-and-endive casserole are more flavorful, less oily, and lighter than those served elsewhere. The trattoria's owner is Raffaelo Fadlon, who was born in Israel and moved to Rome in the early 1980s. He married a Roman Jew from an old Roman family, converted his mother-in-law's retail storefront into a restaurant, and adapted her home-style recipes to create his kosher menu. He uses fine ingredients, including extra virgin olive oil from his in-laws' farm south of Rome. Tradition is the rule; the only Roman-Jewish classic on the menu that has clearly been modified is the fried squash flower. Instead of the usual delicious but powerful mozzarella-and-anchovy filling, Fadlon stuffs his flowers with a sautéed filet of white fish the size of a baby finger. A kosher restaurant must choose whether to serve "flesh" or "dairy," never both. Since Romans are big meat and fish eaters, Fadlon opted for flesh. His clients are a mix of tourists and non-orthodox Roman Jews who nonetheless enjoy keeping kosher. The wine list is short and includes only kosher wines.

VIA DEL PORTICO D'OTTAVIA 8

TEL: 06 688 09771 ✦ WWW.LATAVERNADELGHETTO.COM

OPEN *for* LUNCH *and* DINNER SUNDAY *through* THURSDAY, FRIDAY OPEN *for* LUNCH *and* CLOSED *for* DINNER; SATURDAY CLOSED *for* LUNCH *and* OPEN *for* DINNER. CLOSED *on* JEWISH HOLIDAYS.

MODERATE ✦ *Near: halfway along the Ghetto's main street*

LA VECCHIA BOTTEGA DEL VINO

This fine wine bar/lunch spot is described in detail in the wine section (see page 113).

VIA SANTA MARIA DEL PIANTO 9A/11

TEL: 06 681 92210 ✦ WWW.LAVECCHIABOTTEGADELVINO.IT

CLOSED SATURDAY AFTERNOON, SUNDAY, *and* MONDAY

Near: 100 yards east of Via Arenula, 20 yards west of Via del Portico d'Ottavia, the Ghetto's main street

BREAD, CHEESE, FRESH PASTA, FRUIT ICES, GOURMET FOOD SHOPS, ICE CREAM, PASTRIES

ALBERTO PICA

ALBERTO PICA IS THE LONGTIME PRESIDENT OF THE ITALIAN ICE CREAM MAKERS' ASSOCIATION, AND HIS eponymous ice cream parlor, *caffè*, snack bar, and—incongruously—tobacco shop, is a Rome institution. It's 20 yards off Via Arenula, near the Tiber, facing the Ghetto, and has a pleasant covered terrace, which attracts devoted regulars. The ice cream is reliably good, and some of the fruit flavors are excellent, though often very sweet and intense. Pica does not claim to make "natural" ice cream, though his fruit flavors are made in a respectful, old-fashioned way, without additives. With the exception of the macadamia nut flavor, the other nut-based ice creams are made using high-quality nut pastes. There are usually about 50 flavors available. Specialties include remarkable wild strawberry cream, and *zabaglione* (*crema* ice cream with Marsala and egg yolk).

VIA DELLA SEGGIOLA 12 ✦ TEL: 06 686 8405
OPEN DAILY *except* SUNDAY. *In* SUMMER, *also* OPEN SUNDAY *from* 2PM
Near: the Ghetto and Tiber River

ANTICA NORCINERIA VIOLA

THIS CENTURY-OLD, NARROW LITTLE BUTCHER SHOP SPECIALIZING IN PORK PRODUCTS IS ONE OF THE LAST anchors in the maelstrom of Campo de' Fiori, which has become too popular for its own good. Step into Viola and the tourist crowds disappear. Dangling from steel hooks are *prosciutto*, salami, and *guanciale*. Most of the items fresh or cured that are sold here come from Umbria; all are reliably of very good quality.

CAMPO DE' FIORI 43

TEL: 06 688 06114 ✦ CLOSED *in* AUGUST

Near: on the east side of the market square

ANTICO FORNO DEL GHETTO

SINCE 1927, FOUR GENERATIONS OF THE URBANI FAMILY HAVE TAKEN TURNS RUNNING THIS OLD BAKERY AT THE Ghetto's main crossroads. Though Roman Catholics, current scion Adolfo Urbani and his sons Mario, Marcello, and Mauro make most of the kosher breads and pizza for the city's Jewish community, under the guidance of the Rabbinate of Rome. The dough used is allowed to rise overnight, the olive oil is always extra virgin, and the *pizza bianca* and tomato-sauce-slathered *pizza rossa* in particular are remarkably light and delicious. The Urbani's *pizza bianca* dough also takes the form of a bread roll you'll find in very few other bakeries: *ossi*, meaning bones. When ordering them, local jokesters ask for tibia or fibia. Crisp and crusty outside, porous and soft inside, they're a *pizza bianca* in another form. Non-kosher Jews and

Romans claim they are the perfect envelope for stuffing with a slice or two of *mortadella*, sold in the bakery's small deli section (with the exception of the mozzarella, the products are not kosher; for a kosher deli, go around the corner to Kosher Bistrot, Via Santa Maria del Pianto 68-69). According to the Urbanis, the favorite Jewish bread of Rome is the *treccia*, a pleated loaf that Rome's Jews call *kallota*; the *forno* bakes about 3,000 *treccia/kallota* loaves each Saturday. Note that no animal fats and no dairy products are used in any of the Urbani's breads.

PIAZZA COSTAGUTI 30 ✦ TEL: 06 688 03012
CLOSED WEEKEND AFTERNOONS
Near: 20 yards north of the Ghetto's main street

ANTICO FORNO MARCO ROSCIOLI

ROSCIOLI IS ONE OF ROME'S GREAT INSIDER ADDRESSES FOR EVERYTHING FROM BREAD AND PIZZA BIANCA TO snacks, delicious meals, wine, and upscale deli shopping. It's divided into a bakery/snack bar and deli/restaurant areas, which are separated by about 70 yards of cobbled street, Via dei Chiavari. The bakery side of this family-run operation is perpetually mobbed, but the service is efficient and polite and the experience less traumatic than in other crowded, chaotic shops of this kind. Founded in the 1970s by baker Marco Roscioli, Antico Forno is justly renowned for its luscious *pizza bianca*, which strikes the perfect balance between crispness and tenderness. The secret to making *pizza bianca*, says Pierluigi Roscioli, Marco's son and now head baker here, is the long, laborious kneading and minimum 12-hour rising time, and the large quantities (about 660 pounds) of *pizza bianca* the bakery makes daily, 'round the clock. Regulars here order their *pizza bianca alta* (thick), *bassa* (thin), *croccante* (crispy), *ben cotta* (well done), and some ask for *il culetto* (the heel or butt). Roscioli not only sells *pizza bianca* to the public, but also supplies many of Rome's best *caffè*, snack bars, and restaurants. A thickset, soft-spoken but charming man in his thirties, Pierluigi Roscioli is the scion of the extended Roscioli clan of Rome bakers, originally from the isolated Apennine village of Montemonaco. There are currently five Roscioli bakeries in Rome, each entirely independent (among them is nearby Forno Campo de' Fiori see page 109). Pierluigi's irresistible

croccanella is a crispy flatbread with olive oil in the dough, and a pocked, rough texture. His puffy, light *rosette* are made with sourdough from a decades-old sponge. The bakery also turns out sourdough *pane di Lariano* (which is made with 50-percent whole wheat, 50-percent white flour, both supplied by the excellent Molino del Ferraro mill in Rocca Massima southeast of Rome). The *cruschello di Lariano* is an unusual *filone* loaf with chunky walnuts and chopped olives. The classic sourdough *pane di Genzano* is crusty and porous. Particularly delicious are Roscioli's *rustici*: savory baked turnovers made with *pizza bianca* dough filled with cooked vegetables such as sautéed spinach or chicory, and ham, mozzarella, or provolone cheese. The bakery's cookies, *crostata* tarts and other traditional pastries are excellent. Adjoining the main sales room is a snack bar and *tavola calda* area where customers can enjoy all of the bakery's goods, plus *carciofi alla romana*, grilled vegetables, baked pasta, delicious *porchetta* sandwiches, salads, and a wide range of beverages. For a full meal in casual-hip surroundings, go to the Roscioli deli/restaurant, on Via dei Giubbonari facing Via dei Chiavari, a two-minute walk. See the Roscioli entry in the restaurant listings above (page 90).

VIA DEI CHIAVARI 34 ✦ TEL: 06 686 4045
WWW.ANTICOFORNOROSCIOLI.COM
OPEN 7:30AM *to* 8PM, CLOSED SATURDAY
AFTERNOONS *in* JULY *and* AUGUST, *and* SUNDAY
Near: halfway—about 250 yards—between Campo de' Fiori and the Ghetto

ARTE DEL GUSTO

TWO SLIM CLIENTS CAN FIT SIDE-BY-SIDE IN THIS SHOEBOX-SIZED PASTRY SHOP PRESIDED OVER BY chef Tiziano Cardellicchio. The only business of its kind in the neighborhood, Arte del Gusto is a handy spot to know about if you're hiking between the Forum, Palatine, and Circus Maximus or Aventine Hill. Try a delicious cream-filled *bomba*, *millefoglie*, mini *crostata* or crispy Roman *sfogliatella* filled with ricotta. The flour and yeasts used are organic.

VIA SAN TEODORO 88 ✦ TEL: 06 679 8469
WWW.ARTEDELGUSTO.COM ✦ CLOSED SUNDAY
Near: corner of Via dei Cerchi, kitty-corner to Circus Maximus

BAR DEL CAPPUCCINO

AFFABLE, MUSTACHIOED BARMAN LUIGI SANTORO IS FAMOUS FOR HIS ARTISTIC MANIPULATIONS OF THE foam atop the delicious *cappuccini* he serves at this unpretentious neighborhood coffee spot on busy Via Arenula, facing the bus and streetcar stops near the Tiber. Santoro uses good Danesi coffee, small amounts of powdered semi-sweet chocolate, and lots of frothy hot milk, shaking the jug and folding the foam to create roses, stalks of wheat, apples (New York!), and other elaborate designs (but only upon request). If asked, he will also happily recite the 33 ways that he has counted so far to order coffee in Rome (see page 37). Bar del Cappuccino gets its *pizza bianca*, pastrami, and bread from Roscioli, which explains why they're so good. The pastries are kosher.

VIA ARENULA 50 ✦ TEL: 06 688 06042
WWW.BARDELCAPPUCCINO.COM ✦ OPEN 6:30AM *to* 7:30PM
CLOSED SUNDAY ✦ *Near: Ghetto and Tiber River*

BAR GIULIA—CAFFÈ PERÙ

DIRECTLY ACROSS FROM THIS SMALL NEIGHBORHOOD CAFFÈ ARE SOME OF THE OFFICES OF ROME'S CITY hall. That explains the constant crowds of leisure-struck regulars, who seem to know and love themselves and each other to an extravagant degree. Given the business hours, habitués also include noted night-shift and early-rising journalists from Rome's main daily, *Il Messaggero*, plus garbage collectors, policemen, night clubbers, and the many other friends the *caffè*'s owner Alfredo Mariscoli, his wife, and family have made over the years. Not only is the Caffè Perù brand of coffee strong and good—it comes from the Consorzio Torrefattori, a grouping of coffee roasters out near the slaughterhouse on Via Prenestina. It is also served with panache. The dashing barmen of Bar Giulia are among Rome's swiftest, most professional, and polite. It's thrilling to watch them. Like Luigi Santoro at better-known Bar del Cappuccino, they also make luscious *cappuccini* with clever designs folded into the foam, usually performing this act for first-time female customers. The interior, slightly larger than a shoebox, is usually three-deep at the bar. Sit outside if you can. Beyond the permanent loungers from city hall, many local merchants and a few savvy tourists drop by and occupy the handful of tables set out in Via Giulia, which has no sidewalks, but also very little traffic these days. Alfredo does not charge extra for sit-down service. He is among the only *caffè* owners in Rome to have adopted this radical policy, and has been rewarded by an enviable client-return rate.

VIA GIULIA 84 ✦ TEL: 06 686 1310 ✦ OPEN *from* 4:30AM *to* 8:30PM, CLOSED SUNDAY ✦ *Near: corner of Vicolo delle Palle, and church of San Giovanni dei Fiorentini*

BOCCIONE—IL FORNO DEL GHETTO

BOCCIONE IS THE LAST JEWISH-OWNED-AND-OPERATED PASTRY SHOP IN THE GHETTO, A SMALL, STREET-corner operation seemingly bursting out of the centuries-old palazzo that houses it. The extended Boccione family have been here for countless generations, and continue to work together like relay runners, making the

REFRESHMENTS IN ROME'S MUSEUMS

UNSURPRISINGLY, THE FOOD, WINE, AND COFFEE ARE NOT REMARKABLE IN ANY OF ROME'S MUSEUM *caffè*, but many have spectacular settings and/or wonderful views. For some, a museum entrance ticket is required.

CAPITOLINE MUSEUMS

On the top floor and filling a wide terrace, this *caffè* has one of the city's best views over the roofs of central Rome, from the Ghetto to the Gianicolo. No entrance ticket required.

CAPITOLINE CAFÉ ✦ PIAZZA DEL CAMPIDOGLIO 1
TEL: 06 691 90564 ✦ OPEN 9AM *to* 7PM, CLOSED MONDAY

CASTEL SANT'ANGELO

You'll need a place to rest after exploring the labyrinth of the castle. The view of Rome and the Tiber is magnificent. Entrance ticket required.

CAFFETTERIA, LUNGOTEVERE DI CASTELLO 50
TEL: 06 688 02598 ✦ OPEN 8:30AM *to* 7:30PM, CLOSED MONDAY

CHIOSTRO DEL BRAMANTE

CAFFETTERIA, VIA DELLA PACE ✦ TEL: 06 688 09035
WWW.CHIOSTRODELBRAMANTE.IT
OPEN 10AM *to* 7:30PM, CLOSED MONDAY
NO ENTRANCE TICKET REQUIRED
SEE AREA 2 PAGE 146 *for* COMPLETE LISTING

GALLERIA DORIA PAMPHILI

DORIA CAFFÈ, PIAZZA DEL COLLEGIO ROMANO 2 *or* VIA DELLA GATTA 1 ✦ TEL: 06 679 3805 ✦ OPEN DAILY 8AM *to* 8PM ✦ NO TICKET REQUIRED ✦ SEE AREA 2 PAGE 152 *for* COMPLETE LISTING

MODERN ART MUSEUM

With one of the most pleasant, widest, leafiest terraces in Rome, on the edge of Villa Borghese, plus a handsome interior in a landmark building, this is a great *caffè*, period. No entrance ticket required.

CAFFÈ DELLE ARTI, VIA ANTONIO GRAMSCI 73
or VIA DELLE BELLE ARTI 131 ✦ TEL: 06 326 51236
WWW.CAFFEDELLEARTIROMA.IT
OPEN 8AM *to* 9PM, CLOSED MONDAY

MUSEO MACRO

The *caffè* serves organic coffee from Rome roaster Pinci, and is adjacent to a restaurant with organic food. This is a good place to view Monte Testaccio from an unusual angle. No entrance ticket required.

BIO CAFFÈ, FORMER TESTACCIO SLAUGHTERHOUSE,
VIA REGGIO EMILIA 54 ✦ TEL: 06 671 07900
OPEN 10AM *to* 6PM, CLOSED MONDAY

QUIRINALE STABLES

Come for one of the temporary shows at the magnificent stables of the Quirinal Palace, and the view over the palace and surroundings. If you like Paris's Musée d'Orsay, you'll probably like what contemporary architect Gae Aulenti did to the stables and the *caffè*'s modish interior. Entrance ticket required; the *caffè* closes at 7:30pm, 30 minutes before the closing time of exhibitions (8pm).

CAFFETTERIA DELLE SCUDERIE PAPALI, VIA XXIV
MAGGIO 16 ✦ TEL: 06 696 272216 ✦ OPEN 10AM *to* 7:30PM
DAILY DURING EXHIBITIONS

RISORGIMENTO MUSEUM
COMPLESSO DEL VITTORIANO

On the upper deck of the so-called Typewriter, the wonderfully hideous 1911 monument to King Victor Emmanuel II, above the Forum and flanking the Capitoline, you'll get some of the most stunning views of Rome's ancient monuments and city center. No entrance ticket required.

CAFFETTERIA ITALIA, PIAZZA VENEZIA

TEL: 06 679 3598 ✦ WWW.RISORGIMENTO.IT

OPEN WEEKDAYS 9:30AM *to* 4:30PM OFF SEASON, *until* 5:45PM *in* SUMMER, 9AM *to* 6:45PM WEEKENDS

VILLA GIULIA NATIONAL MUSEUM

Villa Giulia is a handsome park due north of Villa Borghese, where the Villa of Pope Julius III, built in the 1550s, houses the Villa Giulia National Museum of pre-Roman antiquities, now called the Museo Etrusco. Caffè dell'Aranciera is in a leafy winter garden conservatory where citrus fruit trees were grown, a haven of quiet. If you enter from Piazza Thorvaldsen, where the #3 tram stop is found, you need not pay an entrance fee; if you enter the museum's main door at Piazzale di Villa Giulia 9, you must buy a ticket.

CAFFÈ DELL'ARANCIERA ✦ PIAZZA THORVALDSEN

TEL: 06 326 512040 ✦ OPEN 9AM *to* 4PM, CLOSED MONDAY

delicious if weighty Roman-Jewish classics of yesteryear. They range from *pizza dolce ebraica* (a coffee cake with raisins, candied fruit, and dry fruit) to marzipan *amaretti*, and *tozzetti* dry cookies. The *torta di ricotta* is a startling, 33 1/3 LP-sized cake topped by a Pantheon-style dome, and weighs about two pounds. It's filled with sweetened ricotta and sour cherry jam or chunks of chocolate. All of Boccione's goods tend to be baked to the point of charring. This, it's said, is not a sign of incompetence but rather a Ghetto tradition, carried on because regulars demand that their pastries be slightly scorched around the edges. Expect a crowd, and chaos when it comes to ordering and paying. It's worth the trouble.

VIA DEL PORTICO D'OTTAVIA 1

TEL: 06 687 8637 ✦ CLOSED SATURDAY

Near: on the northwest end of the Ghetto's main street

CAFFÈ FARNESE

THE FRENCH OCCUPIED AND THEN "DEFENDED" ROME AND THE VATICAN FOR DECADES, STARTING UNDER Napoleon Bonaparte at the end of the eighteenth century, and managed to claim several pieces of prime real estate, including Palazzo Farnese, the imposing palace facing this *caffè*, with a façade by Michelangelo (grafted onto an earlier structure). French diplomats and embassy staff are just part of the international crowd that fills the outdoor tables of this convenient wrap-around corner *caffè*, which is ideally situated 100 yards south of the chaos of Campo de' Fiori. Skip the ice cream and food; the coffee and pastries are good, the opening hours remarkably long for Rome.

PIAZZA FARNESE 106 ✦ TEL: 06 688 02125
OPEN 7AM *to* 2AM DAILY
Near: on Piazza Farnese, facing Palazzo Farnese

LA DOLCEROMA

LA DOLCEROMA, A MINISCULE BAKESHOP ON THE GHETTO'S MAIN STREET, SELLS NO ROMAN SPECIALTIES other than purely natural, delicious ice creams (from late spring to fall only). But its pastries are so outstanding that they must be tasted to be believed. Pastry chef Stefano Ceccarelli spent years baking in Austria and also traveled and baked in America, and his strüdels, Sacher tarts, cheesecakes, and apple pies are exquisite. His parents own and operate the celebrated trattoria Giggetto, next door. Though the Ceccarelli family is Roman Catholic and not Jewish, Giggetto serves the best traditional Roman-Jewish ricotta cheesecake in town, made by the handsome, self-effacing Stefano. To avoid competition with the only Jewish bakery left in the Ghetto, he doesn't sell ricotta cake at his pastry shop.

VIA DEL PORTICO D'OTTAVIA 20B ✦ TEL: 06 689 2196
CLOSED SUNDAY AFTERNOON *and* MONDAY
Near: on the east end of the Ghetto's main street, next door to Giggetto

FORNO CAMPO DE' FIORI

THIS COMPACT, EVER-CROWDED CULT BAKERY CELEBRATED ITS 200TH BIRTHDAY IN 2004, AND GOT A facelift, which has done little to alleviate the elbow-to-elbow lines. For *pizza bianca*—the bakery's best item—go to the counter on your right as you enter. The other counter is for bread and other baked goods. The current owners have a sardonic sense of humor, reminding curious clients that in the 1500s, the establishment's forebear supplied bread and pastries to the ill-fated Lucretia Borgia, who lived and famously died nearby. Bakers Dino and Fabrizio Roscioli took over from their father Mario. They turn out all the Roman classics, from mini *crostate* and pine nut-sprinkled *pinolata* to some of the best *filone* bread in town. The *pizza bianca* stands out for its degree of paradoxically unctuous crispness. The family, originally from the hills of Le Marche, are cousins of the owners of the area's other illustrious bakery, Antico Forno Marco Roscioli (nearby in Via dei Chiavari). Forno Campo de' Fiori also has a tiny shop across the alleyway at Vicolo del Gallo 14, which sells pastries, cookies, and *pizza bianca* plain or topped and filled with everything from anchovies to mortadella, Nutella to tomatoes.

CAMPO DE' FIORI 22 ✦ TEL: 06 688 06662
WWW.FORNOCAMPODEFIORI.COM ✦ CLOSED SATURDAY
AFTERNOON *in* JULY, AUGUST *and* SEPTEMBER, *and* SUNDAY
Near: on the northwest end of the square, on the corner of Via dei Cappellari

GELATERIA ARA COELI

IT'S EASY TO WALK BY THIS SMALL ICE CREAM SHOP ON THE BUSY, NOISY EDGE OF PIAZZA VENEZIA (HERE called Piazza Ara Coeli). The area is filled with tourist traps, and unfortunately this place looks very much like one. Happily, it isn't. Since 1995 Ara Coeli has been making organic ice creams, *semifreddi*, frozen mousses, *granita*, frozen yogurt (studded with fresh fruit), *tiramisù*, *cassata*, and cakes of very high quality using excellent ingredients. The chocolate is supplied by Valrhona, for instance, and goes into the rich, luscious chocolate flavor. The fruit ices have no milk in them and are always made from fresh, ripe fruit. Unlike several of the city's best natural ice creameries, Ara Coeli does not toast and grind its own pistachios, hazelnuts, and almonds; the nut-based flavors are made using very good nut pastes, and the consistency and fattiness gives them away. There is a small salon where you can have your ice cream on the premises, but you're better off getting a cone or a *coppetta* and strolling up the Capitoline for the view.

PIAZZA ARA COELI 9-10

TEL: 06 679 5085 ✦ WWW.GELATERIAARACOELI.COM

Near: facing the fountain on the piazza below the church of Ara Coeli on the Capitoline

ST. TEODORO CAFFÈ

A CHARMING ISLAND OF THE CITY LIES ISOLATED BETWEEN THE CAPITOLINE AND PALATINE, ABUTTING THE Forum, and that's where you'll find this handsome *caffè*. From the comfortable terrace, which has wooden benches and chairs and canvas umbrellas, the views back on the Capitoline are unexpected and lovely. St. Teodoro belongs to the fashionable restaurant of the same name (see Non-*terroir* tables, page 115), which is at the end of the block, and shares the same kitchen. You can get delicious snacks here at reasonable prices (the restaurant, run by chef Luciano Zaza, is excellent but very expensive). San Teodoro, spelled in the Italian style this time, is also a coffee roaster, based in Livorno, Tuscany; the coffee served here is either San Teodoro's remarkably strong 100-percent, highest-quality, hand-picked Mylatpur Robusta from Karnataka in southern India, or a 100-percent Bettadakhan mountain-grown Indian Arabica. Occasionally, when the owners are experimenting, you'll find a new Robusta/Arabica blend. A pleasant surprise is to be had if you ask for your espresso *macchiato*: it arrives with a tiny dollop of unsweetened whipped cream, at no extra charge. The staff is friendly.

VIA DEI FIENILI 49/50/51

TEL: 06 678 0933 ✦ WWW.ST-TEODORO.IT

CLOSED SUNDAY NOVEMBER *through* APRIL

Near: on elevated sidewalk above Piazza della Consolazione

VITO RUGGERI

FOUNDED IN 1919, THIS HANDSOME OLD-FASHIONED GROCERY SHOP AND DELI HAS EVERYTHING YOU NEED for a picnic, from egg to apple, including wine (and ham and cheese).

CAMPO DE' FIORI 1/2 ✦ TEL: 06 688 01091
CLOSED SUNDAY ✦ *Near: on southwest side of square*

WINE AND WINE BARS

ANGOLO DIVINO

THE OWNER OF THIS SMALL, DARK, CORNER WINE BAR IS MASSIMO CRIPPA, NOT THE FAMOUS SOCCER player, but a rather serious, shy fellow with a wide appreciation for wines from all over Italy and the world, especially France. Now fashionable, the shop was for decades a simple *vineria* run by Crippa's grandmother, who dispensed jug and bulk *vino* to locals. Young Crippa's passion is anything but limited to the Lazio region, the wines of which he largely overlooks. Nonetheless, Angolo Divino is an authentic spot, despite the menu translated into rough English; few tourists set foot here, in part because of the insiderish, clubby atmosphere. Though not really offering a full menu for hungry wine enthusiasts, Crippa does serve very good hams and cheeses, *bruschetta*, *rustici*, salads, and daily specials, which range from the sublimely simple (lasagna with meat sauce) to the ridiculously faux-French (duck breast *tagliata*).

VIA DEI BALESTRARI 12/14 ✦ TEL: 06 686 4413
WWW.ANGOLODIVINO.IT
CLOSED MONDAY LUNCH *and* SUNDAY
Near: about 60 yards south of Campo de' Fiori, on the corner of Vicolo del Giglio

IL GOCCETTO

IL GOCCETTO IS A COZY, CONSPIRATORIAL DEN WITH ONLY A DOZEN SMALL TABLES WHERE ROME'S TOP WINE tasters—sommeliers, journalists, and wine collectors—meet to exchange notes, talk vintages, argue about yeast, clones, and the toasting of barrels, and see which 30 wines the shop's affable owner Sergio Ceccarelli has on the chalkboard that day. The day's selection is available by the bottle or the glass. Now that Italy's public places are smoke-free, Il Goccetto is a delight. The choice isn't vast—Ceccarelli typically stocks wines from hundreds, rather than thousands, of wineries—but you can be sure that the most promising bottlings from established or up-and-coming Italian and French winemakers will be showcased here. There is no lunch or dinner served; however, the hams, cheeses, and snacks are excellent. Il Goccetto is not easy to spot. Look for the worn "Vino Olio" sign on the façade above the main door, on the corner of Via delle Carceri and Via dei Banchi Vecchi, across from the small church of Santa Lucia del Gonfalone.

VIA DEI BANCHI VECCHI 14 ✦ TEL: 06 688 01746
OPEN 11:30AM *to* 2PM *and* 6:30PM *to* MIDNIGHT
CLOSED SUNDAY ✦ *Near: about 200 yards north of Piazza Farnese*

LA VECCHIA BOTTEGA DEL VINO

LA VECCHIA BOTTEGA DEL VINO IS A GHETTO INSTITUTION, AND ONE OF ROME'S FINEST WINE SHOPS AND CASUAL lunch spots. It was founded decades ago by Anacleto Bleve, an animated wine and whisky connoisseur who imparted his enthusiasm for European and American wines and Scottish whisky to his extended family and staff. Bleve's cousins, Gino and Antonio Nutricato, began running the shop nearly a decade ago, and have taken over from Bleve, whose businesses are now elsewhere (area 2 page 162). Wisely, few changes were made, and the friendly atmosphere, excellent simple food, and small but intelligent choice of wines have remained. The range of Lazio offerings is limited to a handful of premium wineries, including Casale del Giglio and Castel de Paolis. As it has been doing for many years, La Vecchia Bottega del Vino serves delicious lunches based around Roman and central Italian traditions; menu items change with the seasons.

VIA SANTA MARIA DEL PIANTO 9A/11
TEL: 06 681 92210 ✦ WWW.LAVECCHIABOTTEGADELVINO.IT
CLOSED SATURDAY AFTERNOON, SUNDAY *and* MONDAY
Near: 100 yards east of Via Arenula, 20 yards west of Via del Portico d'Ottavia, the Ghetto's main street

NON-TERROIR TOP OR TRENDY TABLES

AL BRIC

VIA DEL PELLEGRINO 51 ✦ TEL: 06 687 9533
WWW.ALBRIC.IT ✦ DINNER ONLY, *also* BRUNCH *on* SUNDAY
EXPENSIVE

CAMPONESCHI

PIAZZA FARNESE 50/50A ✦ TEL: 06 687 4927
WWW.RISTORANTECAMPONESCHI.IT
DINNER ONLY, CLOSED SUNDAY ✦ EXTREMELY EXPENSIVE

EVANGELISTA

VIA DELLE ZOCCOLETTE 11/A ✦ TEL: 06 687 5810
DINNER ONLY, CLOSED SUNDAY ✦ MODERATE *to* EXPENSIVE

HOSTERIA DEL PESCE

VIA DI MONSERRATO 32 ✦ TEL: 06 686 5617
DINNER ONLY, CLOSED SUNDAY ✦ VERY EXPENSIVE

IL PAGLIACCIO

VIA DEI BANCHI VECCHI 129/A ✦ TEL: 06 688 09595
WWW.RISTORANTEILPAGLIACCIO.IT ✦ CLOSED SUNDAY, MONDAY *and* TUESDAY *for* LUNCH ✦ EXPENSIVE

IL SANLORENZO

VIA DEI CHIAVARI 4 ✦ TEL: 06 686 5097 ✦ DINNER ONLY
CLOSED AUGUST ✦ EXPENSIVE

MONSERRATO

VIA MONSERRATO 96 ✦ TEL: 06 687 3386
CLOSED MONDAY ✦ MODERATE *to* EXPENSIVE

SANPIETRINO

PIAZZA COSTAGUTI 15
TEL: 06 688 06471 ✦ WWW.ILSANPIETRINO.IT
DINNER ONLY, CLOSED SUNDAY ✦ EXPENSIVE

ST. TEODORO

VIA DEI FIENILI 49/50/51 ✦ TEL: 06 678 0933
WWW.ST-TEODORO.IT ✦ CLOSED SUNDAY *from* NOVEMBER *to* APRIL, EXPENSIVE *to* VERY EXPENSIVE

TAVERNA DEGLI AMICI

PIAZZA MARGANA 36/37 ✦ TEL: 06 699 20637
WWW.LATAVERNADEGLIAMICI.COM
CLOSED MONDAY ✦ MODERATE *to* EXPENSIVE

VECCHIA ROMA

PIAZZA DI CAMPITELLI 18 ✦ TEL: 06 686 4604
WWW.RISTORANTEVECCHIAROMA.COM
CLOSED WEDNESDAY ✦ EXPENSIVE

REGIONAL RESTAURANTS

SARDINIA

IL DRAPPO

VICOLO DEL MALPASSO 9 ✦ TEL: 06 687 7365
WWW.ILDRAPPO.IT ✦ CLOSED SUNDAY *and* AUGUST
MODERATE *to* EXPENSIVE

CHAPTER 2

CAMPO MARZIO, PANTHEON, PIAZZA NAVONA

LIKE THE ABUTTING CAMPO DE' FIORI, GHETTO, CAPITOLINE AREA, THIS NEIGHBORHOOD FALLS WITHIN the wide "C" of the Tiber River's east bank, and is among the city's oldest and most atmospheric. It also shares many of the same challenges as area 1, from the demographics to the mass tourism. Two sights make it impossible to bypass: the Pantheon and Piazza Navona. Also of note, a few hundred yards northwest of Piazza Navona, is the Via dei Coronari, the antique dealers' quarter. On the neighborhood's east side are Piazza Colonna and Montecitorio, site of the Italian Parliament; due north of Montecitorio is Piazza di San Lorenzo in Lucina, the centerpiece of the Campo Marzio district.

Despite the bloom in eat-and-run places and supermarkets, many authentic trattorias and outstanding food-related establishments continue to thrive here, including central Rome's two most accomplished *guanciale* makers, several very good ice cream parlors, and three world-class coffee roasters, two of them (Tazza d'Oro and Sant'Eustachio) within 100 yards of the Pantheon, where the scent of burning wood and toasting beans is tangible. Often, when Tazza d'Oro and Sant'Eustachio

are roasting coffee at the same time of day, and the breeze swirls around the Pantheon's dome, you can see the rival drifts of smoke intermingle.

Administrative buildings abound: in addition to Parliament, the senate, council of ministers, and many of the Italian government's other offices are headquartered in this area, which explains in part the crowds of natty eaters, especially at lunch time, and the high number of fine wine shops, wine bars, chocolate shops, and delicatessens. Some of these establishments, and cult *caffè* and cocktail bars, such as Giolitti, Ciampino, Vitti, and Sant'Eustachio, double as meeting rooms for legions of lobbyists, politicos, and reporters.

Mercatino di Piazza delle Coppelle is the only authentic outdoor market in the area. It's hidden away about 150 yards north of the Pantheon following a zigzag of narrow streets and dog's-leg alleys, and occupies a square the size of a tennis court, framed by picturesque, pastel-hued buildings. The market's fruit-and-vegetable stands are operated by the same extended family, established here since 1957. The quality is particularly high, because Leandra Belli, her husband Alberto Giammatteo, and their children Marco and Sabrina Giammatteo are authentic market gardeners, with a farm near Velletri on the southern edge of the Alban Hills. Prices are competitive, and the selection of freshly picked salad greens, zucchini, tomatoes, and leaf vegetables is outstanding. Savvy locals buy their flavorful buffalo-milk mozzarella and rich burrata here (both the cheeses are made in Battipaglia and delivered daily). The Giammatteo family also sells eggs from their own free-range hens. The

extra virgin olive oil, sold by the liter in unmarked bottles, is made with ripe Leccino olives handpicked in the family olive groves. Milled in the traditional way with millstones and then decanted, the oil is not filtered or pasteurized and has no artificial colorings. It's sweet and delicious. Next to the market's fruit and vegetables, a fish stand with fresh Mediterranean fish plus pre-soaked *baccalà* appears on Tuesdays and Fridays only.

In the afternoon, once the market has packed up, the square is gradually taken over by the terraces of several restaurants; abutting them, the oak wine barrels which serve as the tables of a popular wine bar, **Vinoteca Novecento,** fill daily until 1 or 2am. Further animation is provided by **Myosotis**, an upscale dinner-only restaurant; **Maccheroni**, a neo-trattoria; and **Riccioli Café**, a trendy sushi bar/hangout. A further novelty is **Caffè Universale** (Via delle Coppelle 16A, Tel: 06 40040733, www.caffeuniversale.it, open daily); this trendy, sui generis establishment sells wines, specialty foods, and books; displays contemporary art; serves coffee, snacks, and light meals; and offers spa treatments.

Another street market, with just three fruit and vegetable stands, is on Via della Pace, near the intersection with Vicolo del Corallo, two blocks west of Piazza Navona. An old grocery store, **Ruggieri**, is here. By day, the narrow street has an authentic, neighborhood feel; by night, the grocery stands are replaced by sellers of beads and jewelry, patronized by clubbers and tourists.

RESTAURANTS AND TRATTORIAS

ARMANDO AL PANTHEON

IF LONGEVITY WERE A MEASURE OF EXCELLENCE, ARMANDO WOULD GET ONE OF THE HIGHEST RATINGS IN town. This typical trattoria of decades past has been run since 1961 by the extended Gargioli family. Armando's sons Fabrizio (the manager) and Claudio (the chef) were practically born here. Nowadays, along with Chiara Maria and Andrea, they continue to serve all the Roman classics, which are better than good, starting with the artichokes *alla romana* and other *antipasti* to the lamb chops or tripe. The requisite *cacio e pepe*, *amatriciana*, *carbonara*, salt cod, or oxtails are also very good, and there's a light *tiramisù* with bilberries and red fruit to finish things off. Several house specialties stray perilously from the Roman repertoire, however, and unless you like saffron with your mushrooms, and truffle or gorgonzola in your otherwise delicious hulled wheat *farro* balls, you're better off sticking to the straight and narrow. The welcome and service are friendly, and everyone seems to speak at least a little English, not that it's necessary, since the menu items are translated into the universal language. The impressive wine list features 22 Lazio reds, and ten whites, among the latter the very good Campo Vecchio from Castel de Paolis. Lunch and dinner are served early by Roman standards; the clientele is largely made up of tourists. Though there's no outdoor terrace, and the tables are fairly close and small, the air conditioning keeps the darkish, paneled interior comfortable and pleasant.

SALITA DE' CRESCENZI 31 ✦ TEL: 06 688 03034
WWW.ARMANDOALPANTHEON.IT ✦ CLOSED SATURDAY
NIGHT, SUNDAY *and* AUGUST ✦ MODERATE
Near: 50 yards west of the Pantheon, toward Piazza Navona

CAPRANICA ENOTECA E TAVERNA

FIRST, DO NOT CONFUSE THIS INFORMAL SPOT WITH ENOTECA CAPRANICA, AN UPSCALE INTERNATIONAL-style restaurant with excellent but astronomically expensive fish, located on the same square, on the other side of the Capranica theater. (The lace curtains, forest of wine glasses on each table, and brass doorbell give that address away.) On the Corso side of the Capranica theater, in what was the theater's bar area, you'll find this newish wine bar-pizzeria-restaurant, which has a handful of wooden tables on the street (there is no sidewalk) and a studiously cozy wood-paneled interior made to look like a library, with wine bottles where the books usually go. This is a crossover neo-trattoria and wine bar, not an authentic old Roman place, but as such properties go, it's good. Maurizio Bertusi, his wife Loretta, and his sister Daniela run the show, serve, and cook, in that order. The pizzas, hams, cheeses, and grilled vegetables are good, and so too are the simpler, classic Roman dishes (*cacio e pepe*, *pasta e ceci*). Beware the overly complicated and pricey menu items, such as the *gnocchetti*, which come with *tartufo di Norcia*. Finish off with ricotta cheesecake or wine-dunking cookies. The wine list offers hundreds of Italian bottlings. The terrace and casual, clubby feel appeal to out-of-towners. On weekends, opening time is 5pm (to accommodate American and Northern European guests).

VIA IN AQUIRO 104/PIAZZA CAPRANICA ✦ TEL: 06 679 0860 *or* 335 758 1781 ✦ CLOSED MONDAY *and* AUGUST
MODERATE *to* EXPENSIVE ✦ *Near: on Piazza Capranica*

DA ALFREDO E ADA

AMONG THE ETERNAL CITY'S ETERNAL TABLES, THIS ONE STANDS OUT FOR ITS SIMPLICITY AND PRESERVED-in-amber authenticity. There's no sign on the door, just a card tacked to it. The wooden tables with marble tops and paper mats are probably a century old. Hand-scrawled

mottos decorate the walls. The local regulars and intrepid out-of-towners who eat here are sometimes entertained—if that be the word—by minstrels with acoustic guitars. Since 1946, Sora Ada has been making home-style meals in her tiny kitchen at the back, and keeps working despite her age and the death of her husband Alfredo, who presided over the trattoria's one long, narrow dining room for nearly 60 years. For anyone who's eaten at home with a Roman family, the food will bring back memories: *amatriciana* with short pasta; a red sauce made with Rome's *involtini* beef rolls and used for topping rigatoni or penne; veal stew with peas. Dessert? Fresh fruit and wine-dipping cookies. The wine comes in two colors: red or white, both from the family's small vineyard at Albano, in the Alban Hills. Note: cash only, no credit cards, but the prices are also stuck in amber.

VIA DEI BANCHI NUOVI 14 ✦ TEL: 06 687 8842 ✦ OPEN *for* DINNER FROM 6PM WEEKDAYS ONLY, CLOSED *for* LUNCH, *on* WEEKENDS *and in* AUGUST ✦ VERY INEXPENSIVE ✦ *Near: Tiber River end of street, about 100 yards west of Piazza dell'Orologio*

DA BAFFETTO

GETTING INTO DA BAFFETTO TAKES ABOUT AS LONG AS GETTING INTO THE VATICAN MUSEUMS. Look at the cobbles on the narrow street in front of this cult pizzeria's door: they're scalloped from decades' worth of scuffing feet. Waiting clients nose the air scented by the wood-burning oven. Luigi and Gilberto keep the simple, shared wooden tables filled cheek-by-jowl, herding guests with panache and surprising courtesy. "How many of you are there?" is the refrain. Upstairs, the heavy, centuries-old timbers frame the cramped tables. But no one comes here for the décor. There's a terrace that extends down an alleyway. It can take hours—and luck—to get a seat on it. The classic, crispy Roman pizzas,

bruschetta, stuffed olives, and fried foods—mozzarella-filled rice *supplì*, zucchini flowers, or potato croquettes—are reliably very good, sometimes outstanding, and the house-made *panna cotta*, a fixture for the last 40 or more years, keeps locals and veteran tourists coming back. Note: cash only, no credit cards.

VIA DEL GOVERNO VECCHIO 114 ✦ TEL: 06 686 1617
OPEN DAILY *until* 1AM, CLOSED *in* AUGUST
VERY INEXPENSIVE ✦ *Near: about 200 yards west of Piazza di Pasquino and Piazza Navona*

DA UGO

IT'S EASY TO WALK RIGHT BY THIS TINY, NARROW OLD TRATTORIA, WHOSE DOOR SEEMS TO BE PERPETUALLY hidden by an illegally parked SUV owned by a neighbor. The word "trattoria" is the only thing you'll see above the car's roof. Da Ugo has been here since 1942. Now in their late seventies, Ugo and Maria Velletrani took over from the founder, Umberto, many decades ago, and are assisted by their children, Pietro and Anna, the third generation. They're all rough diamonds, afflicted by the kind of shyness that you can easily mistake for curmudgeonly grumpiness. Despite the vicinity of the Pantheon, few tourists set foot here. For one thing, lunch service starts only at 1:30pm and dinner at 8:30pm. Atop the composite-marble floor is one antique wooden coat rack and a handful of tables, most of them occupied by regulars—the same Italian bureaucrats and newshounds who show up at Gino, the other insiders' trattoria, around the corner. Da Ugo is simple but comfortable and clean, the menu features only a handful of classics, which are made with fresh, seasonal ingredients and served with eye-popping generosity. Unless you're accustomed to mountains of pasta, if you order the perfect *spaghetti alla carbonara* or *bucatini all'amatriciana*, or the spinach-and-ricotta ravioli or gnocchi, you'll be hard pressed to eat much more. You'll certainly want to leave room for the *ossobuco* and beef *involtini*, or the rabbit done *alla cacciatora* with white wine and vinegar. Luckily, no desserts are served, only fresh fruit. The wine is easy: on tap, from the Castelli Romani. Note: cash only, no credit cards.

VIA DEI PREFETTI 19 ✦ TEL: 06 687 3752
CLOSED SUNDAY *and* AUGUST ✦ INEXPENSIVE *to* MODERATE
Near: 300 yards due west of Parliament, between Vicolo del Divino Amore and Via della Lupa

ENOTECA CORSI

NOWADAYS 100 OR MORE TRENDY WINE BARS IN ROME CALL THEMSELVES *ENOTECHE*. THIS IS THE REAL THING, and has been a reliable, reasonably priced bottle shop and great lunch spot for decades. Affable Agostino Paiella left his Appenine village of Leonessa and started working here as a bar boy in 1967, became chef and cooked for 20 years, and then bought out the former owners in 1996. Now he and his family—his daughters Ilaria and Manuela grew up in the shop and are sommeliers—run the show. They've kept the original

ASSOCIAZIONE ITALIANA SOMMELIER
VIN BIANCO
"CASTELLI ROMANI"
"IL CORNO"
€4.00
AL LITRO

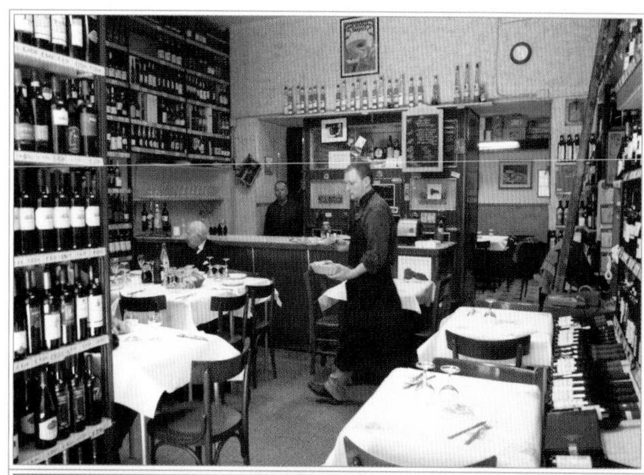

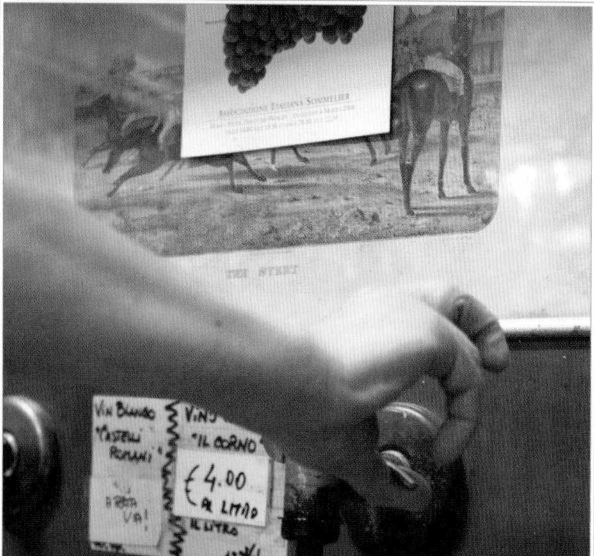

rough 'n' ready *osteria* décor—wooden tables and paper mats, an ancient refrigerator, and a solid old bar out of which the house Chianti and Frascati flow on tap. Because of demand, they've shoehorned a handful of extra tables into the wine sales room. The tables are framed by tall metal shelves filled with hundreds of Italian wines. On the handwritten menu, which changes daily, are delicious, simple classics of the Roman repertoire—the weekly wheel of gnocchi, *baccalà*, tripe, and so forth—plus specials. Among them, oven-baked short pasta with tomato sauce, thick *farro* soup, *ossobuco* with peas and mushrooms, boiled beef with green parsley sauce, roast veal, mixed grill of meat, pan-fried chicory, and more. The servings are copious, especially the *carbonara*, which is a meal in itself. The luscious *pastiera napoletana*—a Neapolitan tart with ricotta, citrus zest, and candied lemon or orange peel—is always house-made; some of the other desserts, all of them good, come from outside suppliers. If you're interested in something more ambitious than the carafe wines, choose any bottle and pay a corkage fee ranging from two to five euros. Most bottled wines are also available by the glass. The service is swift but amazingly friendly, the prices hard to beat. The only sour note is the Musetti-brand coffee, which is like liquified asphalt. Walk over to Tazza d'Oro or Sant'Eustachio instead; both are nearby.

VIA DEL GESÙ 87-88 ✦ TEL: 06 679 0821
OPEN *for* LUNCH ONLY, *from* NOON *to* 3:30PM, WINE SHOP STAYS OPEN *until* 8PM, CLOSED SUNDAY *and* AUGUST ✦ INEXPENSIVE
Near: 100 yards north of the Chiesa del Gesù, 20 yards from Piazza della Pigna

FORTUNATO AL PANTHEON

IF YOU MISSED ATTENDING A SESSION OF ITALY'S PARLIAMENT, NO WORRIES, FORTUNATO IS WHERE REPRESENTAtives and senators waddle to when they want comfortable surroundings, waiters in livery, and reliably edible food, most of it Roman. The tablecloths are starched, the art on the walls is original, and, because of the prices, you won't see the kinds of tourists who favor the snack bars or McDonald's around the corner in the square, facing the Pantheon. The atmosphere is authentically Roman, unchanging, slightly self-important, and fun for people-watching. Stick to *carciofi alla romana*, *puntarella* salad and pan-fried chicory, ravioli, roast lamb, *tiramisù*, and *crostata*, and enjoy the VIP scene.

VIA DEL PANTHEON 55 ✦ TEL: 06 679 2788
WWW.RISTORANTEFORTUNATO.IT ✦ CLOSED SUNDAY
and TWO WEEKS *in* AUGUST ✦ MODERATE *to* EXPENSIVE
Near: the Pantheon

GINO

A NEON SIGN ON VIA DI CAMPO MARZIO POINTS TO THIS CULT TRATTORIA, HIDDEN DOWN THE KIND OF alleyway you would not enter back home. There's no danger: you're in one of Rome's chic central-city neighborhoods, and Parliament is less than 100 yards away. The

predictable crowd of representatives, senators, journalists, and local shopkeepers, plus a few intrepid tourists, keeps the two small dining rooms packed at lunch and dinner. To describe Gino as typical is to do it an injustice. This is *the* archetypal Roman trattoria, a wonderful throwback that has been run since the early 1960s by friendly, diminutive Luigi del Grosso, aka Il Cavaliere Gino, and his wife and children. Fabrizio, Gino's upbeat, happy-go-lucky son, is in charge nowadays, and wouldn't dream of changing anything. The walls are daubed with naïf murals showing grapevines. Starched cloths drape the tables, which are pushed perilously close together. The demand is constant and constantly growing but patient Gino and laid-back Fabrizio rightly refuse to rush clients or turn tables. You'll find all the classics of the Roman repertoire and the Canonical weekly wheel, served in giant portions, but also several delicacies invented over the years by Gino and his chefs. The most famous is *tonnarelli alla ciociara*, now a classic served at many other trattorias. Peas, mushrooms, butter, and *pancetta* are combined to make the luscious sauce, and the pasta is finished in the skillet, with lots of grated parmigiano and pecorino romano tossed and melted into it. The *carbonara*—also made with fresh tonnarelli and *pancetta*, which is skillfully degreased with white wine—is among the most flavorful and perfectly cooked in town. Gino's anchovy gratin, and rabbit or lamb *alla cacciatora*, are to die for, though you will surely want to live in order to savor the vegetable side dishes, such as *carciofi alla romana* or pan-fried chicory, and the homey desserts—from spoon sweets

IN VINO VERIT

like *tiramisù* to *crostata.* The house wine is from the Castelli Romani, served by the carafe. If you have only one trattoria meal in Rome, eat it here. Reserve several days ahead.

VICOLO ROSINI 4 ✦ TEL: 06 687 3434
CLOSED SUNDAY *and* AUGUST ✦ MODERATE ✦ *Near: on a dog's-leg alley directly across from Parliament, north of the Pantheon*

LA CAMPANA

MANY HISTORIANS INSIST THAT THIS CLASSIC, LIKABLE TRATTORIA IS ROME'S OLDEST: THE EARLIEST extant records show it to have been an *osteria* or hostelry in 1518. Unlike a handful of others (such as Ar Galletto), which have come and gone over the centuries, La Campana has been in constant operation. The interior, however, is of the circa mid-twentieth-century variety, with bottles on shelves, a sound-proofed ceiling (presumably hiding ancient timbers), and tables draped in white cloths, surrounded by bentwood chairs. Original art and old maps add a touch of class, to go with the waiters in equally classic outfits. Owner Giuseppe Trancassini is the umpteenth generation of his family to run the place. The relaxed atmosphere and menu have not substantially changed in modern or postmodern times, exception made for the tagliolini with fresh anchovies and pecorino, which can easily be skipped. You'll find the weekly wheel of traditional Roman dishes, most of them very well made, plus seasonal specials such as labor-intensive *vignarola* and *puntarella* salad (both served in spring), or the harder-to-find *galletto alla diavola* (grilled game hen with chili pepper). There are also a few crowd pleasers, such as fettuccine with shaved truffles, or fresh seafood. The desserts, rigorously classic, are house-made and, as long you enjoy things rich and sweet, you won't go wrong with any of them. The wine list is above average, with plenty of solid Italian bottlings. Expect to dine with well-heeled out-of-towners and a few neighborhood regulars. All in all, a meal here is a pleasant if unexciting experience.

VICOLO DELLA CAMPANA 18 ✦ TEL: 06 686 7820, 06 687 5273
WWW.RISTORANTELACAMPANA.COM
CLOSED MONDAY *and* AUGUST ✦ MODERATE *to* EXPENSIVE
Near: equidistant—50 yards—from Piazza Nicosia and Via della Scrofa

LILLI

LILLI IS THE NICKNAME OF AFFABLE LOREDANA, CHEF AND OWNER OF THIS MODEST NEIGHBORHOOD TRATTORIA, which has the distinction of being among the least noisy and most relaxed in Rome—and very hard to find. Sons Dino and Silvio and daughter Beatrice now largely run the operation, which has been a success since 1969 (though not always in these premises). Stick to the classics—everything from *cacio e pepe* to *coratella*, salt cod to roast veal—and you'll be well served. For dessert, luscious spoon sweets, from crumbled *millefoglie* served in a champagne coupe to chocolate mousse or *panna cotta* with red fruit. The street is off the beaten tourist path, and Lilli's clientele is made up almost entirely of Romans and other Italians. Sit outside on the terrace in fine weather.

VIA TOR DI NONA 23 ✦ TEL: 06 686 1916 ✦ CLOSED SUNDAY *and* 2 WEEKS *in* AUGUST ✦ MODERATE ✦ *Near: below Tiber River embankment, 100 yards north of Via dei Coronar*

MACCHERONI

THIS NEO-TRATTORIA WITH A GLASSED-IN KITCHEN AREA COULD BE IN SAN FRANCISCO, SYDNEY, OR PARIS, except that it serves Roman classics (and other more complicated and less successful dishes) such as *cacio e pepe*, *carbonara*, *gricia*, and *amatriciana*, grilled lamb, chicken *alla cacciatora*, and very good house-made desserts. The clientele is predominantly young hipsters and upscale tourists. The atmosphere is jovial and lively, and the outdoor tables on the edge of tiny Piazza delle Coppelle are ideally situated.

PIAZZA DELLE COPPELLE 44 ✦ TEL: 06 683 07895 WWW.RISTORANTEMACCHERONI.COM ✦ OPEN DAILY MODERATE ✦ *Near: 250 yards due north of the Pantheon*

MATRICIANELLA

IN THE MID 1990s, THE AMBITIOUS BROTHER-AND-SISTER TEAM OF GRAZIA AND GIACOMO LO BIANCO TOOK THE helm of this popular, crowded neighborhood trattoria that had lost some of its luster since opening in 1957. They've turned it into one of Rome's favorites for traditional cooking in middling-to-upscale surroundings. The style of the food is that of the Ghetto, with lots of luscious fried tidbits, including salt cod filets, potato skins, artichokes, and three different mixed fries—vegetables; vegetables with potato croquettes and mozzarella balls; and gutsy brains and sweetbreads. The *amatriciana* is delicious. So too are the rigatoni sauced with oxtail stew (and the oxtail stew itself is exquisite), the *pajata*, the buttery semolina gnocchi, the lamb chops, *pollo alla romana*, anchovy and endive casserole, and vegetable side dishes. The desserts feature luscious ricotta-and-chocolate cheesecake, chestnut mousse (in season), and pears poached in wine with cloves and cinnamon. Giacomo, a trained sommelier, has expanded the wine list to around 600 different bottlings, ranging from modest regional favorites to bruisers from Tuscany and Piedmont. Some are available by the glass. You'll dine in the company of Americans and Japanese, and a few Roman food lovers and politicos from Montecitorio; because of the proximity of the tables, and the high decibel level, the fashion and VIP crowd heads elsewhere. Reserve a few days in advance, especially if you'd like a table on the narrow sidewalk terrace, which is open in warm weather only.

VIA DEL LEONE 2/4 ✦ TEL: 06 683 2100
WWW.MATRICIANELLA.IT ✦ CLOSED SUNDAY *and* 3 WEEKS *in* AUGUST ✦ MODERATE *to* EXPENSIVE
Near: equidistant—100 yards—from Piazza di San Lorenzo in Lucina and Piazza Borghese

TONINO—TRATTORIA ANTONIO BASSETTI

ROME USED TO HAVE SCORES OF NO-NAME EATERIES LIKE TONINO: HOLE-IN-THE-WALL OSTERIAS, TRATTORIAS, *tavola caldas*, and such like, with no signs on them and, usually, no telephone either. Everyone in town knows this particular joint is called Tonino. Because of the spot's popularity, these days there's a cardboard sign taped to the window, and a telephone number to call. Cheap and cheery, with standard-issue red-check tablecloths and a no-nonsense décor (if such is the word), Tonino has friendly, casual service and offers the weekly wheel of Roman classics. You'll also find short pasta with eggplant, or with pan-fried broccoli rabe, and the kind of homey Italian-American meatballs the pseudo-sophisticates claim are not eaten in Italy. The desserts are house-made and include the requisite *tiramisù* or *crostata* with pastry cream and pine nuts. Despite the nearness of Piazza Navona, and the increased number of out-of-towners who eat here, the authenticity remains. Even the carafe wines—red or white from the Castelli Romani—are easy to quaff. White-collar employees and local shopkeepers keep Tonino filled. If no one answers the telephone, don't be surprised. Walk by late morning or early evening and reserve one of the 18 small tables.

VIA DEL GOVERNO VECCHIO 18/19
TEL: 06 687 7002 *or* 333 587 0779
CLOSED SUNDAY ✦ VERY INEXPENSIVE
Near: 100 east of Piazza dell'Orologio

BREAD, CHEESE, FRESH PASTA, FRUIT ICES, GOURMET FOOD SHOPS, ICE CREAM, KITCHEN TOOLS, PASTRIES

AI MONASTERI

OWNERS THE NARDI FAMILY FOUNDED THIS WELL-STOCKED, UPSCALE HERB SHOP IN 1894 AND ARE into their fourth generation. They sell natural health care products from the monasteries and other religious institutions of Italy, ranging from honey, herbs, and spices to liqueurs and distilled elixirs (of aniseed, camomile, coffee, or mandarin orange, among others), plus jams, grappas, candy, chocolate, tea, soaps scented with flower essence or honey, perfumes, shaving creams (try the tingling mint variety), and scores of herbal or natural potions and cures.

CORSO RINASCIMENTO 72
TEL: 06 688 02783 ✦ WWW.MONASTERI.IT
CLOSED THURSDAY AFTERNOON *and* SUNDAY
Near: on north end of main thoroughfare 1 block east of Piazza Navona

ANGELO FEROCI

ONE OF ROME'S TOP-THREE BUTCHER SHOPS, ANGELO FEROCI HAS BEEN IN BUSINESS FOR ABOUT A century, and is still in the Feroci family. The marble-clad and paved interior is a landmark and can't be altered. The main counter is a slab of marble about five inches thick, which maintains a constant temperature, and has therefore escaped eviction by European Union health inspectors. If you're renting an apartment in Rome, and cooking there, this is the place to buy excellent fresh lamb and other meat, including beef and veal. Feroci is absolutely reliable. Offal is another specialty; the *pajata* comes from suckling lambs, not veal. Also sold are many ready-to-eat dishes, from starters to main courses.

VIA DELLA MADDALENA 15 ✦ TEL: 06 683 07030
CLOSED THURSDAY *and* SATURDAY AFTERNOONS
and SUNDAY, OPEN MORNINGS ONLY *in* AUGUST
Near: 100 yards north of the Pantheon

ANTICA ERBORISTERIA ROMANA

THE OLFACTORY EXPERIENCE ALONE MAKES A STOP AT THIS HERB-AND-SPICE SHOP A MUST. HIDDEN IN THE drawers of tall cabinets from the 1880s are 300 types of medicinal plant, 50 teas, and 20 to 30 herbs and spices (basil; rosemary; laurel; fennel; curries; chili peppers; saffron; black, white, green, and pink peppercorns; or ground pepper). Small and charming, the shop has been in operation since 1752; the Ospici family took over in 1948. Nowadays, second-generation herb specialists Paolo and Riccardo Ospici work with their partner, pharmacist Gianluca Borgato. The

city's most demanding cooks come here to buy their dry herbs, and some have special infusions and teas mixed for them. If you tell the Ospici or Borgato what kind of digestive, diuretic, or tonic properties you're seeking, they will come up with a personalized herbal or herb-and-spice mix.

VIA DI TORRE ARGENTINA 15 ✦ TEL: 06 687 9493
WWW.ANTICAERBORISTERIAROMANA.IT ✦ CLOSED SUNDAY
Near: Largo di Torre Argentina and the Carilli delicatessen

ANTICA NORCINERIA

ANTICA NORCINERIA IS ONE OF ROME'S OLDEST PORK BUTCHER SHOPS, AND *PROSCIUTTO* AND *GUANCIALE* makers. Fittingly, it's in Via della Scrofa, "Sow Street." Owner Giuseppe Simoni, Umbrian by birth, cures his *guanciale* for ten days and ages it for about 20 days. The resultant jowl is excellent for cooking but too young to be eaten raw. Simoni still hand-slices the hams and jowls he sells; the flavor of hand-sliced *prosciutto*, compared to machine-sliced ham, is more intense, in part because of the slightly uneven texture created by the knife blade. A fine selection of fresh mozzarella, aged cheeses, highest-quality canned foods, dried mushrooms, and pasta is also sold; Simoni and his assistants are always affable, and the shop is full of charm.

VIA DELLA SCROFA 100 ✦ TEL: 06 354 96806 ✦ CLOSED SUNDAY

Near: equidistant—about 300 yards—from the Pantheon and Ara Pacis

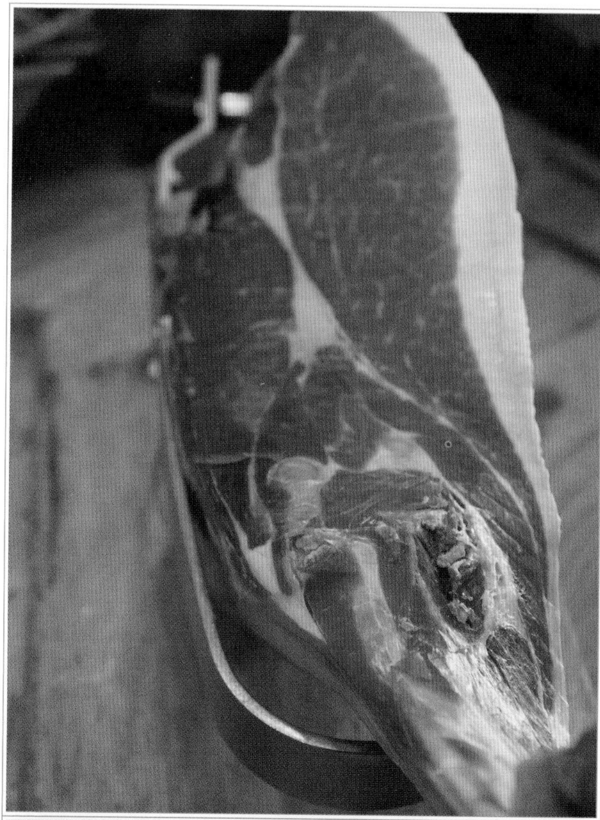

GASSER
SALAME
AL TARTUFO
€ 34,95
AL KG
SALAME
DI CINGHIALE
€ 34,95

LEVONI
FANNO BENE I SALUMI

L'ANTICO FORNO

ROUGH DIAMONDS OWN AND OPERATE THIS PROLIFIC, CLUTTERED, PERPETUALLY MOBBED CORNER BAKERY, the only one left in the Scrofa neighborhood. The classic pastries, pies, tarts, and cookies are often giant-sized, and appear to be on the point of exploding out of the display cases or falling off helter-skelter stacked trays. The goodies are less than light, but they're flavorful and wholesome in a rustic way. The *pizza bianca* is very easy to eat, and comes in a variety of thicknesses and in different degrees of doneness, so ask for a slice the way you like it. Several of the breads are remarkably good, including the multi-cereal Pugliese-style loaf that is baked only in the afternoon. Tourists on the Pantheon-to-Ara Pacis run have discovered L'Antico Forno, which is also popular among locals, in part because of its convenient opening hours.

VIA DELLA SCROFA 33/VIA DELLA STELLETTA 1-2-3
TEL: 06 454 81408 ✦ OPEN DAILY *from* DAWN *to* 8PM, *sometimes later*
Near: next door to Volpetti alla Scrofa and equidistant—about 300 yards—from the Pantheon and Ara Pacis

CAFFÈ DELLA PACE

MOST CUSTOMERS DON'T REALLY GO TO THIS TRENDY, HIPSTER HANGOUT FOR THE QUALITY OF THE MOKarabia coffee, or the drinks and snacks, or even the cozy interior, which hasn't changed appreciably since 1891, when Caffè della Pace opened for business. Multilingual beautiful people with entertainingly outrageous attitude provide the service, such as it is, while they await their next chance to appear in an advertisement or Cinecittà movie. By day, the interior is filled by tourists and locals, who occupy old wooden tables haphazardly arrayed in front of the bar and around the central column that props up the ceiling timbers. The real scene is outside, however, where the tables on the wrap-around terrace are packed until the early hours. A casual visitor will be happy to find a table here not simply for the anthropological value, but also because the street is quiet by Rome standards, and the setting full of character. The view toward the north end of Via della Pace, which frames Bramante's façade on the church of Santa Maria della Pace, is particularly pleasant at sunset, when the street lights and spots pick it out.

VIA DELLA PACE 3/7
TEL: 06 686 1216 ✦ WWW.CAFFEDELLAPACE.IT
Near: 2 blocks west of Piazza Navona

CAFFÈ SANT'EUSTACHIO

CAFFÈ SANT'EUSTACHIO DRAWS DEVOTEES FROM AROUND THE WORLD. MANY COME TO DRINK THE GRAN Caffè, a double espresso with a remarkably foamy head, made according to a secret formula. Screens prevent customers from seeing Sant'Eustachio's barmen—Rome's high priests of coffee—working behind their machines. Brothers Raimondo and Roberto Ricci took over the historic property in 1996, improved the quality of the coffee, and left the original 1938 décor intact. Above the curving, cursive-L-shaped bar (made from a single piece of stainless steel) are vintage black-and-white photographs, hand-cranked coffee grinders, and a large wall clock. The floor has a mosaic showing the stag and crucifix of Saint Eustace, whose church is across the small, busy square. The Ricci brothers come from a family of *caffè* owners, are passionate, knowledgeable and, though secretive about Gran Caffè, are eager to share their passion with connoisseurs. They import the very best, most expensive Arabica beans from Africa (organic Ethiopian Sidamo) and South America (organic, fair trade Poço Fundo Brazilian, among others). The roasting is done several times a week in a small room at the back of the *caffè*, using a manually operated, wood-burning coffee roasting machine from the 1940s. Only a handful of experts still know how to get the

hard-to-use, persnickety machine to work properly, but the results are stunning. Whereas automatic roasters operate on average temperatures and timed programs, this hand-operated machine must be adjusted and tweaked second by second. The smell of the coffee, the sound it makes, its color and shine, are what the shop's veteran roaster goes by. Customers can watch the show from the doorway. The symphonic house blend marries beans from Brazil, Colombia, Santo Domingo, Guatemala, and Nicaragua (most of them organic and fair trade). For those who enjoy mono-varietals, of special note is the Bourbon della Galapágos, a 100-percent organic coffee from the Cobos-Gonzales plantation on San Cristòbal; the plantation's extraordinarily long-lived Arabica plants have been producing beans since 1869. The yield is tiny, the beans small, with amazingly complex, concentrated flavors. The Ricci brothers get this coffee direct from the growers. Note that coffees served at the bar come lightly sugared; ask for yours *senza zucchero* if you prefer it without sugar. Chocolate lovers will want to try the luscious, three-tiered Monachella: espresso, hot chocolate, and whipped cream (the name means "nun with white veil"). Sant'Eustachio pastries and *cornetti* are delicious. Though world-renowned, and frequented by many tourists, the *caffè* is unapologetically Roman and chaotic, with clients perpetually packed several deep at the bar and a line waiting for the few outdoor tables. Don't be surprised if you see Italian senators and political potentates who drift over from Palazzo Madama, the senate building, kitty-corner. Diplomats from nearby embassies, chauffeurs and bodyguards in dark suits and darker glasses, French priests and nuns from the church of San

Francesco dei Francesi, and an international mix of travelers add to the atmosphere. Also sold are a potent coffee liqueur made with the house blend of coffee; irresistible coffee-filled chocolates; chocolate-covered coffee beans and other candies; and vacuum-packed cans of ground Sant'Eustachio coffee. Don't miss it. Sant'Eustachio supplies coffee to restaurant Il Presidente in area 3, and Caffè Piacere e Passione in area 8. Note: head to the cash desk first and get a receipt for your order before lining up at the bar.

PIAZZA SANT'EUSTACHIO 82 ✦ TEL: 06 688 02048
WWW.SANTEUSTACHIOILCAFFE.IT ✦ OPEN DAILY,
SUNDAY *to* THURSDAY 8:30AM *to* 1AM, FRIDAY *to* 1:30AM *and*
SATURDAY *to* 2AM, CLOSED *on* AUGUST 15 *and* CHRISTMAS
Near: equidistant—about 200 yards—from Piazza Navona and the Pantheon

CAFFETTERIA DEL CHIOSTRO DEL BRAMANTE

OPENED IN 2007, THIS SELF-SERVICE MUSEUM CAFETERIA ON THE UPPER FLOOR OF THE GORGEOUS Cloister of Bramante, behind the church of Santa Maria della Pace, is blissfully quiet. Take a seat where men and women of the cloth once paced their lives away, and gaze up at the rooftops around you. The coffee is served in ceramic cups with ceramic lids, and the pastries and American-style muffins are perfectly edible, and will please the homesick traveler. The simple, could-be-anywhere lunch and weekend brunch are popular even with Romans, and, for the pleasure of Internet addicts, there's free WiFi. A bookstore is next to the *caffè*, and high-quality art exhibitions are held in adjoining rooms.

VIA DELLA PACE ✦ TEL: 06 688 09035
WWW.CHIOSTRODELBRAMANTE.IT ✦ OPEN 10AM *to* 7:30PM
CLOSED MONDAY ✦ *Near: 2 blocks west of Piazza Navona*

CARILLI

THIS SMALL, OUTWARDLY UNREMARKABLE DELICATESSEN, BUTCHER'S SHOP AND GROCERY IS THE SOURCE of Rome's most traditional cured pork products, foremost among them *guanciale*. Salvatore Carilli is nearly 80 years old and the eldest of three brothers, all *norcini* pork specialists from a tiny village in Umbria. The family has been in the trade for more generations than anyone can remember. Several times a month, Salvatore and his younger brothers Giulio Cesare and Giovanni fill a truck with free-range, corn- and grain-fed white pigs from Umbria, raised for them by cousins or friends, and take them to the municipal slaughterhouse on Rome's outskirts. The Carilli brothers always walk their hogs through the slaughterhouse themselves to be sure they receive their own sides of

pork at the end. Working on a stainless steel table, they rub sea salt into the hog jowls by hand, coating each thoroughly, and then transfer them to another stainless steel table in the shop's cold room. Here, the jowls wait at just above freezing for 21 days. Once a week, the Carillis flip them and massage any loose salt back in. After three weeks, the salt has been absorbed. The Carillis rinse the jowls in warm water and pat them dry with clean dishtowels. Back on the worktable, they combine garlic powder, roughly ground black pepper or sometimes chili pepper, and more sea salt. They coat the jowls with the seasoning, punch a small hole in the thin tip of each *guanciale,* and run twine through it. At the family's drying facility in Frascaio di Norcia in Umbria, the jowls hang in cool mountain breezes for three to four months. The *guanciali* are then ready to sell, but the largest and thickest improve if they age in a cellar or the shop for another year or more. In part because of the long salting and hanging, the taste of the Carillis' *guanciali* is close to *prosciutto crudo* and, unlike most salt-cured jowls, the Carillis' can be eaten raw. Also sold at this wonderful shop are excellent mozzarella from Aversa, trucked in fresh several times a week, other fine Italian cheeses, *prosciutti,* sausages, fresh pork, and a wide variety of olives, grilled vegetables packed in olive oil, artisanal dry pasta, and sundry groceries.

VIA DI TORRE ARGENTINA 11

TEL: 688 03789 ✦ CLOSED THURSDAY

Near: about 200 yards south of the Pantheon, near Largo di Torre Argentina

CHOCOLAT

CHOCOLAT IS A COMPACT BUT ATTRACTIVELY DECORATED SHOP SCENTED BY A BUBBLING HOT POT OF lightly sugared milk chocolate. With it, clients are invited to make their own *pirottini*, the house specialty, which are white or semisweet chocolate shells into which a candied sour cherry is dropped. You ladle the hot chocolate over the cherry, and sprinkle spices (such as cinnamon, ground ginger, or chili) on top. Another outstanding specialty chocolate you'll find nowhere else is *capezzolo di Venere* ("Venus' nipple"), a fresh strawberry in champagne encased in a dark-chocolate shell. Chocolat is family-run. Affable Lellé Paolini opened for business in 2003, after about 20 years of making chocolate at home and selling it directly to clients. Her son Francesco Colangeli learned from her and took over as chocolatier in 2005. Her daughter Claudia Colangeli makes the cheerfully decorated wooden and ceramic gift boxes and trays. Chocolat uses only fresh ingredients, no concentrates, including freshly brewed coffee, and freshly toasted and ground hazelnuts from the Langhe or pistachios from Bronte, a prime growing area on the slopes of Etna. Even the cherries are candied in-house. The base chocolate here is a 70-percent cocoa from Venezuela supplied by Barry Callebaut. Paolini uses little cocoa butter in her chocolates, and has a dislike for sugary, buttery chocolate. Hers, she says, follows the old Spanish and monastic tradition, meaning it's simple, light, and fresh. Paolini offers two-day intensive chocolate-making courses to groups of six. She also sells delicious coffee cakes flavored with fresh rose petals, violets, jasmine, or lemon, made for her by a baker in Piedmont, as well as unsweetened chocolate-flavored dry pasta, which is unusual, and challenging to sauce, but makes for an intriguing gift.

VIA DELLA DOGANA VECCHIA 12 ✦ TEL: 06 681 35545
OPEN DAILY ✦ *Near: 20 yards north of Piazza Sant'Eustachio, facing Palazzo Madama, 150 yards west of the Pantheon*

CIAMPINI

THE CIAMPINI FAMILY HAS FIVE *CAFFÈ*/COCKTAIL BAR/RESTAURANTS IN ROME, STARTING WITH THE CELEbrated Tre Scalini on Piazza Navona. This, the San Lorenzo in Lucina location, is a favorite among prosperous residents and the fashion crowd, and is comparable to Vitti next door both in style, service, and quality of food and beverages. Ciampini also has waiters in livery, and the seating both inside and out is comfortable, with correspondingly high prices. The main difference between Ciampini and others is that Ciampini serves Morganti coffee, which is coarser and stronger than the Illy coffee at Vitti, and more like the Teichner bar blend offered directly across the square. What you'll find here, but not at the two other famous *caffè* on the piazza, is Ciampini's inimitable Tartufo, the original chocolate-covered truffle ice cream, invented in Rome decades ago. The recipe is the same at all the Ciampini outlets. Another Ciampini bar, with the same food, desserts, and beverages on the menu, but a quieter atmosphere and smaller street-side terrace, is about 50 yards due north of the square, on the corner of Via del Leoncino and Via della Fontanella di Borghese (Tel: 06 68135108, closed Sunday).

PIAZZA DI SAN LORENZO *in* LUCINA 29 ✦ TEL: 06 6876606
CLOSED SUNDAY ✦ *Near: north of the Pantheon and the Italian parliament building, 100 yards west of Via del Corso*

CONFETTERIA MORIONDO E GARIGLIO

THIS IS ROME'S MOST CELEBRATED CHOCOLATE SHOP AND HAS BEEN IN BUSINESS IN A VARIETY OF INCARNATIONS, with different names and in different locations, since 1870. In 1886 Enrico Cuniberti, a Piedmontese, was brought in as chocolate maker. Cuniberti supplied the court of the Savoy kings in Turin. His recipes and techniques are still being used. Wood-paneled and done up like a jewelbox, with scarlet décor, Moriondo e Gariglio always has handsome window displays, and smells intoxicatingly of fresh chocolate, flowers, and spices. The shop's current owner and manager is Pierina Minelli; her son Attilio Proietti is the chocolate maker. Attilio learned from his father Marcello Proietti, who until forced to stop working by a grave illness, was for decades widely recognized as the city's most skilled chocolate artisan. Moriondo e Gariglio is a direct importer of top-quality chocolate beans and bulk chocolate from South America. The solid or filled chocolates come in a wide range of flavors and are made from fresh ingredients, not concentrates, and therefore last only a few days. That explains why a few dozen and not hundreds of chocolate types

are displayed at any one time; regular customers often order their chocolates ahead. The house style is clean and simple, not sugary or creamy (with the exception of the old-fashioned cream-filled *cremini*, which must be special ordered). Moriondo e Gariglio creates wildly wonderful, giant Easter eggs, which they make to order; if requested, they will fill the eggs with a gift brought in by the client. These surprise gifts range from engagement rings to suits of clothes. *Marrons glacés* are also made to order, are exquisite, and, like the house-filled chocolates, are at their best for three days. The candied fruit is delicious, firm, and not overly sweet.

VIA DEL PIÈ DI MARMO 21-22 ✦ TEL: 06 699 0856
CLOSED SUNDAY *and* SATURDAY AFTERNOON,
from MID-JUNE *to* SEPTEMBER
Near: kitty-corner from Palazzo Doria-Pamphili

DA LECCARSI I BAFFI: SQUISITEZZE & CIOCCOLATERIA

THIS SMALL, NEW BOUTIQUE CATERS PRIMARILY TO THE TOURIST TRADE, BUT DOES STOCK GOOD HONEYS, jams, marmalades, fruit gelatins, chocolate, herbs, and spices.

VIA DI PANICO 31 ✦ TEL: 06 979 97935
CLOSED MONDAY MORNING ✦ *Near: at the Castel Sant'Angelo end of Via dei Coronari, 50 yards from the Tiber*

DORIA CAFFÈ

ONCE YOU'VE ADMIRED THE BERNINI PORTRAIT BUST—AND THOUSANDS OF OTHER PRICELESS MASTERpieces—in the Galleria Doria Pamphili, go through the passageway or go outside and around the corner from the main entrance (in Piazza del Collegio Romano) and relax in this *caffè*. It's on the ground floor of the same massive, privately owned *palazzo*. In keeping with the tony setting, with an overlay of Las Vegas glitz, you'll see a niche and a gilded dolphin fountain sunk in the Travertine floor. The ceiling is vaulted, there's woodwork on the walls, green under-cloths and yellow tablecloths on the tables, comfortable armchairs, and a green serpentine bar top, in case you prefer to stand while enjoying your good, strong Danesi coffee. The pastries (from Zio Cornetti) are also very good, the service polished.

VIA DELLA GATTA 1 ✦ TEL: 06 679 3805
OPEN DAILY 8AM *to* 8PM ✦ *Near: inside the Palazzo Doria-Pamphili, kitty-corner to Moriondo e Gariglio*

GELATERIA DEL TEATRO AI CORONARI

THE YOUNG, BRASH OWNER OF THIS HARD-TO-FIND ICE CREAMERY IS STEFANO MARCOTULLI. HE'S BENT ON outdoing his fellow masters of *gelato artigianale naturale* and has installed a Plexiglass window in his kitchen to allow curious customers to see him at work. He claims he has nothing to hide. "The others say they're natural, I show people I'm natural." Marcotulli states clearly that he uses small quantities of guar and carob seed as emulsifiers, and, when necessary, mixes his own freshly toasted and ground nuts (Bronte pistachios, Langhe hazelnuts, and Bari almonds) into the best available nut pastes. The guar, carob, and pastes give a thick, luscious consistency to the ice creams, adding a fatty bass note which most people love, a note absent from the lighter, brighter products of Rome's other supreme ice cream makers, Al Settimo Gelo in particular. Still, Marcotulli's ice creams are remarkably excellent, exceptionally flavorful, and made of fresh, highest-quality ingredients. Illy espresso is brewed to make the *caffè* flavor. The ewe's-milk ricotta transformed into that flavor (and to make *torta di ricotta* cheesecake flavor) is delivered daily by Rome-area cheesemaker Pietro Punturi. The lively, outspoken Marcotulli was a pastry chef at Rome's Marriott Hotel and says his mission is to create "pastry ice creams." So far he has successfully transliterated *zuppa inglese* (trifle), *pan di Spagna* (sponge cake), Sacher Torte, *millefoglie*, and other classics into delicious *gelati*.

VIA DI SAN SIMONE 70 ✦ TEL: 06 454 74880
OPEN DAILY 11:30AM *to* 1AM ✦ CLOSED JANUARY *and* FEBRUARY
Near: across Via dei Coronari on an alley facing the south side of the church of San Salvatore in Lauro

GIOLITTI

ABOUT A CENTURY OLD AND STILL IN THE SAME FAMILY, GIOLITTI IS A POPULAR SIT-DOWN CAFFÈ, TEA salon, and ice cream parlor. The late opening hours mean it's haunted by a mix of policemen, security guards, night clubbers, and jet-lagged tourists. Natty Italian parliamentarians wander down from nearby Montecitorio to meet informally in Giolitti's luxurious, painted rooms, while tourists prefer the narrow street terrace (there are no sidewalks). The stream of pedestrians on the Pantheon-to-Trevi circuit via Piazza Colonna swarms in for take-out ice cream cones. The *gelati* are better than average, and the espressos and cappuccinos and coffee ice cream made with the house Mondicaffè coffee are very good. Other delicious ice cream classics include hazelnut and chocolate; the fresh seasonal fruit flavors such as *mirtillo* (bilberry) can sometimes be excellent, tending to extreme sweetness, which is perhaps why they're popular with young customers. Dozens of flavors are always available.

VIA UFFICI DEL VICARIO 40 ✦ TEL: 06 699 1243
OPEN DAILY, *until* 2AM, *including* SUNDAY
Near: between Montecitorio and the Pantheon

KITCHEN

ROME IS NOT PARTICULARLY WELL ENDOWED WITH SHOPS SELLING KITCHEN TOOLS. THIS TINY, GLASSED-in stand at the very northern end of the area has a limited selection of classic Italian tools, plus the hard-to-find slicer for preparing *puntarella* salad. Another Kitchen outlet is 300 yards due south of the Musei Vaticani/Cipro subway stop on the western edge of Prati (Viale degli Ammiragli 10-12, Tel: 06 397 40597, same hours).

PIAZZA DEL PORTO DI RIPETTA ✦ TEL: 06 688 02244
OPEN 10:30AM *to* 2:30PM *and* 3:30 *to* 7:30PM,
CLOSED MONDAY MORNING *and* SUNDAY
Near: facing Ara Pacis on the Tiber River at Ponte Cavour

PASTICCERIA LA DELIZIOSA

A HOLE IN THE WEATHERED WALL, ON A NARROW ALLEY-WAY, THIS WONDERFUL PASTRY SHOP IS EASY TO MISS. Owned by the Di Salvo family, it's a favorite of locals and savvy Romans with a sweet tooth. All the delicious, homey Roman classics are made here daily, from shortbread cookies to outstanding ricotta cakes with chocolate or jam. Pre-modern, cream-filled pastries such as *profiteroles* and *bignè* are a house specialty.

VICOLO SAVELLI 48-50 ✦ TEL: 06 803155 ✦ CLOSED MONDAY
Near: about 250 yards west of Piazza di Pasquino, near the corner of Via di Parione

PASTICCERIA ROCCO

FOUNDED IN THE 1920s AND STILL RUN BY THE SAME FAMILY (NOW FALCIONELLI), THIS HARD-TO-FIND PASTRY shop has a huge back workroom fronted by a retail sales area the size of a broom closet. It's the ultimate insider's address, supplying restaurants, trattorias, and delis all over Rome with those luscious cakes, pies, and butter cookies which so many restaurateurs pretend to have made themselves. The miniature ricotta-and-chocolate tarts are sublime, but so too are the chocolate-dipped shortbread sandwich cookies filled with jam, the many different kinds of *crostata*, and the other simple, classic Roman sweets. The jovial owners, Gina and Susanna, are living testimonials to the irresistibility of their own products.

VIA DEI PIANELLARE 22/23 ✦ TEL: 06 686 5600 ✦ OPEN DAILY
Near: about 250 yards north of the Pantheon, flanking the church of Sant'Agostino in Campo Marzio

PATRIZIA ONORATI

STEP INSIDE THIS CENTURY-OLD, UPSCALE, FAMILY-OWNED CANDY AND SWEETS SHOP AND SNIFF THE timeless atmosphere. The chocolate bars are high quality, ditto the bonbons, licorice, boiled sweets, and suckers. The family no longer candies the fruit it sells, but buys in from reliable suppliers, and the dried fruit is always delicious. Though located on a thoroughfare near Piazza Navona, the shop is easy to miss.

It's on the south end of the street, near the traffic-clogged "piazza" facing the massive church of Sant'Andrea della Valle.

CORSO RINASCIMENTO 8 ✦ TEL: 06 686 5268 ✦ CLOSED SUNDAY
Near: ten yards north of Piazza Sant'Andrea della Valle

LA TAZZA D'ORO

LA TAZZA D'ORO AT THE PANTHEON IS ONE OF ROME'S BUSIEST, MOST POPULAR *CAFFÈ*. DON'T CONFUSE IT with the many other Tazza d'Oro espresso bars around town; all belong to the same extended, fractious family. Only at the original Pantheon location is the coffee still roasted on site five times a week, and only here will you find the justly celebrated Miscela Regina house blend. The interior of the *caffè* is clad in stone and decorated with un-PC bas reliefs showing South American natives hefting bags of coffee beans. Many Romans feel that this is the source of the city's most luscious, smoothest cappuccino, and that may well be true. The foam is tiger-striped, frothy, and stiff. The milk used is extra rich by Italian standards (it's called *speciale bar* and is 3.6-percent fat, like most American milk). The sour notes at Tazza d'Oro are the perpetual crowds and long lines, and the elbow-to-kidney competition at the bar. In summer, when the ambient temperature is high and the bodies wrestle each other three-deep, the espresso machines sometimes overheat, and the coffee comes out overly strong and tar-like. The frozen *granita al caffè* is always outstanding, however. Miscela Regina is used at the bar and sold over the counter in the roasting area behind the cash register. It's composed of excellent, 100-percent Arabica coffees from South America, and its exact composition is a closely guarded secret. It was perfected, the management claims, in 1946, when Tazza d'Oro opened, and the percentages have remained unchanged since. Given that the quality and characteristics of coffee beans vary from harvest to harvest and place to place, and most coffee plants only produce for a few decades before being replaced, the claim seems of dubious value. However, from the marketing standpoint, it is a winner: Tazza d'Oro customers clearly enjoy being reassured that they're drinking coffees concocted using a secret, vintage formula. All Tazza d'Oro blends and single-plantation coffees are imported directly. Of special note are the Maragogype Guatemala and Jamaican Blue Mountain mono-varietals (also available at the bar for a premium). The 1946 gas-fired roaster runs every weekday at 8am one week, 2pm the following week. Customers are welcome to watch. Note: make sure to get a receipt for your order at the cash register before lining up at the bar.

VIA DEGLI ORFANI 84 ✦ TEL: 06 678 9792
WWW.TAZZADOROCOFFEESHOP.COM ✦ OPEN 7AM *to* 8PM
MONDAY *through* SATURDAY ✦ CLOSED SUNDAY
Near: about 100 yards east of the Pantheon's colonnade

TEICHNER

TEICHNER IS A *CAFFÈ* AND COCKTAIL BAR, UPSCALE DELICATESSEN, AND COFFEE ROASTER. MANY OTHER *caffè* in Rome use Teichner blends to make their bar coffees. Oddly, the blend served here is not outstanding, and contains a high proportion of very strong, dark-roasted Robusta. It's okay for a cappuccino, which you can happily sip at a table set out in the handsome Piazza di San Lorenzo in Lucina. But if you buy take-out coffee to brew at home, make sure to get the 100-percent Arabica blend, which is exceptionally good: mild, complex, and chocolatey. The roasting is done in a cramped back workroom on the premises, using an old-fashioned machine of uncertain age, probably 50 years old or more. Theoretically the roasting facility is off limits to customers, but when asked politely, the men in charge have been known to allow enthusiasts to watch from the threshold. Roasting is usually done early in the morning; there is no precise schedule. Teichner is one of the square's trio of hangouts—the other two are Ciampini and Vitti—where a mix of locals and tourists lounge under sun umbrellas, enjoying everything from breakfast to lunch, cocktails to light dinners. Of the three, Teichner is the most relaxed, with casual, sometimes lackadaisical or confused service, but very good snack food. The *pizza bianca* comes from Antico Forno Marco Roscioli, and there's a fine selection of high-quality hams, salamis, cheeses, and grilled vegetables in olive oil, plus a wide range of sandwiches, including one particularly delicious variety made with authentic spit-roasted *porchetta* from the Alban Hills.

PIAZZA DI SAN LORENZO IN LUCINA 17 ✦ TEL: 06 687 1449
SHOP OPEN 8AM *to* 8PM, CAFFÈ OPEN 8AM *to* 11PM,
BOTH CLOSED SUNDAY *in* JULY *and* AUGUST
Near: north of the Pantheon and the Italian parliament building, 100 yards west of Via del Corso

TRE SCALINI

VARIOUSLY DESCRIBED AS A PAPERCLIP OR AN ELONGATED OVAL, PIAZZA NAVONA IS JUSTLY RENOWNED for being built atop Emperor Domitian's circus; for Giovanni Lorenzo Bernini's Four Rivers fountain; and for the church of Santa Maria in Agone, designed by rival architect Francesco Borromini. Food lovers know that the Tre Scalini *caffè* and ice creamery facing the Four Rivers fountain, while often written off as a pricey tourist trap, is where the now world-famous Tartufo ice cream was invented in 1931 by the establishment's first owner, Francesca Colasanti-Ciampini. *Tartufi*, as they've been made here for nearly 80 years, are lumps of dark chocolate ice cream with a candied sour cherry in the center and semi-sweet chocolate hunks inside and out. In Italian, a *tartufo* is a truffle. Francesca's husband Giuseppe Ciampini, who was born and raised in Umbria, where black truffles grow wild, gave Tartufo ice cream its name. Their son Nando still runs the *caffè* (and the restaurant next door), presiding over the daily production of its 500 or so truffles. The family also makes truffles at its other *caffè*-restaurant in the Piazza di San Lorenzo in Lucina, serving them there and at two other Ciampini locations in central Rome. It's undoubtedly true that the prices are high and the tourists thick at Tre Scalini, but of all the *caffè* on Piazza Navona (with the possible exception of modish, touristy Caffè Bernini, practically next door), this is the most pleasant. It certainly has the best ice creams, which are made in the old-fashioned way, using wholesome ingredients.

PIAZZA NAVONA 30 ✦ TEL: 06 687 9148

WWW.RISTORANTE3SCALINI.COM

OPEN 9AM *to* 1:30AM DAILY ✦ *Near: on square, facing Four Rivers fountain and practically flanking Santa Maria in Agone*

VITTI (1)

NOWADAYS A CHIC *CAFFÈ*, LIGHT LUNCH OR DINNER SPOT, AND COCKTAIL BAR, VITTI STARTED OUT OVER a century ago as a pastry shop, and then added coffee, snacks, ice cream, and finally food and wine to its offerings. The *cornetti* and other breakfast rolls and pastries are very good and are house-made, as are the tarts and other classic desserts, and the very good ice creams. Vitti serves Illy coffee; the barmen here are among the most skilled and polite in Rome, and espressos and cappuccinos are perfectly made and served in properly warmed cups. The bar area at the back of the long, narrow, stone-clad interior of Vitti is often mobbed by fashion moguls from the Piazza di Spagna side of Via del Corso, just east of the square, and by politicians from the Italian parliament down the street. Vitti's outdoor terrace flanks Ciampini and is across from Teichner; of the three it is the most stylish, with waiters in livery, and comfortable seating. The selection of food is also wider here than at the other two, and while the pasta isn't memorable, it isn't bad, either. Note: Vitti operates caffè in the Feltrinelli bookstore on Largo di Torre Argentina and inside the Galleria Colonna/Galleria Alberto Sordi (on Via del Corso, facing Piazza Colonna); it also has a restaurant-caffè in Piazza Capranica (see below).

PIAZZA DI SAN LORENZO IN LUCINA 33 ✦ TEL: 06 687 6304
WWW.VITTI.IT ✦ OPEN DAILY ✦ *Near: north of the Pantheon and the Italian parliament building, 100 yards west of Via del Corso*

VITTI (2)

VITTI IS A LOCAL MINI-CHAIN OF *CAFFÈ*, WITH FOUR DIFFERENT LOCATIONS, THREE OF THEM RECENT. UNLIKE the others, this one, in Piazza Capranica, is first and foremost a full-blown restaurant which, during off hours, doubles as a *caffè*, and serves the same excellent Illy coffee as the other Vittis. The managers claim a distant date of founding (1898), when Vitti began operating as a *caffè*, ice creamery, and pastry shop in Piazza di San Lorenzo in Lucina. This attractive addition to the Vitti portfolio opened only in late 2007. The setting is hard to beat: a pocketsized square with relatively little traffic and plenty of charm. Handsome canvas umbrellas shade the sturdy tables and chairs, which are a nice change after the ubiquitous plastic buckets. They're set at a safe distance from passing cars and stampeding tour groups. At night, with candles lit at each table, and the illuminated façade of the church of Santa Maria in Aquiro across the way, the scene is magical. The dining room is also appealing, decorated in cream and scarlet tones, and furnished with comfortable chairs around well-spaced tables. The multilingual waiters, dressed in chic gray suits, deal mostly with tourists, politicians, and business people, and do their job with professionalism. Vitti has adopted Roman food as its theme; the menu, which changes daily, is a parade of well-executed, lightened-and-brightened classics of the kind you find on many more authentic trattoria menus. The *amatriciana* and *carbonara*, *coda alla vaccinara*, and *saltimbocca* are better than competent and the wine list more than adequate. Desserts include delicious pastries and cakes made by Vitti at its Piazza di San Lorenzo in Lucina location. Though Mamma isn't rolling out the pasta in the kitchen or grating the lemon zest into the *crostata*, as far as upscale, neo-Roman places go, Vitti is a success.

PIAZZA CAPRANICA 75/77 ✦ TEL: 06 699 21720
WWW.VITTI.IT OPEN DAILY ✦ *Near: 100 yards northeast of the Pantheon, around the corner from Tazza d'Oro*

VOLPETTI ALLA SCROFA

SMALLER, LESS CROWDED, LESS DYNAMIC, AND LESS WELL-STOCKED THAN COUSINS E. VOLPETTI & C. IN THE Testaccio area, this long-established deli, wine shop, *gastronomia*, and restaurant is nonetheless a good source for high-quality hams, cheeses, take-out dishes, and other delicacies. Though somewhat charmless, the handful of tables in the dining room abutting the deli are a good place to chill out and have a light meal or a snack. The prices are correspondingly high.

VIA DELLA SCROFA 31/32 ✦ TEL: 06 683 00334
WWW.VOLPETTISHOP.COM ✦ CLOSED SUNDAY *from* JULY *to* APRIL
Near: across from Antica Norcineria and equidistant—about 300 yards—from the Pantheon and Ara Pacis

WINE AND WINE BARS

ACHILLI—ENOTECA AL PARLAMENTO

LONG ESTABLISHED AND JUSTLY RENOWNED, ACHILLI CATERS TO SERIOUS WINE CONNOISSEURS WITH THICK wallets and international appetites. Parliamentarians, lobbyists, and apolitical devotees of Bacchus prop up the small bar in this cavernous old wood-paneled shop, in business for over four decades. French and Italian premium vintages, and Madeira and Porto (often a century old), are the specialty. But there is also a wide selection of up-and-coming wines from Lazio and other Italian regions. Available to anyone tasting wines at Achilli are 65 types of delicious snack *tartine*, which are slices of bread or toast topped with everything from olive paste to anchovies. The shop also sells quite an array of high-quality specialty food items including caviar, smoked salmon, chocolate, and the authentic (and very expensive) balsamic vinegar of Modena.

VIA DEI PREFETTI 15 ✦ TEL: 06 687 3446
WWW.ENOTECAALPARLAMENTO.IT
CLOSED SUNDAY *and* AUGUST
Near: about 150 yards north of the Italian parliament building, halfway between the Pantheon and Piazza di San Lorenzo in Lucina

CASA BLEVE

CASA BLEVE IS A VAST, LUXURIOUS WINE SHOP AND WINE BAR. THE YAWNING SALONS OF THE PALAZZO feature marble columns, arches, and a stained-glass skylight, and are built atop Roman ruins. A visit of the spot-lit basement, set among cyclopean foundations, is a surprising delight. The dynamic owner is Anacleto Bleve. He has imparted his enthusiasm for European and American wines and Scottish whisky to his family—particularly his son Alessandro—and his staff. The choice of bottlings at Casa Bleve hovers around 1,000—not as wide as in some of Rome's mega wine emporiums; however, the quality is peerless, the service and advice exceptional, and the prices competitive. Every day, a different, limited selection of wines is available by the glass. Anacleto's wife Tina is in charge of the kitchen, and her food is largely traditional, delicious, simple, and abundant. She excels in particular at making *involtini*, which, as she sees them, are rolls of grilled sweet peppers, veal, or turkey stuffed with cheeses and herbs. Her homey spoon sweets and tarts are also delicious. The hams, salamis, and cheeses are always excellent, and the straightforward daily lunch or dinner specials are reliably good.

VIA DEL TEATRO VALLE 48-49
TEL: 06 686 5970 ✦ WWW.CASABLEVE.IT
Opening hours are complicated and vary WINE SALES *and* TASTINGS *are from* 11AM *to* 3:30PM *and* 7 *to* 11:30PM TUESDAY *through* SATURDAY LUNCH IS SERVED TUESDAY *through* SATURDAY; DINNER WEDNESDAY, THURSDAY, *and* FRIDAY.
CLOSED SUNDAY, MONDAY, *and* AUGUST
Near: about 100 yards east of Piazza Navona, and 50 yards south of Caffè Sant'Eustachio

ENOTECA CORSI

(see page 125)

MR. WINE

MORE THAN 1,300 DIFFERENT WINES FROM AROUND THE WORLD ARE SOLD AT THIS RELATIVELY RECENT and showily upscale shop, whose customers include many Italian Parliamentarians. The Lazio wines number only 20, which indicates what the thrust really is here: high-priced champagnes, Sauternes, and other French cash-crop bottlings (with a high mark-up), plus Super Tuscans and Piedmont's grapey giants. The personnel is qualified, but used to dealing with VIPs and politicos. Also sold are excellent olive oils from Lazio, Tuscany, and elsewhere, and many luxury specialty food items, at stiff prices.

PIAZZA DEL PARLIAMENTO 7 ✦ TEL: 06 681 34141
WWW.MR-WINE.COM ✦ CLOSED MONDAY MORNING
Near: facing the Italian parliament building, corner Via in Lucina

IL VINAIO

A FRIENDLY, CLUTTERED LITTLE NEIGHBORHOOD BOTTLE SHOP, IL VINAIO STOCKS A LIMITED BUT WELL-CHOSEN selection of Lazio wines plus quaffable wine on tap from Olevano Romano, made by Azienda Vinicola Mattei (it's also sold in many open markets, and served at *osterias* and trattorias in and around Rome). There's a decent selection of artisanal dry pastas, and canned and bottled or packaged specialty foods, which are stacked and wedged among the cases and bottles. No frills, no pretensions, great prices, and very helpful service, make this a favorite with locals.

VIA DEI PORTOGHESI 5 ✦ TEL: 06 689 74068
CLOSED THURSDAY AFTERNOON *and* SUNDAY
Near: around the corner from Antica Norcineria and Volpetti alla Scrofa, and equidistant – about 300 yards – from the Pantheon and Ara Pacis

NON-TERROIR TOP OR TRENDY TABLES

ALCESTE AL BUON GUSTO

CORSO RINASCIMENTO 70 ✦ TEL: 06 686 1312
CLOSED SUNDAY *and* AUGUST ✦ VERY EXPENSIVE

BOCCONDIVINO

PIAZZA IN CAMPO MARZIO 6 ✦ TEL: 06 683 08626
WWW.BOCCONDIVINO.IT ✦ CLOSED SATURDAY LUNCH *and* SUNDAY ✦ MODERATE *to* EXPENSIVE

HOSTARIA DELL'ORSO

VIA DEI SOLDATI 25/C ✦ TEL: 06 683 01192
WWW.HDO.IT ✦ DINNER ONLY ✦ ASTRONOMICALLY EXPENSIVE

IL CONVIVIO TROIANI

VICOLO DEI SOLDATI 31 ✦ TEL: 06 686 9432
WWW.ILCONVIVIOTROIANI.COM
DINNER ONLY, CLOSED SUNDAY *and* AUGUST
ASTRONOMICALLY EXPENSIVE

L'ALTRO MASTAI

VIA G. GIRAUD 53 ✦ TEL: 06 683 01296
WWW.LALTROMASTAI.IT ✦ DINNER ONLY, CLOSED SUNDAY, MONDAY, EARLY JANUARY *and* MID-TO-END AUGUST
EXTREMELY EXPENSIVE

LA ROSETTA

VIA DELLA ROSETTA 8 ✦ TEL: 06 686 1002
WWW.LAROSETTA.COM ✦ EXTREMELY EXPENSIVE

OSTERIA LE STREGHE

VICOLO DEL CURATO 13 ✦ TEL: 06 687 8182 ✦ CLOSED SUNDAY
MODERATE *to* EXPENSIVE

QUINZI E GABRIELI

VIA DELLA COPPELLE 5 ✦ TEL: 06 687 9389
WWW.QUINZIEGABRIELI.IT ✦ CLOSED MONDAY
EXPENSIVE *to* EXTREMELY EXPENSIVE

RICCIOLI CAFÉ

VIA DELLE COPPELLE 13 ✦ TEL: 06 682 10313
WWW.RICCIOLICAFE.COM ✦ OPEN DAILY *except* SUNDAY
9AM *to* 1AM ✦ MODERATE

TRATTORIA

VIA DEL POZZO DELLE CORNACCHIE 25 ✦ TEL: 06 683 01427
WWW.RISTORANTETRATTORIA.IT ✦ CLOSED SATURDAY
LUNCH, SUNDAY ✦ EXPENSIVE

REGIONAL RESTAURANTS

SICILY

TRATTORIA

(SEE NON-TERROIR TOP OR TRENDY TABLES, ABOVE)

TUSCANY

PAPÀ BACCUS

VIA TOSCANA 36 ✦ TEL: 06 427 42808 ✦ WWW.PAPABACCUS.COM
CLOSED SATURDAY LUNCH, *and* SUNDAY
EXPENSIVE *to* VERY EXPENSIVE

CHAPTER 3

PIAZZA DEL POPOLO/PINCIO, PIAZZA DI SPAGNA, FONTANA DI TREVI

FASHION AND HIGH-END TOURISM ARE WHAT THIS CENTRAL ROME AREA IS ALL ABOUT. IT HAS A DISTINCTLY international feel and, unsurprisingly, fewer *terroir* addresses than other districts of Rome. Picturesque and full of monuments, its wide main street—Via del Corso—is off limits to cars each afternoon and teems with shoppers. Bernini's Barcaccia fountain graces Piazza di Spagna; the scroll-like Scala di Spagna monumental stairway unrolls itself up the hillside behind. Also here are the gushing, overblown Fontana di Trevi, and the handsome oval of Piazza del Popolo, now almost entirely pedestrianized. The landscaped, panoramic Pincio, part of the Villa Borghese park, spreads above and to the east of Piazza del Popolo; Rome's city walls and Porta Flaminia city gate mark the square's (and the ancient city's) northern edge. Recently rebuilt by American architect Richard

Meier, the museum housing the Ara Pacis—Emperor Augustus' temple to the goddess of peace—has focused attention on Piazza Augusto Imperatore. This arcaded, Mussolini-era square spreads between Via del Corso and the Tiber. Food lovers began rediscovering it over a decade ago, when 'Gusto, the innovative complex comprising restaurants, a cooking tools shop, wine emporium, and specialized gastronomy bookstore, opened for business on the square's north side.

There is no longer a true outdoor market in this area. A few greengrocers' stands still set up along the north end of Via Bocca di Leone between Via Vittoria and Via della Croce. Two more stands operate out of the old market structure at pocket-sized Piazza di Monte d'Oro on the south side of Via Tomacelli, between Via del Corso and the Tiber. A handful of historic *caffè* continue to thrive on Piazza del Popolo and near Piazza di Spagna, as do several authentic trattorias, one of Rome's best butcher shops and *pasta fresca* shops, two outstanding chocolate shops, a fine wine shop, and what might be the city's most successful and imitated artisanal ice cream maker.

RESTAURANTS AND TRATTORIAS

AL 31

IN THE HAUTE COUTURE DISTRICT, WHERE HIGH-HEELED FASHION VICTIMS AND OVER-BRONZED PLAYBOYS PREEN and prance, this neighborhood spot serving traditional Roman and Umbrian food is perpetually thronged by local regulars and tourists hungry for authenticity. The Mari family—originally from Umbria—opened Al 31 decades ago; cousins Umberto and Angelo took over a few years back and remodeled with simple good taste. Take a table outdoors in fine weather and watch the peacocks as you savor the Roman classics—from artichokes and *puntarella* to a very good *amatriciana*, *gricia* or *carbonara*, not to mention oxtails or tripe. The owners' Umbrian origins are evident in the quantity and quality of dishes with mushrooms, the wide pappardelle pasta (sauced with a rich *sugo* of wild boar), the sausages and Norcia hams, and the occasional black truffle.

Fish is also served, but clearly, the meat dishes shine brighter. The desserts are equally classic (the *tiramisù* is luscious), the wine list short but well chosen.

VIA DELLE CARROZZE 31 ✦ TEL: 06 678 6127
CLOSED SUNDAY *and* JULY ✦ MODERATE
Near: between Via Bocca di Leone and Via Mario de' Fiori

ANTICA HOSTARIA AL VANTAGGIO

THIS FAMILY-STYLE TRATTORIA-PIZZERIA HAS BEEN AROUND SINCE 1920; ALBERTO DE VINCENTI TOOK OVER in 1963 and eventually handed over to his sons, the current owners, Luigi and Costantino. The naïf murals, motel art, and braids of garlic give it away as a favorite among tourists, as do the please-all menu items (the inevitable spaghetti with mussels, clams, and shrimp, for instance). However, the shady outdoor terrace is pleasant, and the Roman classics are reliably edible. The family is originally from Calabria, so you'll also find spicy *salame*, sun-dried tomatoes in olive oil, and Calabrian headcheese. Not the best choice in Rome, but a good fallback in this food-challenged neighborhood.

VIA DEL VANTAGGIO 35 ✦ TEL: 06 323 6848
WWW.ALVANTAGGIO.IT ✦ CLOSED TUESDAY *in* JULY *and* AUGUST, *and* JANUARY ✦ MODERATE
Near: between Via di Ripetta and Via del Corso

GIOIA MIA PISCIAPIANO

LIKE HOSTARIA ROMANA (SEE BELOW), THIS PIZZERIA-TRATTORIA IS JUST FAR ENOUGH OFF THE TOURIST beat to maintain a reasonable balance of locals and out of towners, miraculous given the nearness of the Trevi fountain. Loosely translated, the curious name means "pee slowly, my dear," and while it sounds unappetizing, it's actually a little-known Umbrian wine from Lake Trasimeno (and is revelatory of owners Walter Nobili and Achille Stopponi's wicked sense of humor). The wood-burning oven is used by skilled *pizzaioli* to make crispy classic pizzas (and lots of other, less successful, complicated ones)—but not only. Out of it also come tasty vegetable gratins. In addition to well-made Roman classics—from *gricia* and *amatriciana* to *carbonara*, *abbacchio*, and *saltimbocca*—you'll find a variety of dishes designed to please all tastes, and others that suggest Tuscan-Umbrian origins (veal with peas and mushrooms, *bistecca alla fiorentina*). One wonderfully old-fashioned dish invented in Rome in the 1930s which you'll find here and practically nowhere else these days is *fettuccine alla papalina*, a caloric bomb made with Parma ham and a creamy egg-and-cheese sauce. Desserts are equally pre-modern and possibly dangerous for those with cholesterolemia: creamy house-made *millefoglie*, Pere alla Gioia (baked pears with chocolate, whipped cream, and sponge cake), and *zuccotto* (as made here, a frozen cake with jam, sponge cake, and ice cream).

VIA DEGLI AVIGNONESI 34 ✦ TEL: 06 488 2784
CLOSED SUNDAY *and* 3 WEEKS *in* AUGUST
EXPENSIVE *to* MODERATE
Near: 1 block southeast of Via del Tritone, near the corner of Via dei Serviti

HOSTARIA ROMANA

HIDDEN DOWN A STAIRCASE AT THE BASE OF THE QUIRINALE, THIS FAMILY-RUN TRATTORIA IS FAR enough from the Trevi fountain to have retained its authenticity, drawing journalists from the nearby *Il Messaggero* newspaper headquarters, and more locals than out-of-towners. It's been around for decades, but was thoroughly remodeled in 2006, with a new glassed-in terrace. Upscale and comfortable, with lots of light, Hostaria Romana does a fine job with Roman classics, and has won a well-deserved reputation for outstanding *carbonara*. The dish is rushed piping hot in a bowl from the kitchen to your table, where the affable chef, his wife, or a waiter finishes tossing and flipping the pasta before your eyes. The desserts are house-made and delicious, the wine list better than average.

VIA DEL BOCCACCIO 1 ✦ TEL: 06 474 5284 ✦ CLOSED SUNDAY
MODERATE ✦ *Near: corner Via Rasella and Via dei Giardini, 100 yards east of Via del Traforo car tunnel*

OSTERIA DELLA FREZZA

(see 'Gusto shop entry page 189)

OTELLO ALLA CONCORDIA

IN THE CAPORICCI FAMILY SINCE 1948 AND GOING STRONG, ESPECIALLY AMONG FOREIGN TOURISTS, OTELLO ALLA Concordia is a likeable, easy address and does all the things an Italian trattoria is supposed to do—fill you with good, fresh, simple food and quaffable, affordable house wine, with professional but casual service and a pleasant setting. The patio tables in the mossy courtyard are set around an ancient, leafy wisteria and a marble basin; the crowded, vaulted dining rooms are

handsome and lively, and stuck in a pre-modern time warp, with half-paneling and starched tablecloths, and naïf paintings and old prints on the walls. The menu changes with the seasons, offering most of the Roman favorites, plus *fettuccine all'Otello* sauced with fresh tomatoes, and enough pan-Italian dishes (from pasta *alla bolognese* on up) to lure in neophytes. Note: the fresh pasta is delicious, and comes from the Massimiliano Guerra pasta shop across and up the street. Otello's house-made desserts are rich and satisfying, especially the crostata and the lemon custard tart. Still drinkable and a bargain, the Frascati on tap goes with everything.

VIA DELLA CROCE 81 ✦ TEL: 06 679 1178
MODERATE ✦ CLOSED SUNDAY *and* FEBRUARY
Near: the corner of Via Mario de' Fiori

DAL POLLAROLO

A NEIGHBORHOOD FIXTURE SINCE 1936, THE NAME MEANS "THE POULTRY MAN'S PLACE." THE SERPILLI family started out here serving spit-roasted chicken and snacks. Ludovina, granddaughter of the founder, now presides over a simple but full-service trattoria serving all the classics of Rome and the Ciociara district, plus crispy pizzas (dinner only). The artichokes and *puntarella* salad are very good, and this is one of the only places in town that still serves the 1960s summer favorite, pasta *alla checca*—elbow pasta with raw tomatoes, basil, capers, olives, and fennel seeds. Tourists keep Dal Pollarolo busy, but local shopkeepers and Roman families still come in.

VIA DI RIPETTA 4/5 ✦ TEL: 06 361 0276
CLOSED THURSDAY *and* AUGUST
INEXPENSIVE *to* MODERATE ✦ *Near: Via Borghese*

TRATTORIA DA UGO AL GRAN SASSO

THE DOLCE VITA AND ROME'S FLOWER CHILDREN WERE IN FULL BLOOM WHEN THIS NEIGHBORHOOD TRATTORIA opened in the mid 1960s. The décor has changed, Ugo is no longer, but his wife Mimma and children Andrea and Giuseppe are still at it. They've redone the interior, which is lighter and brighter and looks distinctly upscale, with giant contemporary photo-art pieces. Out-of-towners enter easily, mistaking this trattoria for a trendy international-style spot. Happily the prices haven't risen appreciably in years, and while the clientele is a mix of tourists and regulars, the food has remained uncompromisingly Roman (with a touch of the Abruzzi—Ugo's native region). You'll find the hit list of perennials, including that endangered soup of skate and broccoli that sounds so unlikely but is remarkably delicious. The *bucatini all'amatriciana* are outstanding—the sauce cooks down for hours, and the cheese is melted into the hot pasta seconds before it's served. The desserts are house-made and classic (the *tiramisù* is particularly creamy, rich, and delicious). Lovers of Lazio wines will be well served.

VIA DI RIPETTA 32 ✦ TEL: 06 321 4883 ✦ CLOSED SATURDAY
INEXPENSIVE *to* MODERATE ✦ *Near: Via Borghese*

CHEESE, CHOCOLATE, COFFEE, HAM, ICE CREAM, MEAT, PASTA

L'ALBERO DEL CACAO

THERE MIGHT JUST BE A SMALLER CHOCOLATE SHOP IN ROME, BUT IN ANY CASE THIS ONE STANDS OUT for its spartan interior and unusually difficult-to-spot location. It's due south of Piazza di Spagna, due north of Via del Tritone, and just far enough off the beat to defeat most seekers. A pity, because the handmade, highest-quality artisanal chocolates from several chocolatiers are outstanding. The *marrons glacés* are made here daily—or often enough to fill orders—and displayed like jewels. If you enjoy your chocolate in the shape of kitsch statuary, you'll be happy to know that L'Albero del Cacao sells chocolate cityscapes, a white chocolate vision of Saint Peter's, melt-in-the-mouth Michelangelo sculptures, and little green frogs.

VIA CAPO LE CASE 21 ✦ TEL: 06 679 5771
OPEN MONDAY *through* FRIDAY 2PM *to* 7:30PM,
SATURDAY 10:30AM *to* 7:30PM ✦ CLOSED SUNDAY
Near: between Via dei Due Macelli and Via Gregoriana

ANNIBALE

IN THE 1960s, YOUNG ANNIBALE MASTRODDI STARTED WORKING AT THIS HISTORIC BUTCHER SHOP, WHICH OPENED FOR business in 1898, and eventually took over the business. He and his family still run it today, with extraordinary passion, courtesy, and professionalism. Even if you're not doing your own cooking while in Rome, it's worth a detour to see the small shop's gorgeous Carrara marble-clad interior, particularly the counter with bronze ormolu bas-reliefs and sculpted scrolls. Annibale always has a smile on his face, possibly because he's won every imaginable award for courteous service and the best meat in Rome—from the milk-fed Lazio lamb to the wild game, offal, free-range pork, and old-fashioned, dry-aged beef. The shop is a registered landmark.

VIA DI RIPETTA 236 ✦ TEL: 06 361 2269 ✦ WWW.ANNIBALE.COM
OPEN 6AM *to* 2PM MONDAY *through* SATURDAY, CLOSED SUNDAY
Near: 20 yards north of the corner of Via del Vantaggio

BABINGTON'S

CAN AN ENGLISH TEA SALON BE TYPICALLY ROMAN? THE ANSWER IS, YES. BABINGTON'S IS NOT ONLY Roman; it's unique. Housed in the same handsome, luxurious landmark premises since 1893, serving the same scrumptious hot buttered crumpets, scones, biscuits, breakfasts (omelets, muffins, waffles), cucumber or club sandwiches, "high tea," light lunches, and 70 varieties of tea, and owned by the same Anglo-Italian family, now into its fourth generation, this is one of the city's gustatory wonders, with an enchanting atmosphere of yesteryear. The elegantly framed prints of old Rome hanging on the walls are originals. The herringbone oak parquet and turn-of-the-century cane chairs with cushions creak

softly but do not exude dust, for Babington's is as popular as ever. Its long, narrow rooms are haunted these days by members of Rome's intelligentsia and fashion world, as well as business people, TV personalities, and journalists in seach of a quiet spot in which to hold an interview. A certain jeweler whose shop is nearby, whose last name begins with "B" and whose brand is known world over, enters Babington's kitchen door at 8am every weekday to have breakfast, unnoticed, amid the memorabilia. History or not, the tea (and the coffee) is excellent, and so too are the delicious chocolate-covered biscuits, each hand-dipped and beautifully presented. Even the green Ginori china is unique, made exclusive for Babington's. Don't miss it.

PIAZZA DI SPAGNA 23 ✦ TEL: 06 678 6027
WWW.BABINGTONS.COM ✦ OPEN 9AM *to* 8:15PM
Near: the bottom of the Spanish Steps

CAFFÈ GRECO

TOO FAMOUS TO NEED MUCH INTRODUCING, THIS OLDEST OF ROME'S COFFEEHOUSES, SOMETIMES REFERRED to as Antico Caffè Greco, has been in constant business since 1760. Though it describes itself as a literary *caffè*, the last time a bona fide Roman intellectual was seen entering was about 50 years ago. Jokes aside, you might expect the ghosts of former regulars—everyone from Byron and Gogol to Goethe and Goldoni—to flit past, but somehow they don't. The crowds are raucous and foreign, composed almost entirely of Americans, British, Northern Europeans, and Japanese—in other words, the clientele of the neighborhood's fashion boutiques and luxury hotels. Though not a gourmet experience, the pastries, tarts, sandwiches, *tramezzini*, and pizza are perfectly good. Beyond the food, Caffè Greco is the proverbial feast for the eyes. The lavish décor is from the 1700s and 1800s, and in excellent repair, with well over 100 original paintings, drawings, and vintage prints. In keeping with the traditions of the period during which it was built, there is no outdoor terrace, but the mirrored, gilded salons with their wall sconces and chandeliers are cozy and comfortable. In other words, Caffè Greco is a must for those attracted by landmark properties and gilded reputations. Speaking of which, the beverages and snacks are remarkably expensive. It's the memories and the atmosphere—entirely smoke-free nowadays—that you're paying for.

VIA CONDOTTI 86 ✦ TEL: 06 679 1700 ✦ OPEN TUESDAY *through* SATURDAY 9AM *to* 7:30PM, SUNDAY *and* MONDAY 10:30AM *to* 7PM

CAFFÈ TREVI E TRITONE

IN 2003, WHEN THE LATE-1800s GALLERIA COLONNA COVERED SHOPPING GALLERY REOPENED AFTER YEARS of restoration work, Romans were surprised and delighted to find two identical, free-standing espresso bars in the center of each of the arcaded gallery's two wings. The bars are run and staffed by the same team, and both serve Illy coffee. The name Trevi e Tritone refers to the nearby fountains of Trevi (150 yards east) and Tritone (at the top of Via del Tritone, which flanks the north side of the complex). Neither bar resembles those fountains. Rather, they're shaped like Bernini's Barcaccia—the famous Drunken Boat fountain in Piazza di Spagna. The clientele is mostly tourists with some locals, mainly politicos headquartered at Parliament, which is across the street. Both espresso bars are packed at lunchtime. One well-known Italian magazine has boasted that the coffee here is the best in town—better than La Tazza d'Oro's or Sant'Eustachio's. That's nonsense. The Illy served is the same great blend of Arabicas found all over the world; the barmen of Trevi e Tritone are in no way superior in skill to those of Rome's other top *caffè*. This is a good place for a break in summer's heat or winter's cold. The snack food and light meals are fine, with a nod to Roman tradition: *cacio e pepe* and *porchetta* sandwiches. Note: confusingly, the shopping gallery is called both Galleria Colonna (the original name) and Galleria Alberto Sordi.

GALLERIA ALBERTO SORDI 52 ✦ TEL: 06 678 0617
OPEN FROM 10AM *to* 10PM ✦ *Near: in the covered shopping gallery that faces Piazza Colonna, on the corner of Via del Corso and Via del Tritone*

CANOVA

THE ONLY THING THAT MAKES THIS HISTORIC CAFFÈ STILL WORTHY OF YOUR ATTENTION IS ITS LONG OUTDOOR terrace on the east side of the square, where you can opt for sun or shade, depending on the season and the hour of the day. Since the Via del Babuino and Piazza del Popolo are now largely traffic-free, the sole impediment to your view of the obelisk,

lions, and fountain in the center of the square is the rank of taxis across from the *caffè* terrace. The interior of Canova was recently and entirely redone is an anodyne, arrivals-hall style intended, perhaps, to rival 'Gusto and other trendy hangouts. The food and beverages are of acceptable quality, nothing more; the coffee, roasted by Trombetta, is fearfully strong, though some Romans clearly love it. You're paying—dearly—for the atmosphere and view. Still, enjoying a cappuccino in the morning or a cocktail at sunset is a very pleasant experience, and the service at Canova is affable and professional.

PIAZZA DEL POPOLO 16 ✦ TEL: 06 361 2227
WWW.CAFFECANOVA.IT ✦ OPEN DAILY
Near: on northeast side of the square

LA CASINA DELL'OROLOGIO

BUILT IN 1922 AND LAVISHLY RESTORED IN 2003, THIS WONDERFUL, SURPRISINGLY LUXURIOUS *CAFFÈ* HOUSED in a little green kiosk on the main pedestrian road running across the Pincio park is a favorite among local dog-walkers, cyclists, and out-of-town visitors. It's a pleasant place to sip a cappuccino made with strong Bondolfi-brand coffee, and to nibble a delicious pastry (from the Faggiani bakery in Prati, area 8). The mood-music tells much about the setting and clientele: *As Time Goes By* plays on a spool, followed by Frank Sinatra crooning. There are lovely, floral-pattern mosaics on the floor; the bar top is green serpentine, the chandelier Murano glass. In fine weather you can sit on the terrace under umbrellas, surrounded by spreading old bay and ilex trees, and enjoy snacks and light meals. The food is perfectly okay, the service friendly, and the atmosphere, well, timeless. La Casina dell'Orologio is named for the mossy antique water clock nearby.

VIALE DEI BAMBINI/VIALE DELL'OBELISCO, PINCIO
TEL: 06 679 8515 ✦ WWW.LA-CASINA-DELL-OROLOGIO.IT
OPEN DAYLIGHT HOURS SPRING *through*
SUMMER, OFF-SEASON HOURS VARY WIDELY
Near: on east side of Pincio park, near bridge over Viale del Muro Torto

CASINA VALADIER

FEW RESTAURANTS ARE HOUSED IN A LOVELIER OR MORE HISTORIC PIECE OF PROPERTY, AND ARGUABLY none has a better view over Rome's rooftops and cupolas or a setting as gorgeous as the Villa Borghese and panoramic Pincio garden. Marriages, anniversaries, graduations, and such keep the chef busy. The food served at the Casina Valadier is often fussy, complicated, and overpriced, and while a table on the restaurant terrace (or one facing a picture window) is achingly romantic, you're better off seeking elsewhere. Luckily, you can enjoy the *caffè* and cocktail bar in the landscaped garden surrounding this grand garden folly, which was designed in 1816 by Giuseppe Valadier, finished only in 1837, and thoroughly restored a few years ago.

PIAZZA BUCAREST, PINCIO ✦ TEL: 06 699 22090
WWW.CASINAVALADIER.IT ✦ CAFFÈ TERRACE OPEN
in WARM-WEATHER MONTHS ONLY, HOURS VARY
Near: in Pincio park, above Piazza del Popolo

CIAMPINI

THE SUAVE SCION OF ROME'S FAMOUS BAR-CAFFÈ-RESTAURANT FAMILY, MARCO CIAMPINI OWNS AND operates this perched Dolce Vita hangout, once famously haunted by Sophia Loren and other Cinecittà movie stars. The view of Rome's rooftops from the raised, glassed-in kiosk is lovely; the tables below on the rambling garden terrace offer a more intimate setting, with turtles and water lillies in gently splashing fountains, and ivy-draped pergolas. Though Ciampini serves full lunches and dinners, the style of cooking is a mite inventive; stick to the *tramezzini* sandwiches (a house specialty), pastries, ice creams (including the authentic Tartufo, made by Marco's father at Tre Scalini on Piazza Navona), snacks, and wine or cocktails. The cappuccino and espresso here are good and strong, made with Morganti Miscela d'Oro, which is dark roasted and highly caffeinated. Unsurprisingly, it contains a whopping 63 percent Robusta.

PIAZZA TRINITÀ DEI MONTI
TEL: 06 678 5678 ✦ WWW.CAFFECIAMPINI.COM
CLOSED MID-NOVEMBER *to* MID-FEBRUARY
Near: facing Villa Medici north of the Spanish Steps and Trinità dei Monti

FRATELLI FABBI

THIS SHOP'S RESEMBLANCE TO SALUMERIA FOCACCI, WHICH IS ONE BLOCK WEST, IS UNCANNY. FABBI HAS been around since 1937 and in the same family, and is a good source for caviar, *bottarga*, San Daniele *prosciutto*, champagne, truffles, and a handful of wines (including several Brunello di Montalcinos)—everything, in other words, you need to prepare a picnic in the neighborhood's style, to enjoy, perhaps, under the umbrella pines of Villa Borghese.

VIA DELLA CROCE 27 ✦ TEL: 06 679 0612 ✦ WWW.FABBI.IT
CLOSED SATURDAY AFTERNOON *in* SUMMER *and* SUNDAY YEAR ROUND
Near: on the corner of Via Bocca di Leone, 2 blocks east of Via del Corso

IL GELATO DI SAN CRISPINO

WHEN IT OPENED IN 1993, IL GELATO DI SAN CRISPINO BROKE NOT THE ICE BUT THE ITALIAN ice cream establishment. Brothers Pasquale and Giuseppe Alongi and their partner Paolo Nesci rejected the received wisdom about how to run a moneymaking, modern Italian *gelateria*. They decided to produce peerless ice cream from wholly natural ingredients, without compromises or shortcuts. The reception in Rome by other *gelatai* was chilling, but the public responded immediately. With the exception of small amounts of powdered low-fat milk in its cream-based flavors, San Crispino uses only fresh ingredients of the highest quality, no artificial anything, and no additives or preservatives of any kind. The only thickeners are egg white, carob seeds, agar-agar, and flour, in minute quantities. The Alongis were slated to be, respectively, doctor and lawyer. They brought no prejudices to the venture but rather a determination to demonstrate that cutting corners and using processed, chemical ingredients were antithetical to good taste, good sense, and good business. The Alongis are from Alto Adige, a Germanic enclave in Italy's far north. Their steely efficiency and scientific rigor manifest themselves in the spartan atmosphere of their shops. They refused from the start to serve ice cream in cones, because, they claim, the cones interfere with the ice cream's pure flavor, so only paper cups are available. Luckily, the *gelati* are luscious, delicious, and satisfying, never cloying, and always balanced. The house speciality—Il Gelato—is an arbutus honey-based *crema*. The Alongi brothers were inspired to make it by a sixteenth-century recipe; it is exceptionally good. The *crema* flavor with ginger and cinnamon is out of this world, as is *nocciola*, made not with a nut paste but with artisanally toasted fresh Tonda Gentile hazelnuts from the Langhe (Piedmont), which are crushed exclusively for San Crispino. Ripe, untreated Amalfi lemons go into the lemon *gelato*; excellent Jamaican Blue Mountain coffee is freshly brewed for the *caffè* (and served to sit-down customers in the form of espresso); the rum and Marsala that go into, respectively, rum-chocolate and *zabaglione* are vintage, excellent, and expensive. About 20 flavors are available at any one time. They follow the seasons and the owners' inspiration. It is said that all the ice creams are made fresh daily; leftovers—if there are any—are thrown away. Note: San Crispino has two outlying locations in the Appio and Fleming neighborhoods.

VIA DELLA PANETTERIA 42 ✦ TEL: 06 679 3924
WWW.ILGELATODISANCRISPINO.COM
OPEN NOON *to* 1AM, CLOSED TUESDAY *in* AUTUMN *and* WINTER
Near: 150 yards east of Fontana di Trevi

PASTA FRESCA GUERRA MASSIMILIANO

FAMILY-RUN, MULTI-GENERATIONAL, AND THOROUGHLY TRADITIONAL, WITH MACHINERY FROM DECADES PAST, this is the neighborhood's last authentic *pasta fresca* shop, founded way back in 1918. It supplies many nearby trattorias

and restaurants, including Otello alla Concordia, which is on the opposite side of the street. The pasta is cut to order for all clients. Also sold are many types of packaged artisanal dry pasta, in case you want to stock up before flying home.

VIA DELLA CROCE 8 ✦ TEL: 06 679 3102
CLOSED SUNDAY ✦ *Near: 50 yards west of Via del Babuino*

PASTATECA

IT HAD TO HAPPEN. THE UBIQUITOUS *ENOTECA* FOR WINE AND *OLIOTECA* FOR OLIVE OIL HAVE GIVEN RISE TO ROME'S first *pastateca*—a boutique selling only high-quality artisanal dry pasta. To name at random a few of the producers: Rustichella, Santa Rita, Latini, Benedetto Cavalieri, Antico Pastificio Umbro, Cavaliere Giuseppe Cocco, and dozens of others. Displays are divided by region, with the entire country covered. So far, only seven shapes of egg pasta from Lazio are available, all very good, and all from the little-known company Papi (www.pastapapi.it). Beyond the usual durum wheat and egg pastas, you'll find many types made with whole wheat, kamut, spelt, and *farro*.

VIA DELLA VITE 44-45 ✦ TEL: 06 454 91431
WWW.PASTATECA.IT ✦ OPEN TUESDAY *to* SATURDAY
10AM *to* 8PM, SUNDAY 11AM *to* 8PM *and* MONDAY 3PM *to* 8PM
Near: about 150 yards south of Piazza Mignanelli

QUETZALCOATL CHOCOLATIER

THE NAME IS AZTEC AND THIS CHIC SHOP FEELS LIKE A SLICE OF PARIS IN THE HEART OF ROME'S FASHION district. However, at least some of the excellent chocolates sold here are distinctly Roman, not French. Among them is the dark-chocolate *cioccolatino* with a rich, dark-chocolate filling seasoned with fresh chili powder. The shop's owner is Ida Petrillo; she speaks Italian with an unmistakably French accent and claims to have invented chili chocolate, which is now widely imitated in Rome and the rest of the world, but rarely attains the excellence found here. Elegant, tall, and thin, Petrillo opened this lavishly luxurious boutique in 1998. The décor features black stone cladding and vaguely Aztec-style display cases. Demand is such nowadays that the chocolates are no longer made on the premises by Petrillo, but rather by her son, who operates the family's chocolate factory in Nettuno, a small city south of town in the province of Rome. The base chocolate used contains 72 percent cacao, and is supplied by Valrhona. All the ingredients are fresh, not concentrated, and the chocolates are uniformly exquisite and well balanced in flavor and richness. Especially delicious are the filled pralines with flavors Americans know, but which seem surprising to conservative, traditionalist Roman palates. Among them are fresh thyme and honey; balsamic vinegar; dark chocolate with Bourbon vanilla; figs and red wine; cappuccino (made with freshly brewed coffee); and passion fruit. Also sold are fresh strawberries dipped in dark chocolate, and imported *marrons glacés* and *calissons d'Aix*, both from Provence.

VIA DELLE CARROZZE 26 ✦ TEL: 06 692 02191
CLOSED SUNDAY *and* AUGUST
Near: about 200 yards west of the Spanish Steps

ROSATI

FACING THE TWIN CHURCHES OF PIAZZA DEL POPOLO, WITH HISTORIC RIVAL CANOVA DIRECTLY ACROSS THE wide way, Rosati is one of Rome's celebrated hangouts, popular since it opened in 1922. Its heyday was the Dolce Vita, when Fellini, Sophia Loren, and others were regulars. Hardly anyone bothers to step inside, so inviting is the outdoor terrace, but if you do, you'll discover a long, serpentine-topped bar and original period pieces, from the grandfather clock and cash desk to the display case in which the delicious pastries are stored.

Rosati still makes its own breakfast rolls and desserts, and they're better than those served elsewhere in the neighborhood; the coffee is very good and comes from Tazza d'Oro (the mini-chain, not the original Tazza d'Oro near the Pantheon). If the weather is cold or wet, no worries: the downstairs salon is comfortable, with its molded plasterwork ceilings, peach-colored walls, big mirrors, and pistachio-hued felt upholstery. A smaller upstairs room offers nice views of the square in relative quiet. Full meals are served at Rosati, but the international-style food isn't the real draw, it's the atmosphere. Umpteen hipper, younger places in town attract today's Dolce Vita set; Rosati remains the perennial favorite of many well-heeled Romans and visitors. Dal Bolognese—the VIP restaurant serving specialities from the Emilia region—is right next door, and much of its glitzy, politico-showbiz clientele heads to Rosati for a pre-prandial cocktail or an after-dinner drink.

PIAZZA DEL POPOLO 5 ✦ TEL: 06 322 5859
OPEN DAILY ✦ *Near: on the corner of Via di Ripetta*

SALUMERIA FOCACCI

THIS ATTRACTIVE, LONG-ESTABLISHED CORNER DELI STOCKS THE KIND OF SPECIALTY FOODS YOU'D EXPECT to find in this neighborhood of movie stars and billionaires: caviar, smoked salmon, and other smoked fish, top Parma or San Daniele ham, fine cheeses, excellent olive oils, artisanal pasta, and wines from prestige wineries. The Fabbi family deli one block east is on a par with Focacci.

VIA DELLA CROCE 43 ✦ TEL: 06 679 1228 ✦ CLOSED SUNDAY
Near: on corner of Via Belisiana, 1 block east of Via del Corso

WINE AND WINE BARS

BUCCONE

BUILT CENTURIES AGO AS A CARRIAGE HOUSE, THIS CAVERNOUS NEIGHBORHOOD WINE SHOP HAS BEEN pouring and selling *vino* for over a century. Domenico and Maddalena Buccone took over in the 1960s. Their affable sons Vincenzo and Francesco now run the show, serving food amid the wine displays (stick to the simple snacks and Roman classics). Many of the shop's decorative and functional features go back to the late 1800s, from the cash register to the wrought-iron chandeliers, which are so high up you probably won't notice them, or the massive exposed timbers. The ceilings are about 20 feet high, with tall shelves below, and tall ladders leaned against the shelves, where thousands

of Italian and foreign bottlings repose. Luckily, the many excellent Lazio offerings are easy to inspect and reach at chest or belly level; wineries include Casale del Giglio, Falesco, Camponeschi, Colacicchi, Casale Marchese, Conte Zandotti, Castel de Paolis, and Sant'Andrea. There's also a good selection of honeys (among them, hard-to-find bitter honey from arbutus blossoms), olive oils made in half a dozen Italian regions, balsamic and herb- or raspberry-flavored vinegars, and other specialty food items, plus corkscrews and bottle openers.

VIA DI RIPETTA 19-20 ✦ TEL: 06 361 2154
WWW.ENOTECABUCCONE.COM ✦ CLOSED SUNDAY,
LUNCH SERVED WEEKDAYS *and* SATURDAY, DINNER
FRIDAY *and* SATURDAY ✦ MODERATE

'GUSTO WINE BAR, OSTERIA DELLA FREZZA AND NEGOZIO DI VINI

WELCOME TO TRIBECA-ON-THE-TIBER: 'GUSTO IS A VAST, TRENDY, MODISH COMPLEX, WITH NINE distinct sections, including a luxury restaurant, a simple *osteria*, a pizzeria, a "cheese bar" and wine bar, a pastry and bread shop, and a fish-and-vegetable restaurant (located across the square). The wine bar has the kind of brick walls painted white, and the looming overhead lamps, black tables, and stools, that you'd find in an outer-borough pool hall or poker club. On Tuesdays and Thursdays there's live jazz. Most customers and seemingly all of the studiously cool staffers dress in shades of black, and groove on the 'Gusto magic, which appears able to dematerialize and transport them to New York, San Francisco, Paris, London, or Sydney—anywhere but Rome. Still, there's a buried vein of *terroir* running through slick, corporate 'Gusto. The quality of the ingredients is high, and you can get snacks (salami, ham, cheese, tapas, and more) while sipping a glass of fine wine. You can also merge seamlessly into the faux-early-1900s Osteria della Frezza for a (putatively) Roman meal of fried delicacies, *cacio e pepe*, *amatriciana*, and wine on tap in the best retro style. Over 1,000 different wines are stocked, and there's always a wide range of them available by the glass. The cook shop and bottle shop on the Tiber River end of the complex has every imaginable kitchen tool in the world, and hundreds of bottlings to choose from; the bookstore carries about 5,000 titles on food and wine subjects.

VIA DELLA FREZZA 23 *and* 16, *and* PIAZZA AUGUSTO IMPERATORE 7/9 ✦ TEL: 06 322 6273 *and* 06 322 6363 WWW.GUSTO.IT ✦ WINE BAR OPEN NOON *to* 1AM DAILY WINE SHOP/BOOKSTORE/KITCHEN SUPPLIES STORE OPEN DAILY 10:30AM *to* 12:30AM ✦ *Near: On north and east sides of the square*

PALATIUM

WHAT BEGAN AS A GOOD IDEA—A STATE-OF-THE-ART REGIONAL WINE INFORMATION CENTER, BOUtique, and restaurant underwritten by the Italian regional government and private investors—has faced a dizzying political-administrative roller-coaster ride, as the Lazio regional assembly falls and rises. In theory, about 600 winegrowers from Rome's region are represented at this trendy, chic wine bar, which serves a changing, seasonal menu of classic Lazio foods and snacks (Gaeta olives, organic pickled vegetables), in an ultra-modern, modish setting. In practice, the number of wines available by the glass is limited to five each of red and white, and some of the staff seem less than conversant with local gastronomy and oenology. An address to watch, with some trepidation.

VIA FRATTINA 94 ✦ TEL: 06 692 02132
OPEN 11AM *to* MIDNIGHT, CLOSED SUNDAY
Near: corner Via Belsiana, 250 yards west of Piazza di Spagna

IL TINO DI VINO/FRATELLI CIAVATTA

THIS SMALL BUT WELL-STOCKED WINE SHOP IS OWNED BY THE CIAVATTA FAMILY, WHOSE DELI-GROCERY IS around the corner, one block closer to the Trevi fountain. The location is problematic in terms of authenticity—tourist mobs are constant—and clearly was made for strategic marketing reasons: Il Gelato di San Crispino is next door, and savvy ice cream lovers often also appreciate fine wine. The choice of Lazio bottlings isn't wide, but you can enjoy your wine with a high-quality snack on site—everything from hams and cheeses to mozzarella balls or pastries. Essentially, whatever you see at the deli you can eat here with a glass or bottle of wine. Also sold are chocolates and candies, caviar, *bottarga*, foie gras, and other specialty foods.

VIA DEL LAVATORE 31 *and* VIA DELLA PANETTERIA 42B
TEL: 06 679 2935 ✦ CLOSED SUNDAY
Near: respectively 2 and 3 blocks east of Fontana di Trevi

NON-TERROIR TOP OR TRENDY TABLES

AL MORO

VICOLO DELLE BOLLETTE 13 ✦ TEL: 06 678 3495
CLOSED SUNDAY *and* AUGUST ✦ EXPENSIVE *to* VERY EXPENSIVE

AL PRESIDENTE

VIA IN ARCIONE 95 ✦ TEL: 06 679 7342 ✦ WWW.ALPRESIDENTE.IT
CLOSED MONDAY *and* AUGUST ✦ VERY EXPENSIVE

BABETTE

VIA MARGUTTA 1 ✦ TEL: 06 321 1559
WWW.BABETTERISTORANTE.IT ✦ CLOSED MONDAY
and 3 WEEKS IN AUGUST ✦ MODERATE *to* EXPENSIVE

IMÀGO

PIAZZA TRINITÀ DEI MONTI 6 ✦ TEL: 06 699 34726
WWW.HOTELHASSLER.COM ✦ CLOSED *for* LUNCH *in* SUMMER
ASTRONOMICALLY EXPENSIVE

JARDIN DE RUSSIE

VIA DEL BABUINO 9 ✦ TEL: 06 328 88870
WWW.ROCCOFORTEHOTELS.COM
EXTREMELY *to* ASTRONOMICALLY EXPENSIVE

LE SORELLE

VIA BELSIANA 30 ✦ TEL: 06 679 4969 ✦ WWW.LESORELLE.IT
CLOSED TUESDAY, 3 WEEKS *in* AUGUST *and* 1 WEEK *in* JANUARY
EXPENSIVE

REGIONAL RESTAURANTS

CALABRIA

SACRO & PROFANO

VIA DEI MARONITI 29 ✦ TEL: 06 679 1836
CLOSED AUGUST ✦ EXPENSIVE

CAMPAGNA

RECAFÉ

PIAZZA AUGUSTO IMPERATORE 36 ✦ TEL: 06 681 34730
CLOSED AUGUST ✦ MODERATE

EMILIA ROMAGNA

LE COLLINE EMILIANE

VIA DEGLI AVIGNONESI 22 ✦ TEL: 06 481 7538
CLOSED SUNDAY DINNER *and* MONDAY
MODERATE *to* EXPENSIVE

DAL BOLOGNESE

PIAZZA DEL POPOLO 1/2 ✦ TEL: 06 361 1426
CLOSED MONDAY *and* AUGUST ✦ VERY EXPENSIVE

TUSCANY

MARIO

VIA DELLA VITE 55 ✦ TEL: 06 678 3818
CLOSED SUNDAY *and* AUGUST ✦ EXPENSIVE

NINO

VIA BORGOGNONA 11 ✦ TEL: 06 679 5676
CLOSED SUNDAY ✦ EXPENSIVE

VENETO

EL TOULÀ

VIA DELLE LUPA 29B ✦ TEL: 06 687 3750
CLOSED SUNDAY *and* AUGUST ✦ VERY EXPENSIVE

LA DOLCE VITA AND THE TREVI FOUNTAIN

BUILDING THE FONTANA DI TREVI, WHICH IS TUCKED INTO A TANGLE OF STREETS OFF VIA DEL Tritone and Via del Corso, took the luckless sculptor Nicola Salvi several changes of pope and precisely 30 years (1732-62). He grafted the fountain's giant mock-boulders, urns, horses, and mythological figures onto the back of a Renaissance building in a dauntingly restricted space. Few visitors to the famous site realize that Trevi was already a drinking fountain before Salvi arrived. The original, conceived nearly 2,000 years ago, was the monumental terminus of Agrippa's Aqua Virgo aqueduct. Despite its history, the Fontana di Trevi is famous today as the backdrop to Anita Ekberg's frolic in Fellini's *La Dolce Vita*, and as the romantic wishing well in the Hollywood melodrama *Three Coins in a Fountain*. You can still drink the water, which gushes from a drinking fountain built into the rockery in front of the basin's north side.

CHAPTER 4

MONTI, QUIRINALE, SALARIA, SALLUSTIANO, VIA VENETO

THOUGH A FIGUREHEAD, THE PRESIDENT OF ITALY IS FORTUNATE: HIS RESIDENCE, IL QUIRINALE, DUE EAST of the Trevi neighborhood, is among Rome's most splendid, poised atop the Quirinal Hill. This eminence is also known to locals as Monte Cavallo. "*Cavallo*"—horse—refers to the twin steeds on the obelisk monument to Castor and Pollux, in the square facing Il Quirinale. Popes lived in the palace for centuries, before Italian Unification was completed in 1870. Anyone who has hiked east uphill from the Trevi Fountain knows how steep Monte Cavallo is, and how few places there are on it to slake the thirst, snack, or dine. In fact, the Quirinal Hill is covered almost entirely by the presidential palace and the nearby Palazzo della Consulta, the constitutional courthouse. Luckily, when art exhibitions are being held at the Quirinal Stables, you can get a cup of coffee and a snack at the cafeteria inside.

Behind and to the east of Monte Cavallo begins the Monti neighborhood, a favorite among Romans not for its beauty or history, but because it is quiet and has few monuments, and therefore has largely been spared the attentions of mass tourism. A handful of streets afford keyhole views of the Coliseum or Trajan's Market, on the edge of Monti. It's named for the church of Madonna dei Monti, one block north of Via Cavour, the neighborhood's focal point. On the piazza facing the church, two modish *caffè* are favorite hangouts among the area's younger, newer residents. Government offices, small businesses, and residential buildings fill the surrounding, sloping streets, between Via del Quirinale (which becomes Via XX Settembre) and Via Nazionale. A handful of excellent food-related businesses found here make a detour to Monti worthwhile.

Northeast of Monti is the Via Veneto neighborhood, which spreads on either side of this curving boulevard, Rome's answer to the Champs-Elysées. Most Americans know Via Veneto because the US embassy is here. The street's heyday was the Dolce Vita; its luxury hotels, restaurants, and *caffè* still attract an international crowd. Abutting its east side is the Sallustiano neighborhood, so called for the small, handsome Piazza Sallustio, which wraps around the subterranean ruins of the Horti Sallustiani and Villa of Sallustius. Within 100 yards of this untouristed square you'll find one the city's best cheese shops; a handful of pleasant, traditional restaurants and trattorias; and several fine gourmet food and wine boutiques. What may just be Rome's top wine shop, Trimani, is also nearby, on the area's southern edge, where the streets begin to merge with the tatty surroundings of Termini train station.

The Via Salaria—the ancient salt route linking Rome to the Appenines and the Adriatic—begins on the northeastern edge of the Sallustiano neighborhood; on or near the Via Salaria are Piazza Fiume and Piazza Alessandria. Though not particularly aesthetic, this area too is authentically Roman, with much good food.

Mercato coperto di Piazza Alessandria is among the city's most appealing small neighborhood marketplaces. Its wrought-iron gates and metalwork, and the soaring nave-like interior toppped by skylights, make it an attractive place to shop. The greengrocers sell high-quality produce; the neighborhood is solidly middle class, and the shoppers are of the demanding variety. Facing the market's north side is one of Rome's better upscale pizzerias, Giggetto, and around the corner from it on Via Bergamo is historic pastry shop Caffè Pannocchi.

RESTAURANTS AND TRATTORIAS

CANTINA CANTARINI

ALSO KNOWN AS DA MARIO, FOR ITS CURRENT OWNER, MARIO FATTORI, THIS OLD TRATTORIA WITH A SINGLE, vaulted dining room and a pleasant terrace on Piazza Sallustio serves all the Roman classics plus many dishes from Le Marche, the region Fattori comes from (and the Cantarini family Fattori bought out). Fattori worked his way up from busboy; this is his home. The spartan décor is the same as ever: half-paneling, brass coat hooks, murals, and old wooden tables. A few years back, Fattori decided that instead of the weekly wheel of Canonical classics, he'd divide up the days of the week into meat or fish. So on Thursday at dinner, and on Friday and Saturday at lunch and dinner, you eat fresh fish from the Adriatic—the sea that bathes the beaches of Le Marche. Expect to find fish grilled, pan-fried with butter and lemon, flash-fried as *fritto misto*, or stewed in *guazzetto*. Fish pasta dishes include succulent spaghetti with baby octopus, clams, or shrimp. Lovers of *amatriciana*, *carbonara*, and the like (and veal stews, steaks, chicken with bell peppers, rabbit in spicy white wine sauce, and more) should reserve from Monday to Thursday (lunch). The desserts—*tiramisù*, *crostata*—are classic and house-made and served whether it's a meat or fish day. The wine list features many bottlings from Lazio and Le Marche, including a very nice house Verdicchio. Note that, though tourists are few, Cantina Cantarini starts serving lunch from 12:30pm and dinner from 7:30pm.

PIAZZA SALLUSTIO 12 ✦ TEL: 06 474 3341
CLOSED SUNDAY *and* AUGUST ✦ MODERATE
Near: on south side of square

EST! EST!! EST!!! FRATELLI RICCI

THIS CULT *OSTERIA*-PIZZERIA OPENED IN 1905, AND THOUGH IT'S NO LONGER IN THE RICCI FAMILY, THE handsome turn-of-the-century décor is intact, from the outsized brass lamps, bevelled mirrors, brass coat hooks, and overhead fans to the chairs and tables and the detailing that makes it so cozy. Now that smoking is no longer allowed, you can actually see across the dining room. The small sidewalk terrace is flanked by an old street lamp, which casts a timeless glow, and since the street is a dead end, there's no traffic noise. The unusual name of the establishment refers to the celebrated wine of Montefiascone, Est! Est!! Est!!!, which is still served here, along with mugs of beer. The chummy atmosphere and mixed crowd—tourists from nearby hotels or Termini station, plus Ministry of the Interior regulars—makes it an easy place in which to feel comfortable, even if you're on your own. Don't come here expecting a gourmet experience. The food is tasty, from the 20 or so pizzas on offer, to the *crostini* (with anchovies and mozzarella) and *calzoni*, or the delicious flash-fried filets of salt cod. *Antipasti* are a specialty: stuffed olives, *supplì*, *carciofi alla giudia*, and fried broccoli or zucchini. You can also get a good plate of *amatriciana* and *carbonara*, or try the house specialty pasta, *spaghetti alla sorrentina* (with Pachino tomatoes, mozzarella, and fresh basil). There are no second courses, but rather vegetable side dishes such as plump Tuscan beans or mushrooms in oil. Desserts are house made; the sour cherry *crostata* is up to Rome standards, the *panna cotta* with ricotta rich and satisfying, the *tiramisù* and *bacio al cioccolato* guaranteed to please those who like thick, chocolatey sweets. If you're having trouble finding the address, you'll easily spot the unlikely Mr. Chow, a Chinese restaurant, directly across the way.

VIA GENOVA 32 ✦ TEL: 06 488 1107 ✦ OPEN *for* DINNER ONLY 7PM *to* MIDNIGHT ✦ CLOSED MONDAY *and* AUGUST INEXPENSIVE ✦ *Near: 1 block south of Via Nazionale, on a dead-end street, abutting the foundation wall of the Viminale (Ministry of the Interior) and the gateway to the building's underground telephone center*

FIASCHETTERIA MARINI

RUN BY THE SECOND, THIRD, AND FOURTH GENERATIONS OF THE MARINI FAMILY, THIS WONDERFULLY SIMPLE, family-style eatery has changed little since it opened for business in 1913. The white-veined, gray marble table tops with butcher paper on them, the bentwood chairs, antique documents and wall clocks are original. Every faux

retro trattoria in town tries to replicate the look; this is the real thing. The menu changes regularly, but has been offering the same round of satisfyingly simple dishes for nearly a century. Among them are *pasta e fagioli*, chickpea soup with barley, cuttlefish with peas, lamb *alla cacciatora*, and grilled provola cheese. Vegetable sides are generously served, and range from the surprisingly delicious cabbage cooked in red wine (with orange zest), to broccoli drizzled with lemon juice, or strips of baked bell pepper with olives and plump capers; the pan-fried *misticanza* field greens and zucchini sautéed with olive oil and garlic are especially good. Marini's *torta di ricotta*, *torta* with pastry cream, and sour cherry *crostata* are house made and round off a meal nicely. On tap from the old-fashioned bar come Cesanese red and white, plus a Tuscan red, served by the flask. A few bottled wines are also available. The final, unchanging touch is the good, strong coffee, which is served *in vetro*—in a glass. Local office workers pack out Marini, but lunch starts at 12:15pm and if you get here before 1pm you'll have no trouble finding a table. Note: no credit cards are accepted, but the prices are extremely low. Also worthy of note: the bathrooms are big, and amazingly spic'n'span.

VIA R. CADORNA 7/11 ✦ TEL: 06 474 5534 ✦ OPEN *for* LUNCH ONLY, EXCEPT FRIDAY, CLOSED SUNDAY ✦ VERY INEXPENSIVE
Near: 80 yards from Piazza Sallustio

GIGGETTO PIZZERIA

FACING THE PIAZZA ALESSANDRIA COVERED MARKET, GIGGETTO IS A CROSSOVER PIZZERIA-RESTAURANT, with a handsome, traditional, vaulted interior, a brass plaque outside the door, and frosted windows to keep prying eyes out. That's because, for the last 40 years, it's been a favorite haunt of politicians, journalists, and mid-to-upper-level white collars. You ring the bell to gain entry. As if that weren't enough to keep out tourists, the pizzas are expensive (though not unreasonable, given the excellent quality of the ingredients used, the setting, and professional service). There are usually 35 to 40 different pizzas available, from crispy, thin Roman-style pizzas to a few softer, doughy Neapolitan-style types, plus delicious *bruschetta* rubbed with garlic and drizzled with good olive oil, and perfect *crostini* with anchovies and provolone. You can also savor classic *antipasti* like grilled vegetables or mushrooms in olive oil, hams, salami, and cheese, as well as good pasta dishes and steaks, and luscious house-made *tiramisù* or *crostata*. There's wine and beer on tap, and a short but adequate wine list. Reserve ahead.

VIA ALESSANDRIA 43/49 ✦ TEL: 06 841 2527
OPEN DAILY *for* DINNER ONLY ✦ CLOSED AUGUST
INEXPENSIVE *to* MODERATE ✦ *Near: facing Piazza Alessandria*

SANTOPADRE

THE NAME MEANS "HOLY FATHER" BUT THE POPE HAS NEVER BEEN HERE, AND THIS CURIOUS TRATtoria-restaurant has nothing to do with the Vatican. Every evening except Sunday, Rome's tony, horsey set trots to Santopadre, the ultimate insider's address, to feast under jockeys' shirts which dangle overhead like the *gonfaloni* at the Palio di Siena. There is no horsemeat served, but rather all the Roman classics, plus offal (*coratella* with artichokes, tripe), all of them seasonal and very good indeed. This unusual, clubby establishment was founded in 1947 by Vincenzo and Assunta Santopadre, and it's now run by their male children, Bruno, Ennio, and Tonino, who still write the menu by hand, and slap their thighs with hilarity if you ask about their email address or website. Not only do they not have any such thing, they also decided long ago to take their time and enjoy life. Hence their decision to open for dinner only, and to decorate the grotto-like rooms with paintings, photographs, trophies, jockey shirts, and knick-knacks evoking their passion for the equestrian scene. Make sure to get an Italian speaker to reserve ahead for you (you might even want to give a false Italian name). Guests are vetted, and it's amazing how few get through the front door without a reservation; often the restaurant is fully booked, far ahead. Is it worth the bother? That depends. Certainly, if you like horses and racing you'll feel right at home. And if you want to experience something absolutely Roman, including the insouciance, the answer is yes. Note: next door are Il Genovino d'Oro and Micocci.

VIA COLLINA 18 ✦ TEL: 06 474 5405 ✦ OPEN *for* DINNER
ONLY MONDAY *through* SATURDAY ✦ MODERATE
Near: facing the northeast side of Piazza Sallustio

TAVERNA ROMANA

WHITE-HAIRED TONINO D'ANNIBALE AND HIS WIFE LUCIA CALVINI HAVE BEEN RUNNING THIS SMALL, corner trattoria for decades, and locals usually refer to it as either "La Taverna," as if there were only one in the city, or "Da Tonino e Lucia." The couple comes from the Alban Hills, and they and their families are winemakers. Their Velletri house wines, while simple and quaffable, are reliably good. Tonino runs the show, towering over the ten small tables in the small, cluttered dining room. It has the requisite non-décor typical of such neighborhood places. Lucia, whose raucous voice sounds like something from a Fellini film, still rolls out the pasta fresh daily, and makes from scratch just about everything else on offer. The perennial house antipasto—the only one available—consists of otherwise impossible to find *coppiette*—spicy jerky—a few rounds of salami, a chunk of grana or other cheese, and some olives. The weekly wheel of classics is what you come for, plus *carbonara*, *cacio e pepe* and so forth, veal stew with peas, *saltimbocca*, lamb chops, oxtail stew, and homey, equally house-made desserts such as *crostata* or apple pie. Some tourists gird up their loins and find the courage to enter this tiny, Roman-looking institution and are well received. Otherwise you'll see locals, workmen, and white collars feeding happily. One great advantage for those who like to eat early: Taverna Romana starts serving lunch at noon; dinner is from 7pm.

VIA MADONNA DEI MONTI 79 ✦ TEL: 06 474 5325
CLOSED SUNDAY ✦ INEXPENSIVE *to* MODERATE
Near: 1 block north of Via Cavour, corner Via dell'Agnello

TRATTORIA CADORNA

THE TUDINI FAMILY HAS BEEN RUNNING THIS UPSCALE TRATTORIA SINCE IT OPENED HERE IN 1947. THEY serve luscious, traditional Roman food with a few winks to other regions. Current scion Marco Tudini was born here, and while he has painted the walls chiffon yellow, and added quality original modern artworks and comfortable chairs, the place has changed very little. The service is particularly smooth and affable; Marco or another family or staff member will tempt you to try the "*antipasti sfiziosi*" for which Cadorna is known. They include *fritelle*, what we'd call fried bread or plain fritters, made with bread dough, and flanked by classic meat sauce and herbs. Don't overdo it. There's plenty to come. The wildly delicious house first course, which has been on the menu since day one, is *pappardelle alla Cadorna*, a kind of kitchen-sink *carbonara* sauced with bacon, mushrooms, peas, eggs, and parmigiano. But the *gricia*, *carbonara*, and *amatriciana* are memorable, too, and if you like *pajata* or oxtails, the rigatoni with either are excellent. The weekly wheel of trattoria classics is respected at Cadorna. Lovers of meat—from steaks and stews to roasts, pork meatballs, and skewered strips of mutton, to offal—will be delighted. Cadorna also serves a limited number of fish dishes, however, and one you'll find here and nowhere else is grilled tiny fresh anchovies with lettuce and quail-egg-sized tomatoes. The desserts are homey, simple, and house made. The wine list isn't as wide or deep as you'd expect, given the excellence of the food, but the house white and red from the Castelli Romani will go with anything. There's a narrow, covered terrace on the sidewalk for fine weather dining.

VIA RAFFAELE CADORNA 12 ✦ TEL: 06 482 7061
CLOSED *for* LUNCH *on* SATURDAY *and* SUNDAY
MODERATE *to* EXPENSIVE ✦ *Near: 20 yards from Piazza Sallustio*

CHEESE, COFFEE, COOKIES, GOURMET FOOD SHOPS, ICE CREAM, PASTRIES

ANTICO CAFFÈ DEL BRASILE

THE COLISEUM AND QUIRINAL AREAS OFFER TRICKY NAVIGATING FOR FOOD LOVERS. LUCKILY, IN THE HEART of Monti, several fine addresses such as this one are still to be found. In addition to its decades of service as a neighborhood hangout, the main claim to fame of this busy, family-owned *caffè* and coffee-roasting establishment is its Miscela del Papa (the "pope's blend"), a strong, dark-roasted animal of 70-percent Arabica and 30-percent Robusta, both types of bean from Brazil and other South American countries. The formula is a secret. Why the pope's blend? When he was still a theology student, the late pope Karol Wojtyla lodged nearby and was a regular. Whether he particularly approved of the *caffè*'s subsequent trade in his name, or knew anything about the quality of coffee, is an open question. A 100-percent Arabica blend (South American beans, mostly from Brazil) is also available and a better choice for anyone who prefers delicacy. Cagey Andrea Di Nucci has been roasting the coffee here since 1993, and claims the machinery is in the back of the shop, but off limits to visitors; others in the business claim the coffee is now roasted in the suburbs. Does it matter? As is often the case when Robusta is involved, the bar cappuccinos are delicious, the Robusta's defects foiled by plenty of rich, fatty foam. Antico Caffé del Brasile pastries are many, and tempt even the most zealous pilgrims into committing the mortal sin of gluttony.

VIA DEI SERPENTI 23 ✦ TEL: 06 488 2319

CLOSED SUNDAY AFTERNOON

Near: between Via Cavour and Via Nazionale

BAR—TORREFAZIONE DELLA MANNA

A NEIGHBORHOOD FIXTURE SINCE 1939, THIS FAMILY-RUN SHOP SELLS CANDY AND BOXED CHOCOLATE, BUS tickets, tobacco, and knick-knacks, and is in the process of becoming a full-service espresso bar once again (a death in the family precipitated the closure of the *caffè*). Above all, the coffee roasted here in the original 1939 manually operated machine, which is in full view of clients, is remarkably excellent. Only a few pounds are roasted at a time, several times a week, to keep the product fresh. Order the Miscela Manna, which is 100-percent Arabica, take it home and brew it in your Moka. Manna may be plain and in an unsung area, but its coffee is some of the best in town.

VIA SALARIA 79 ✦ TEL: 06 841 6689 ✦ CLOSED SUNDAY

Near: just south of entrance to Villa Albani, 200 yards north of Piazza Fiume

LA BOTTEGA DEL CIOCCOLATO

THIS SMALL, HANDSOME SHOP'S INTERIOR IS RED AND BLACK AND HAS A CHINOISERIE THEME. LA BOTTEGA del Cioccolato opened for business in 1996, when owner Maurizio Proietti, a master chocolatier of a chocolate dynasty, "cut the umbilical cord," as he puts it, and went independent. Maurizio is the eldest son of Marcello Proietti, formerly Rome's top chocolate maker and longtime owner of Moriondo e Gariglio (area 2). Maurizio uses Barry Callebaut Venezuelan chocolate as a base, and usually sells about 50 different chocolates at any one time. Some flavors are only available seasonally. Le Parisien, made using a 1920s recipe, is a luscious filled chocolate combining hazelnut-chocolate gianduja in the style of Turin with fresh cream; it has a short shelf life and is offered in cool-weather months only. Maurizio loves Asian spices, and his dark-chocolate filled chocolates with chili or ginger are outstanding. Especially delicious are the organic candied oranges, apricots, lemons, and clementines, where the flavor of the fruit shines through. Other old-fashioned specialties include candied violets, marzipan, *marrons glacés,* chocolate figurines, and Easter eggs.

VIA LEONINA 82 ✦ TEL: 06 482 1473
WWW.LABOTTEGADELCIOCCOLATO.IT
CLOSED SUNDAY YEAR ROUND, *for* 6 WEEKS *in* MAY *and* JUNE, *and on* SATURDAYS *in* SEPTEMBER
Near: 1 block north of Via Cavour, 20 yards west of Via del Boschetto

DE ANGELIS

EVEN IF YOU'RE NOT DOING ANY COOKING AT HOME WHILE IN ROME, YOU'LL WANT TO VISIT THIS BUTCHER shop for the splendor of the interior, and the entertainment value of the clientele. Marble-clad from floor to ceiling, spotlit, and animated by expert butchers in pristine white outfits, this is Rome's most luxurious *macelleria.* The meat and gourmet foods are displayed like jewelry, and cost nearly as much, but the quality is impeccable. Blueblood Roman matrons and their gentlemen, cooks, butlers, and servants, are always to be seen, sometimes with lap dogs in tow. The outstanding chicken comes from Bresse, in Burgundy. There are many ready-to-eat take-out dishes. Also sold are foie gras, caviar, excellent olive oils, and a few fine wines, cookies, and sweets.

VIA FLAVIA 74 ✦ TEL: 06 420 12192
CLOSED SATURDAY AFTERNOON *and* SUNDAY
Near: 120 yards southeast of Piazza Sallustio

FASSINO

THIS SMALL *CAFFÈ*, SNACK BAR, AND ICE CREAMERY IS OWNED AND OPERATED BY COUSINS OF THE BIGGER, more famous Palazzo del Freddo, near the Esquilino market south of Termini train station (area 5). The family name is the same—Fassi—and this place has been in business since 1880. The coffee, pastries, and simple dishes are good, the seating comfortable, and the ice creams artisanal and satisfying, though not in the same league as the greats.

VIA BERGAMO 24 ✦ TEL: 06 854 9117 ✦ OPEN DAILY
Near: half a block north of the northeast side of Piazza Alessandria

IL GENOVINO D'ORO

FRANCO CALAFATTI IS A WILDLY ENERGETIC, TALKATIVE, AND KNOWLEDGEABLE FOOD EXPERT WHO RUNS THIS unusual, miniscule shop next door to Santopadre restaurant. He stocks precisely 1,000 different items—the best of the best of Italy's regions. You'll find a selection of excellent olive oils, for instance, a handful from each of the top olive oil producing areas. The offerings vary constantly. For Lazio oils, you might find medium-bodied, flavorful extra virgin from the 1,000-year-old Isoletta estate at Buon Riposo near Aprilia (south of Rome), or La Mola, a remarkable DOP Sabina oil, or an outstanding organic oil such as Colle San Lorenzo, from Cori, near Latina. Among the 100 outstanding wines, you'll encounter not the usual Super Tuscans and brawny Piedmontese Bs—Barolo, Barbaresco, Barbera—but rather a modest Frascati Superiore made by the cousin of the famous Costantini family of wine merchants and wine makers (whose amazing huge emporium is in the Prati district, area 8). Stacked and squirreled away are delicious tiny asparagus or baby artichokes packed in excellent extra virgin Canino olive oil. Calafatti is from Genoa, via Marseille, and he's completing a thesis on the philosophy of food and "sensorial arts." Spices are another of his many passions. He mixes up dry condiments for everything from baked potatoes to fish, using the known, scientifically proven properties of herbs, spices, and aromatic plants to create amazing combinations. In summer, he sets up a "spice tent" on the banks of the Tiber near Piazza Trilussa and Ponte Sisto, on the Trastevere side of the river. If you ask him about Leonardo da Vinci and food, you risk spending several hours talking about the *Codex Romanoff*, Renaissance recipes, and conspiracy theory. Calafatti appears to speak all languages, and his enthusiasm is as genuine as his knowledge of Italian food. Not to be missed.

VIA COLLINA 22 ✦ TEL: 06 454 75983
WWW.GENUINESTORE.IT ✦ CLOSED SUNDAY
Near: facing the northeast side of Piazza Sallustio

MICOCCI—CASA DEI LATTICINI

THE FINEST CHEESES OF ITALY, FRANCE, AND ENGLAND ARE TO BE FOUND IN THIS SMALL BUT LUXURIOUS shop, which—along with E. Volpetti & C. and La Tradizione—is probably the best place in Rome to discover Italian curds and whey. Most cheesemongers get mozzarella several times a week, a few get it daily; Micocci takes delivery twice a day from a small mozzarella maker that sells only through them (in Rome). And so it is with many other cheeses. You'll also find fabulous caciocavallo, pecorino di fossa, Tuscan or Sardinian pecorino, ricottas of various types, cheeses crusted with herbs, blue cheeses, goat's milk cheeses—hundreds and hundreds of them. Used to prickly VIPs and the exigent bluebloods that live around Piazza Sallustio, the proprietors aren't exactly warm and cuddly, but they're very knowledgeable and, often, on Saturday mornings will offer tastings of cheeses and the condiments to go with them.

VIA COLLINA 14 ✦ TEL: 06 474 1784 ✦ CLOSED SUNDAY
Near: facing the northeast side of Piazza Sallustio,
next door to Santopadre and Il Genovino d'Oro

PALOMBI

THE GLITZ AND GLAMOR OF VIA VENETO, ONCE HAUNT OF FEDERICO FELLINI, SOPHIA LOREN, AND THE Cinecittà-Hollywood gang, may have faded, replaced by the petro-dollar and Russian mafia-oligarch crowd, but Palombi, a decades-old bakery, is little changed. It still serves tea and coffee to white-gloved ladies and gentlemen enjoying their Roman Holiday, and bakes delicious Roman butter cookies, *crostata*, and cakes and tarts of all kinds, plus the requisite muffins and newfangled pastries demanded by the street's international clientele. Palombi's savory snacks are fine, but there are many other places (not in this neighborhood) to enjoy better focaccia or pizza.

VIA VENETO 114 ✦ TEL: 06 488 5817
CLOSED SUNDAY ✦ *Near: the north end of the boulevard*

PASTICCERIA PANNOCCHI

THE PANNOCCHI FAMILY OPENED THIS ARCHLY TRADITIONAL PASTRY SHOP, ICE CREAMERY, AND ESPRESSO bar back in 1927 and, into their fourth generation, they run it to this day. Locals come here for the classics—cakes, tarts, and pastries, such as *maritozzi* buns filled with dense, lightly sweetened whipped cream, and rich *krapfen* bursting with pastry cream. The coffee is good and strong, just what you need to cut through the buttery calories. Pannocchi also serves snacks such as *tramezzini*, and is known for its *aperitivi*, when the bar is covered with bowls of olives, potato chips, and finger foods. There's nowhere to sit, the atmosphere is a constant bustle, and you'll be hard pressed to spot a tourist among the crowd.

VIA BERGAMO 56/56A/58/60 ✦ TEL: 06 855 2109
OPEN 7AM *to* 8:30PM ✦ CLOSED MONDAY
Near: around the corner from the northeast side of Piazza Alessandria

PUNTURI

THIS HIGH-END *GASTRONOMIA* USED TO BE A CHARMING, FAMILY-RUN BUSINESS LIKE E. VOLPETTI & C. IN Testaccio, or La Tradizione in Prati, but has evolved—if such be the word—into a luxury mini-market and deli, of the kind found on Manhattan's Upper East Side. Efficient staff supply you with very good hams, salami and cheeses, breads and pastries, and the self-serve shelves and refrigerated display cases offer everything from breakfast cereal or cookies to milk, yogurt, and smoked salmon. This is a good place to buy picnic supplies, or pick up a snack as you explore the area.

VIA FLAVIA 48 ✦ TEL: 06 481 8225
CLOSED SATURDAY AFTERNOON *and* SUNDAY
Near: 80 yards southeast of Piazza Sallustio

SESTO GIRONE

TOO MINISCULE TO IMAGINE AND LOCATED ON AN UNFASHIONABLE STRETCH OF VIA SALARIA, THIS HIGH-end deli opened in late 2007 but has already won itself a fine reputation for friendly service, top-quality hams (including *culatello di Zibello*) and cheeses (among them several otherwise unfindable artisanal goat cheeses from the Lazio and mozzarella from Latina), and a small but well-chosen selection of wines and olive oils. Among them are excellent DOP Sabina oils, and one from the Sezze area (Lazio's artichoke capital). Wineries featured include Casale del Giglio, Falesco, and Pallavicini. Among the shop's curiosities are local black chickpeas, *cece nero della Tuscia*, and other Lazio heirloom dry beans and lentils. If you're hungry, the affable proprietors will make you a delicious sandwich, which you can eat while perched at a tall, magic-mushroom-like table facing the wine racks.

VIA SALARIA 91 ✦ TEL: 06 855 1970
OPEN 8:30AM *to* 9:30PM CLOSED SUNDAY
Near: facing entrance to Villa Albani, 250 yards north of Piazza Fiume

WINE AND WINE BARS

ENOTECA CAVOUR 313

THE WOODEN BOOTHS, A WIDE ANTIQUE SHOP COUNTER, AND CONVENIENT BUSINESS HOURS KEEP THIS longtime wine bar filled much of the time. It serves a wide variety of high-quality hams, salamis, cheeses, salads, snack foods, and upmarket dishes—*bottarga, carpaccio*—but is not a full-service restaurant with cooked-to-order meals. The wines on offer by the bottle range across Italy and abroad, with hundreds to choose from. A limited, often-changing selection is available by the glass, and horizontal or vertical tastings can be arranged. This is a user-friendly, easy address, not far from the Coliseum and train station, and it draws a mixed crowd of regulars and tourists.

VIA CAVOUR 313 ✦ TEL: 06 678 5496
CLOSED SUNDAY LUNCH *and* AUGUST
Near: 50 yards west of Via dell'Agnello

ENOTECA MARCHETTI

IN ROME, TWO MARCHETTI ARE HIGHLY REGARDED WINE EXPERTS; ROBERTO OWNS AND OPERATES THE TRENDY wine bar-restaurant Al Bric (near Campo de' Fiori, area 1). This modish wine shop-wine bar, where regular clients still buy bottles to take home, is the fief of Marco Marchetti. His passion ranges far beyond the Lazio, and his selection of superb bottlings from Burgundy and Alsace make this a mecca for lovers of French wine. Piedmont and Tuscany also play major roles on the list, as do whiskies and Scotch. You can snack on savory or sweet delicacies while you sip, or buy a precious bottle to go.

VIA FLAVIA 28 ✦ TEL: 06 487 2028
CLOSED SATURDAY AFTERNOON *and* SUNDAY
Near: 100 yards southeast of Piazza Sallustio

ENOTECA ROCCHI

ABOUT 3,000 DIFFERENT WINES FILL THE SHELVES OF THIS UPSCALE, FAMILY-OWNED WINE SHOP, WHICH has been in business since 1904 and is strategically located near the Zecca, where Italy's euros are minted. The usual bureaucrats, VIPs, and well-heeled locals—Villa Borghese is only a few hundred yards away—seek out the current generation of proprietors Roberto and Giovanna Rocchi not only for their champagne and Super Tuscans, but also for their advice about *terroir* wines. Among the fine Lazio wineries represented here are Falesco, Mottura, Marco Carpineti, Castel de Paolis, Camponeschi, Colle Picchioni, Principi Pallavicini, and Fontana Candida. Rocchi also has shops in several other outlying areas (see website for details).

VIA A. SCARLATTI 7 ✦ TEL: 06 855 1022
WWW.ROCCHIENOTECA.IT ✦ CLOSED THURSDAY AFTERNOON *and* SUNDAY ✦ *Near: 150 yards south of Piazza Verdi and the Italian mint*

TRIMANI

TRIMANI IS ROME'S ETERNAL WINE SHOP, IN BUSINESS SINCE 1821 AND OWNED AND OPERATED BY THE SAME passionate, wine-loving family. The generations can no longer be counted without using a calculator. Trimani started as a *vineria*—a bulk wine shop—serving simple food, and

then evolved into a bottle shop catering to newly-united Italy's bourgeosie. Trimani has been in its current, now-lavish premises since 1876, with a top-to-bottom remodeling in the early 1990s that transformed it into something resembling the lobby of a grand hotel, with a dazzling two-level wine bar/restaurant next door. Current owners Marco Trimani and his wife Rosalena are very much present, running the retail shop and wine bar with their children Paolo, Carla, Francesco, and Giovanni. The range and number of wines are still the city's biggest, with some 4,500 different labels totaling tens of thousands of bottles from around the world. The choice of affordable and medium-priced wines is remarkable. Despite the baggage of centuries, the Trimanis are trailblazers, and they've been much imitated. They were the first in Rome to promote new and improved—read: new and Americanized—Lazio wines. The selection of them is still the city's widest and deepest. Theirs was Rome's first real full-service wine bar serving lunch and dinner, and it remains one of the best (with cheeses, hams, salamis, appetizers, traditional pasta and fish dishes, and good grilled meats).

Theme tastings and wine seminars are held regularly in the wine bar's upstairs conference room. Even if you're not a wine lover, you'll want to visit the Trimani shop to see the landmark wine "fountain," used for decades to distribute naturally chilled wines on tap. The Acqua Felice aqueduct runs under the building, and its cold waters flowed through the handsome, sculpted marble contraption. The Trimani are also winemakers; they own and distribute Cantina Colacicchi Anagni, which produces four highly drinkable wines, all of them Lazio IGTs: Schiaffo (Cabernet Sauvignon, Merlot, and Cesanese) has the merit of being spared oaking, and is drunk young; Romagnano Rosso (the same blend, but oaked for a year and therefore less typical of the region); Torre Ercolana (ditto, but made from the best grapes, and bottle-aged, and more interesting than the previous); and Romagnano Bianco (Malvasia del Lazio, Passerina del Frusinate, and Romanesco grapes), which is surprisingly well-structured yet easy to drink when young and frisky. The family's olive groves at Torri in Sabina now produce certified organic DOP Sabina olive oil, under the label San Vittore degli Uccellatori. Made from Carboncella, Frantoio, Moraiolo, Leccino, and Pendolino olives from about 2,000 trees spread across 15 acres, the oil is a sunny greenish-yellow, medium-bodied, full of ripe fruit and flowery flavors, and almost entirely free

of the rustic, earthy defects of many Central Italian oils. That's because the olives are hand-harvested slightly immature, and rushed to the mill within eight hours of picking. In short, anyone who wants to get the breaking news on Lazio wines and oils needs seek no further than Trimani.

VIA GOITO 20 ✦ TEL: 06 446 9661 ✦ WWW.TRIMANI.COM
STORE HOURS 9AM *to* 1:30PM *and* 3:30 *to*
8:30PM MONDAY *through* SATURDAY

The wine bar is around the corner (Via Cernaia 37B) and OPEN *from* 11:30AM *to* 3PM *and* 5:30 *to* 12:30AM, BOTH *are* CLOSED SUNDAY
TEL: 06 446 9630 ✦ *Near: 150 yards south of Via XX Settembre, a quarter mile northwest of Termini train station*

NON-TERROIR TOP OR TRENDY TABLES

BRUNELLO

VIA VENETO 70A ✦ TEL: 06 489 02867
WWW.BRUNELLORESTAURANT.COM
CLOSED SUNDAY ✦ EXTREMELY EXPENSIVE

GEORGE'S

VIA MARCHE 7 ✦ TEL: 06 420 84575
WWW.GEORGESRISTORANTE.IT ✦ CLOSED SUNDAY
and AUGUST ✦ EXTREMELY EXPENSIVE

LA TERRAZZA DELL'HOTEL EDEN

VIA LUDOVISI 49 ✦ TEL: 06 478 121
WWW.STARWOODHOTELS.COM ✦ OPEN DAILY ✦ EXPENSIVE

MIRABELLE

HOTEL SPLENDIDE ROYAL, VIA DI PORTA PINCIANA 14
TEL: 06 421 68838 ✦ WWW.MIRABELLE.IT
OPEN DAILY ✦ EXTREMELY EXPENSIVE

TRATTORIA MONTI

VIA SAN VITO 13A ✦ TEL: 06 446 6573
CLOSED SUNDAY DINNER *and* MONDAY ✦ EXPENSIVE
ALSO REGIONAL FOOD FROM THE MARCHES

VIVENDO DEL ST. REGIS GRAND

VIA V.E. ORLANDO 3 ✦ TEL: 06 470 92736
CLOSED SATURDAY LUNCH *and* SUNDAY ✦ VERY EXPENSIVE

REGIONAL RESTAURANTS

THE MARCHES

TRATTORIA MONTI

(see Non-Terroir Top or Trendy Tables, above)

CANTINA CANTARINI

(see page 197)

CHAPTER 5

ESQUILINO, CELIO, TERMINI, SAN LORENZO, SAN GIOVANNI

VISITORS OFTEN OVERLOOK THE UNGLAMOROUS, LARGELY UNSUNG EASTERN AND SOUTHEASTERN areas of central Rome. That's a pity. They're worth exploring, particularly if you love good food. The boundaries are, roughly, the massive churches of Santa Maria Maggiore and San Giovanni in Laterano, the Porta Maggiore city gate, and the small, Romanesque church of San Lorenzo Fuori le Mura—so named because it stands outside the Aurelian Walls, which gird the historic center of town. Much real estate is covered by the handsome Colle Oppio parklands (site of the Domus Aurea); the Università La Sapienza campus; and the Policlinico, a municipal hospital. The area's biggest occupant, however, is sprawling Termini train station, whose elevated tracks isolate the San Lorenzo neighborhood.

Since the mid-1990s, San Lorenzo has been a favorite among the party crowd, and is, transliterated, Rome's answer to New York's East Village. On its southern edge, at Porta Maggiore, stands the celebrated Baker's Tomb, a must-see for bread lovers. The ancient mausoleum was built by a wealthy baker, and its bas reliefs show scenes of bread being made and baked. For a flavor of San Lorenzo's trendy edginess, from Piazzale Tiburtino walk south on the wild side of the city walls, along an impressive bulwark of ancient brick, with menacing, crenellated towers. The abundant graffiti, nightspots (with names such as Hurly Burly), and slummy-trendy neo-trattorias, are typical of the neighborhood.

Framing the eastern curve of the Coliseum are the Esquilino and Celio, two of Rome's seven hills. They harbor a handful of authentic trattorias, one of the city's great nineteenth-century ice cream parlors, an equally venerable cookie factory, and an impressive new covered market complex. Also to be found are wonderful pastries, bread, and salami. Due south of San Giovanni in Laterano, beyond the city walls, is the Appio-Tuscolano neighborhood, which has many gourmet food shops, several good places to eat, and an authentic neighborhood market at Piazza Epiro. The Appio is the gateway to both the Via Appia Antica and Via Appia Nuova, described in area 10.

For over a century, the Esquilino Hill's alimentary focal point was mercato di Piazza Vittorio Emanuele II, south of Termini station. The outdoor market no longer exists, but you can still enjoy a coffee, drink or a typical fruit-flavored Roman ice at **Grattachecca Romana all'Esquilino**, a sidewalk stand on the south side of the piazza; it's open 24/7 in spring, summer, and early fall (and closed in winter). The **Nuovo Mercato Esquilino**

(Via Principe Amedeo 184 and other street numbers), which opened in 2006, is a vast complex in a former military barracks, located one block northeast of Piazza Vittorio Emanuele II. It comprises several courtyards, one of them showcasing contemporary artwork, and also houses the Oriental Studies Department of the University of Rome. Open daily 7am to 3pm, it is among Rome's biggest and least expensive markets, and has the city's largest number of stands selling Asian and African specialties. This reflects the demographics of what Romans call the Quartiere Vittorio, home nowadays to many working class immigrants. Imported herbs and spices flank the traditional necklaces of local *peperoncino* chili peppers or triangles of jowl bacon, and there's as much cilantro on offer as spearmint or rosemary. At least half of the stands sell non-Italian items. The main access to the food emporium, in Building #2, is entrance #11. Dozens of stands in Building #1 sell clothing and accessories, much of it from China and India.

A mile farther south, the **mercato rionale di Piazza Epiro** is another new covered market in the long, narrow square formed by a swelling in Via De Mattias. The postmodern market structure is painted a loud, unmistakable burnt Siena color. Its stands sell the requisite selection of fruit and vegetables, dry goods, and household cleaning products, plus quaffable wine on tap. Each stand within the market is called a "box," using the English word; **Cantine D'Offizi**, a winery, has its stainless steel tanks in Box 11 (Tel: 339 667 3783). The Falanghina white comes from the IGT Beneventano appellation. The others, white or red, are innocuous Castelli Romani wines.

The San Lorenzo neighborhood still has an appealing, small outdoor market, **mercato rionale di Piazza Osci**. It faces the south side of the Chiesa dell'Immacolata, a remarkably hideous nineteenth-century church. Clothing and sundries are sold from makeshift stands on the south end of the square, while the fruit-and-vegetable stalls are permanent, painted green, and were remodeled a few years ago to meet European Union hygiene standards.

RESTAURANTS AND TRATTORIAS

ANTICA HOSTERIA DA ANGELINO

SINCE 1899 THE SAME FAMILY HAS RUN THIS SMALL, ARCHETYPAL ROMAN TRATTORIA, A NEIGHBORHOOD favorite for its simplicity and authenticity. Despite the disappearance of the outdoor market, which drew most of the trattoria's clients, the show goes on. Stefano De Paoli helps his mother, Ilde, who's in her eighties and still does the cooking; she's been working in the kitchen here since 1939. There are red-and-white checked tablecloths atop 1950s tables, turn-of-the-century tiles, wainscotting, a 1950s ice box, and a relaxed, timeless atmosphere to match. There's no fish on the menu, other than *baccalà*, and that only when the cook is in the mood, and the day of the week permits fish. The meat comes from the butcher shop across the street; it has been supplying the trattoria for generations. As you might expect, the Canonical calendar of classics is respected, so prepare to savor thick *pasta e fagioli* on Monday; perfect, meltingly tender *coda alla vaccinara* on Wednesday; house-made gnocchi on Thursday; *pasta e ceci* on Friday; and tripe on Saturday. Every day you'll find Roman beef *involtini*, addictive *saltimbocca,* and rustic omelets, plus seasonal greens, from artichokes to *puntarella.* The desserts are simple and house made. The wine list is short; stick to local bottlings. There's nothing fancy about the food or the décor or the service—or the prices. This is the kind of place many claim no longer exists. Note that, because many of the clients are early risers who get hungry early, you can have lunch starting at 12:30pm, dinner from 7:30pm.

VIA MACCHIAVELLI 64 ✦ TEL: 06 446 7555
CLOSED SUNDAY ✦ INEXPENSIVE *to* MODERATE
Near: 100 yards southwest of Piazza Vittorio Emanuele II

DANILO

THE DYNAMIC PROPRIETOR OF THIS SMALL BUT INCREASINGLY POPULAR FAMILY-RUN NEO-TRATTORIA IS DANILO Valente, who seems to know how to market his establishment to the right people in Rome's trendy, chummy food world, but has resisted the temptation to go too far down the creative food road. Valente and his wife are out front, in the dining room, which has a less-than-trendy look: yellow tablecloths atop checkered undercloths, white walls, a wagon wheel, farm implements, and oddments that add rusticity to this patently urbane address. The real secret is Danilo's mother, who makes the pasta by hand, and does the cooking. She is a master of the Roman classics, but has added fashionable diversity to the menu. Her rustic *strozzapreti* are dressed not with equally rustic *guanciale* and pecorino romano but rather with fancy, expensive *lardo di Colonnata* and pecorino di fossa, and the *cacio e pepe* are tossed and amalgamated with cheese inside an excavated wheel of pecorino. Also available seasonally are giant ravioli with buffalo-milk ricotta, artichokes and truffle shavings, or big, short paccheri pasta with arugula, mozzarella, and *pachini*. There's a stilted summertime "*carbonara estiva*," with bacon and zucchini and a pinch of saffron; the normal *carbonara* is more satisfying. If you stick to the simple *abbacchio scottadito*, the tripe, oxtails, slow-cooked beef stew, *puntarella* salad, *crostata* with *pinoli*, or triangles of ricotta and chocolate, both house made, you certainly won't be disappointed. On Tuesday and Friday fresh fish is served—simply grilled or roasted is best. Among its 250 entries, the wine list features dozens of the Lazio's best. Note that Valente also owns the nearby casual-hip wine bar **Wine Art** (Via Bixio 93).

VIA PETRARCA 13 ✦ TEL: 06 772 00111
WWW.TRATTORIADADANILO.IT ✦ CLOSED MONDAY LUNCH, SUNDAY, *and* AUGUST ✦ MODERATE ✦ *Near: in the Vittorio neighborhood, next door to Ciamei, 100 yards west of Piazza Dante*

DOMENICO DAL 1968

WHILE STUDENTS WERE BURNING CARS AND BUILDING BARRICADES ACROSS TOWN IN THE POLITICAL heat of 1968, Domenico Compagnucci, from a village near Rieti, was already a veteran of trattoria kitchens, and kept out of harm's way. He opened this cult restaurant on a tree-lined avenue to preserve, not dismantle, Lazio traditions. His children Lia and Arnaldo, the second generation, were born here and have been in charge for some time now. The décor is more upscale and sleek than it was 40 years ago, with cane chairs and starched white tablecloths, but the spirit of the place and the menu have changed little, exception made for the fresh fish dishes. They range from salads with shrimp and sliced baby artichokes, to spaghetti with clams and *bottarga*, or grilled or whole roasted fish. Though very well prepared, with the freshest ingredients, fish is not really where the heart of the house beats strongest. This is among the few restaurants in town where you can still eat the delicious small, striped *rigatella* snails of Lazio, served in late spring and early summer in a red sauce made piquant by spearmint and chili. The *carbonara* is remarkable, the *amatriciana* as good as you'll find. There's skate soup with broccoli, as popular today as it was 40 years ago. The oxtail stew, or the breaded, pan-fried fresh anchovies, and, of course, *baccalà*, are irresistible. House-made desserts include simple tarts and rich spoon sweets with fresh seasonal fruit. The wine list features between 70 and 80 bottlings, all (or nearly) from Lazio. In warm weather, you can take a table on the sidewalk, but the interior is appealing and considerably less noisy.

VIA SATRICO 23-25 ✦ TEL: 06 704 94602 ✦ CLOSED SUNDAY DINNER, MONDAY, *and* AUGUST ✦ MODERATE *to* EXPENSIVE

Near: 100 yards southeast of the Piazza Epiro market

LUZZI

YOU'LL SPOT THE POMPEIAN RED BUILDING HOUSING THIS CULT TRATTORIA-PIZZERIA, WHICH HAS BEEN RUN by the Luzzi family since 1945, a block west of the handsome Romanesque church of San Clemente. There are niches on the façade, one with a small statue of Padre Pio. You have a view of the back of San Clemente from Luzzi's coveted sidewalk terrace, though you'll probably have difficulty seeing through the crowd of diners and people waiting for a table. Inside, the yellow checked tablecloths, wainscotting, and black-and-white photos of old Rome tell you that Luzzi is an unpretentious neighborhood eatery where clients feel at home. There's a wood-burning oven, and out of it come delicious pizzas and *bruschetta*, the simpler the better. The menu also features plenty of authentic Roman dishes from gnocchi on up, and good, solid desserts—*tiramisù*, chocolate cake, *crostata* with pine nuts, and lemon custard. Stick to the beer or wine on tap.

VIA SAN GIOVANNI IN LATERANO 88, *and* VIA CELIMONTANA 1
TEL: 06 709 6332 ✦ CLOSED WEDNESDAY ✦ VERY INEXPENSIVE
Near: 150 yards east of the Coliseum

POMMIDORO

"POMMIDORO" IS AN OBSOLETE YET EUPHONIC VARIANT ON POMODORI—TOMATOES. LIKE THE NAME, LONGTIME owners Aldo and Anna keep the flame burning and pot bubbling—the flame of the old, authentic, working-class San Lorenzo, a neighborhood now overrun by the grunge-slum-club set, whose neo-, retro-trattorias are self-conscious shadows of their former selves. The best place to dine and observe the area's fauna is Pommidoro's glassed-in terrace on the edge of this homely square, which is really a crossroads that doubles as a parking lot. The interior of the restaurant, with its soaring arches, white tablecloths, and old-fashioned cooler case in wood and glass, is also pleasant, especially in bad weather—meaning when it's too sunny and bright inside the terrace, despite the air conditioning. At Pommidoro the service is polished but friendly, without being invasive, and those who enjoy an early lunch

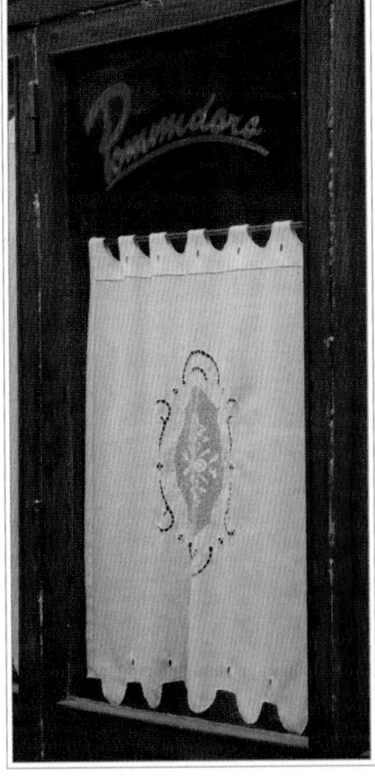

will be pleased: the official opening time is 1pm, but if you come at 12:30pm you'll be seated and served. As to what you should eat: fish is available and fresh, and the Roman classics are hard to beat, particularly the artichokes, *spaghetti alla gricia* and *carbonara* (long held to be the most luscious in the city), which is usually made with *pancetta* and not *guanciale*. There's *coda* and lamb and *pajata* too. The grilled meat (including offal) is Aldo's specialty. In fall, wild game steals the show, from luscious wild boar stewed so long at low heat that it flakes at the flick of your fork, to roast quail or pheasant. The ricotta cheesecake comes from Ciccioscake (a pastry shop around the corner) and is remarkably flavorful; the house-made *tiramisù* is always a rich, caloric winner. Regional wines by the bottle are your best bet. Expect to dine in the company of well-heeled Roman regulars, business people, professors from La Sapienza, and a mix of Italian and international visitors. For fans of the late, great Pier Paolo Pasolini, Pommidoro is a place of pilgrimage and memory: the cult film director ate his Last Supper here the night he was murdered.

PIAZZA DEI SANNITI 44 ✦ TEL: 06 445 2692
CLOSED SUNDAY *and* AUGUST ✦ MODERATE *to* EXPENSIVE
Near: in the San Lorenzo neighborhood, the square is the crossroads of Via dei Volschi and Via degli Ausoni

TAVERNA DEI QUARANTA

THE RED-CHECKED TABLECLOTHS, HIGH CEILINGS, OLD PRINTS, WORN WOODEN TABLES, CANE CHAIRS, AND half-paneling give this away as a typical neighborhood trattoria. It's just far enough in the wrong direction from the Coliseum that tourists don't usually see it—or they simply walk by. The locals like the taverna because it's friendly, cheap, and cheery, and so will you, if you enjoy Roman classics, and the occasional dish or variation on a theme from Sardinia and the Abruzzi. The fried zucchini flowers and tiny skewers of mutton, and the seasonal salads that combine arugula with tomatoes or nuts, are tradition-based and good though not thoroughly Roman. One old-fashioned, rib-sticking dish you're not likely to find elsewhere is gnocchi sauced with short ribs and sausage meat—a variation on the classic *fettuccine alla romana*, often served at home on Sunday. The desserts are rich—creamy spoon sweets or apple tarts and ricotta cheesecake. The choice of wines is limited; pick an uncomplicated Italian bottling and you'll be fine.

VIA CLAUDIA 24 ✦ TEL: 06 700 0550 ✦ OPEN DAILY
INEXPENSIVE *to* MODERATE ✦ *Near: in the Celio neighborhood, 100 yards due south of Piazza del Colosseo, corner Via Annia/Piazza Celimontana*

TRAM TRAM

THE TELEPHONE NUMBER—ONLY SIX DIGITS AFTER THE "06"—AND THE FADED STENCILING, GIVES THIS AWAY as an old address. But don't be fooled: Ramponcino, the *osteria* whose ghostly name on the façade evokes memories of a premodern San Lorenzo neighborhood, is part of the décor. Tram Tram is a neo-trattoria, which serves some very good Roman classics and a mix of Pugliese and other central-southern Italian dishes plus a few tamely creative originals. It's the best, and most raucous, of the neighborhood's faux eateries, and has been around long enough to have earned its own pedigree. Spicy, highly flavorful, often salty, and often eclectic combinations come out of the kitchen. They range from authentic *polipetti alla Luciana* (or *alla Lucana*, if you prefer), which are baby octopus in a red sauce with chili, to orecchiette with eggplant, more red sauce, and ricotta salata. The *amatriciana*

and *coda* are very good, but the modish San Lorenzo clientele seems to prefer muddled offerings such as linguine with pesto and baby squid, or *involtini* made not with veal or beef, carrots, and celery, but with swordfish. Desserts are rich and sweet and creamy, from the *panna cotta* to the *zabaglione*. The wine list is longer than you'd find in an authentic trattoria, with a wide range of Lazio and other bottlings. Note that the wooden tables and bentwood chairs are crammed into a single,

SHOP TILL YOU DROP, ANCIENT ROMAN STYLE

WHERE BULLS, BEARS, GOATS, AND SHEEP WERE ONCE SLAUGHTERED, NOW STANDS THE curious round fifth-century church called Santo Stefano Rotondo. It's in the street of the same name, facing the Celio Park, south of the Coliseum, and is due to reopen after years of restoration. The church was built over the ancient Macellum Magnum, Rome's main market and slaughterhouse during the reign of Emperor Nero (later transformed, claim some scholars, into the Castra Peregrinorum, a military barracks for foreign soldiers). Inside, the restored frescoes by Pomarancio, Antonio Tempesta, and Niccolò Circignani show the Martyrdom of the Saints in thirty grisly panels. There are saints crushed by rolling boulders, burned alive, or maimed with a surprising array of instruments. Others drown with weights around their necks or are torn limb from limb by lions, presumably brought in for the purpose from the Coliseum. For those interested in ancient market structures and slaughterhouses, however, it's the floorplan and colonnades of the church that make it worth visiting: they appear to follow very closely the original layout from Nero's day.

remarkably noisy dining room and a tiny hallway, so prepare to shout to be heard. You won't be alone. Everyone shouts, and the trams—numbers 3, 5, and 9—thunder merrily by. Tram Tram is as much a happening as an eatery; it's also a cute play on words, meaning "daily grind" or "routine." Though not easy to find for those unfamiliar with the neighborhood, you'll have no difficulty spotting the building across the street: it is one of Rome's most egregious 1960s eyesores.

VIA DEI RETI 44/46 ✦ TEL: 06 490 416
CLOSED MONDAY *and* MID AUGUST ✦ MODERATE *to* EXPENSIVE
Near: in the San Lorenzo neighborhood, on the corner of Via dei Piceni

BREAD, CHEESE, FRUIT ICES, GOURMET FOOD SHOPS, GUANCIALE, ICE CREAM, KITCHEN TOOLS, PASTRIES

L'ANGOLO DEI GOLOSI

THIS SMALL NEIGHBORHOOD PASTRY SHOP WAS TAKEN OVER IN 2003 BY A YOUNG SARDINIAN COUPLE named Demontis. She makes the coffee and serves the pastries and snacks. He trained as a pastry chef and ice cream maker, and his butter pastries and *crostata* are rich, satisfying, and made with at least 50-percent pure butter. The jams used are also house-made; the plum flavor is excellent, replacing the classic Roman sour cherry jam in the *crostata*. At Eastertide, Demontis turns out fluffy, delicious Colomba—dove-shaped *panettone*—studded and/or topped with chocolate. The house coffee is good and strong, made with Teichner's Oro blend. In warm-weather months, Demontis makes very good artisanal ice creams, from luscious coffee and chocolate flavors to seasonal fruit done in the Sicilian-Sardinian style—meaning brilliant and sweet. You can also get savory snacks, crêpes and fruit milkshakes. Lovers of Sardinian specialty foods can buy them here, including bitter arbutus honey. This is the best place in the Piazza Epiro area for a pick-me-up after shopping at the market.

VIA SATRICO 7D/E/F ✦ TEL: 06 772 03483
OPEN DAILY ✦ *Near: 1 block east of Piazza Epiro*

CECCACCI

ONCE A SIMPLE NEIGHBORHOOD BAKERY, CECCACCI HAS MORPHED INTO A DELI AND FOOD EMPORIUM serving *tavola calda*-style dishes both indoors and on a small sidewalk terrace. The breads—some made with organic whole wheat, emmer, rye, even chickpea flour—are very good, and the *crostate*, cakes, pies, and tarts are always delicious. The postmodern décor is more evocative of an airport coffee shop than a Roman cake shop, but regulars crowd in, and the atmosphere is as chummy as it gets for the kind of neo-cafeteria Ceccacci has become.

VIA LICIA 9 ✦ TEL: 06 704 92755 ✦ CLOSED SUNDAY
Near: 100 yards northwest of Piazza Epiro

CECCHINI & C.

NOW IN HIS 40s, VIRGILIO CECCHINI HAS TAKEN OVER HIS FAMILY'S AUTHENTIC *SALUMERIA*, WHICH HAS BEEN in business here since 1930, and is known for its jowl bacon, salami, and hams, all made and aged on the spot. Virgilio's roots are in Collazzoni di Preci, a village six miles from Norcia, in Umbria, and his hogs are raised in the Umbrian mountains and the adjacent Marche region. Mild and fresh-tasting, Cecchini *guanciale* gets a sprinkling of mashed fresh garlic and sea salt before spending a week in a vat at just above freezing. Coated with black pepper or crushed chili flakes, it hangs for a week or two in the shop's marble-clad back room, so it's too young to eat raw like *prosciutto* and must be cooked before it is eaten. Cecchini & C. also sells hams from Parma and San Daniele, and excellent deli products, and is a full-service *gastronomia*. The service is friendly, the prices reasonable, and the clientele of regulars deeply attached to Rome and its foodways.

VIA MERULANA 85 ✦ TEL: 06 772 07535 ✦ CLOSED SUNDAY
Near: in the Vittorio neighborhood, on the corner of Via Macchiavelli

CIAMEI

CIAMEI IS A FAMILY OF ROUGH DIAMONDS WHO ROAST ROUGH COFFEE—PLUS SOME VERY GOOD, 100-PERCENT Arabica coffee, too. That's what makes a detour here worthwhile (that and the fact that Danilo, the trattoria, is right next door). A neighborhood *caffè*-bar/coffee-roasting establishment, Ciamei has been around since 1930, and the décor and service show considerable wear. In theory, four coffee options are available at the bar, but in practice, for reasons of supply and demand, the standard bar blend is what you'll be served much of the time, no matter what you request. It contains a high percentage of powerful Robusta and will take the skin off your tongue. The pure Arabica blend—the owners would rather die than reveal its make-up—is excellent, however, and you should buy a bag of it to go. Dark roasted yet smooth, it competes with some of Rome's best. Also sold are Ciamei's coffee liqueur, and good chocolates and cookies from outside suppliers.

VIA EMANUELE FILIBERTO 57 ✦ TEL: 06 704 95230
WWW.CIAMEI.COM ✦ CLOSED SATURDAY AFTERNOON
and SUNDAY ✦ *Near: in the Vittorio neighborhood, on the corner of Via Petrarca, 100 yards east of Piazza Dante*

CICCIOSCAKE

PARDON THE SILLY, PSEUDO-ENGLISH NAME. IF YOU ENJOYED THE *CROSTATA DI RICOTTA* AT POMMIDORO, the fine restaurant on the square around the corner from this small bakery, Ciccioscake is the reason. They supply it. As the name suggests, this is a neo-place that has tapped into the trendiness of the San Lorenzo area. It changed hands in 2005, after umpteen decades of normality, but the new, eager young owners still make the same delicious pastries, cookies, cakes, and ice creams (in warm weather only), and haven't even changed the minimalist shopfront. That makes it a true paradox: an authentic, faux-retro property. The ricotta cake really is excellent.

VIA DEGLI AUSONI 46 ✦ TEL: 06 495 7895
CLOSED MONDAY ✦ *Near: in the San Lorenzo neighborhood, 20 yards southeast of Piazza dei Sanniti*

CIPRIANI

THIS ARTISANAL COOKIE FACTORY AND PASTRY SHOP, TUCKED DOWN A QUIET SIDE STREET SOUTH OF PIAZZA Vittorio Emanuele II, is over 100 years old and still in the same family. You can smell its irresistible scent from blocks away. The shop's retail sales area is handsome but the size of two telephone booths lashed together, which can become problematic when local regulars waddle in to stock up. Behind and atop a glass counter are beautiful antique cookie tins, and inside two other display cases are tarts and cakes—all of them Roman classics fashioned by hand and cooked to perfection. Of

the dozen or more types of cookie, all of which are made with a mix of butter and margarine, the most popular are dove-shaped *colombe*, chocolate *stelline*, and aniseed or wine-flavored *ciambelline*. The *crostata* and *torta di ricotta* are crisp-crusted and heavenly. In a city full of helpful merchants, the sales staff are remarkably friendly and helpful, and appear to genuinely enjoy giving you tempting tastes of delicacies to get you hooked.

VIA BOTTA 21 ✦ TEL: 06 704 53930
CLOSED MONDAY MORNING *and* SUNDAY
Near: in the Vittorio neighborhood, between Via Poliziano and Via Guicciardini west of Via Merulana

DOLCI TENTAZIONI

THIS NEIGHBORHOOD PASTRY SHOP IS A GOOD PLACE TO TRY ALL THE ROMAN CLASSICS, FROM MINI *CROSTATE* to cookies, pastries, and breakfast rolls. You can knock back a coffee while you're at it. Directly across busy Piazza Tuscolo is rival **Pasticceria Valentini** (Piazza Tuscolo 1, Tel: 06 772 09677; open daily), which is slightly larger, and also has savory snacks, but is in all other ways comparable.

VIA GALLIA 230/234 ✦ TEL: 06 700 3421 ✦ CLOSED SUNDAY
Near: in the Appio/Tuscolo neighborhood, 30 yards west of Piazza Tuscolo

IL GELATO DI SAN CRISPINO

THIS IS ONE OF THE TWO OUTLYING-NEIGHBORHOOD SHOPFRONTS OF ROME'S CELEBRATED ICE CREAM MAKER (See area 3 listings, page 181).

VIA ACAIA 56-56A ✦ TEL: 06 704 50412
WWW.ILGELATODISANCRISPINO.COM
OPEN 11AM *to* MIDNIGHT ✦ CLOSED TUESDAY
Near: in the Appio/Tuscolo neighborhood, 100 yards south of Via Satrico

NICOLA PREZIOSO & FIGLI

FOUNDED IN 1872 AND STILL IN THE SAME FAMILY, THIS CLASSY COOKING TOOLS SHOP WAS REDONE A FEW years back and now has sparkling marble floors and sliding wooden panels which hide the scores of knives and specialized kitchen utensils stocked here. One typically Roman tool you can usually find at Prezioso is the *taglia puntarella*, a cutter especially designed for slicing *puntarella* chicory. Many of Rome's top chefs buy their knives here. Next door is Agata e Romeo, the highly regarded gourmet restaurant, which continues (misleadingly) to call itself an *hostaria*.

VIA CARLO ALBERTO 41/41A ✦ TEL: 06 446 5797
CLOSED SATURDAY AFTERNOON *and* SUNDAY
Near: 100 yards north of Piazza Vittorio Emanuele II

PALAZZO DEL FREDDO GIOVANNI FASSI

THE FASSI FAMILY OPENED ITS FIRST *GELATERIA* IN 1880 AND HAS BEEN IN THESE CAVERNOUS PREMISES since 1928. This was long Rome's top ice cream parlor, and is still a favorite hangout for families and the young, in part because it's spacious and friendly, in part because the prices are lower than at the newer rivals such as San Crispino or Al Settimo Gelo. What you'll find here and nowhere else are curious ice cream bars made to look like paving stones (*sanpietrini*) or *tramezzini* sandwiches (they're assembled from sliced *pan di Spagna* sponge cake, and filled with *bacio* ice cream with hazelnuts, or *frutti di bosco* red fruit ice cream). There are also classic ice cream sandwich cookies, *cassata*, and a dozen types of frozen cake, in addition to the scores of "normal" ice cream flavors. This is no longer a cutting-edge place, and doesn't claim to make totally natural ice creams with everything from scratch, but the quality is good, the atmosphere fun. Note: the US Army occupied the Palazzo del Freddo during and immediately after

World War Two, and a plaque attests to the American presence—as welcome liberators. Fassi franchise ice cream shops are found in a variety of places abroad.

VIA PRINCIPE EUGENIO 65-67A ✦ TEL: 06 446 4740
WWW.PALAZZODELFREDDO.IT ✦ OPEN NOON *to* MIDNIGHT
DAILY EXCEPT MONDAY ✦ *Near: between Via Bixio and Via Cairoli, 100 yards southeast of Piazza Vittorio Emanuele II*

PANELLA

LONG-ESTABLISHED AND WIDELY IMITATED, BACK IN THE MID-1990s PANELLA WAS THE FIRST BAKERY IN ROME to transform itself into a high-end boutique operation, with French-style bread racks, track lighting, and a wide selection of pizzas by the slice, plus breads baked in regional Italian styles. All are very good, a few are excellent. Coffee, soft drinks, and snacks are also sold and can be eaten on the premises or taken out.

VIA MERULANA 54-55 ✦ TEL: 06 487 2344
CLOSED THURSDAY AFTERNOON *and* SUNDAY; *in* AUGUST,
CLOSED SATURDAY AFTERNOON *and* SUNDAY
Near: in the Vittorio neighborhood, on Largo Leopardi, about 300 yards south of Santa Maria Maggiore

IL PASTAIO

THE CLASSIC HOLE-IN-THE-WALL FRESH PASTA SHOP, THIS FRIENDLY PLACE HAS BEEN SERVING NEIGHBORhood regulars for decades, and makes all the Roman and pan-Italian pasta shapes.

VIA LICIA 4 ✦ TEL: 06 772 04340 ✦ CLOSED MONDAY
AFTERNOON *and* SUNDAY ✦ *Near: 30 feet northwest of Piazza Epiro*

PASTICCERIA PACI

ONE OF SAN LORENZO'S LAST AUTHENTIC, OLD-FASHIONED, FAMILY-RUN BUSINESSES, PACI HAS BEEN around since the late 1950s and shows no signs of fatigue. In addition to the Roman classics, which are about as good as you can get anywhere, try the flaky apple-and-cream pastry squares with crunchy apple bits layered with crispy dough. The plump *bombole* with pastry cream are Rome's answer to the *krapfen* of northern climes.

VIA DEI MARSI 35 ✦ TEL: 06 495 7804 ✦ OPEN *from* 7:30AM *to* 8:30PM, CLOSED MONDAY ✦ *Near: in the San Lorenzo neighborhood, 30 feet northeast of Piazza dei Campani*

PIETRO ROSCIOLI

A NEIGHBORHOOD BAKERY AND MORE, WITH *RUSTICO*-FELL-OFF-THE-BACK-OF-A-TRUCK DÉCOR, PIETRO Roscioli is what the more famous Antico Forno Marco Roscioli near Campo de' Fiori was like only ten years ago, before Pierluigi and Alessandro Roscioli took over from their father Marco and modernized. Mustachioed Pietro Roscioli is Marco's brother, and looks and sounds startingly like him. It's no wonder that many of the same savory *rustici* turnovers and delicious, simple snacks, desserts, and breads you find at the celebrated Roscioli are also found here, plus cookies and groceries.

VIA BUONARROTI 46/48 ✦ TEL: 06 446 7146 ✦ CLOSED SUNDAY *Near: 50 yards southwest of Piazza Vittorio Emanuele II*

REGOLI

REGOLI HAS BEEN IN THE SAME TINY, UNPRETENTIOUS BUT ATTRACTIVE PREMISES SINCE 1916, WHEN UMBERTO and Narcisa Regoli began baking *maritozzi*, *stelle* (star-shaped brioches filled with whipped cream or zabaglione), *millefoglie*, *crostate*, *torte della nonna* (lemon-flavored pastry cream and pine nuts on a shortbread pastry shell), and *profiteroles*. Their son Ermete and his wife, Rita, were the second generation, and for the last 40 years it's been Carlo and his wife, Agnese. Their children Laura, Valentina, and Alessandro are gradually taking the reins. Amazingly, they work together happily, and make all the same exquisite desserts Umberto and Narcisa made 90 years ago, plus mini-tarts with wild strawberries from Lake Nemi, and *sfogliata romana*, a sweetened ewe's milk ricotta-filled turnover that's to die for. Don't miss it.

VIA DELLO STATUTO 60 ✦ TEL: 06 487 2812 ✦ CLOSED TUESDAY *Near: in the Vittorio neighborhood, 200 yards south of Santa Maria Maggiore*

SAID—ANTICA FABBRICA DEL CIOCCOLATO

FOUNDED IN 1923, BUT TOTALLY REMODELED AND TRANSFORMED INTO A MODISH BOUTIQUE AND CHOCOLATE-theme restaurant, this family-owned chocolate factory is a San Lorenzo institution. The chocolates are still made by hand, and run the gamut from simple bars to fancy filled chocolates with spices, chili, liqueurs, and more. The new spotlights, trendy display cases, and a dark cavernous interior give the remodeled space a surreal quality. Dazzled by the lights, sales staff in black outfits serve similarly dressed local trendies, and the occasional old timer who wanders in. There's a fledgling restaurant hidden away behind the sales area, in part of the factory complex, and it serves sui generis, creative cooking with a chocolate theme, including chocolate pasta.

VIA TIBURTINA 135 ✦ TEL: 06 446 9204 ✦ CLOSED MONDAY MORNING *and* SUNDAY ✦ *Near: in the San Lorenzo neighborhood, down an alley from Via Tiburtina, the main thoroughfare*

NON-TERROIR TOP OR TRENDY TABLES

AGATA E ROMEO

VIA CARLO ALBERTO 45 ✦ TEL: 06 446 6115
WWW.AGATAEROMEO.IT ✦ CLOSED WEEKENDS *and* 3 WEEKS *in* AUGUST ✦ EXTREMELY EXPENSIVE

ARANCIA BLU

VIA DEI LATINI 55/65 ✦ TEL: 06 445 4105
OPEN DAILY ✦ MODERATE

CRAB

VIA CAPO D'AFRICA 2 ✦ TEL: 06 772 03636 ✦ CLOSED MONDAY LUNCH, SUNDAY, *and* AUGUST ✦ EXPENSIVE *to* VERY EXPENSIVE

MOMA

VIA SAN BASILIO 42 ✦ TEL: 06 420 11798
CLOSED SUNDAY ✦ EXPENSIVE *to* VERY EXPENSIVE

ROBERTO E LORETTA

VIA SATURNIA 18 ✦ TEL: 06 772 01037
WWW.ROBERTOELORETTA.IT
CLOSED MONDAY *and* AUGUST ✦ MODERATE

UNO E BINO

VIA DEGLI EQUI 58 ✦ TEL: 06 446 0702
DINNER ONLY, CLOSED MONDAY *and* AUGUST
EXPENSIVE *to* VERY EXPENSIVE

VINARIUM

VIA DEI VOLSCI 103/107 ✦ TEL: 06 446 2110 ✦ CLOSED MONDAY *and* TWO WEEKS *each in* AUGUST *and around* CHRISTMAS
EXPENSIVE *to* VERY EXPENSIVE

REGIONAL RESTAURANTS

PUGLIA

TRAM TRAM

(see page 225)

SARDINIA

CRAB

(see Non-terroir Top or Trendy Tables, above)

SICILY

IL DITO E LA LUNA

VIA DEI SABELLI 51 ✦ TEL: 06 494 0726
OPEN DINNER ONLY, CLOSED SUNDAY *and* AUGUST
MODERATE *to* EXPENSIVE

CHAPTER 6

TESTACCIO, OSTIENSE, GARBATELLA

Until the postwar building boom of the 1950s, the Testaccio neighborhood marked the southeast edge of town, bounded by the austere curtain of the Aurelian city walls. Rough-and-tumble Testaccio's air smelled of blood around the clock, because the city's central slaughterhouse operated here from the 1890s to the 1970s. The name "Testaccio" is much older, however, coming from Monte Testaccio, a manmade hill composed entirely of broken terracotta amphorae accumulated for nearly 500 years, from the late Republic forward. Ancient Rome's dock and warehousing facilities for wine, oil, and grain—all transported in amphorae—were also at Testaccio, on the banks of the Tiber. As dead as the amphora dump of antiquity are Testaccio's blue-collar days. The neighborhood is gentrified. Former tenements make sought-after apartments for the upwardly mobile young Roman. Reconverted, the former slaughterhouse compound includes Macro Future, a contemporary art museum; a senior center; and the Città dell'Altra Economia–Eco Mercato, a fair-trade, organic, co-op supermarket, which might as easily be found on Manhattan's Upper West Side, or in Berkeley, California. (www.cittadellaltraeconomia.org). It is flanked by a well-meaning restaurant with organic food, and **Bio Caffè**, which serves healthful organic coffee from local roaster Pinci (www.pincicaffe.it). For now, the best thing about the fledgling complex, beyond its good intentions, is the view of Monte Testaccio's avalanches of shards.

The contrasts are many. Along the southwest side of the hill are half a dozen nightclubs. They've replaced the workshops that operated there, often in association with the slaughterhouse. Most of the horses that pull Rome's tourist carriages, plus the city's donkeys and donkey-carts, are kept in the stalls which have been here for centuries. One can only hope the noise from the nightclubs doesn't disturb the animals' sleep. An encampment of Rom (Gypsies) and their considerable herd of goats occupies the derelict, southern portion of the slaughterhouse compound, along the railway viaduct and city walls.

Broad and busy, Via Marmorata, the area's main street, runs along Testaccio's northern side, at the foot of the Aventine Hill, a fashionable, residential neighborhood remarkable for its lack of food and wine shops. At the southeastern end of the thoroughfare, facing the Ostiense area, rises the white marble pyramid of Caius Cestius, and the so-called Protestant cemetery or Campo Cestio, whose caretakers describe it as "the old cemetery for non-Catholic foreigners." The tombs of Keats, Shelley, and Goethe are found here (not to mention Gramsci, an Italian, but an avowed atheist).

Ostiense lies beyond the pyramid and the Aurelian walls and is home to the busy train station and subway stop of that name, capping the main road, Via Ostiense, which leads south ten miles or so to the coast at Ostia. The wholesale food markets of Rome were on Via Ostiense for nearly a century; in 2003 they relocated farther out of town, and the old market structure is being converted into a new food emporium, with theme restaurants. The former municipal gas and electricity generating facility across the street from it is now a spectacular museum of ancient art (officially, Museo Capitolino Centrale Montemartini). As in Testaccio, the gentrification of Ostiense and the abutting Garbatella area is nearly complete. An outdoor market still operates on the southern end of the neighborhood, in Via di San Galla.

Despite these changes, many popular trattorias are to be found in this area. The authentic ones still serve gutsy Quinto Quarto, the offal-based cooking from slaughterhouse days. Most of the neo-trattorias shy away from innards, preferring fish, truffles, and other fashionable, high-margin ingredients.

Mercato coperto di Piazza Testaccio was long the city's most authentic and dynamic covered market, because of the presence

PORCHETTA
DAL NORCINO

TESTACCIO

PANE PIZ
E DOLC
La Contea del Pane
CAFFE' DOLCIU

of the slaughterhouse, 200 yards south, and the nearby wholesale food markets. Faced by competition from supermarkets, Testaccio's *mercato coperto* holds on thanks to longtime customers. For the time being, its rough-and-ready atmosphere is intact. The century-old structure's iron uprights and glass roof are in dire need of repair; a planned remodel was delayed indefinitely. The city then announced that it was building a new market-cum-shopping mall, with an archeological "park" and parking garage, kitty-corner to the former slaughterhouse; it is expected to open in 2009–10. The ultimate fate of the historic covered market has yet to be decided. In the half-light seeping through the structure's grimy glass panes, several dozen food stands sell produce, meat, fish, and cheese of very good quality—Testaccio oldtimers are demanding customers. One pork butcher, **Dal Norcino** (at the market's northwest corner), specializes in *porchetta*, but also sells ready-to-eat pig's trotters, tails, and hard-to-find pork jerky. While the market is open (Monday through Saturday 7am to 1/1:30pm), the streets bordering the square fill with sellers of clothing, kitchen utensils, and household accessories, shoes, and sundry cleaning and other products—a colorful, festive scene.

RESTAURANTS AND TRATTORIAS

AGUSTARELLO

FOUNDED DECADES AGO BY AGOSTINO "AGUSTARELLO" COMMENTUCCI, AND NOW RUN BY HIS SON ALESSANDRO (and Alessandro's wife, Antonella), this simple, archetypal Testaccio trattoria has one large, unadorned room, and is frequented by a mix of older working class and trendy neighborhood clients. Tourists are few; the windows are frosted, to keep prying eyes out. The atmosphere is convivial, the service at times jocular. Typical Roman dishes such as *bucatini all'amatriciana*, *spaghetti alla carbonara*, and *saltimbocca alla romana* or *involtini* are reliably good. Many Quinto Quarto classics are available daily, including *pajata* with rigatoni, grilled or in tomato sauce, *animelle* (sweatbreads), *coratella*, and *coda alla vaccinara*. The wine list is longer than you'd expect, but you'll be equally well served if you order the house Sangiovese red, which comes in a bottle; the innocuous house whites from the Castelli Romani are also sold by the bottle.

VIA GIOVANNI BRANCA 98 ✦ TEL: 06 574 6585
CLOSED SUNDAY ✦ MODERATE
Near: Piazza Santa Maria Liberatrice, 2 blocks in from the Tiber

AL BIONDO TEVERE

THE BASILICA OF SAN PAOLO FUORI LE MURA IS A FEW HUNDRED YARDS SOUTH OF THIS HISTORIC trattoria, on a particularly unappealing stretch of Via Ostiense. Once through the gate and across the terrace and split-level dining room of Al Biondo Tevere, you will understand the establishment's main draw: an edgy view of the Tiber, industry, and housing projects. The other attraction is the family-style atmosphere and food. The Panzironi clan has been here for the better part of a century, and Roberto is the third generation to run the place. All the Roman classics are cooked up and served with competence, and the menu follows the Canonical calendar (fish, such as *baccalà*, on Friday). Pizza is also served, and is good and crisp-crusted, in the Roman tradition. The desserts are house made (the *panna cotta* is very good). The wine list features affordable, drinkable bottlings from Italy. Expect to lunch or dine in the company of professors from Rome university's architecturally egregious faculty #3, across the street, plus a mix of pilgrims, lost tourists, business people, and Romans heading to or from Ostia.

VIA OSTIENSE 178 ✦ TEL: 06 574 1172 ✦ CLOSED TUESDAY
MODERATE ✦ *Near: on the Tiber side of the thoroughfare, on the edge of Piazza Parco San Paolo*

BUCATINO

THIS ANIMATED, POPULAR OLD CORNER TRATTORIA RUN BY THE EXTENDED DI STEFANO AND DI CESARE families is justly known for its *bucatini all'amatriciana*, a dish which draws neighborhood regulars and a sprinkling of foreign tourists. Neither chic nor hip—the cloth-draped wooden tables are pushed close together, forcing you to eat cheek-by-jowl with other diners—Bucatino has so far been spared the attentions of the neo-Bohemians who have taken over nearby refurbished tenements. It serves all the delicious Roman classics, from crispy fried artichokes to creamy *zabaglione*; the rabbit *alla cacciatora* is pleasantly piquant. Quinto Quarto dishes include a very good, thick, sumptuous oxtail stew. The fish is fresh and affordable; the skewers of grilled calamari are blessedly simple. The ground-floor dining room, with its black-and-white photos, and the small sidewalk terrace, are to be preferred to the stuffy, echoing cellar rooms. The wine list offers many drinkable low- to medium-priced wines from around Italy. Reserve ahead and expect to have plenty of time to admire the décor; Bucatino is perennially packed. Even with a booking, you'll probably have to wait for your table.

VIA DELLA ROBBIA LUCA 84/86 ✦ TEL: 06 574 6886
CLOSED MONDAY ✦ MODERATE
Near: two blocks from the marketplace toward the Tiber River

CHECCHINO DAL 1887

OWNED AND OPERATED BY THE FIFTH GENERATION OF THE MARIANI FAMILY, CHECCHINO DAL 1887 IS justly recognized as Rome's premier Quinto Quarto restaurant, specializing in otherwise unfindable classic Roman dishes. The dining room is barrel-vaulted and built into the base of Monte Testaccio. With its wall sconces, starched white tablecloths, waiters in white livery, and a wine list with over 600 different bottlings, Checchino is atypical for the Quinto Quarto genre, which was long associated with the working class. Politicians, executives, and well-heeled tourists outnumber neighborhood clients. The luxurious setting and reverent silence makes the gutsy menu all the more surprising. One classic first course is *insalata di zampi*: flavorful, tender morsels of meat and nerve stripped from calves' trotters, braised, cooled, and set in aspic. The appearance, texture, and taste of the *zampi*—literally hooves—evoke delicate headcheese or braised beef cheeks. *Rigatoni con la pajata* are tubular pasta and milk-filled lamb intestines simmered in tomato sauce. The milk contained in *pajata* has been digested and is in the process of becoming curd. That explains the unexpected, delicious creaminess, ricotta-like consistency and flavor. Whereas other Roman restaurateurs buy innards from butchers or wholesalers, the Mariani brothers get Quinto Quarto direct from longtime "inside" suppliers. The daily deliveries from the Prenestina slaughterhouse across town arrive quivering. If served with rigatoni, *pajata* is cut into sections two to three inches long. They look like beige

Vienna sausages, and are cooked in the fresh tomato sauce. *Pajata* can also be prepared in tomato sauce in lengths of about eight inches, like sausages, and served without pasta. Another popular recipe is to sprinkle uncut coils with salt and pepper and grill them. The decisive yet delicate taste is reminiscent of liverwurst and ricotta. Until Mad Cow disease, veal *pajata* was more common than *pajata* from lamb. Veal *pajata* produced in the European Union is currently unavailable, not for health concerns, but because boilerplate EU laws passed after Mad Cow struck do not ponder its existence as a food for humans, and it is thown away. Romans are among the only Europeans who continue to eat it. Some chefs in Rome buy frozen *pajata*, imported from Argentina, but connoisseurs and most reputable restaurants disdain it, using suckling lamb intestine instead. Oxtails are equally difficult to procure in Europe (and America) for a different reason: oxen have largely disappeared. With rare exceptions, only steer, heifer, or cow tails are available. The younger the animal, the smaller the tailbone, the less flavorful the meat. The Mariani brothers get tails from mature cows and when possible oxen or bulls. Their *coda*—short for *coda alla vaccinara*—is without question among the most delicious in town. At the flick of a fork, hazelnut-sized chunks of meat easily detach from the tailbones. They are tender, moist, and rich without excess fattiness. The thick tomato sauce smells lightly of cloves, black pepper, and bitter chocolate, heightening the lusciousness of the meat. The celery stalks, still crunchy, provide a foil. Be sure to ask to visit Checchino's remarkable wine cellar, flanking the dining room. It was excavated 200 years ago or more from Monte Testaccio, and is ideal for storing the restaurant's excellent bottlings, with a constant temperature of 12-13 degrees C. Checchino is expensive, and formal, but the food, wine, setting, and service are exceptionally fine.

VIA DI MONTE TESTACCIO 30 ✦ TEL: 06 574 3816, 06 574 6318
WWW.CHECCHINO-DAL-1887.COM ✦ CLOSED SUNDAY, MONDAY *and* AUGUST ✦ EXPENSIVE *to* VERY EXPENSIVE
Near: facing the former slaughterhouse

DA OIO A CASA MIA

THIS NEIGHBORHOOD TRATTORIA WITH A PLEASANT IF NOISY SIDEWALK TERRACE SHADED BY OLD PLANE trees has an even more animated dining room filled with

Roman eaters who come here for the Quinto Quarto, which is always available, and other Roman classics. The veal roast wrapped with bacon is remarkable. The servings tend to be copious, the food salty and on the rib-sticking side, but flavorful and fresh. Popular and unpretentious, with raucous waiters and waitresses, it attracts few tourists. The wine list is minimal. Prefer the reliably quaffable, medium-priced bottles of Lazio and Umbrian wines.

VIA GALVANI 43-45 ✦ TEL: 06 578 2680
CLOSED SUNDAY ✦ INEXPENSIVE *to* MODERATE
Near: halfway between the ex-slaughterhouse and the Aventine

DAR MOSCHINO

FACING A PARK, ON AN EMINENCE, WITH A FOUNTAIN AND UMBRELLA PINES, DAR MOSCHINO IS SET IN ONE OF Rome's most unexpected, endearing, outlying neighborhoods, built entirely in the early 1920s in an ecclectic Liberty or Jungenstil style. Unfortunately it's difficult to reach, and fronted by blight. No matter. This premodern, family-run trattoria seems set in amber—or aspic. The white paper atop plastified, red-and-white checked tablecloths, the wooden tables, and brick vaults, and the black-and-white photos with a horse racing theme, haven't changed in years, though the place is a tiny bit nattier than it was back in the 1970s, when owner Franco "the fly" Perugini set up here. Neither has the menu changed: it is strictly Roman, and gutsy, from oxtails and tripe to *pajata* and *il padellotto*—a hearty panful of sautéed inner organs. The pasta courses—*gricia*, *cacio e pepe*, pasta with oxtail sauce—are also classic and good. Desserts are homey and house made, and include memorable sour cherry or ricotta *crostata*, and peaches poached in wine. Speaking of which, stick to the house wines. A final nostalgic touch: the coffee is served *in vetro*—in a glass.

PIAZZA BENEDETTO BRIN 5 ✦ TEL: 06 513 9473
CLOSED SUNDAY *and* AUGUST ✦ INEXPENSIVE *to* MODERATE
Near: due east and over the railway tracks from Piazza Parco San Paolo; half a mile south of the Gasometro; north about 250 yards of Via delle Sette Chiese

FELICE A TESTACCIO

FAMOUSLY MISNAMED, GRUMPY FELICE "HAPPY" TRIVELLONI IS NEARING 90. HE NO LONGER RUNS THE LONG dining room of this cult eating-place. He shows up regularly, however, to supervise, observing every detail from his table near the entrance. For decades, Felice delighted Roman insiders with his gruffness, often refusing to seat or serve certain clients, particularly those out-of-towners he thought might not eat a full meal, from artichoke *alla romana* via mountains of *carbonara* through oxtail stew to giant-sized dessert. His long-suffering son Franco, flanked by Maurizio, the family's third generation, are ostensibly in charge, and carry on the crabby tradition. Perhaps in view of the neighborhood's new yuppie population, or as a way of signaling a break with the tyrannical past, Maurizio revolutionized the décor, from standard, fluorescent-lit Roman-Spartan to an attempt at modishness. The exposed iron I-beams and frosted picture windows clash with the Torero-red of the tablecloths, however, and the less-than-trendy tile floor. Grumpy exclusivity is still *de rigueur*: the "We're full!" sign hangs at the ready behind the bar. Instead of snapping as Felice did at unwanted customers, the new team merely sets "reserved" plaques on each table, removing them with a remarkable lack of graciousness, once they've decided on the customers' fate. Why do people bother? A mix of nostalgia and wanting to be part of a hip scene. Felice's already considerable fame soared among yuppies when actor-director Roberto Benigni became a regular. His ode to Felice is framed and on the wall. Benigni fans, and those in search of a thrill, continue to fill the establishment. The food is the same as before, a roll call of reliably edible Roman classics. Skip the occasional out-of-region offerings (the pesto is truly forgettable). Stick to the Quinto Quarto and other safe bets. A word to the wise: get a Roman to reserve ahead for you.

VIA MASTRO GIORGIO 29 ✦ TEL: 06 574 6800

WWW.FELICEATESTACCIO.COM

CLOSED SUNDAY *and* AUGUST ✦ MODERATE

Near: one block southeast of the market, toward Via Galvani

LO SCOPETTARO

ANTONELLO FIORELLI IS THE SECOND GENERATION OF THE SAME FAMILY TO RUN THIS POPULAR, HIP, and slightly modish trattoria, among the first in the area to attract bigwigs, savvy tourists, politicos, and sports and media stars. The décor may be a bit studied by Testaccio standards, and the customers not necessarily neighborhood regulars, but the Roman classics are authentic and well prepared. The roast veal and pork shortribs *alla cacciatora*, stand out, for instance, and the house made desserts are delicious, particularly the *panna cotta*. The wine list is better than average; you'll find some good regional bottlings, and others from further afield.

LUNGOTEVERE TESTACCIO 7 ✦ TEL: 06 575 7912, 06 574 2408
OPEN DAILY ✦ MODERATE *to* EXPENSIVE
Near: on the riverside drive, directly across the Tiber from Porta Portese

PERILLI

PERILLI OPENED FOR BUSINESS IN 1911 AND IS IN THE SAME FAMILY. CAVERNOUS, LOUD, DUSKY, AND DAUBED with primitive murals, this cult restaurant is thronged lunch and dinner by voracious Roman families. The windows on Via Marmorata are frosted, to keep paparazzi and PIs from spying on customers. A kitchen buzzer and pay phone—mounted on a column, in the center of the dining room—ring insistently. The look and feel of the place is out of a Federico Fellini film (and guess what: Fellini was a regular). Third-generation owner Bernardino Perilli is large, jolly, and well past retirement age. He squeezes through tables piled with platters of braised artichokes or grilled lamb, bowls of tripe, mountains of *spaghetti alla carbonara* and daunting scoops of *tiramisù*. Bernardino and his middle-aged, remarkably slender son Maurizio, flanked by a cousin named Ferdinando, take turns serving clients. The Quinto Quarto, available daily, is very fresh, and comes from one of Rome's premier butchers, Annibale (near Piazza del Popolo, area 3). One hard-to-find appetizer from the variety-meats repertoire that you can occasionally enjoy here is *zinna fritta dorata*—deep-fried cow's teets. They look, and feel to the tooth, like fried octopus tentacles, but taste like veal cutlets. The grilled *animelle* veal sweetbreads—alias thymus glands—seasoned with salt and pepper, and served with a wedge of lemon, are sublime in their simplicity. The house *coratella*, made from the organs of very young milk-fed lamb, is dark, has unusual textures and rich aromas, and is a revelation. Desserts are rich and generously served. The service is cheerfully rough-and-ready. Roman families, local merchants, and tourists make up the clientele. Perilli's house wines arrive picturesquely in barrels, which are lashed to a truck, dispatched from the Castelli Romani. Despite the short distance, the wines don't travel very well. Order a bottle from a recognized Italian winery instead.

VIA MARMORATA 39 ✦ TEL: 06 574 2415
CLOSED WEDNESDAY *and* AUGUST ✦ MODERATE *to* EXPENSIVE
Near: a few shop fronts from E. Volpetti & C., on the southeastern (Ostiense) end of the road

VOLPETTI PIÙ

THIS IS THE SPARTAN, SELF-SERVICE *TAVOLA CALDA*/PIZZERIA OF THE VOLPETTI FOOD EMPORIUM DOWN the street—a great place to have a snack, pizza by the slice, or a full meal of simple Roman classics. The products are the same as at the Volpetti shop, and the quality is very high.

VIA A. VOLTA 8-10 ✦ TEL: 06 574 4306 ✦ INEXPENSIVE
Near: two shopfronts west of Emilio Volpetti & C.

ZAMPAGNA

ZAMPAGNA RINGS LIKE *CAMPAGNA*, AS IN COUNTRYSIDE, AND THIS VENERABLE TRATTORIA, IN THE SAME FAMILY since 1924, feels like a roadside inn lost in outer Lazio. A few tables stand on the sidewalk under an awning, presumably to lure students from the university 200 yards north, or pilgrims from the outsized basilica 150 yards south. Do as the local blue collar regulars do, and sit inside, where the handful of small tables are dressed in the standard green-and-white checked coverings, with butcher paper on top, and mismatched napkins. The house wine is from the Castelli Romani and is on tap, the menu follows the Canonical calendar, and is recited patiently by the slow-moving owners, who were literally born and weaned within these narrow but friendly walls. Cook Maria Elena claims that the house specialties are *fettuccine alla gricia*, *gnocchi alla romana* and *bucatini all'amatriciana*, but you'll also find *baccalà* with rich tomato sauce, veal done in a piquant *cacciatora*, and delicious *picchiapò*—chunks of boiled beef sautéed with onions, tomatoes, and a pinch of chili. The sour cherry *crostata* is delicious, and the strong, dark coffee is made by the *caffè* next door and walked over on a covered tray. Few Rome trattorias are more authentic or less expensive; no credit cards are accepted.

VIA OSTIENSE 179 ✦ TEL: 06 574 2306 ✦ CLOSED SUNDAY, EVENINGS *and* AUGUST; LUNCH ONLY ✦ INEXPENSIVE
Near: kitty-corner to the basilica of San Paolo fuori le Mura, facing Parco Schuster, near the corner of Via delle Sette Chiese

BREAD, CHEESE, FRESH PASTA, FRUIT ICES, GOURMET FOOD SHOPS, ICE CREAM, PASTRIES

ANDREOTTI

YET ANOTHER FAMILY-RUN OSTIENSE INSTITUTION FAMED, SINCE 1931, FOR ITS CLASSIC PASTRIES AND handmade, artisanal ice cream, has shed its likeable mom-and-pop skin, emerging as a trendy, 1960s revivalist, modish *caffè*, and snack-and-aperitif bar, where neighborhood oldtimers mix with Bobos, clubbers, university students, and lost tourists. Jazz or lounge music plays. Purplish fiber-optic lights glow above the white epoxy bar. The current scion of the pastry-making dynasty is Marco Andreotti, a consummate PR meister; luckily, his mother, pastry chef Miranda Andreotti, still runs the back shop areas, so this is more than just another Ostiense hot spot long on looks and short on excellence. The *millefoglie* and *crostata*, and gorgeous cakes and tarts, and even the old-fashioned ice creams (made in spring and summer only), are as good as ever. The Illy coffee is made and served with professional flair.

VIA OSTIENSE 54B ✦ TEL: 06 575 0773
CLOSED MONDAY *and* SUNDAY *in* JULY *and* AUGUST
Near: about 100 yards south of the Ostiense railway viaduct

CAFFÈ AVENTINO

TONY AVENTINE RESIDENTS MIX WITH BUREAUCRATS FROM FAO AT THIS CORNER *CAFFÈ* AND SNACK BAR ON busy Viale Aventino (here called Piazza Albania), halfway between the FAO and the Pyramid of Cestius. The coffee and pastries are good, and you might be glad to know of this spot, and its clean facilities, if you're hiking back into central Rome from the baths of Caracalla or the Circus Maximus.

PIAZZA ALBANIA 1/2 ✦ TEL: 06 574 3865 ✦ OPEN DAILY
Near: FAO headquarters and Circo Massimo

CHIOSCO TESTACCIO GRATTACHECCA

LOCAL SCHOOL KIDS LINE UP BY DAY, AND THE TRENDY NIGHTCLUBBING CROWD STAGGERS IN BY NIGHT: THIS seasonal sidewalk fruit ice stand stays open until the wee hours. The ices tend to be very sweet, especially the cola flavor. The best flavors are the simple fruit ones, especially the lemon.

VIA G. BRANCA, CORNER VIA FRANKLIN ✦ NO TELEPHONE
OPENING HOURS VARY, CLOSED OCTOBER *through* APRIL
Near: Piazza Santa Maria Liberatrice

EMILIO VOLPETTI & C.

EMILIO VOLPETTI & C. STARTED OUT IN THE 1970s IN THE PRATI AREA ACROSS TOWN, AS A HUMBLE *norcineria* selling salami and groceries, but soon evolved into the city's premier *gastronomia*. It moved to the Testaccio neighborhood in the early 1980s. The elder of two brothers, Emilio Volpetti, pioneered the concept of highest-quality products—*prosciutti* and *formaggi* in particular—and attentive personal service in a boutique setting. Younger, outgoing brother Claudio spent years traveling through Italy finding excellent producers of everything from mozzarella to tuna, truffles

to capers, hams to cheeses. The shop is hung with *guanciali*, platters of dried *porcini*, salamis, and chilis in the style of an old-fashioned Italian grocery, but like other luxury *gastronomie* is air-conditioned and clad in stone, beautifully appointed and maintained, and sparkling clean. The eye-catching displays are edible works of art. Though compact it has always had a disproportionately large staff, and it's Volpetti service and the advice provided by the expansive Claudio, Emilio, and his affable son Alessandro, and the highly professional *banchisti* behind the counter, that draw devoted regulars. Other *gastronomie* may be bigger and more lavish nowadays, but Emilio Volpetti & C. remains a top reference. The *corallina* salami, sold at Eastertide, is crafted especially for Volpetti by Maletti, in Modena, and is noticeably more tender, sweet, and full of pea-sized chunks of luscious fat than the *corallina* found elsewhere. The olive oil made by artisanal producer Bruno Battaglini in the Canino district near Lago di Bolsena is full-bodied and outstanding, and, in Rome, difficult to find; Volpetti has it. Ditto the excellent organic *orzo* (toasted barley) recognized by connoisseurs as a worthy beverage and not merely a coffee substitute. A decade ago, Claudio Volpetti started the craze in Rome for pecorino di fossa, an ewe's milk cheese from Tuscany produced in March. Volpetti has it made to order by the Caseificio Sociale di Manciano, a top co-op cheesemaker, picks it up in August, and ages it underground in rock grottoes at Venturi di Sogliano al Rubicone until November, when it goes on sale at the shop in Rome.

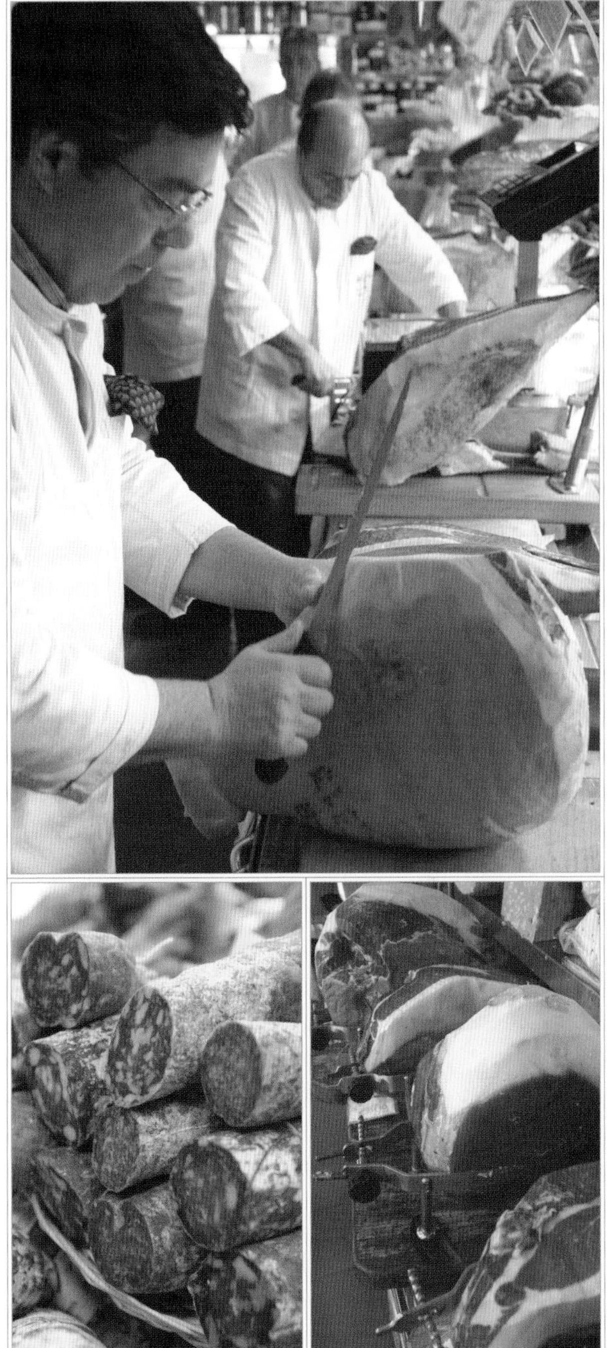

Many other hard cheeses sold here are aged in Volpetti's cellar in Rome. The mozzarella di bufala is some of the most flavorful anywhere, handmade at Caseificio Terra Felice in Cancello Arnone, in the province of Caserta; it arrives at Volpetti every Monday, Wednesday, and Friday morning (and sometimes on Tuesdays) and is often sold within minutes. All told, Volpetti displays about 150 cheeses from all over the world, and 150 types of salami and *prosciutto*. The take-out foods are delicious, especially the ready-to-dress chicory and salads. Baked goods include some of the city's most crisp yet unctuous *pizza bianca*, as well as irresistible tarts and pastries. A fine selection of Italian wines (among them, many of the Lazio region's best) is also sold. **Volpetti Più**, a cafeteria-style *tavola calda*, is two shopfronts away, toward the Testaccio market, and serves tasty classic Roman food (*supplì* stuffed with mozzarella, *arancini di farro*, artichokes *alla romana*, etc.) and many of the delicacies sold in the shop.

VIA MARMORATA 47 ✦ TEL: 06 574 2352
WWW.VOLPETTI.COM ✦ CLOSED SUNDAY
Near: facing the Aventine, between the Pyramid of Cestius and the covered market

FATAMORGANA

ONE OF THE PROPHETS OF *GELATO ARTIGIANALE NATURALE* IS MARIA AGNESE SPAGNUOLO, OWNER OF this second branch of her Fatamorgana mothership, whose original shop is in the Nemorense district (area 10). The ingredients are wholesome, and most come from small suppliers or growers in Italy; the methodology is rigorously non-industrial, and the results are often outstanding, but sometimes baffling. Simpler flavors such as sublime pistachio (made with fresh Bronte pistachios from Sicily), strawberry (from Terracina berries, in strawberry season only), or coffee (with freshly brewed Illy espresso) are flanked by a myriad of imaginative combinations, from Porto with pear and elderberry, to lime and celery, or tobacco-flavored chocolate, basil, cheese, and more. At least one new-fangled flavor is sublime: *pimento*. It merges dark chocolate with freshly ground black pepper and cloves. The consistency of the ice creams is pleasantly soft, almost like *semifreddi*, and they're rarely overly sweet or fatty. The shop has a modish, minimalist look that matches the neighborhood's new fauna, and the *gelati* are served in colorful plastic cups.

VIA OSTIENSE 36E ✦ TEL: 06 863 91589
WWW.GELATERIAFATAMORGANA.IT
OPEN DAILY NOON *to* MIDNIGHT
Near: about equidistant—250 yards—from the Ostiense railway viaduct and the Pyramid of Cestius, near the corner of Via dei Conciatori

GATTI—PASTA ALL'UOVO

SINCE THE 1960s, OWNER MASSIMO VENTURINI, A COLORFUL TESTACCIO CHARACTER, ALIAS IL GATTO (THE cat), has been turning out excellent fresh pasta at this small, old-fashioned, friendly shop. You'll find everything from agnolotti or cannelloni to fettuccine, ravioli, tagliolini, and tonnarelli.

VIA G. BRANCA 13 ✦ TEL: 06 574 0595 ✦ OPEN *from* 7AM *to* 1:30PM, *and on* FRIDAYS *and* SATURDAYS (*from* SEPTEMBER *to* MAY), ALSO *from* 5 *to* 7:30PM; CLOSED SUNDAY ✦ *Near: Via Marmorata*

ICE E COFFEE

THE NAME IS NEW AND, BECAUSE IT'S IN ENGLISH, TRENDY, BUT THIS CORNER FRUIT ICE STAND-CUM-*CAFFÈ* has sheltered hot, thirsty locals since 1903. It's still run by the same family, and the orange or sour cherry ices are as good as ever. Nowadays it's like a lantern to moths, catering to the pub-crawling, nightclubbing set, and stays open until at least 2am, serving shakes and alcoholic drinks alongside the old-fashioned treats.

VIA MARMORATA, CORNER LARGO MANUO GELSOMINI NO TELEPHONE ✦ OPENING HOURS VARY, CLOSED OCTOBER *through* APRIL ✦ *Near: facing the fire station, next to Testaccio's landmark Razionalista-style post office*

LA FROMAGERIE—CASA DEL FORMAGGIO

OWNED BY THE PALOMBI WINE SHOP NEXT DOOR TO IT (SEE PAGE 259), THIS UPSCALE DELICATESSEN is bursting with hundreds of great Italian and imported cheeses. The selection of ham and salami is also very good. You'll find specialty dry goods, jams, jellies, pickled or candied fruit, sauces, and more. Everything sold here can be eaten next door at Palombi, which not only sells wine and beer, but also doubles as a pleasant spot for a light lunch or aperitif.

PIAZZA TESTACCIO 35 ✦ TEL: 06 451 0992 ✦ CLOSED SUNDAY

Near: facing the Testaccio covered market on the north side

LINARI

FAMILY-RUN FOR SEVERAL GENERATIONS, FRIENDLY, UNGENTRIFIED, AND POPULAR WITH LONGTIME RESIDENTS, THIS big old Testaccio pastry shop, ice creamery, and *caffè* is a good place to throw back a strong, dark-roasted Marziali coffee, devour a delicious *cornetto* or two, or a Danish, or a cream- or jam-filled *bomba* donut (not to mention a classic *crostata*), and watch the locals interact. There are a few sidewalk tables, with views of an eyesore church, where you can take the air, but the real action is at the bar, where polished pros crank out the espresso with panache. The ice creams (available from late spring to early fall) are good, made with a mixer from the 1950s, and do not have the showy, sugary quality of other "artisanal" *gelati* dispensed in the neighborhood.

VIA NICOLA ZABAGLIA 9/A/B ✦ TEL: 06 578 2358

CLOSED TUESDAY *and* AUGUST

Near: kitty-corner to the church of Santa Maria Liberatrice

PANIFICIO PASSI

PASSI IS A LONG-ESTABLISHED, UNGENTRIFIED CORNER BAKERY IN A STRATEGIC LOCATION IN TESTACCIO, NEAR the market. It offers a wide selection of good Roman breads and excellent *pizza bianca*, but its real draw is *scrocchiarella*, a very crisp, very thin and wavey flatbread somewhat similar to Sardinian *carta da musica*. Few bakeries make *scrocchiarella*, and Romans will cross town to buy it here.

VIA MASTRO GIORGIO 87 ✦ TEL: 06 574 6563 ✦ CLOSED SUNDAY,

and SATURDAY AFTERNOON *in* JULY *and* AUGUST

Near: one block northwest of the Testaccio covered market

PASTA FRESCA MEA

ONE OF TWO REMAINING FRESH PASTA SHOPS IN THE TESTACCIO NEIGHBORHOOD, MEA HAS BEEN IN business since 1947 in the same small premises, turning out very good classics from the Roman (and pan-Italian) repertoire. Novelty is not in this shop's vocabulary, which is probably why the regulars keep coming, ensuring a high turnover and therefore fresh products. MEA is spartan. A simple glass display case out front holds trays of fettuccine, potato gnocchi, maltagliati (roughly cut strips, like pappardelle), quadrucci (tiny squares, for soup), ravioli, tagliatelle, and tonnarelli. Owner Pier Paolo Campeggiani was an employee for decades before taking over in 2004. The ribbon pasta is cut to order. Also sold are good, ready-to-fry *supplì*.

PIAZZA TESTACCIO 3 ✦ TEL: 06 575 0843
CLOSED THURSDAY AFTERNOON *and* SUNDAY
Near: across the street from the Testaccio covered market

L'URTO

LIKE ICE E COFFEE, THIS OLD (FORMER) *GRATTACHECCA* ICE STAND, LONG KNOWN AS NONNA GINA, HAS BEcome a nightclubber's hangout, with a small range of classic ices and just as many easy-to-drink, sweet, highly alcoholic beverages that Roman hipsters call "*shottini*," as in shots of liqueur. Stomach-filling snacks like crêpes are also served. The current name, L'Urto, means "crash" and is appropriate, particularly after midnight or around 5am, when shock victims stagger in from the clubs. The early evening hours instead offer a jovial, harmless atmosphere for those heading to or returning from a meal in the Garbatella/Ostiense area, or a visit to the nearby Centrale Montemartini ancient art museum.

VIA DEL PORTO FLUVIALE, CORNER VIA DELLE CONCE
NO TELEPHONE ✦ OPEN 24/7 *in* SUMMER, *from* 6PM *to* 6AM DAILY *the* REST *of the* YEAR ✦ *Near: in the Garbatella neighborhood, facing the Gasometro (former gas storage facility) along the railroad viaduct*

WINE AND WINE BARS

PALOMBI—L'OASI DELLA BIRRA

KNOWN FOR ITS AMAZING SELECTION OF EXCELLENT BEER—DEPENDING ON THE SEASON, UP TO 700 BEERS from 400 to 500 breweries, worldwide—Palombi is an atmospheric, cavernous old shop stuffed with other delights, including a vast array of wines. Mario Palombi always has bottlings from the top ten wineries of Lazio—Conte Zandotti, Castel de Paolis, Casale del Giglio, Santa Teresa, and others—plus fine wines big and small from other regions of Italy, and the world. Beer by the bottle and wine by the glass may be enjoyed at one of a handful of tables indoors or, better, on the sidewalk terrace facing the covered market. Here Palombi serves outstanding cheeses, good hams, and delicious snacks and finger foods, plus classic first courses, all made next door at the family's delicatessen, La Fromagerie (see page 256).

PIAZZA TESTACCIO 38-41 ✦ TEL: 06 574 6122
OPEN MONDAY *through* SATURDAY NOON *to* 1AM,
CLOSED SUNDAY *and* AUGUST
Near: facing the Testaccio covered market on the north side

NON-TERROIR TOP OR TRENDY TABLES

DOC

VIA BENIAMINO FRANKLIN 9 ✦ TEL: 06 574 4236
WWW.OSTERIADOC.IT ✦ MODERATE *to* EXPENSIVE

THE KITCHEN

VIA DEI CONCIATORI 3M ✦ TEL: 06 574 1505
WWW.THEKITCHENROMA.COM ✦ MODERATE *to* EXPENSIVE

CHAPTER 7

GIANICOLO, MONTEVERDE, TRASTEVERE

IL GIANICOLO—THE JANICULUM IN ENGLISH—IS A HANDSOME, HILLY DISTRICT THAT STRETCHES ALONG THE ridge behind Trastevere on the west side of the Tiber River. To the north is the Vatican. Monteverde lies south, while the immense Villa Doria Pamphili parklands begin a few hundred yards to the west. Only a handful of places to eat and drink are on the Gianicolo, which is primarily a pleasant place for a panoramic stroll. The famous belvedere, with a towering monument to Giuseppe Garibaldi in its center, has two kiosks. **Copacabana Café** is where you can shoot down a tarry espresso while taking in the view; nearby is the usual Roman refreshments stand selling not just overpriced bottle water but also the difficult-to-find *fusaie*—white lupins—and olives. You can get a decent coffee and a *cornetto*, and still enjoy a good, if lower, view, at **Bar Tasso**, on the gravel esplanade facing the upper exit of the children's hospital, Ospedale Bambino Gesù.

Trastevere wraps around the Gianicolo's eastern foot and is a large, disjointed neighborhood. It is directly across the Tiber River from Campo de' Fiori, the Ghetto, and Testaccio. The backbone of Trastevere is Viale di Trastevere, a wide, tree-lined boulevard. North of it is the liveliest, most crowded part of the district, while south of it you will find many quiet streets and squares. Trastevere was where Rome's Jewish community first settled in antiquity. Like the Ghetto, it is widely held to be one of the keepers of the flame of authentic Roman cooking. Though the neighborhood has changed a great deal in recent years, with an influx of street people and Rome's young party crowd, many traditional trattorias and pizzerias and a few long-established gourmet food artisans still thrive. Several classics of the Roman repertoire are identified with an "*alla trasteverina*" suffix, which suggests that they were invented or perfected here centuries ago. *Spinaci alla trasteverina* (spinach sautéed with raisins and pine nuts) and *pollo alla trasteverina* (chicken stewed with bell peppers, onions, and tomatoes) are merely the best known of many. As they do in the Ghetto, some residents continue to make homemade *coppiette* beef or horse jerky here, which, however, is not officially available in shops and restaurants, because of EU hygiene laws. A discrete request for *coppiette* can sometimes yield a delicious sample.

For a thousand years or more, a frenzied festival was held annually in Trastevere on June 24. For the last few centuries, the Festa de' Noiantri, which means "Our Festival" and is meant to underscore how different Trasteverini are from other Romans, has been held for eight days in the second half of July. It brings even more animation, more musicians, jugglers, and fire-eaters, and more stands selling beads, crafts, and knickknacks, to Trastevere's already chaotic labyrinth of medieval alleys and piazzas.

....

Above Trastevere on the hillside, south of the Gianicolo, the Monteverde neighborhood seems staid by comparison. Its wide, winding, or grid-block streets are lined with handsome apartment buildings, villas, and gardens, and while the number of food-related businesses is small, several are worth a detour. Monteverde is actually two neighborhoods side-by-side: Monteverde Vecchio and Monteverdo Nuovo—old and new. The age of the buildings, and the pedigrees of the inhabitants, reflect the nomenclature. Monteverde Vecchio is charming, with a nice outdoor market, **mercato rionale di Via G. B. Nicolini**, running several blocks south from Via Enrico Torre, and a main shopping street, Via Barrili, with several pleasant *caffè*, pastry shops, bakeries, and groceries. The newer Monteverde Nuovo has larger, more modern buildings, is less alluring, and has few remarkable food addresses. However, on its western edge lies **mercato rionale di Piazza di San Giovanni di Dio**, and Via Federico

Ozanam, a fine shopping street (see area 10 for details).

Mercato rionale di Piazza di San Cosimato in the lively, jigsaw neighborhood north of Viale di Trastevere occupies the better part of a triangular piazza. It is located about 250 yards south of Trastevere's main piazza, Santa Maria in Trastevere. In 2005-2006, the market's rundown stalls were replaced by postmodern structures that might as easily be on a South Pacific island, and the piazza was repaved with flagstones. When the new market reopened for business, it was smaller in size and less diverse than before, though some of the same greengrocers, butchers, fishmongers, and grocery owners came back. Like much of Trastevere, Piazza di San Cosimato is one-part gentrified, two-parts seedy, a contemporary court of miracles.

Another area market, the tatty but lively **mercato rionale di Via Ettore Rolli**, hugs an abandoned train viaduct south of the sprawling Porta Portese flea market and is unknown to those from outside this blue-collar bastion.

RESTAURANTS AND TRATTORIAS

AUGUSTO

A DOZEN TABLES ON A SMALL SQUARE, WHICH IS STILL A PARKING LOT AND ONLY PARTLY GENTRIFIED, SIGNAL the presence of this beloved Trastevere trattoria. It's been in the same family since 1954, and though the current owner (Sandro) and his sister (Anna) are young and appear cut from the same blue jeans cloth as the neighborhood's new Bobo

residents, they've left things largely unchanged and unadorned. There are linoleum-topped wooden tables, cane chairs, and zigzag patterned tiles on the floors. Cheap, cheery, and full of regulars, Augusto also attracts jazz and folk musicians who show up with their acoustic guitars and basses, whisking the hoarse clientele back several decades. Clients are hoarse because the decibel levels can get very high. Certainly, there are novelties at Augusto: you can now see into the kitchen, if you're seated at the rear of the single, small dining room. But out of that kitchen come the same delicious *bollito*—boiled meats served with condiments—and *brasato*—beef stewed in wine, a Roman version of the Piedmontese classic. There are artichokes and anchovies, *amatriciana* and *cacio e pepe*, *baccalà*, rabbit *alla cacciatora* and *pollo alla trasteverina* with sweet peppers. The desserts are simple and good, especially the *tiramisù*. Stick to the quaffable house wines and you'll be all right. Note: no credit cards are accepted, but the prices are astonishingly low.

PIAZZA DE' RENZI 15 ✦ TEL: 06 580 3798 ✦ CLOSED SATURDAY NIGHT, SUNDAY *and* AUGUST ✦ INEXPENSIVE
Near: on the corner of Vicolo de' Renzi and Via della Pelliccia, 100 yards north of Santa Maria in Trastevere

CHECCO ER CARRETTIERE

THE PORCELLI FAMILY HAVE RUN THIS CELEBRATED TRASTEVERE INSTITUTION SINCE THE PRE-WAR YEARS, when Francesco, nicknamed Checco, actually rattled across Rome and into the Castelli Romani several times a week in his wooden *carretto*—wagon—and returned laden with wine. Displayed like a memento mori, his *carretto* is now in the lobby of this labyrinthine restaurant, which fills several dining rooms, and is flanked on one side by a bar/pastry shop/ice creamery, and by an *osteria* on the other side. All are owned and operated by the Porcelli. There are wine barrels in the cellar, which is visibile through the glass flooring in the *osteria* area. The requisite braids of garlic, bushels of artichokes, and decorative ceramic plates adorn the wood paneling, exposed timbers, and wooden buffets. If Walt Disney had been Roman, he might've invented Checco er Carrettiere to go on Main Street, Italy. The thing is, Checco looks phony, and it sometimes feels phony, but it's authentic. The family and staff are here daily, plucking and trimming the artichokes, baking the pastries, and making the ice cream. What distinguishes this from other Trastevere trattorias is the high degree of professionalism, the polished, wanton kitsch, and the excellence of the ingredients used. The food is very good, no matter what is said of the touristy experience. You won't find many Romans here anymore—it's too expensive, for one thing. But plenty of out-of-town Italians (and an international mix of well-heeled tourists) keep the tables filled. Stick to the Roman classics, from anchovies or offal to oxtails and *tiramisù*, and you'll have a fine meal. The wine list is long, but the house red and white, in keeping with family traditions, are perfectly good.

VIA BENEDETTA 10/13 ✦ TEL: 06 580 0985
WWW.CHECCOERCARETTIERE.IT ✦ OPEN DAILY *in* SPRING, SUMMER *and* FALL, CLOSED MONDAY *in* WINTER
EXPENSIVE *to* VERY EXPENSIVE ✦ *Near: right behind Piazza Trilussa*

DA ENZO

LIKE OTHER ARCHETYPAL FAMILY-STYLE TRASTEVERE TRATTORIAS, DA ENZO HAS A HANDFUL OF TABLES OUTside on an atmospheric alleyway, this one south of Viale di Trastevere and relatively quiet. The single, simply decorated dining room of this century-old favorite packs out at lunch, when the tables are covered with thick white paper, and blue-collar workers vie with local residents for a spot. At dinner, the noise level goes down marginally, the white tablecloths come out, and the menu and wine list increase in length. Fried artichokes and *baccalà* rank high among the perennials to try here day or night, plus all the Roman weekly wheel classics, not to mention ricotta- and spinach-filled ravioli, and the house specialty: pasta elbows with puréed bell peppers and sausage meat. The *ossobuco* with peas, the grilled lamb, the roast veal, and milkfed lamb, and even the meatballs with zingy lemon zest, are very flavorful. Teodoro Filippini does the cooking and his wife Tiziana makes the desserts—from perfect *crostata* and *torta di ricotta* to luscious *tiramisù* and *torroncino semifreddo*. Their teenage daughter is responsible for the cat-related artwork on the walls and shelves. She also helps in the dining room, lending an endearing touch to an authentic Roman experience.

VIA DEI VASCELLARI 29 ✦ TEL: 06 581 8355 ✦ CLOSED SUNDAY *and in* AUGUST ✦ INEXPENSIVE ✦ *Near: on the southeastern end of Trastevere, between Via dei Salumi and Via dei Genovesi*

DA GILDO

THERE ARE OLDER, BETTER-KNOWN PIZZERIAS IN TRASTEVERE—NOT TO MENTION SEVERAL VERY RECENT ones, including Bir & Fud, mobbed by a modish crowd—but unsung Da Gildo has been making reliably very good pizzas, at lunch and dinner, since 1958. There's a wood-burning oven, and a comfortable, simple dining room through whose large windows you can observe the neighborhood fauna. All the classics come out of the oven piping hot and are delivered efficiently, which is not always the case in Trastevere, and there's an unusual but only-in-Rome house specialty found here: pizza topped with Jewish-style fried artichokes. If you're up for more than mere pizza, the classic pastas and vegetable side dishes are delicious, ditto the desserts, equally classic and all house-made. The clientele is a mix of tourists and regulars.

VIA DELLA SCALA 31/A ✦ TEL: 06 580 0733
CLOSED THURSDAY *and* AUGUST ✦ INEXPENSIVE
Near: facing Porta Settimiana

DA GIOVANNI

OFTEN UNNOTICED BY PASSERSBY, WHO ARE GENERALLY EAGER TO GET OUT OF THE WAY OF SPEEDING police cars and paddy wagons on this, the most unappealing stretch of street in Trastevere, Da Giovanni is a neighborhood institution, in the same family since 1951. There's one small, vaulted room of the most basic kind, made cozy by wine bottles and wooden tables. Don't be put off by the "English" menu, which is posted outside. Slightly surreal, it is titled "Lista on the week" and features "roast troux" and "squid in tomato sauce with pease." Luckily, you needn't take English lessons from the rough diamond of an owner. In addition to the weekly wheel of well-made Roman classics, you can get deliciously simple roast fish whenever it's fresh, or spaghetti with lightly spicy tuna and tomato sauce, usually served on Friday (and always at Christmastide). There's often only one dessert made per day—a classic. You might want to reserve a portion ahead, since Da Giovanni fills up with locals, turnkeys from Regina Coeli, students, and intrepid tourists, sometimes turning the tables several times at lunch and dinner. That's why certain dishes, especially desserts, tend to disappear before you can get to them. The house wines are typical Castelli Romani in red or white, but there's also a surprisingly long and decent wine list—surprising because Da Giovanni is one of the cheapest trattorias in Rome, an amazing bargain. Note that lunch starts at 12:15pm, a good time to show up (or better yet, to reserve), because you're sure to be able to order everything you want to eat.

VIA DELLA LUNGARA 41A ✦ TEL: 06 686 1514
CLOSED SUNDAY *and* AUGUST ✦ VERY INEXPENSIVE
Near: 200 yards north of the botanical gardens, 300 yards south of the Vatican; Rome's main prison, Regina Coeli, is practically next door

DA OLINDO

THIS LITTLE OLD FAMILY RUN TRATTORIA, ON A BACK STREET AT THE BASE OF THE GIANICOLO, HAS BEEN around for 60 years. It's the closest thing to eating at home—a modest home—that you'll find these days in Trastevere, and reminiscent of nearby Sora Lucia before Lucia died and her young nephew took over. Da Olindo starts serving at 7:30pm, which is the best time to show up (since the crowds grow thicker as the evening goes on, and the service is likely to be cordial but unrushed in the extreme). There's a tiny outdoor terrace, with tables cheek-by-jowl fronting the building's pink façade. When you step inside the entrance area, you can see right into the kitchen, but it's not the fancy San Francisco/New York/Sydney-style open kitchen. It's tiny and cluttered and how anything good can come out of it is a mystery. But good things do, from the classic *carciofi alla romana* to the perfect *cacio e pepe* or *amatriciana*, the *saltimbocca* or *involtini* and the grilled lamb or stewed chicken. Skip the Bindi desserts—they come from Milan and are best left in the refrigerator case that occupies part of the entrance room. The house-made spoon sweets and *crostata* are perfectly good, as is the house wine. No credit cards are accepted.

VICOLO DELLA SCALA 8 ✦ TEL: 06 581 8835 ✦ DINNER ONLY, CLOSED SUNDAY *and* AUGUST ✦ INEXPENSIVE *to* MODERATE

Near: 100 yards west of Piazza della Scala

DAR CORDARO

DAR CORDARO DOES NOT LOOK LIKE A PROMISING ADDRESS—A FORMER ROPE FACTORY BUILT UP against the city walls, with a gas station/garage next door. You step through Porta Portese, face right and sigh. But Dar Cordaro has nothing at all to do with the garage or flea market, which is held when the trattoria is closed, and is anything but seedy. Though a trattoria, it's nicely furnished, without kitsch; there's plenty of light; and linen tablecloths are draped on the tables. The extended Dori family has run Dar Cordaro with courteous professionalism since 1922. The weekly wheel of Roman specialties is featured, and it's a good idea to follow the offerings. Skip the house appetizer and go right for the pasta—*cacio e pepe*, *amatriciana*, *gricia*, *carbonara*, gnocchi—and segue with meat loaf, tripe, *involtini* with carrots and celery, oxtails and, if you have room, a vegetable side. The house specialty vegetable is *fagioli con la scarola*—beans and escarole—an old fashioned recipe you won't encounter elsewhere. The chocolate desserts are rich, you might even say rib-sticking, but there's usually a nice, light lemon sorbet on offer too. The wine list isn't: you have a choice of red or white house wine on tap, or house wine in a bottle. Drunk in moderation, none will harm you. Expect to dine with a mixed crowd of Romans and savvy tourists. Reserve ahead; Dar Cordaro gets very busy.

PIAZZALE PORTUENSE 4 ✦ TEL: 06 583 6751
CLOSED SUNDAY *and* MONDAY ✦ MODERATE
Near: by the Porta Portese city gate where the Sunday flea market is held

IL CORTILE

THE MONTEVERDE VECCHIO NEIGHBORHOOD ISN'T EASY WHEN IT COMES TO RESTAURANTS. THIS SPLIT-level, stylish, upscale spot is good if you're exploring the area or shopping at the nearby open market. Though the menu includes many pan-Italian dishes, you can happily eat an antipasto composed of grilled vegetables and such like, displayed temptingly downstairs, and order very good fried artichokes, a classic pasta dish, and a simple main course such as *saltimbocca* or grilled fish. The desserts range from spoon sweets like *tiramisù* or *panna cotta*, to lighter seasonal sweets with fresh fruit. The wine list is adequate, the service professional, the atmosphere clubby.

VIA ALBERTO MARIO 26 ✦ TEL: 06 580 3433 ✦ CLOSED SUNDAY NIGHT, MONDAY, *and* AUGUST ✦ MODERATE *to* EXPENSIVE
Near: on the corner of Via Felice Cavallotti, near Monteverde Vecchio's open market

IVO A TRASTEVERE

UNCHANGED FOR THE LAST 50 YEARS, THIS CULT PIZZERIA IS THE TRASTEVERE EQUIVALENT OF DA Baffetto, near Piazza Navona (area 2). Standing in line is part of the experience, as are the perennial stuffed olives, *bruschetta, supplì* and other good *antipasti* to keep you going while you wait. There are classic pastas and vegetables sides, not to mention 35 to 40 pizzas on offer. They range from the sublime (*alla romana, margherita*) to the ridiculous (with caviar or Nutella). Stick to the beer or Castelli Romani wine, both on tap.

VIA SAN FRANCESCO A RIPA 158 ✦ TEL: 06 581 7082
DINNER ONLY ✦ CLOSED TUESDAY ✦ VERY INEXPENSIVE
Near: 150 yards south of Piazza San Callisto, 150 yards east of Piazza di San Cosimato

PARIS

THE NAME HAS NOTHING TO DO WITH PARIS, FRANCE. THE FOUNDER OF THIS 90-SOME-YEAR-OLD LANDMARK, celebrated for its upmarket, traditional Roman-Jewish cuisine, was named Silvano Paris. It's no longer in the Paris family, but is family-run. The contrast between Paris and the scruffy, beloved bar/ice cream shop/hangout next door, Bar San Calisto, could not be more complete. Both places are fronted by a group of more or less permanent local boozers, who pitch their nomadic settlement on the edge of the square, which is really a glorified parking lot, and spend much of the year panhandling and strumming guitars, surrounded by lazy dogs. This is what you behold if you take a table on the terrace of Paris. The interior is cozy, with a fireplace in the front dining room, and the requisite clutter of objects and art on walls and shelves. There's air conditioning, so in hot weather the dining rooms are comfortable. Most of all, the service is professional and courteous, the wine list long, with plenty of good bottlings, and the unchanging Roman menu features all the classics, all of them very good, some excellent, from the *carne secca* beef *prosciutto* on up. The fried artichokes or other fried vegetables, and the *carbonara*, are remarkable, and the fried veal meatballs are outstanding. The potato gnocchi and pasta are house made, ditto the rich and creamy classic desserts. Yes, you'll pay more here than in many other Roman places for this style of cooking, but the quality makes the premium worth paying.

PIAZZA DI SAN CALISTO 7/A ✦ TEL: 06 581 5378
CLOSED SUNDAY DINNER *and* MONDAY ✦ EXPENSIVE
Near: 100 yards from Piazza Santa Maria in Trastevere

PIZZERIA AI MARMI—L'OBITORIO PANATTONI

ASK FOR PIZZERIA AI MARMI—THE OFFICIAL NAME—AND PEOPLE WILL SHRUG. THAT'S BECAUSE EVERYone in Rome refers to this longtime cult pizzeria as Panattoni or L'Obitorio. The first reference is to the name of the family that owns it, the second means "the morgue." Step inside and you'll know why. The tabletops are marble, with paper mats and napkins atop them, and the clinical, tiled interior is downright chilling. That's fine in hot weather, but in hot weather you'll want a table outside on the wide sidewalk, where trams rattle past, and crowds walk by until the small hours. Panattoni is open until 2am, and has some of the crispiest classic pizza in Rome, plus very good garlicky *bruschetta*, plump *supplì*, fried salt cod fillets, and stuffed zucchini flowers, and hearty dishes like giant Tuscan beans with sausages and pork rinds. The desserts are homey and simple, the beer and wine are pulled from a tap. Expect to wait in line.

VIALE DI TRASTEVERE 53-55 ✦ TEL: 06 580 0919 ✦ DINNER ONLY, CLOSED WEDNESDAY *and* AUGUST ✦ INEXPENSIVE

Near: 100 yards south of Piazza Sidney Sonnino

BREAD, CHEESE, FRESH PASTA, FRUIT ICES, GOURMET FOOD SHOPS, ICE CREAM, PASTRIES

ANTICA CACIARA TRASTEVERINA

DON'T MISS THIS HISTORIC ADDRESS: FILLING THE DISPLAY CASES FACING THE SIDEWALK ARE HUGE loaves of country bread and baskets of freshly made ricotta. Strung from the threshold are pork jowls. Drum-sized rounds of pecorino romano are stacked just inside. Friendly, soft-spoken Roberto Polica and his equally polite wife Anna Chieruzzi run Antica Caciara, which has been in his family

PROVATE IL
VERO
PECORINO
ROMANO

SALSICCE
FRESCHE
€ 9,00
PRIMO SALE
€ 13,00
FONTINA

since 1900. The third generation of Policas to work here, he started at age 13, in 1962, and comes in every day but Sunday, which he usually spends traveling around, picking up merchandise. The couple's day typically starts at 4:45am and ends around 9pm. Why do they do it? They're passionate, love food, and love their jobs. Their jobs are their life, a source of joy and satisfaction, not oppression. Everything in this exquisitely old-fashioned cheese shop/deli bears the marks of the artisans who make it—nothing is standardized or predictable. The pecorino and ricotta come from Roberto's uncle's cheese factory in the suburban Boccea neighborhood. The salt-free *pane sciapo* bread is made for Antica Caciara by Artema in the Castelli Romani, and is delivered early each morning. The *guanciale* comes from small, trusted producers in Lazio and Umbria. There are hams and salamis, artisanal pastas, dry mushrooms, and a wide variety of fresh or aged cheeses, including excellent burrata from Puglia. Antica Caciara is a Trastevere touchstone.

VIA SAN FRANCESCO A RIPA 140A ✦ TEL: 06 581 2815
WWW.ANTICACACIARA.IT ✦ CLOSED SUNDAY ✦ *Near: 150 yards southeast of Piazza di San Cosimato, 50 yards northwest of Viale di Trastevere*

BAR GIANICOLO

A HANDFUL OF GREEN PLASTIC TABLES AND CHAIRS, DRAPED WITH BLINDING ORANGE TABLECLOTHES, FACE the entrance to the Villa Sciarra park and the Porta San Pancrazio city gate on busy Piazzale Aurelio. Inside this welcoming neighborhood *caffè*, snackbar, and all-around hangout

are knick-knacks, artwork, and graphics whose theme is Italian Risorgimento hero Giuseppe Garibaldi. He and his 1,000 valiant men not only helped unite Italy in the 1860s; Garibaldi was also key to freeing Rome from the papal grasp, and opening the walled Vatican City to the world. Many of the heroic events in this struggle took place hereabouts. Sergio Meloni and Fabrizia Coccia have been running Bar Gianicolo for the last 30 years or so, and have made it the focal point for artists and intellectuals, students and professors, without a hint of persnickety snobbery. Poet Joseph Brodsky sang the praises of the bar (and Piazza San Pancrazio), and Sergio and Fabrizia will proudly show you the lines he penned. The Negresco coffee served here may be stronger than some like, but the *pizza bianca* sandwiches (with mozzarella, anchovies, zucchini flowers, and arugula) and the tiny finger sandwiches meant to be eaten in a bite, the simple pasta dishes and salads, are remarkably good.

PIAZZALE AURELIO 5 ✦ TEL: 06 580 6275
CLOSED MONDAY ✦ *Near: facing Porta San Pancrazio city gate*

DA SAVERIO AL N. 1

THIS OTHERWISE UNREMARKABLE *CAFFÈ*, WITH A PLEASANT OUTDOOR TERRACE, IS REMARKABLE BECAUSE IT serves the excellent pastries of Checco er Carrettiere. The establishment's owner is Stefania Porcelli, who's also part-owner of the celebrated restaurant and pastry and ice cream shop 200 yards away.

VICOLO DELLA SCALA 1 ✦ TEL: 06 583 32008 ✦ CLOSED WEDNESDAY
Near: on the northwest side of Piazza della Scala

DOLCI DESIDERI PASTICCERIA GELATERIA

ATOP THE PLATEAU IN MONTEVERDE VECCHIO, THIS UPSCALE NEIGHBORHOOD BAKERY AND ICE CREAM shop makes all the Roman and Italian classics, including cakes, tarts, and mini-tarts; in season don't miss those with exquisite tiny strawberries from Lake Nemi. The ice creams are old-fashioned and luscious.

VIA A. G. BARRILI 60/66 ✦ TEL: 06 589 7709 ✦ OPEN DAILY
Near: in Monteverde Vecchio, 1 block west of the open market

I DOLCI DI CHECCO ER CARETTIERE

CHECCO ER CARRETIERE, THE RESTAURANT, IS FLANKED BY THIS SMALL PASTRY SHOP AND BAR, WHICH MAY be crowded and short on charm, with no place to sit, but has remarkably good tarts, *crostata*, and *cornetti*. The coffee is the best pure-Arabica blend made by local roaster Mondicaffè, and is also good. The handmade ice creams are some of the best in Trastevere, especially the fresh fruit flavors.

VIA BENEDETTA 7 ✦ TEL: 06 581 1413
WWW.CHECCOERCARETTIERE.IT ✦ OPEN DAILY *in* SPRING, SUMMER, *and* FALL, CLOSED MONDAY *in* WINTER

FIOR DI LUNA GELATO E CIOCCOLATO

LOCATED IN THE NOISIEST, MOST CROWDED PART OF TRASTEVERE, THIS SMALL, TAKE-OUT-ONLY ICE CREAM and chocolate shop opened here recently, though it was already in business in an outlying area back in 1994. The wooden shelves are stacked with fair trade honey and chocolate—one of the shop's ethical, organic specialties. Distinct cocoas are used here in the ice creams and to fashion chocolate bars, ingots, and tablets: pure Criollo; or Criollo-and-Trinitario from Madagascar, Venezuela, Dominican Republic, and Equador. The recipe used to make the chocolates is from the 1500s and was devised by Spanish nuns in Mexico. The ingredients are simple: pure, organic cocoa, and pure, unrefined cane sugar, and that's it. There's no added butter or fat. The result is grainy, almost granular, bittersweet, and with a vaguely medicinal yet marvelous flavor. Using these ingredients, Fior di Luna makes five different dark chocolates, two milk chocolates, and one white chocolate. The chocolates and ice creams with vanilla beans are wildly good: "friends" of the shop bring in the beans fresh—not dried—direct from Mauritius. The ice creams are outstanding, though the texture and appearance give them a homemade feel not everyone loves. There's no powdered or concentrated milk (the milk-powdering process was perfected "only" in 1842, and is therefore recent, and an unwelcome shortcut, in the owners' view). Fior di Luna uses exclusively organic milk from the Agro Romano district south of the city (Latte Sano is the brand name). The hazelnuts that go into that flavor are of the Tonda Gentile variety from the Langhe in Piedmont, the pistachios are of the Smeraldo variety and come from Bronte, in Sicily; the plump pine nuts are from the Parco Migliarino San Rossore abutting Pisa. All the nuts used here are bought raw and toasted for Fior di Luna by a small, specialized firm based in northern Italy. No semi-processed nut pastes are used. As the owners go out of their way to explain, they don't make Roman or Italian but rather Mediterranean ice creams, meaning they use no eggs, except in the *crema* flavor, and no dairy products in the fruit flavors, which contain only fresh fruit, water, and raw cane sugar. Happily, the results are not only ethical, organic, and well-intentioned—they're delicious.

VIA DELLA LUNGARETTA 96 ✦ TEL: 06 645 61314
OPEN DAILY NOON *to* MIDNIGHT (*until* 1:30AM *in* SUMMER)
Near: three blocks south of Piazza Santa Maria in Trastevere

FRONTONI

THIS OLD, FAMILY-OWNED FORMER GROCERY HAS EVOLVED INTO A SPRAWLING PIZZERIA, *CAFFÈ*, AND snack bar, catering to the tourist and commuter trade—the #8 tram stops out front. Surprisingly, sacks of fresh coffee beans are still roasted on site by the somewhat surly staff, and the 100-percent Arabica blend is very good. The bar blend has a little too much Robusta in it for those with sensitive palates, and packs a tremendous caffeine punch. It's worth noting that this is the only coffee-roasting establishment still operating in Trastevere.

VIALE DI TRASTEVERE 52 ✦ TEL: 06 581 2436
WWW.FRONTONI.IT ✦ OPEN 9AM *to* 11PM MONDAY *through* SATURDAY, CLOSED SUNDAY MORNING
Near: 200 yards southwest of Piazza di San Cosimato, on the corner of Via di San Francesco a Ripa

IL MARITOZZARO

THE AGOSTINI FAMILY HAVE RUN THIS CORNER *CAFFÈ* FOR DECADES, AND ARE FAMOUS FOR SERVING SOME of the best *maritozzi* in Rome, the kind that look like old-fashioned sweet buns and are split open and filled with fresh, lightly sweet whipped cream. The *maritozzi*, *cornetti*, and *lieviti* aren't made on the premises any longer, but rather in a nearby pastry factory. This out-of-the-way address is worth seeking out if you happen to be at the street market, or have strayed south of the giant Porta Portese flea market.

VIA ETTORE ROLLI 50 ✦ TEL: 06 581 0781
CLOSED WEDNESDAY, OPEN UNTIL 1AM *to* 3AM
Near: Ettore Rolli street market, corner Via Crescenzo Del Monte

INNOCENTI

THE OFFICIAL NAME IS BISCOTTIFICIO ARTIGIANO INNOCENTI, AN AUTHENTIC, SMALL-SCALE, FAMILY-RUN cookie factory in the heart of Trastevere. An old continuous-oven measuring about eight yards long runs from the back of the workshop to the level of the sales counter. The air in and near the factory is scented by freshly baked cookies and the happy accumulation of a century's worth of good baking smells. Smiling and handsome, Stefania Innocenti is the third generation to own and run the shop. She serves customers but also does the baking, and when she's not filling orders can be seen hefting the large, heavy iron cookie trays off the conveyor belt and setting them aside to cool. Other large display trays are covered with mounds of tongue-shaped *lingue di gatto* (cookies the size and shape of a cat's tongue), *stelline* (small stars, with a candied cherry in the

center), chocolate-coated crescents, *baci di dama* (plump, round hazelnut sandwich cookies with hazelnut-chocolate cream), *straccetti* (almond, hazelnut, or pine nut cookies the size of a baby finger), dozens of other "butter" cookies (all made with vegetable shortening), plus delicious *crostate* and merengues. Innocenti cookies are light, crisp, and thoroughly addictive, and so are the tarts.

VIA DELLA LUCE 21 ✦ TEL: 06 580 3926 ✦ CLOSED SUNDAY AFTERNOON; CLOSED ALL DAY SUNDAY *in* JULY

Near: 150 yards south of Viale di Trastevere, near Via dei Genovesi

INNOCENZI

STACKED ON THE FLOORS AND CRAMMED INTO THE WINDOW DISPLAY AREAS ARE ARTISANAL PASTAS, DRY BEANS, boxed candies, *panettone*, liqueurs, sacks of tea, cans of coffee, boxes of breakfast cereal, biscuits, cookies, jams, honeys, and much, much more. The shelves and counters overflow with packaged or bulk dry herbs and spices. This magical shop is the proverbial Aladdin's Cavern of dry goods—the archetypal *drogheria*—and it has been around for over a century. Predictably, a discount supermarket opened across the street to drain off customers, and business wasn't boosted by the fact that the outdoor market in front, on the square, was closed for two years for renovations. But Innocenzi has survived, and loyal customers keep it afloat. Don't miss it.

PIAZZA DI SAN COSIMATO 66 ✦ TEL: 06 581 2725
CLOSED THURSDAY AFTERNOON *and* SUNDAY; *in* SUMMER, *also* CLOSED SATURDAY AFTERNOON
Near: on the corner of Via Natale del Grande

NORCINERIA IACOZZILLI

THE TRASTEVERE NEIGHBORHOOD WAS ROME'S ORIGINAL JEWISH QUARTER, SETTLED IN IMPERIAL TIMES BY Jewish immigrants from Jerusalem, and that might explain the dirth of pork butchers and salami or *guanciale* makers here: the tradition simply never took root. Iacozzilli is the only one of note in Trastevere. Family-run and in business for decades, Iacozzilli makes very good *guanciale* in the traditional way with sea salt, and ages it long enough to give it flavor. But unless a particularly large specimen happens to have been air-dried for 90 days or more and is available for purchase on the day you visit, most of Iacozzilli's jowls must be cooked to be used and cannot be eaten

raw. The salami, sausages, and *prosciutto* are excellent and all are made by the Iacozzilli family, on site. The atmospheric old shop is remarkable for its selection of cheeses, which include some of the most flavorful, fresh buffalo-milk ricotta (from Battipaglia) anywhere; the fragrant, crusty breads are baked in a wood-burning oven. On sale year 'round and by the slice is traditional, rosemary-stuffed, whole, spit-roasted *porchetta*. The recipe used is that of Ariccia, a town in the Castelli Romani, about ten miles from downtown Rome. *Porchetta* was once sold everywhere in the city, but has largely disappeared because few shops have rotisseries or ovens big enough for roasting whole pigs, and the practice is discouraged by municipal authorities. Iacozzilli has its *porchetta* roasted outside the city limits and trucked in fresh. Get a sandwich made to order and savor it on a bench on the heights of the Gianicolo.

VIA NATALE DEL GRANDE 15 ✦ TEL: 06 581 2734
CLOSED TUESDAY ✦ *Near: 80 yards southeast of Piazza di San Cosimato*

PASTICCERIA ARTIGIANALE GIOVANNI CECERE

LONG, NARROW, AND PERPETUALLY CROWDED, CECERE HAS BEEN AROUND FOREVER, SERVING NEIGHBORHOOD regulars and the mobs that arrive Sunday morning for the Porta Portese flea market. This is a pastry shop, and they don't serve coffee, so choose a handful of pastries or cookies and eat them elsewhere. Among the scores of house specialties are cookies flavored with orange, pistachio, or cream-and-coffee, plus the fan-shaped ethereal *ventaglio* cookie hardly anyone makes anymore, jam-filled "bull's eye" *occhio di bue* cookies, classic *maritozzi*, and rock-hard, nut-filled *tozzetti*, not to mention the lumpy, ugly but delicious *brutti ma buoni*.

VIA B. MUSOLINO 25/33 ✦ TEL: 06 589 5014
WWW.PASTICCERIECECEREGIOVANNI.IT ✦ OPEN DAILY, CLOSED SUNDAY *and* HOLIDAY AFTERNOONS
Near: in the Trastevere/Portese neighborhood, two blocks northwest of the Porta Portese flea market

PASTICCERIA TRASTEVERE DI FABRIZIO MATTEI

FACING THE IACOZZILLI DELI, THIS TINY, FAMILY-RUN NEIGHBORHOOD PASTRY SHOP BAKES SOME OF THE best desserts in Trastevere. Ultra-traditional, the butter-crust *crostata*, buttery cookies, and luscious cakes of all kinds are sensational. The *cornetti* are remarkably light, and would pass muster in Paris.

VIA NATALE DEL GRANDE 49/50 ✦ TEL: 06 581 8719
CLOSED TUESDAY ✦ *Near: 100 yards southeast of Piazza di San Cosimato*

LA RENELLA

A CAVERNOUS TRASTEVERE BAKERY AT LEAST A CENTURY OLD, LA RENELLA WAS TAKEN OVER IN THE LATE 1990s by young, energetic baker Massimo Arnese. He quickly developed a reputation for his crisp, slightly chewy yet flavorful *pizza bianca*, his traditional *filone* bread, and his sourdough loaves made in the style of Umbria and the Alban Hills. The breads are excellent, handmade, allowed to rise overnight or all day, and baked in old brick ovens. In recent years the variety of Massimo's *pizza al taglio*—huge trays of pizza sold by the slice—and *pizza bianca* with toppings of all kinds, has grown. Customers now perch on stools or lean on counters in the sales area as they savor their mouth-watering pizzas topped with zucchini or tiny fresh tomatoes. In many ways, La Renella resembles the by-the-slice pizza joints that were found on every street in Rome in the 1960s and '70s. Also sold is a wide variety of good, classic cookies.

VIA DEL MORO 15 ✦ TEL: 06 581 7265 ✦ OPEN DAILY 9AM *to* 9PM
Near: equidistant—200 yards—from the Tiber River and Piazza Santa Maria in Trastevere

SORA MIRELLA LA GRATTACHECCA

DON'T MISS THIS HISTORIC KIOSK, WHICH SELLS SHAVED ICE FLAVORED WITH SYRUPS AND/OR FRESH fruit, plus decent coffee. It's been here since 1915, though it was rebuilt a few years ago, in the early twenty-first century, and has gone upscale. Nowadays there's a granite counter top and canvas awnings, and the prices are correspondingly high. The quality of the ices is good. Get your ice to go and eat it on the Ponte Cestio, which links the Tiber Island to Trastevere.

LUNGOTEVERE DEGLI ANGUILLARA/PONTE CESTIO ✦ NO TEL
OPEN *in* FINE WEATHER ONLY; HOURS VARY WIDELY
Near: on the sidewalk where Ponte Cestio reaches Trastevere

VALZANI

VALZANI HAS BEEN IN THE SAME ECHOING PREMISES, WITH HIGH CEILINGS AND ANTIQUE DISPLAY CASES, since 1925. If Morpheus were to choose a resting spot among pastry shops, this would be it. Paradoxically lively and talkative, Virginia Valzani is in her eighties; her shy, quiet son Giovanni makes the pastries, though he, too, is now beyond retirement age. Locals come here to buy simple, traditional *cioccolatini* (individual filled chocolates), Easter eggs, archly traditional Italian pastries (Sicilian *cannoli, torrone*) and, especially, the premodern candies and cakes of Rome and the

Lazio. These include *panpepato* (firm, peppery finger cookies), *pangiallo* (dense, sticky loaves of candied fruit, dry fruit, and nuts), and *mostaccioli* (hard honey candies that come in a variety of shapes, and are also available covered with chocolate). An experience.

VIA DEL MORO 37A/B ✦ TEL: 06 580 3792 ✦ WWW.VALZANI.IT
CLOSED MORNINGS *on* MONDAY *and* TUESDAY, *and from* JULY 1 *to* SEPTEMBER 3 ✦ *Near: 100 yards north of Piazza Santa Maria in Trastevere*

WINE AND WINE BARS

FERRARA STORE

TRENDY, WITH A CHIC, MODERN DÉCOR, THIS SPECIALTY FOOD AND WINE SHOP FREQUENTED BY HIGH-SPENDING hipsters is associated with the equally trendy and shockingly expensive Enoteca Ferrara wine bar and restaurant next door. The selection of highest-quality artisanal candies, chocolates, hams, cheeses (including fresh mozzarella), sauces and dry pasta is excellent, and the wines available come from all over Italy and the world. The prices match the jewel-like displays.

VIA DEL MORO 1A-3 ✦ TEL: 06 583 33920
WWW.ENOTECAFERRARA.IT
OPEN DAILY *from* LATE MORNING UNTIL LATE AT NIGHT
Near: 20 feet south of Piazza Trilussa

NON-TERROIR TOP OR TRENDY TABLES

ALBERTO CIARLA

PIAZZA DI SAN COSIMATO 40 ✦ TEL: 06 581 8668
WWW.ALBERTOCIARLA.COM ✦ DINNER ONLY, CLOSED SUNDAY NIGHT, VERY EXPENSIVE *to* EXTREMELY EXPENSIVE

ANTICO ARCO

PIAZZALE AURELIO 7 ✦ TEL: 06 581 5274
DINNER ONLY, CLOSED SUNDAY, EXPENSIVE *to* VERY EXPENSIVE

ASINOCOTTO

VIA DEI VASCELLARI 48 ✦ TEL: 06 589 8985
WWW.ASINOCOTTO.COM ✦ DINNER ONLY, CLOSED MONDAY
EXPENSIVE ✦ ALSO REGIONAL FOOD FROM LOMBARDY

BIR & FUD

VIA BENEDETTA 23 ✦ TEL: 06 589 4016
DINNER ONLY, CLOSED MONDAY ✦ INEXPENSIVE

ENOTECA FERRARA

PIAZZA TRILUSSA 41 ✦ TEL: 06 583 33920
WWW.ENOTECAFERRARA.IT ✦ DINNER ONLY, DAILY
VERY EXPENSIVE *to* EXTREMELY EXPENSIVE

GLASS

VICOLO DEL CINQUE 58 ✦ TEL: 06 583 35903
WWW.GLASS-HOSTARIA.COM ✦ DINNER ONLY, CLOSED MONDAY, LATE JANUARY, *and* MID-AUGUST ✦ EXPENSIVE

REGIONAL RESTAURANTS

CAMPANIA

MONZÙ VLADÌ

PIAZZA SAN GIOVANNI DELLA MALVA ✦ TEL: 06 581 4024
DINNER ONLY *except* SUNDAY LUNCH, CLOSED SUNDAY DINNER *and* AUGUST ✦ MODERATE *to* EXPENSIVE

LOMBARDY

ASINOCOTTO

(see Non-Terroir Top or Trendy Tables, above)

CHAPTER 8

CASTEL SANT'ANGELO, PRATI, VATICANO

NORTH OF TRASTEVERE AND THE GIANICOLO HILL, THE PRATI AREA FRONTING THE VATICAN IS A vast flatland that until the mid 1800s was swampy pastureland—*prati* means fields. The Vatican occupies the extreme western portion of Prati, with Castel Sant'Angelo on the Tiber banks connected to it by the popes' "secret" elevated walkway. The streets between the castle and Saint Peter's are lined by the medieval, Renaissance, and Baroque buildings that survived the "modernization" and "rationalization" of the neighborhood carried out under Mussolini, with wide Via della Conciliazione the result. Because of the millennial tides of pilgrims and tourists, the area immediately around the Vatican is the most difficult of all Roman neighborhoods when it comes to authentic, truly Roman food and wine addresses. Not so the further you travel from the walled city: Prati (and the abutting Trionfale/Mazzini neighborhoods in area 9) is home to many of Rome's best food and wine shops, restaurants, and trattorias.

Beyond the orbit of Vatican City, the remainder of the area is a grid of wide, tree-lined streets and boulevards, with several diagonals and a handful of squares to bring diversity to the cityscape. The northern dividing line is Via Candia, which changes name as it heads east from the Vatican, becoming Viale Giulio Cesare. The *metropolitana* (subway) runs under this wide boulevard.

Handsome and also wide, Via Cola di Rienzo is Prati's main shopping street, and on it you'll find great gourmet food emporiums and a wonderful vintage ice cream parlor. Prati was developed largely after Italian Unification, so the *palazzi* tend to be grand, some might say pompous, but well-constructed and luxurious by modern standards. The whole area is middle and upper middle class and notoriously conservative politically and otherwise. Rome's main courthouse (I Tribunali) is a massive, gloomy white pile on Piazza Cavour, near Castel Sant'Angelo and the Tiber.

Mercato rionale di Prati, an upscale covered market in Piazza Unità, between Via Cola di Rienzo and Via dei Gracchi, is less than half a mile south of the much bigger Trionfale market, on Via Andrea Doria (area 9). Most shoppers here are well-off local residents. The prices are higher than at Trionfale and there are no market gardeners. However, the quality of the produce and the cheese, meat, *prosciutto*, and pasta is uniformly high, and the displays are gorgeous.

SICILSAPORI
EUROFRU
0.99

RESTAURANTS AND TRATTORIAS

L'ARCANGELO

"BOURGEOIS CHIC" MAY BE THE MOST ACCURATE WAY TO DESCRIBE L'ARCANGELO, WHICH IS OFTEN RIGHTLY cited as the best place in Rome for traditional Roman cooking that has been lightened and updated without fuss. The dining room, with its tiled floors, wood panels, and peach-colored walls hung with old prints, might be that of a tasteful Prati-neighborhood home, and the food is what might be served in just such a home, if the cook happens to be world-class. L'Arcangelo is run by Arcangelo Dandini, a fourth-generation restaurateur, and his soft-spoken wife Stefania. In his forties, he wears a stylish salt-and-pepper beard, sports natty jackets, and has a suave manner. One of his passions is for updated Quinto Quarto cooking—the gutsy slaughterhouse cuisine usually associated with Testaccio (area 6). Dandini's mission is not merely to please his guests but also to educate them. With Mozart coming through the sound system, he might tell you, for instance, that putting artichokes *in coratella*—formerly a dish eaten by the poor—makes no sense in these days of prosperity. When the recipe was invented centuries ago, artichokes grew wild, and the organ meats that were cooked with them had little or no value. He's convinced they add bitterness. So he often uses premium sweet, white onions from the village of Cannara in Umbria instead, and the results are excellent. The *coda alla vaccinara*, *pajata*, and *coratella* made here are simply exquisite. L'Arcangelo also serves what is possibly the best tripe in town, on a par with Checchino dal 1887, using fresh spearmint, chili, tomatoes, and grated pecorino romano to elevate something many find unappetizing into the empyrean. For those who prefer tamer food, the menu ranges from other Roman classics—*amatriciana*, *cacio e pepe*, grilled lamb, grilled fish—to foie gras. Yes, foie gras. Dandini knows the ancient Romans invented it, and feels no compunction about serving it. Quiet, comfortable, and favored by serious food lovers, this is the opposite of a roistering Roman trattoria. Every dish at L'Arcangelo is beautifully presented on bone china. The service is seamless and friendly without being obsequious. Of particular note is the wine list, which includes many Lazio wines plus some of Italy's finest (and most expensive) bottlings, such as a Barolo Riserva 1971 made by Giacomo Borgogno, several top offerings of Brunello di Montalcino, and Burgundian classics like Clos de Vougeot Vieilles Vignes Chateau de la Tour. To go with your luscious fresh chestnut mousse, apple pie, or handmade ice cream, try a glass of organic Ludum, an Italian sweet wine made by excellent winemaker Marco Carpineti from heirloom Arciprete grapes with noble rot.

VIA GIUSEPPE GIOCCHINO BELLI 59/61 ✦ TEL: 06 321 0992
CLOSED *for* LUNCH *on* WEEKENDS, *and* DURING
the SECOND HALF *of* AUGUST ✦ EXPENSIVE
Near: one block north of Piazza Cavour

AL RAGNO D'ORO DA MARCO E FABIO

THIS SMALL, SIMPLE NEIGHBORHOOD RESTAURANT-PIZZERIA IS LESS FANCY AND LESS EXPENSIVE THAN many others in Prati. It caters to a mix of residents and out-of-towners, is reliable, and has been run for 50 years by the same friendly family. Cook Marco Formichella, his wife Anna, and their son Fabio, are passionate professionals with a light touch, from the simple white-and-beige tablecloths and walls to the food. The crispy Roman pizzas are delicious and never heavy. You can have them at lunch, which is rare (most pizza is baked only in the evening). For more than a pizza, stick to the classics, from the fried artichokes or *supplì* to the *amatriciana* and *carbonara*, roast suckling lamb, grilled meat or fish, *baccalà*, squid with peas, and vegetable sides such as pan-fried chicory and *puntarella* with anchovy dressing. The "inventive" specials come and go, and are sometimes good, sometimes infelicitous. The classic *crostata*, *torta di ricotta*, and *millefoglie*—all made by Anna and Fabio—are remarkable. You can also get a plate of *dolcetti misti*, a sampler of pastries, pies, and cookies. The wine list is short—about 20 bottlings—and has a few from Lazio, the rest from around Italy. There are tables outside, but the interior is air-conditioned and pleasant in hot weather. Note: this is not Il Ragno d'Oro, a bigger, glitzy, tourist-oriented operation near Colle Oppio and the Coliseum, with a website that shows up in all the searches.

VIA SILLA 26 ✦ TEL: 06 321 2362 ✦ CLOSED MONDAY LUNCH *and* SUNDAY ✦ INEXPENSIVE *to* MODERATE
Near: between Via degli Scipioni and Via Germanico

DA CESARE

DON'T BE FOOLED BY THE FLEUR-DE-LYS COAT OF ARMS, AND THE HANDSOME TURN-OF-THE-CENTURY lamps and ironwork: Da Cesare won't bankrupt you, and the pizzas here, baked in a wood-burning oven, are as delicious as the well-prepared fresh local fish (get it grilled or roasted). The official designation is *hostaria*-pizzeria, but Da Cesare is one of those perennial please-all *ristoranti* that's best defined as simply a Roman eating institution. It's been around since 1966, serving the same reliable classics of the Roman repertoire, from anchovy and artichoke to *zabaglione* and zucchini, plus pan-Italian and Tuscan favorites such as *prosciutto* from heirloom *cinta senese* pigs; Tuscan steaks and tagliata; and dozens of types of pizza. The mixed clientele includes local professionals, judges, lawyers, lobbyists, and shopkeepers, and better-heeled tourists, especially Americans, French, and Japanese. The service is smooth, the seating comfortable, the view not of monuments, but rather of lobsters and fish in the restaurant's aquariums. For dessert? Fresh fruit and more. The coffee flavor ice cream and lemon sorbet are house-made and very good, and there's always a daily dessert or three. What's noteworthy for a pizzeria is the wine list, which has about 300 bottlings on it, most of them from Tuscany; the Chianti house wine is fine, and there's a daily selection of wines served by the glass. Beer is on tap (Peroni, Spaten) or by the bottle.

VIA CRESCENZIO 13 ✦ TEL: 06 686 1227
WWW.RISTORANTECESARE.COM ✦ CLOSED SUNDAY DINNER *and* AUGUST ✦ MODERATE *to* EXPENSIVE
Near: 30 feet northwest of Piazza Cavour

FRANCHI

This deli is a great place to have a simple, quick lunch on the hoof. See page 296 for details.

VIA COLA DI RIENZO 200-204 ✦ TEL: 06 687 4651
WWW.FRANCHI.IT ✦ OPEN 8:15AM *to* 9PM ✦ CLOSED SUNDAY
Near: on the corner of Via Terenzio

IL MATRICIANO

MUCH OF THE YEAR, YOU'LL SEE WHITE CLOTHS DRAPED OVER THE TABLES ON IL MATRICIA-no's long, inviting sidewalk terrace, and uniformed waiters rushing to and fro. The cloths are linen, the uniforms white, but the outdoor chairs are plastic. Given the price, and the excellent reputation of this Prati institution, you'd expect something better. Upscale, classic, and comfortable inside, Il Matriciano is over 100 years old, a favorite among the neighborhood's conservative residents, Roman business people, and well-heeled visitors. Tradition reigns supreme, from the efficient service to the wide-ranging menu, which follows the seasons and respects many Canonical weekly specials, including just about every Roman favorite. Among them is the house specialty, *amatriciana*, which is thickly sauced and rich and spicy—among the best in town—and the now-endangered *quadrucci in brodo*—that simplest of soups, a meat-and-chicken broth, really, with tiny tatters of pasta. The pasta is still house made. The fried starters are remarkably good, too, from the artichokes and potato croquettes to the luscious zucchini flowers stuffed with lots of good mozzarella and anchovy. The desserts are equally classic and Roman, though Il Matriciano is celebrated for its French-style *crème brûlée*. The wine list is long and includes the best Italian regional bottlings, plus many from further afield.

VIA DEI GRACCHI 55 ✦ TEL: 06 321 2327 ✦ CLOSED WEDNESDAY *in* WINTER, SATURDAY *in* SUMMER, *and* AUGUST ✦ EXPENSIVE
Near: one block north of Via Cola di Rienzo, corner Via Silla

BREAD, CHEESE, FRESH PASTA, FRUIT ICES, GOURMET FOOD SHOPS, ICE CREAM, PASTRIES

ANTONINI—GRAN CAFFÈ ESPERIA

PRATI'S BEAUTIFUL PEOPLE HOBNOB HERE WITH POLITICOS, LAWYERS, JUDGES, AND LOBBYISTS—THE CITY'S eyesore main courthouse is right across the street. You can spot Antonini from far away by the number of flashy SUVs and seven-figure sports cars double-parked insouciantly out front, complete with bodyguards and drivers in wraparound sunglasses. The terrace on the wide sidewalk is populated by plastified rattan chairs and mushroom-shaped tables, where the regulars preen themselves, shoot down strong Fantini coffee and cappuccino, or complicated cocktails, accompanied by savory snacks, delicious classic pastries—all house made—and perfectly good artisanal ice creams. A real Roman experience.

LUNGOTEVERE DEI MELLINI 1 ✦ TEL: 06 320 3971 ✦ OPEN DAILY

Near: on the riverside boulevard, kitty-corner to Ponte Cavour

APISTICA ROMANA

BEES IN ROME? WELL, NOT EXACTLY. BUT THE HONEY SOLD HERE IS GATHERED FROM HIVES KEPT IN RELATIVELY unpolluted rural areas outside the city, and handled by beekeeper-biologist Dr. Domenico Licastro. He and his softspoken wife run this upscale, handsome boutique, which always has about two dozen types of honey in stock, plus royal jelly, pollen, and propolis—and scores of honey-based cosmetics, health-care products, and lozenges. The Licastros are passionate, and will tell you everything you ever wanted to know about honey and related products, their history, and uses.

VIA ULPIANO 55/57 ✦ TEL: 06 686 8004 ✦ CLOSED SATURDAY AFTERNOON *and* SUNDAY ✦ *Near: facing the east side of Rome's main courthouse, 100 yards south of Piazza Cavour*

CASTRONI

CASTRONI OPENED IN 1932 AND HAS REMAINED A FAMILY-OWNED *DROGHERIA*, MEANING A DRY GOODS, spices, and specialty packaged and canned foods grocery. This is a wonderful, more-is-more emporium, stacked and piled full of culinary delights. The handsome décor is original, with period furnishings, and includes a bustling *caffè* area favored by local residents. Half a dozen other Castroni stores are scattered around town (see website for more addresses). Everything from the breakfast cereals and pastries at the bar, to the canned tuna and spices, is of high quality, and the coffee sold in all Castroni outlets is the same, toasted by Torrefazione Augusta (in the small suburban city of Pomezia, about 13 miles south of Rome). Though Castroni no longer has outstanding coffee, the 100-percent Arabica blend is good. When drunk on site, the bar blend is tasty and rich in caffeine, and goes down well in the form of a cappuccino. Above all, shopping at Castroni is an only-in-Rome experience of the most enjoyable kind.

VIA COLA DI RIENZO 196 ✦ TEL: 06 687 4383
WWW.CASTRONIGROUP.IT ✦ OPEN 8AM *to* 8PM, CLOSED SUNDAY
Near: on Prati's main shopping street, near the corner of Via Terenzio

LA CONFETTERIA

THIS CHARMING CORNER CANDY AND CHOCOLATE SHOP OPENED IN 1905, AND THOUGH IT NO LONGER ACTUALLY makes its own goods, it sells very good candied fruit and flowers, bars of pure chocolate, *cioccolatini, marrons glacés*, Irish whiskey, Scotch, and many other fattening delights. You'll have no difficulty finding it. Across the street on the opposite corner is one of Rome's ugliest Brutalist buildings.

VIA LUCREZIO CARO 24/26/28 ✦ TEL: 06 321 2503
CLOSED SUNDAY ✦ *Near: on the corner of Via E. Q. Visconti*

FORNO PASTICCERIA ANGELO COLAPICCHIONI

FOUNDED IN 1934 AND NOW INTO ITS THIRD GENERATION OF THE SAME HARDWORKING FAMILY, COLAPICCHIONI IS a two-in-one: a cult bakery and deli-grocery (in Via Tacito) and a bakery/pastry shop/gourmet food shop with scores of Lazio specialties, including wines (in Via Properzio). Both are upmarket and attractive though small and cluttered, and run with professionalism and panache. The most ancient and famous dessert Colapicchioni makes is *pangiallo*, a dense loaf of sultanina raisins, honey, walnuts, almonds, pine nuts, hazelnuts, candied citron and orange, pistachios, powdered almonds, dark chocolate drops, powdered cocoa, eggs, flour, and natural flavorings. The *panpepato* is similar, but has lots of black pepper in it. Only a handful of bakers in Rome still make *pangiallo* and *panpepato*. Alongside all the classic breads you'll find baguettes, excellent *pizza bianca* and *pizza rossa*, and filled *rustici* turnovers. The choice of hams and salamis is wide (don't miss the *prosciutto di Bassiano* and *salame di Amatrice*). Of the many cheeses, you'll want to try the remarkable Tuscan pecorino di Volterra. All the high-class picnic supplies you'll need are here, from the smoked salmon to the champagne. The coffee comes from Torrefazione Perù and is excellent. At the Via Tacito store, which is dedicated to Lazio regional products, you'll discover dozens of the best Lazio wines: DOP Sabina, Tuscia, and Frusinate olive oils; jams, honeys, and specialty foods, including organic delicacies from the Trappist monks at the Lanuvio monastery; plus artisanal dry pastas, breads, cookies, and pastries. In short, Colapicchioni is a must.

VIA TACITO 76/78 *and* VIA PROPERZIO 23/25
TEL: 06 321 5405 *and* 06 688 01310 ✦ WWW.COLAPICCHIONI.IT
CLOSED SATURDAY AFTERNOON *and* SUNDAY ✦ *Near: the Via Tacito location is one and a half blocks north of Piazza Cavour, the Via Properzio location is near the corner of Via Crescenzio and the Prati covered market*

FRANCHI

FRANCHI IS A PRATI INSTITUTION, A TRADITIONAL GROCERY-DELI THAT EVOLVED BEFORE MANY OTHERS INTO a high-end *gastronomia* and *tavola calda*. It's been owned by the Franchi family for about a century, and is run nowadays by seasoned professional managers. L-shaped and on Prati's main shopping street, Franchi is always mobbed around lunch time, when white collar regulars show up to savor the fried foods—including some of Rome's most flavorful and crisp mozzarella-filled rice *supplì*—and any number of classics from the Roman repertoire: *pasta e ceci* (short pasta and chickpea stew), stuffed veal breast, or sweet and sour salt cod. The selection of high-quality hams, cheeses, wines, and specialty foods of all kinds is very good, the atmosphere lively and fun.

VIA COLA DI RIENZO 200-204 ✦ TEL: 06 687 4651
WWW.FRANCHI.IT ✦ OPEN 8:15AM *to* 9PM ✦ CLOSED SUNDAY
Near: on the corner of Via Terenzio

LE GÂTEAU

A SHORT FLIGHT OF STAIRS LEADS DOWN FROM THE SIDEWALK INTO A SMALL BASEMENT SHOP WHERE Giuseppe Di Sisto makes some of the best *marrons glacés*, fruit gelatins, candied fruit, Easter eggs, chocolates, and candies in town. This insider's address has been here since 1927, supplying restaurants, candy and chocolate shops, caterers, wholesalers, and a few savvy retail clients. Spartan is too lavish a word to describe the premises. Di Sisto's confections are anything but.

VIA DEGLI SCIPIONI 228 ✦ TEL: 06 324 2107 ✦ CLOSED SUNDAY
Near: between Via Fabio Massimo and Via Paolo Emilio

GELATERIA DEI GRACCHI

GELATERIA DEI GRACCHI, A SMALL, TAKE-OUT-ONLY SHOP THAT OPENED IN 2000, IS INCREASINGLY recognized as one of Rome's most outstanding producers of excellent natural ice cream. Affable, energetic owner Alberto Manassei insists that he uses only fresh ingredients "for everything," and even toasts and grinds the fresh, top-quality pistachios (from the Bronte area, on the slopes of Etna, in Sicily), hazelnuts (Tonda Gentile variety, from the Langhe), and almonds (from southern Italy), on site, for those flavors. He brews fresh coffee for his remarkable *gelato al caffé* flavored with star anise (he calls the combination Mistrà). Gracchi ice

creams are consistently among the smoothest, richest, and most satisfying in Rome, and perhaps in all of Italy. From the texture and intensity of the nut-based flavors, it's easy for a skeptic to wonder whether the freshly toasted and ground nuts are bolstered and thickened by highest quality nut pastes, but that's something Manassei vehemently denies. In any case, the fruit flavors are entirely fresh and available only seasonally. In 2006 the Prati shop's huge success spawned a second, similar outlet across town on Viale Regina Margherita near Via Salaria (area 10); it serves the same excellent ice creams as in Prati.

VIA DEI GRACCHI 272 ✦ TEL: 06 321 6668 ✦ OPEN DAILY *from* MID- *to* LATE MORNING *to* LATE *at* NIGHT ✦ *Near: equidistant—250 yards—from Piazza Cavour and Viale delle Milizie*

GIULIO GIULIANI—FABBRICA MARRONS GLACÉS

FOUNDED IN 1948 AND STILL RUN BY GIULIO GIULIANI, HIS WIFE AGNESE, AND THEIR CHILDREN GIOVANNI AND Anna Maria, this wonderful candy shop is a Prati touchstone, its big "Marrons Glacés" sign visible from half a block away. The interior was redone in the Age of Ugly—there's remarkably hideous 1960s faux paneling—but the candied chestnuts, chestnut cream, real candied violets, candied fruit of all kinds, *torrone* in eight different flavors—from classic white with hazelnuts, to dark with rum, or *gianduia* with hazelnuts—are excellent. The chestnuts are from the Avellino region of central-southern Italy and candied—impregnated with sugar—for two weeks, and then hand brushed with a glistening sugar coating.

VIA PAOLO EMILIO 67 ✦ TEL: 06 324 3548
WWW.MARRONGLACES.IT ✦ CLOSED BETWEEN JULY 12 *and* AUGUST 31 ✦ *Near: the corner of Via degli Scipioni*

GRAN CAFFÈ BORGO

BORGO PIO IS THE QUIET, CAR-FREE STREET JUST NORTH OF BUSY VIA DELLA CONCILIAZIONE, AND, LIKE MOST of the Vatican area, is short on authentic properties. This *caffè* caters to pilgrims and tourists, but it's also patronized by locals, in part because it's been in the Scialanga family since 1947, but mostly because the house-made pastries and ice cream are very good, the Illy espresso and cappuccinos excellent, and the shaded outdoor tables a welcome refuge.

BORGO PIO 170/173 ✦ TEL: 06 686 5539 ✦ OPEN DAILY
Near: the corner of Vicolo d'Orfeo/Via degli Ombrellari

PELLACCHIA

HISTORIC, MUCH-LOVED ICE CREAM PARLOR PELLACCHIA HAS BEEN AROUND SINCE 1900 AND IS AS famous as Giolitti as a *caffè* and late-night hangout. It's off the usual tourist routes, toward the Tiber end of Prati's main shopping street. Roman regulars wait in long lines at the counter to order takeout cones and *coppette*, or sit on the sidewalk terrace and consume banana splits and elaborate 1950s ice cream concoctions topped with mountains of whipped cream. Creamy and rich, the vanilla is particularly good, and the fresh fruit ice creams are also noteworthy. A recently added curiosity is Pellacchia's frozen yogurt, made with goat's milk; it's tangy and utterly unlike bland frozen yogurt made from cow's milk. The classic coffee *granita* is also very good. Most of all, Pellacchia is an atmospheric, fun place, a real Roman experience.

VIA COLA DI RIENZO 103/107 ✦ TEL: 06 321 0807
WWW.PELLACCHIA.IT OPEN 6AM *to* 1AM ✦ CLOSED MONDAY
Near: on the corner of Via Ezio

PICA—LA PASTA ALL'UOVO

SOME OF THE BEST FRESH PASTA IN THE PRATI AREA HAS BEEN COMING OUT OF THIS SMALL, FAMILY-RUN PASTA factory for the last 70 years or so. All the traditional Roman shapes are available, plus many pan-Italian varieties. Affable owners Felice and Massimiliano Giovannetti are sticklers, and claim (correctly) that what Romans nowadays call "tonnarelli"—the long, square-shaped pasta often used for *cacio e pepe*, *gricia* and *carbonara*—are in fact none other than "fettuccine alla chitarra," from the Ciociara area of Lazio. That's what they call them, so if you want them, don't ask for tonnarelli.

VIA DEGLI SCIPIONI 11/13 ✦ TEL: 06 397 22556
CLOSED THURSDAY AFTERNOON *and* MONDAY
Near: on the western end of the road, near the Vatican's walls

PIZZARIUM

THIS HOLE-IN-THE-WALL PIZZERIA FACING THE DREARY CIPRO/VATICAN MUSEUM SUBWAY STOP BAKES AMAZINGLY good pizza by the slice, Roman fried delicacies such as *supplì* and *arancini*, focaccia, and savory vegetable tarts. The award-winning *pizzaiolo* is Gabriele Bonci. He also cooks the food and makes the pizzas for Bir & Fud, the trendy pizzeria-hangout in Trastevere (area 7 page 285). Bonci's trick isn't a trick at all: he uses the best, freshest ingredients possible, from the mozzarella to the tomatoes, plus natural, organic yeast and flour, and lets his pizza dough rise for a very long time. When you eat a slice, you recognize the ethereal lightness not only of the bready part of the pizza but also of what goes on top. Though this storefront is about the size of a large refrigerator, also stocked are excellent extra virgin olive oils, artisanal pastas, vegetables preserved in olive oil, and chocolate.

VIA DELLA MELORIA 43 ✦ TEL: 06 397 45416 ✦ CLOSED SUNDAY
Near: 20 feet from the corner of Via Cipro, 100 yards south of Cipro/Vatican Museum subway stop

SCIASCIA

A CHARACTERFUL THROWBACK AMONG COFFEE ROASTING HOUSES, SCIASCIA HAS BEEN RUN BY THE SAME family of grumps since 1922. The coffee is no longer roasted on the premises, but family members do the buying and oversee production at a suburban plant, or so they claim. The small yet elegant shop area where the roasted coffees (and candies) are displayed and sold is backed by an equally compact rear *caffè* invisible from the street. Here, well-heeled locals gather to sip coffee and potables, snack on pastries, and chat, undisturbed by passing throngs. Sciascia offers a handful of very good blends for the coffee lover, the best of which is 100-percent Arabica, composed of five different Central- and South American beans—the owners will say no more. The bar blend is also delicious, though it has Robusta in it; amounts vary from 20- to 40-percent—again, the owners are secretive, refusing to give details. The bartenders are more forthcoming about the use of Robusta. Most customers, they claim, like a foamy head on their espresso, and a caffeine kick, and the Robusta provides both.

VIA FABIO MASSIMO 80A ✦ TEL: 06 321 1580 ✦ OPEN 8AM *to* 8PM MONDAY *through* SATURDAY, CLOSED SUNDAY ✦ *Near: 30 feet from the corner of Via degli Scipioni, just south of Viale Giulio Cesare*

TADDEI

TADDEI IS A SPARTAN, HOLE-IN-THE-WALL RETAIL OUTLET AND PASTA-MAKING FACILITY. THOUGH ABOUT A century old, it has been run for the last decade or so by affable Franco Bonacei. He makes very good ravioli, tortellini, quadrucci, and potato gnocchi every day, and excels with his cut-to-order fresh ribbon pasta in all the classic Roman shapes (fettuccine, spaghetti, tagliatelle, tonnarelli). The reason Taddei is popular is simple: its *pasta fresca* contains a higher proportion of durum wheat flour (50 to 70 percent) to standard bread flour than most fresh pasta (which, in Rome, is usually 20- to 30-percent durum wheat). That's why it's noticeably elastic, firm to the tooth, and flavorful. Bonacei goes to the expense and trouble of using lots of durum wheat because he sells almost all of his pasta to demanding local restaurants such as Da Gianni–Cacio e pepe, Ai Villini, Gallo Brillo, and Osteria dell'Angelo. As the name suggests, the signature dish at Da Gianni–Cacio e pepe is fresh tonnarelli, the thick, square ribbon pasta, which, when dressed solely with coarsely ground black pepper and mountains of grated pecorino romano, is *cacio e pepe*. The *pasta fresca* has to be good. Taddei's always is.

VIALE DELLE MILIZIE 9G ✦ TEL: 06 372 9853 ✦ OPEN DAILY CLOSED *on* SATURDAY AFTERNOONS *in* JULY *and* AUGUST *Near: facing Via De Sanctis; Rome's main army base is a block away*

WINE AND WINE BARS

DEL FRATE

THIS WELL-STOCKED, HANDSOME OLD WINE SHOP RUN BY FABIO DEL FRATE (AND FLANKED BY THE FAMILY'S newish wine bar) has been a neighborhood fixture for decades. Local residents and restaurateurs buy from Del Frate. The choice among hundreds of wines includes a good selection of Lazio and other Italian bottlings, plus champagne, liqueurs, excellent olive oils, vegetables preserved in oil, and boxed chocolates and candies. At #122 in the same street is the **Del Frate wine bar** (expensive to very expensive), where you can enjoy delicious hams, salami, and cheeses, savory snacks of all kinds, or a full—some might say lavishly baroque—meal. Other than the downscale table settings and paper napkins, the wine bar is upscale and pricey, in keeping with the tony neighborhood. The menu follows the market. You're better off sticking to Roman classics, unless you crave an Italian interpretation of Asian fusion cuisine, with spices and soy sauce and stir-fried vegetables, meat, or chicken.

VIA DEGLI SCIPIONI 118/128A ✦ TEL: 06 321 1612
SHOP CLOSED MONDAY MORNING *and* SUNDAY
WINE BAR CLOSED SUNDAY LUNCH *and* SATURDAY; BOTH
CLOSED 2 WEEKS *in* MID AUGUST ✦ *Near: the corner of Via Silla*

ENOTECA COSTANTINI

ENOTECA COSTANTINI IS THREE BUSINESSES IN ONE: AN EXTRAORDINARY WINE EMPORIUM; THE ROME headquarters of winery Villa Simone; and a wildly expensive, over-the-top wine bar-restaurant (Il Simposio di Costantini). You can't miss it: just look for the garish, bronze-patina wrought-ironwork grapevines on the façade. The retail floorspace alone—800 square meters—would swallow up many other Rome wine shops combined. About 100,000 bottles from 1,000 winemakers across Italy and the world are on display, in handsome, wood-paneled rooms and a vaulted cellar. Piero and Rosy Costantini opened Enoteca Costantini in 1972 and ever since have been stocking up on rare vintages, and adding promising new wines by innovative winemakers, some of them advocating a return to native varieties and yeasts. Labyrinthine gigantism can be daunting, however, and it's essential to get help from the staff to find the right wine and vintage, including many interesting Lazio wines rarely sold outside the region. As winemakers, the Costantinis somehow find time to make six distinct wines of their own at Villa Simone, which they also own. It's located in Monte Porzio Catone, a village northeast of Frascati in the Alban Hills. The full range of fine white and red wines from the winery is available here. Il Simposio di Costantini wine bar next door to the shop offers a mix of delicious snacks, innovative dishes, and some traditional Roman food, in a luxurious setting.

PIAZZA CAVOUR 16 ✦ TEL: 06 320 3575 *and* 06 321 11131
WWW.PIEROCOSTANTINI.IT ✦ WINE SHOP HOURS *are* 9AM *to* 1PM *and* 4:30 *to* 8PM, CLOSED MONDAY MORNING *and* SUNDAY; WINE BAR IL SIMPOSIO DI COSTANTINI *is* OPEN *for* LUNCH (12:30 *to* 3PM), *and for* TASTINGS *and* DINNER (6 *to* 11PM) MONDAY *through* SATURDAY, CLOSED SUNDAY ✦ VERY EXPENSIVE
Near: on the corner of Via Tacito, directly opposite Rome's main courthouse

FORNO PASTICCERIA ANGELO COLAPICCHIONI

(see shop listings, page 296)

NON-TERROIR TOP OR TRENDY TABLES

DA BENITO E GILBERTO

VIA DEL FALCO 19 ✦ TEL: 06 686 7769
WWW.DABENITOEGILBERTO.COM
CLOSED SUNDAY, MONDAY, CHRISTMAS HOLIDAYS *and* AUGUST
EXPENSIVE *to* VERY EXPENSIVE

IL SIMPOSIO DI COSTANTINI

PIAZZA CAVOUR 16 ✦ TEL: 06 321 11131
WWW.PIEROCOSTANTINI.IT ✦ OPEN *for* LUNCH 12:30 *to* 3PM, *and for* WINE TASTINGS *and* DINNER 6 *to* 11PM MONDAY *through* SATURDAY, CLOSED SUNDAY ✦ EXPENSIVE *to* VERY EXPENSIVE

CHAPTER 9

PIAZZA MAZZINI, TRIONFALE

THIS LARGE, FLAT AREA ABUTTING PRATI AND THE VATICAN STARTS ON THE NORTH SIDE OF VIA Candia (which becomes Viale Giulio Cesare as it heads east) and reaches north to the foot of Monte Mario. The northeast sector, comprising leafy Piazza Mazzini and its surroundings, is among Rome's most tony neighborhoods, with wide, green-belt boulevards and squares lined by imposing *palazzi* from the late 1800s to the 1940s. Urbanistically, culturally, and politically this is a continuation of the Prati area. The headquarters of RAI (Italian State Television and Radio) are here, as well as various Italian government ministries, and the offices of lobbyists, lawyers, and other professionals.

The Trionfale neighborhood, closer to the Vatican, is different, with buildings from the 1920s and 1930s, and a more popular feel. Its former low-cost housing projects were privatized and renovated in recent decades, and are now condominiums. The sprawling military base between major thoroughfares Viale Giulio Cesare and Viale delle Milizie is gradually being downsized. Much of it will be redeveloped as condominiums.

The area's biggest food market by far, known as **mercato Trionfale** or **mercato Andrea Doria**, is currently on the sidewalks on both sides of Via Andrea Doria, between Piazza degli Eroi and Largo Trionfale. A new, covered market structure has

FRESCHE
Peso M
PEPPINO
UOVA

been built on the southside of the street, and the temporary stalls are moving into it. The process will be completed in 2009–2010. For now, Trionfale remains central Rome's liveliest, most authentic neighborhood outdoor market. It has few tourists. Some Romans travel from across town to shop here for produce; the Cipro-Musei Vaticani subway stop makes for easy access. At the market's western end are the stands of market gardeners, known as vignaroli, officially Produttori Agricoli in Vendita Diretta or Coltivatori Diretti. Each generally grows just two or three crops at a time. That means that to buy the full range of seasonal produce, customers must visit several stands. Despite this inconvenience, the *vignaroli* do a brisk business. Their prices are about a third lower than those of normal retailers, and the *vignaroli* pick their produce early on the same morning that it's sold. They also gather or grow wild greens and lettuces for *misticanza* (a mix of chicory, endive, escarole, borage, turnip tops, purslane and arugula) and herbs important to Roman cuisine such as *menta romana* (spearmint) and *mentuccia* (the scientific name is *Nepitella*, a form of mint). Wine on tap is sold on the south side of the street, in front of Via Andrea Doria #77-79, near Antico Caffè Doria (a neighborhood institution since 1922, serving and selling good Marziali coffee).

South of the octopus-like Piazza Mazzini, with its many radial boulevards, you'll find an authentic, small open market, **mercato rionale di Via Tito Speri**, between Via Giuseppe Ferrari and Via Settembrini. Northwest of Piazza Mazzini, on Via Sabotino, between Viale Angelico and Via Monte Santo, another open market offers several dozen stands selling clothing and sundries. Food and produce stalls are inside the covered market, which is officially called **mercato rionale Vittoria**, and is housed in a typical Razionalista building, with entrances at Via Sabotino 2E or Via Monte Santo 41.

RIANA
OVA
UOVA DA
COLTIVAZIONE
E ALLEVAMENTO
BIOLOGICO
SPEZIE
UOVA
BIOLOGICHE
ALL. A TERRA
€ 0,30

UOVA
UOVA ITALIANE
CAT. A
DA BERE
€ 0,25
UOVA ITALIANE
CAT. A
€ 0,20
UOVA ITALIANE
CAT. A
€ 0,18

RESTAURANTS AND TRATTORIAS

ANTICO FALCONE

MANY TRATTORIAS CALL THEMSELVES *ANTICO*. THIS ONE IS THE GENUINE ARTICLE. EVEN THE NAMESAKE stuffed falcon, mounted on a wall, out of feather-duster range, exudes age. The *palazzo* and adjoining buildings housing Antico Falcone were built in the Renaissance and owned by the Strozzi and Borgia clans. For something like the last 500 years they have been, in succession, a coaching inn for mail carriers and pilgrims entering Rome on the Via Francigena (the road's medieval name), a tavern and, since at least the 1930s, an historic, cult trattoria, which is a registered landmark. Owners Pietro Fazi and his wife Rita Paci have "only" been here since precisely September 15, 1971, though several of the house specialties were invented before World War II by the previous owners. History and age are writ large, like the fading, peeling black letters taped to the glass over the door, spelling out the trattoria's name. You step down from the sidewalk into an entrance where delicacies beckon from a glass case. The cavernous kitchen is to the right, the long, arcaded dining room (and dusty falcon) to the left. Though a modest trattoria, with mismatched chairs at big, heavy old wooden tables, there are ironed white tablecloths, and solid tableware, the service is efficient, and everything is clean. Rough diamonds Pietro and Rita are not exactly spring chickens, yet, amazingly, Rita's mother, who is far beyond retirement age, still does the cooking. Out of the kitchen come all the Roman classics, many following the weekly wheel of Canonical tradition. The two dishes you'll find only here are *rigatoni alla nasona* (with mozzarella, fresh tomatoes, basil, and lots of parmigiano) and *gnocchetti agli spinaci* (exquisite spinach-and-ricotta dumplings that look like green eyes, and are dressed with melted butter and sage, or a light tomato sauce). Fried appetizers are a house specialty: the zucchini flowers, *baccalà,* and *carciofi alla giudia* are remarkably good. The *carbonara* is a meal in itself, a giant bowlful of perfectly cooked pasta, dressed traditionally with smoked *pancetta* and a whole egg, with lots of black pepper and grated

cheese. It's among the best in town. The *baccalà* stewed with potatoes and onions in tomato sauce, and the old-fashioned *picchiapò* beef stew, also with onions and tomatoes, and a pinch of chili, are the ultimate comfort food. House-made desserts include rich *panna cotta* and *crostata* with apricot jam. Antico Falcone is among the few places still serving *caffè casareccia*, meaning coffee made with a stovetop Moka machine. The Palombini-brand espresso used is dark, strong, and rich in Robusta. Expect to share the dining room with local regulars. Tourists rarely venture this far out. Note: you can lunch from 12:30pm and dine from 7:30pm.

VIA TRIONFALE 60 ✦ TEL: 06 397 43385
CLOSED TUESDAY, JULY, *and* AUGUST ✦ MODERATE
Near: 200 yards northwest of Largo Trionfale

CACIO E PEPE—DA GIANNI

BEARDED, BOUNCY, AND COURTEOUS, OWNER GIANNI BENEDETTI IS A MASTER AT KEEPING CLIENTS HAPPY as they wait for a table at this tiny, modest trattoria, an insider's address mobbed at lunch and dinner by a mixed crowd of local professionals, politicians, and hipsters. Gianni worked in the fashion business and took over the helm from his parents in the mid 1980s. One of Italy's former prime ministers lives 100 yards away, and is a regular, but despite the VIPs and their bodyguards, Cacio e pepe remains a singularly casual, authentic, and friendly place, with simple food and remarkably low prices. The house specialty is, as you'd suspect, *tonnarelli cacio e pepe* (it's worth noting that all the excellent fresh pasta for the trattoria is supplied by Taddei; see page 303). They're served in huge portions, and are mild by Roman standards, dusted with grana or parmigiano and little or no pecorino romano. The *carbonara* and *gricia* are also popular, generously served

and mild. Cacio e pepe has a short menu, with half a dozen starters and as many second courses, all of them Roman, satisfying, and homey. The veal stew, meatloaf or meatballs with lemon zest, not to mention the chicken *alla cacciatora* in a white wine vinegar sauce, are very good. If Gianni has found perfectly fresh offal at the wholesale market, he'll serve a classic *coratella* or tripe, and if you enjoy such hearty fare, don't miss them. The desserts are of the most basic variety, the house carafe wine is quaffable, and the strong, dark-roasted coffee is served in a glass, as it always has been at Cacio e pepe. Arrive early for lunch or dinner, or expect to wait for your table. Note: credit cards are not accepted.

VIA AVEZZANA 11 ✦ TEL: 06 321 7268 ✦ CLOSED SATURDAY DINNER, SUNDAY, *and* AUGUST ✦ INEXPENSIVE

Near: on the corner of Via Settembrini

DA DANTE

WITH A MERE 36 SEATS IN THE UNADORNED DINING ROOM OF THIS LONGTIME TRATTORIA, AND MANY more than 36 VIPs and hungry locals trying to get in, Da Dante is always packed. The headquarters of Italian State TV and Radio are nearby, which is why so many peacock-like personalities flock here. They also come for the authentically good, *casareccia* food. Despite the mixed, often chic clientele, the family that has owned and operated Da Dante for decades is welcoming. Among the weekly wheel of Roman classics, the suckling lamb *coratella* with artichokes stands out as excellent, but the oxtails, *saltimbocca*, and *baccalà* with red sauce are also delicious. Because of demand from tony celebs and the after-theater crowd, there's more fish on the menu than you'd expect in a trattoria like this, from tonnarelli with seafood and linguine with lobster, to roast whole fish. The wine list is adequate. Stick to regional bottlings. Note: this is one of the few traditional restaurants in Rome that stays open very late—until 2 or 3am.

VIA MONTE SANTO 36/38 ✦ TEL: 06 375 15537 ✦ CLOSED SUNDAY *and* AUGUST ✦ MODERATE ✦ *Near: half a block north of the Via Sabotino open market, near the corner of Via Vodice*

MICCI

ALMOST 20 YEARS AGO THE SECOND GENERATION OF THE MICCI FAMILY—ANGELO AND MARCELLO—TOOK over from founders Armando and Valeria Micci, and have slowly nudged this neighborhood restaurant, a fixture since 1951, upward and onward. The service is affable and professional, the white tablecloths starched, the interior unremarkable, except for a remarkably unattractive mirrored wall. Eat outside if you can. Micci is a good place for lunch when you're shopping at the Andrea Doria market. The pleasant outdoor terrace is hedged by potted pittosporum and bay trees, amid the hustle and bustle of the market stalls (80 yards east is the new market's high-rise home). The produce couldn't be fresher, which is one reason the artichokes *alla romana* or *alla giudia* and the *puntarella* salad with anchovy dressing are so perfect. The potato gnocchi are house-made, the *gricia*, *cacio e pepe*, and *carbonara* reliably very good, the tripe, *saltimbocca* and veal stew all homey and comforting. Micci also offers seafood pasta, grilled or fried fish, or whole fish roasted in a shell of coarse salt, sautéed shellfish or calamari, and more. For dessert, there's classic Roman apple pie, *crème brûlée*, chocolate soufflé, *crostata* with sour cherry jam, pears with *zabaione*, and fresh, seasonal fruit. The wine list has plenty of Lazio bottlings to choose from, and there are always several whites and reds available by the glass. Expect to dine with regulars, shoppers, and a sprinkling of tourists.

VIA ANDREA DORIA 55A ✦ TEL: 06 397 33208
WWW.FRATELLIMICCI.IT ✦ CLOSED MONDAY ✦ MODERATE
Near: fronts the Trionfale market

OSTERIA DELL'ANGELO

SOME PEOPLE THINK THAT THE OWNER OF THIS *OSTERIA*, ANGELO CROCE, WAS A BOXER, BECAUSE OF HIS build and the pugilistic outlines of his face and physique. In reality he and many of the waiters at this one-of-a-kind eatery were professional rugby players, which explains the skill with which they weave among the stone-topped tables, which are in turn topped with paper mats. Local regulars sit elbow-to-elbow, and the banter gets lively. "Cheap and cheery" might be a three-word gloss of Osteria dell'Angelo. The menu is printed on the table mats, and it rarely changes, starting with the house *antipasto*—small *salamini*, white beans and garlicky *bruschetta* or *crostini*, and *finto pesce*, "mock fish," which is none other than potato mixed with tuna and pickles. The cooking is basic—*cacio e pepe*, *carbonara*, *gricia*, gnocchi (with clams, tomato sauce, and zucchini). Veal or beef stew comes with tomato sauce and chili, there's good, gutsy tripe, tasty roast rabbit or veal shoulder, and other straightforward dishes. The dessert consists of wine-dipping cookies and a glass of red fortified wine from Olevano Romano, made with Cesanese grapes, which, like all such mysteriously strong wines, should be consumed with moderation. The house red and white won't

hurt you. At lunch you must order à la carte; at dinner there's a prix fixe menu and you pay for everything whether you eat it or not. The price is very low, however. There's a pleasant sidewalk terrace, which is considerably less noisy than the two echoing dining rooms. Note: credit cards are not accepted.

VIA GIOVANNI BETTOLO 24/28 ✦ TEL: 06 372 9470
CLOSED SUNDAY *and in* AUGUST ✦ INEXPENSIVE
Near: one block north of Viale delle Milizie, near Via S. de Saint Bon

CHEESE, COFFEE, FRESH PASTA, GOURMET FOOD SHOPS, ICE CREAM, PASTRIES

AL SETTIMO GELO

IN PHILOSOPHY AND APPROACH, AL SETTIMO GELO IS THE CLOSEST ICE CREAMERY IN ROME TO FIOR DI LUNA Gelato e Cioccolato and Il Gelato di San Crispino. Everything is uncompromisingly natural, fair trade, and organic. The results are distinctive. Al Settimo Gelo ice creams levitate with lightness and have a brilliancy found nowhere else. They tend toward sweetness, to compensate for a lack of fatty substances. These may be the most authentically old-fashioned ice creams in Rome (and perhaps Italy) because of their apparent artlessness. For instance, the nut flavors are pale in color, but they taste of the freshly toasted and ground nuts the owners buy and transform themselves. They're the best nuts on the market, from Bronte, the Langhe, and Southern Italy. Even the peanut butter flavor—usually a clunker—is weightless and fresh-tasting. The fruit flavors have no dairy products in them and approach the simplicity and purity of Roman *cremolato*. The *caffè* is made with freshly brewed coffee from the excellent family-run Torrefazione Olimpica in Rieti. The shop's name is authentically funny in Italian—a play on Settimo Cielo (Seventh Heaven), and it captures the sunny character of both owners. The Vatican isn't far away, and if the Holy Ghost was a *gelataio* and had a sense of humor these ethereal creations would be his. Pierpaolo Agostini was a furniture restorer and cabinetmaker before turning to ice cream. He brings his perfectionism and love of craft to his job. His significant other, Mirella Fiumanò, ran a hardware shop with her father before reinventing herself. The pair also love spices and herbs. If it's available, don't miss the chocolate with *peperoncino* chili, or the cardamom flavor. The sumptuous yet heavenly vanilla is made with fresh vanilla beans and is flecked black with them.

VIA VODICE 21A ✦ TEL: 06 372 5567 ✦ WWW.ALSETTIMOGELO.IT
OPEN 10AM *to* 10PM TUESDAY *to* SATURDAY, 10AM *to* 1:30PM *and* 4 *to* 10PM SUNDAY, CLOSED MONDAY
Near: 200 yards due north of Piazza Mazzini

ANTONINI

THIS LONG-ESTABLISHED, MUCH-LOVED PASTRY SHOP, CAFFÈ, COCKTAIL BAR AND ICE CREAMERY HAS ONE of the classiest and longest sidewalk terraces in town. On it are rather hideous but comfortable plastified rattan chairs, and tables draped with red tablecloths, among which busy waiters in livery weave with their silver trays. The Fantini coffee is not among the best in town, but the choice of peerless pastries, cakes, and pies is vast and irresistible. They're displayed temptingly behind picture windows, making it difficult to get by without stepping into the long, luxurious interior, lined with refrigerated cases also artfully filled with desserts. Pointing at the strawberry *millefoglie* or delicate chocolate layer cakes, perhaps, with their bejeweled fingers, are the same well-heeled, conservative Romans who haunt Vanni and the many Cartier-style food shops nearby (not to mention the other Antonini establishment, Gran Caffè Esperia, area 8, page 288). The ice creams are fluffy and colorful here, but the owners swear they are entirely artisanal and wholesome, and they certainly taste delicious. Many Roman connoisseurs say they are to be preferred to the newfangled, organic, fair-trade ice creams of Al Settimo Gelo, which is only 150 yards away. Maybe. Maybe not. In any case, Antonini is lovely for a pick-me-up or a cocktail.

VIA SABOTINO 19/29 ✦ TEL: 06 372 4354 ✦ OPEN DAILY
Near: kitty-corner to the covered market, 200 yards northwest of Piazza Mazzini

DOLCE MANIERA CORNETTERIA

GROTTO-LIKE, THIS TAKE-OUT-ONLY PASTRY SHOP IS IN THE CELLAR OF THE BUILDING NEXT DOOR TO IL Ciociaro, a perfectly all right Roman/Lazio restaurant with an outdoor terrace. Dolce Maniera makes every imaginable type of Italian pastry, cake, pie, cookie, savory baked snack, and even *tramezzini* and panini. Mobbed by commuters, students, and soldiers, Dolce Maniera is a good place to pick up a *maritozzo* or a *bomboletta* filled with white chocolate, a *ciambellina* or apple strudel. In theory, Dolce Maniera is always open (in practice, one wonders whether anyone has checked at 3:30am).

VIA BARLETTA 27 ✦ TEL: 06 375 17518
WWW.DOLCEMANIERA.IT ✦OPEN DAILY, ROUND *the* CLOCK
Near: facing the military barracks just north of Viale Giulio Cesare

ERCOLI

THOUGH THE PIAZZA MAZZINI NEIGHBORHOOD AS A WHOLE IS UPSCALE, ERCOLI IS IN THE MOST EXPENSIVE section of it. Next door to this palatial, stone-clad food emporium is a car dealership selling Ferraris, Porsches, and Mazeratis. The shop was founded in 1928 by Leonardo Ercoli and took off because the studios of RAI set up across the street. Spend long enough in Ercoli and you're pretty much guaranteed to see a media diva swan in. Salamis, sausages and hams, and packages of dried wild mushrooms, dangle temptingly from overhead racks. But they and the vast selection of cheeses are not the shop's main draw. The city's widest selection of champagne, foie gras, and caviar is here. Ercoli is a direct importer of Iranian caviar, and owner Sandro Massari, alias the Caviar King, thrills in explaining the differences between Asetra, Beluga, and Sevruga (and sells around one metric ton of caviar a year, most of it from wild fish). In his early sixties, dapper and charming, Massari is from the landlocked Norcia area in mountainous Umbria, and his original expertise lies in the realm of Norcia black truffles and ham. On display are dozens of hams, from Parma and Norcia to Jamon Patanegra. The selection of Italian wines is extravagant, and includes Super Tuscans, vintage Vino Nobile di Montepulciano, Brunello di Montalcino ,and Chianti, making this the best source for wine in the area.

The polished, professional service is what you'd expect given the posh premises, and the matching prices. A recent addition is a handsome if staid *sala degustazione* (tasting room) at the rear of the shop, where you can savor any of the hundreds of delicacies and wines on offer, or have tea or coffee and wait for a TV star to show up.

VIA MONTELLO 22/26 ✦ TEL: 06 372 0243 ✦ WWW.ERCOLI1928.IT
OPEN 7AM *to* 8:30PM ✦ CLOSED SUNDAY ✦ *Near: Piazza Mazzini*

F. DE CAROLIS SALUMERIA GASTRONOMIA

IN ROME, WHEN IT COMES TO FOOD, TO SAY "FRANCO DE CAROLIS" IS TANTAMOUNT TO SAYING BULGARI OR CARTIER for jewelry. The neighborhood's prosperous residents, and the politicos and lobbyists who drop by to buy gifts, know De Carolis as among the prime sources—along with Ercoli, E. Volpetti & C., and La Tradizione—for caviar, smoked sturgeon, goose or salmon, *bottarga*, truffles, and pedigreed hams and cheeses from all over Europe, all of peerless quality and corresponding price. Locals also know, however, that some of the most flavorful and fresh mozzarella available in Rome is sold here (it arrives daily), not to mention earthy *guanciale* from the top artisanal producers of Lazio, Tuscany, and Le Marche, excellent olive oils and vinegars, plus artisanal dry pastas and even a handful of kosher delicacies. Whether or not you buy a thing, it's worth detouring here to glance at the gorgeously appointed picture-window displays, and the handsome, marble-clad interior. The service is courteous and professional, as one might expect.

VIA F. P. DE' CALBOLI 40 ✦ TEL: 06 372 4050
CLOSED SUNDAY ✦ *Near: 20 yards from Via Sabotino*

FAGGIANI

THIS CORNER *CAFFÈ*/PASTRY SHOP HAS BEEN AROUND FOREVER BUT CHANGED HANDS IN 2007, MUCH TO THE alarm of devoted regulars. Wisely, the new owners have altered little, from the good coffee and cappuccino on up. The *parigino*—a special *cornetto* with cream inside and a sugary, twisted crust—is still the house specialty, and you'll also find sugar donuts, other filled or plain *cornetti*, cakes, *occhi di bue* jam-filled pastries, mini-*crostate pinolate*, decent artisanal ice cream, boxed chocolate, candies, and wine. The floor is still paved in stone, and the handful of tables on the sidewalk are still fought over by the TV crowd from RAI up the street, plus local business people and bureaucrats.

VIA GIUSEPPE FERRARI 23 ✦ TEL: 06 397 39742
OPEN DAILY ✦ *Near: 200 yards due south of Piazza Mazzini*

GIOLITTI

IN NO WAY ASSOCIATED WITH THE HISTORIC GIOLITTI ICE CREAM SHOP NEAR THE PANTHEON, THIS SLICK, TRENDY cocktail bar, tea room, ice cream shop, pastry shop, and restaurant is the latest incarnation of "the other" Giolitti, which has been in these premises for decades, but has changed hands many times. Crowded and noisy inside, the sidewalk terrace is the opposite—a great place to rest your heels and have a drink or a snack. Take a mauve, orange, or white bucket seat at one of the glinting stainless steel tables, and enjoy a decent cup of coffee, a pastry, or a light lunch. The food is edible, and the self-adoring atmosphere pure Prati-Mazzini. Note that this Giolitti belongs to the same group that owns similarly trendy La Buvette, Dolci & Doni, and Mignanelli (all three are near Piazza di Spagna, in the fashion district).

VIA LUIGI SETTEMBRINI 19/23 ✦ TEL: 06 326 00374
OPEN DAILY ✦ *Near: 200 yards southeast of Piazza Mazzini*

GRAN CAFFÈ MAZZINI

THE RIVAL TO FAGGIANI AND GIOLITTI, THIS DELIGHTFULLY PRETENTIOUS NEW *CAFFÈ* ON THE CORNER OF Piazza Mazzini and Via Giuseppe Ferrari serves better than decent Mokarabia coffee and good pastries and savory snacks. Inside: chandeliers, a gleaming bar-top, and marble floors. Outside: rattan chairs, and tables that wrap around the corner of Via Giuseppe Ferrari. The staff is used to serving VIPs and TV celebrities, so if the servers forget that you exist, don't hold it against them. If nothing else, Gran Caffè Mazzini is a comfortable perch from which to watch the neighborhood's self-conscious, entertaining bigwigs.

PIAZZA MAZZINI 9-11 ✦ TEL: 06 321 7502
OPEN DAILY ✦ *Near: on the south side of the piazza*

PIACERE E PASSIONE CAFFETTERIA

THE LOCAL HIPSTERS WHO HANG HERE CALL PIACERE E PASSIONE "DUE P"—TWO Ps. TINY, WITH A MINIATURE sidewalk terrace, and a black-and-gray interior the size of a shoebox, in which a handful of staff wearing black-and-gray clothing make espressos for clients also wearing black or gray, Due P has one major draw: it serves excellent Sant'Eustachio coffee, and sells Sant'Eustachio beans (or ground coffee) to go. The wide, park-boulevard out front is equipped with gorgeous parasol pines and benches, so if there's nowhere to perch on the terrace, get a cappuccino or an espresso to go. If it's snack time, you can have a Häagen Dazs ice cream, buy a bar of excellent Amedei chocolate, or nibble a sandwich, and feel like you're in Santa Monica or maybe on Beacon Hill.

VIA M. PRESTINARI 27 ✦ TEL: 06 320 4780
CLOSED SUNDAY ✦ *Near: the corner of Via Monte Zebio*

L'ANGOLO DEL GELATO

THIS LONGTIME, UNPRETENTIOUS, FAMILY-RUN NEIGHBORHOOD ICE CREAM PARLOR IS NOW BRACKETED by the loud and sassy Mizzica 3, a mini-chain of Sicilian snack places. It faces a modern courthouse building—an unmistakable eyesore. There's a tiny outdoor terrace, but you're better off getting a cone and walking with it, though the area isn't exactly scenic. The ice creams here are handmade using high-quality ingredients, with no shortcuts, right down to the cracked, crushed nuts for pistachio or hazelnut, and while the *gelati* are not quite as wildly excellent as those of Al Settimo Gelo or Gelateria dei Gracchi, they're very, very good indeed. The texture is soft, and they have volume, which is often a bad sign, but in this case is the result of vigorous whipping, which incorporates lots of air, and makes the ice creams fluffy.

VIA TRIONFALE 75C ✦ TEL: 06 397 338818 ✦ CLOSED TUESDAY
Near: 150 yards north of the Circonvallazione Trionfale

LA BONTÀ DEL PANE

THIS WONDERFUL BAKERY IS RIGHT NEXT DOOR TO LA TRADIZIONE AND MANZO (A FINE BUTCHER SHOP), a few storefronts southwest of the Zoldo ice cream parlor. At La Bontà you'll find all the classic Roman and Italian breads, pastries, and cookies, all of them perfectly baked and delcious. The service is particularly friendly.

VIA CIPRO 8B/C/D ✦ TEL: 06 397 20351
WWW.LABONTADELPANE.IT ✦ CLOSED SUNDAY
Near: facing Cipro-Musei Vaticani subway stop

LA TRADIZIONE

LA TRADIZIONE IS RIGHT: THIS TRADITIONAL GASTRONOMIA IS OWNED AND RUN BY RENZO FANTUCCI AND his wife Franca Cozzari, and Valentino Belli and his wife Santina Truffeli. Renzo is the official spokesman for La Tradizione, and a frequent food commentator on Italian TV and radio. Despite his celebrity and success he's still a charming, simple country fellow from Vallo di Nera, a village in the Valnerina Valley not far from Norcia. You'll find him with Valentino behind the shop counter six days a week, cheerful and eager to please. Among the displays of about 300 cheeses are several house specialties, among them Campa Vallo caciocavallo, a large, pear-shaped cheese of cow's milk made by Renzo's family in Vallo di Nera; it's aged in the family's mountain grottoes for an astonishing three to seven years and for the last six months of the process, is stacked with walnut leaves and wild herbs and sealed in oak barrels. The hams and salamis are equally exceptional. The Fantucci family's Ciauscolo di Vallo di Nera is a mild,

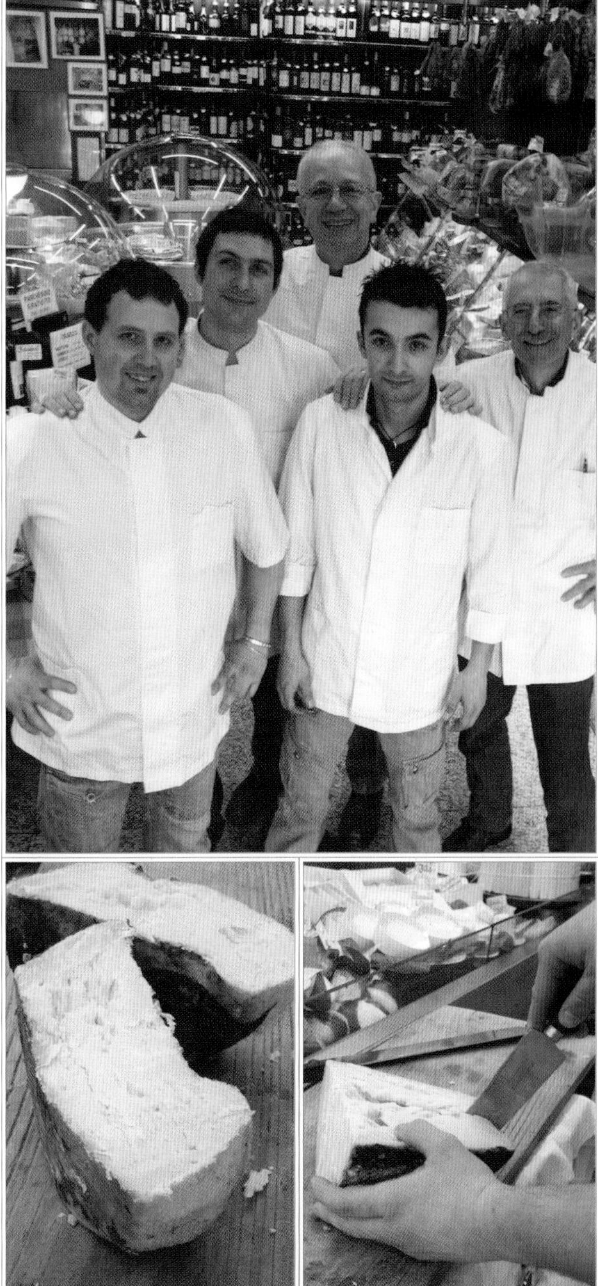

kg 32,00
Ventricina
Salsiccia
di Guilmi
DA MAIALI BRADI
kg
55,00

Kg 38,00
Salsiccia
Aquilana
Kg 33,00
Salsiccia

soft salami made of finely ground shoulder, thigh, and belly of pork with garlic, salt and pepper, and white wine, lightly smoked over a juniper-berry fire and then air-dried for about three months. Like the other exceptionally good *gastronomie* in Rome, La Tradizione sells delicious ready-to-eat salads and prepared foods, and offers a fine selection of pasta, wine, and canned or dried goods.

VIA CIPRO 8E ✦ TEL: 06 397 20349 ✦ WWW.LATRADIZIONE.IT
OPEN 7AM *to* 7:30PM ✦ CLOSED SUNDAY
Near: 150 yards southwest of Piazza degli Eroi and the Trionfale open market, across from the Cipro-Musei Vaticani subway stop

VANNI

VANNI IS A MODISHLY CONSERVATIVE, UPSCALE *CAFFÈ*, PASTRY SHOP, ICE CREAMERY, PIZZERIA, AND SELF-styled "steak and lobster house." The understated gray tables and chairs of the steakhouse blend in with the slate-paved sidewalk, and the business suits and *tailleurs* of free-spending bureaucrats who pack out Vanni, especially on weekdays. The wood-burning oven churns out very good pizza, but the stone-paved snack bar and *pasticceria* next door are more fun. The Kimbo Blu coffee served there is remarkably strong. The ice creams look and taste positively pneumatic and psychedelic, but the pastries and *cornetti* are delicious, and so are the chocolate-coated ice cream bonbons called *vannini*, meant to be devoured in a single bite.

VIA COL DI LANA 10 ✦ TEL: 06 326 49012 ✦ WWW.VANNI.IT
OPEN DAILY ✦ *Near: one block northeast of Piazza Mazzini, on the corner of Via Monte Zebio*

ZOLDO IL GELATIERE

THE CONVENIENT LOCATION OF THIS ARTISANAL ICE CREAM PARLOR IS AS MUCH A DRAW AS THE ICE CREAMS it makes, which are very good but not exceptional, with the possible exception of some of the fresh, seasonal fruit flavors.

VIA CIPRO 6A/B ✦ TEL: 06 397 40839
WWW.ZOLDOILGELATIERE.IT ✦ OPEN DAILY
Near: facing the Cipro-Musei Vaticani subway stop

WINE SHOPS

ENOTECA DI GREGORIO

STEP INTO A TIME-TUNNEL AND ALIGHT IN THE YEAR 1936, WHEN THIS FAMILY-RUN BOTTLE SHOP OPENED FOR business. Even the dust motes are vintage. The wines on tap, pulled from a spigot, come from suburban Olevano Romano, and you can choose from red or white. Oh, there's also the Cesanese dolce—a sweet red sometimes referred to as Romanella, and dispensed on tap at trattorias and *osterias* (such as Osteria dell'Angelo). The bottled wines are of the simplest, good for a picnic on a sunny day.

VIA TRIONFALE 50 ✦ TEL: 06 397 42353 ✦ CLOSED SUNDAY
Near: on the corner of Via Buccari, half a block south of trattoria Antico Falcone

ERCOLI

(See detailed description on page 320)

NON-TERROIR TOP OR TRENDY TABLES

SETTEMBRINI

VIA SETTEMBRINI 25/27 ✦ TEL: 06 323 2617
WWW.SETTEMBRINIROMA.IT
CLOSED SATURDAY LUNCH, SUNDAY, *and* AUGUST
EXPENSIVE *to* VERY EXPENSIVE

REGIONAL RESTAURANTS

CAMPANIA

PAPÀ GENNARO

CIRCONVALLAZIONE TRIONFALE 59A ✦ TEL: 06 397 27511
CLOSED AUGUST ✦ MODERATE *to* EXPENSIVE

CHAPTER 10

OUTLYING AREAS

ROME'S HISTORIC CENTRAL DISTRICTS ARE SURROUNDED BY DOZENS OF OUTLYING NEIGHBORHOODS, MANY built from the early to mid-twentieth century. Beyond them are the so-called *borgate* low-cost housing projects from the postwar era, and other, even further-flung suburbs that have wrapped themselves around what were independent villages. Each of these outlying neighborhoods has its charms. A few are worth visiting for their food or wine.

APPIA ANTICA

THE VIA APPIA ANTICA (IN ENGLISH, THE APPIAN WAY) OFFICIALLY BEGINS AT THE BASE OF THE PALATINE Hill near the Circus Maximus. It runs due south past the Baths of Caracalla, through Porta di San Sebastiano and Rome's third-century Aurelian city walls on the southeastern edge of town, and then continues south several hundred miles to Brindisi on Italy's southern Adriatic coast. Built by consul Appius Claudius in 312 BC, the 14-foot-wide straightaway is shaded for several miles as it leaves Rome by twin rows of umbrella pines. Under them are timeworn mausoleums and monuments. The first ten miles or so of the roadway have been preserved as a park. They are flanked to the east by the Caffarella Valley nature reserve and Park of the Seven Aqueducts. These parklands, and the grounds of abutting villas, olive tree orchards, pastures, and farmland constitute a greenbelt traversed by hiking trails and bike paths. The road itself has little traffic. It's closed entirely to cars on Sunday, and is a favorite destination for outings and picnics.

Appia Antica Park headquarters is a few hundreds yards south of the Aurelian walls (Via Appia Antica 42, Tel: 06 512 6314 or 800 02 8000, www.parcoappiaantica.org). Free maps and brochures are available here. This is also where you sign up for guided visits to the area's sights, the roadway, and the aqueducts (10am and 3pm Sundays). You can rent a bike (Sundays only, 9:30am to 4pm). Normal city buses 118 and 218 stop in front of the headquarters. The Archeobus, a special bus service, links central Rome to the Appia Antica, Caffarella Valley, and Park of the Seven Aqueducts. Archeobuses leave Piazza Venezia every hour on the hour daily 10am to 5pm (information and reservations, 9am to 2pm, Tel: 06 469 54695).

There are several serviceable trattorias within 100 yards of the headquarters. Though not outstanding, the best of the bunch is **Trattoria di Priscilla** (Via Appia Antica 68, Tel: 06 513 6379, closed Sunday, inexpensive to moderate). However, better food is served a few minutes away on foot or by bike (see below). About 50 yards south of the park headquarters is Domine Quo Vadis church, where Peter is believed to have asked Jesus, "Lord, whither goest thou?" Cinecittà (Italy's Hollywood), which produced dozens of sword-and-sandals "Peplums" like the 1951 *Quo Vadis*, is a few miles southeast of here, beyond the pastures of the Caffarella Valley.

A few hundred yards south of the church, up the sloping, cobbled way, is a columbarium-monument to Emperor Augustus' Freedmen. It once held the cremated remains of Roman citizens. Since 1796, this peculiar site's courtyards and their 3,000 sepulchral niches have housed a restaurant, **Hostaria Antica Roma** (Via Appia Antica 87, Tel: 06 513 2888, www.anticaroma.it, closed Mondays, expensive to very expensive). For its first hundred years, the *hostaria* doubled as a depot for the wine carts that shunted between Rome and the Castelli Romani. You might expect to find a certified tourist trap, but what you'll discover instead is a family-run restaurant with good food, made from excellent ingredients, and an upscale clientele one part Roman, two parts out-of-towners. The family grows some of their own produce and herbs, and keeps hens out back, which produce the eggs that go into many recipes, including remarkable *carbonara*, and an exquisite *tiramisù*. The roast suckling pig, lamb, and veal are particularly tasty. In addition to the usual Roman classics, you might find spinach-and-ricotta filled crêpes, or risotto with artichoke hearts. The wine list is long, and boasts many fine Italian and some foreign bottlings. You'll soon forget that soldiers and citizens were once entombed here: the courtyards are shaded by old wisteria vines, and there's a handsome, glassed-in dining room.

Sheep graze not only in the Caffarella Valley due east of the restaurant. They also nibble on the fields and even the lawns of the San Callisto catacombs and affiliated religious institution, on the west side of the road, which extend from Domine Quo Vadis to the top of the rise. Ancient quarries here were transformed into Christian burial grounds and called catacombs, and it's their presence that has kept the area as a whole from destruction and redevelopment. The Catacombe di San Callisto (named for Calixtus, pope from 217-222 AD) offers a chilling 13-mile labyrinth of half a million wall tombs. More atmospheric and less crowded, the smaller San Sebastiano catacombs are a few hundred yards further south. They house delicate second-century frescoes of doves, their necks iridescent, and lovely coffered stuccowork. In the basilica atop the catacombs are the saint's relics.

Directly across the Via Appia Antica from the basilica is aptly named **Archeologia** (Via Appia Antica 139, Tel: 06 788 0494, www.larcheologia.it, closed Tuesday, expensive to very expensive), the area's most upscale gourmet restaurant, also atop an ancient funerary site. Formerly a roadside tavern, Archeologia has been in the Casaveccio family since 1890, and in the last decade or so has become a serious restaurant favored by the Roman business crowd, politicians, celebrities, and well-heeled tourists. The interior is lavish yet cozy, with a fireplace, original Piranesi prints, open timbers, and Pompei red walls and matching undercloths, with white tablecloths on top of them. Some might prefer the garden terrace, where you dine under umbrella pines, and watch lobsters and fresh fish dueling it out in large aquariums. Current scion Marco-Vinicio Casaveccio runs Archeologia with aplomb, serving a wide range of Lazio specialities featured on daily theme menus. Not only will you find the classics of Roma Urbis, you'll also discover rural specialties from the Ciociara, Alban Hills, and other districts. The excellent, authentic seafood soup from the southern coast of Lazio around Gaeta, or the linguine with garlic, zucchini blossoms, and clams, are delicious. You might also be offered thick *farro* soup with black truffles from the Sabine Hills, or wild boar sauce atop fresh pasta such as gnocchetti, from the region's Tuscia district. Casaveccio's grandparents were artichoke farmers, and though the cooking is sophisticated and lightened nowadays, it retains an earthy authenticity. In summer the wood-burning oven in the garden is used to make delicious focaccia and bread. Casaveccio takes an archeological or anthropological approach not only to the region's food, but also to its wine. There are 70 different Lazio wines on the list, and five reds and five whites are available by the glass daily. Ask the affable Casaveccio to show you the *cantina*, accessed via a spiral staircase. Once there, among the burial niches, he might thrill you by casually holding up the human femur he found a few years back when the cellar was remodeled. Candlelit wine tastings are held here. It's a one-of-a-kind place to sip a selection of the 370 different Italian and foreign wines the restaurant stocks.

Continuing south, past the imposing round Mausoleum of Cecilia Metella, you'll find **Appia Antica Caffè** (Via Appia Antica 175, corner Via Cecilia Metella, Tel: 338 346 5440, www.appiaanticacaffe.it, closed Monday in winter). This is a friendly, casual spot to enjoy a snack, sandwich, daily pasta dish, cold refreshments, or a decent cup of coffee on a shaded terrace, without going broke. You can also rent a bike, or talk for hours to the idealistic, affable owner, a lover of quality literature: he maintains a small lending library.

Head east about 300 yards on Via Cecilia Metella to the corner of the Via Appia Pignatelli and enter the Caffarella Valley by crossing a field, usually planted with wheat. Lush and leafy, this ostensibly wild wetlands valley was reputedly the model for the gardens of many Renaissance and later villas, and, some historians claim, for Central Park in New York City. A distressingly polluted stream runs down the middle of the Caffarella nowadays, but from the western flank of the valley, about 100 yards below the church of Sant'Urbano, springs a pristine fountainhead. This is the sacred spring of the water nymph Egeria, and it is clearly marked as such. A recumbent effigy of the nymph, looking rather worse for wear, is framed by a mossy grotto. Watercress grows wild.

Flocks of sheep roam throughout the valley. They're herded by a family of shepherds and cheesemakers who live in the Casale della Vaccarella (or Vacareccia), a semi-ruined 1500s farmstead in the valley bottom, set against an only-in-Italy, surreal backdrop: the high-rise apartment buildings of the Appio

district, perched on heights near the modern Via Appia Nuova. Casale della Vaccarella is one of Rome's last working dairy and lamb farms. Its official name is **Azienda Agricola La Caffarella** (Via della Caffarella 40, Tel: 348 918 6964, always open, phone if no one is in the farmyard). The farmers keep about 1,100 sheep of the Sicilian and Sardinian Comisana breeds. You can buy fresh handmade ewe's milk ricotta, primo sale, pecorino fresco, or rounds of caciotta the size of 45 rpm records (and, in spring, sides of freshly butchered suckling lamb). Also sold are free-range guinea fowls and chickens.

THE APPIO DISTRICT AND VIA APPIA NUOVA

IF YOU'VE VISITED THE VIA APPIA ANTICA AND CAFFARELLA VALLEY, YOU MIGHT WISH TO RETURN TO CENTRAL ROME via the modern, working- and lower-middle-class Appio district and Via Appia Nuova. The subway runs underneath Via Appia Nuova, and the nearest stops are Colli Albani and Furio Camillo. You can also access the area from the other direction, coming from San Giovanni in Laterano or piazzas Tuscolo and Epiro, in area 5.

The Appio isn't aesthetic, but has a handful of addresses worth seeking out. First, the more central of the two local street markets, **mercato rionale Appio I**, on Via Valesio and Via Capponi, starting on the Via Appia Nuova at Piazza C. Finocchiaro Aprile, is authentic, lively, and fun. While the market is on, locals gather at **Gran Caffè Alberone**, on the corner of Piazza Alberone and Via Appia Nuova. It's unremarkable, other than the fact that its pleasant small terrace is shaded by an ilex tree that has replaced a much older, larger specimen that gave the square its name (*alberone* means big tree). On the same piazza, which is not a piazza at all but rather a swelling in the very wide Via Appia Nuova, about 50 yards north of the ilex tree, is the excellent, pocket-sized *caffè* and pastry shop **Le Delizie dell'Alberone** (Piazza dell'Alberone 25, Tel: 06 786 012, closed Monday). There are only two tables on the unappealing sidewalk, but the interior sparkles, the house coffee is Illy, and the pastries are remarkably flavorful and light. The dough for the *cornetti* and other breakfast rolls and pastries rises for 24 hours.

Petrini (Piazza dell'Alberone 16A, corner Via Veturia, Tel: 06 786 307, closed Monday), directly across from Gran Caffè Alberone, is a pint-sized but classy take-out ice cream shop. It's been in the same family since 1926 and is now run by third-generation master *gelataio* Mauro Petrini. When Petrini opens at 11:30am there's usually a long line of regulars waiting. You'll spot the brass plaque and the single wooden bench on the sidewalk. Like cult ice creamery Il Gelato di San Crispino, which Petrini resembles in many ways, this establishment emanates cleanliness, not to say sterility, and deep seriousness. Luckily, the ice creams are outstandingly flavorful and wholesome, especially the seasonal fruit and creamy nut-based flavors.

Heading back into central Rome toward Piazza Epiro from the Via Appia Nuova and Piazza C. Finocchiaro Aprile, in what appears to be the middle of nowhere, look out for the authentic trattoria **Ada e Mario** (Circonvallazione Appia 81, between Via Tabarini and Via Baccarini, Tel: 06 786 615, closed Sunday, inexpensive to moderate). A tattered Italian flag flaps from a short flagpole, there are several pine trees, and across the street is the homely Istituto Antoniano Femminile, a religious institution. Ada and Mario Mazzelli and their three children have run this neighborhood eatery for nearly 30 years now. The prices are low, the setting casual—green tablecloths and simple wooden chairs on what is essentially a reconverted street-side terrace, and a small back dining room—and the clientele strictly local, composed of habitués young and old. Though you'll find a few proprietory recipes such as rich *tonnarelli alla boscaiola* (with mushrooms, peas, and a little too much heavy cream), or very good fresh fish (on Tuesdays and Fridays), the best things here are, unsurprisingly, the classic Roman meat or vegetable dishes, which are always luscious. Desserts are straightforward but satisfying. The house wines are fine.

SALARIA-TAGLIAMENTO-NEMORENSE

ROME'S CELEBRATED VIA SALARIA LIES ATOP A MAJOR ROMAN ROAD THAT PREDATES THE EARliest Republican-era consular roads. The Via Salaria grew from an unpaved Bronze Age path linking the mouth of the Tiber River to Rome and Rieti, capital of the

Sabine people, whose womenfolk were, according to legend, "raped" or carried off by the followers of Romulus. Up the Via Salaria went Mediterranean salt, followed by Roman legions. Nowadays the road looks much like any other contemporary Roman radial artery. However, if you follow it east past the ring road called Viale Regina Margherita, where streetcars run, you'll cross the Rubicon—Via Rubicone—and discover the fantastic turn-of-the-nineteenth-century Quartiere Coppedè. Its streets are lined by massive Italian Art Nouveau buildings designed by architect Gino Coppedè. This alone would make a detour to the Salaria area worthwhile. Happily, there are several other reasons to explore the district's stately streets. Vast, hilly, and dotted with ruins, the parklands of Villa Ada flank the Via Salaria, and include the unsung Catacombs of Priscilla, which are less grand than the catacombs of the Via Appia Antica, but are also much less crowded. Once you're within the walls of Villa Ada, you can walk for hours on looping, leafy paths, under towering bay trees, and climb to the top of Monte Antenne for an unexpected view of the Tiber and the posh Parioli neighborhood.

Perhaps even more important to food lovers, the Salaria area boasts many excellent bakeries and pastry shops, one of Rome's best coffee roasters and ice cream makers, several good places to eat, and a fine open market. Almost all of these are found along a radial artery parallel to and south of Via Salaria called Via Tagliamento. It changes names several times as it runs northeast, becoming Via Sabino and then Via Nemorense.

Start on Via Salaria just southwest of the corner of Viale Regina Margherita. Here you'll find **Cerasari** (Via Salaria 280A/B-288, Tel: 06 841 6447, closed Sunday, open all day Tuesday and Friday), a long-established deli and grocery, with fine artisanal pastas, a fair selection of wine, plus hams, cheeses, and countless gourmet foods. Next door is Cerasari's fruit and vegetable shop, and next door to it, the Cerasari *caffè* and pastry shop (try the jam-filled *occhi di bue*, the house specialty). As the Häagen-Dazs dispenser indicates, not everything here is artisanal. However, the locally roasted Caffè Peru served at the bar is very good, and will appeal to those who like dark-roasted, powerful Arabica blends.

Walk southeast from Cerasari on Viale Regina Margherita toward Piazza Buenos Aires. Before reaching the square, at Via Garigliano, the first cross street parallel to Via Salaria, cross the boulevard and walk northeast several shopfronts to **Cooperativa Stella** (Via Garigliano 68, Tel: 06 854 2681, closed

Tuesday afternoon and Sunday), which sells its own handmade buffalo-milk mozzarella from the village of Patrica, southwest of Frosinone, in the Ciociara district. The mozzarella arrives daily, and is outstanding.

Next door to the cheese shop is the good Sardinian restaurant **Garigliano** (Via Garigliano 70A, Tel: 06 855 1077, www.ristorantegarigliano.com, closed Sunday, moderate).

Backtrack to Viale Regina Margherita. Walk southeast again one block. On the west side of the boulevard the cross street is named Via Po; on the east side it's called Via Tagliamento. Walk back a short distance toward central Rome to the wonderful old *caffè* and pastry shop **Natalizi** (Via Po 124, Tel: 06 853 50736, closed Monday). Tastefully restyled, this neighborhood institution makes some of the best whipped cream-filled *maritozzi* and breakfast rolls in Rome, plus very good artisanal ice creams (in summer only). It's a great place for a cappuccino and a snack, whether sweet or savory.

Turn around and walk up Via Po again to Viale Regina Margherita. Turn right and head southeast four and a half blocks to #212, where you'll find **Gelateria dei Gracchi**, one of Rome's top natural ice cream makers (for a complete description, see entry in area 8, page 297). Cross to the other side of Viale Regina Margherita and backtrack to Via Tagliamento. Head up Via Tagliamento to the corner of Via Adige. **Panis** (Via Tagliamento 62, Tel: 06 841 7029, closed Sunday) is an upmarket bakery that's been around for over a century with the name Gentilini, but was renamed and remodeled recently into chic banality. The dozen or more types of bread are very good; the house specialty remains breadsticks and Fette Biscottate Gentilini (the brandnamed toasted slices of bread), the kind Romans and most Italians favor as a snack or breakfast food (often mounded with jam). Panis also makes excellent savory snacks such as spinach and cheese-filled *rustici* turnovers.

Next door to Panis is **Carnidea** (Via Tagliamento 70, Tel: 06 841 7639, closed Thursday afternoon and Sunday all year, plus Saturday afternoon in summer), a reputable butcher shop with premium veal, beef, and lamb, and good take-out dishes you can reheat at home. Next door to Carnidea is **Specialità d'Abruzzo** (Via Tagliamento 72/74, Tel: 06 841 7636, closed Thursday afternoon and Sunday), the classic neighborhood *norcineria* and deli, with very good *guanciale*, pecorino di Atri, fresh mozzarella, and a wide variety of dry or canned foods, many from the Abruzzi region. A few shops further out is **F. Boni** (Via Tagliamento 84,

Tel: 06 855 1146, closed Tuesday), a small pastry shop with all the Roman treats, plus the house specialty, *castagnole.*

Next door to F. Boni is **Giovanni De Sanctis** (Via Tagliamento 88, Tel: 06 855 2287, closed Sunday all year, from July to September closed on Saturday afternoon, from October through June closed Thursday afternoon), an enchanting, handsome early-1900s shop selling sweets, chocolates, teas, and remarkably good house-roasted coffees. Romans will cross town to buy the coffee here, for good reason. The gas-fired coffee roaster in the shop's back room dates to 1924, the year the De Sanctis family took over the business. Giovanni De Sanctis or his son toast only a few pounds of beans at a time, daily, to ensure freshness and flavor. Their minute attention to the sounds and smells of perfect roasting help make their coffees outstanding. The other factor is uncompromising quality. They buy only top Arabicas from Ethiopia and South America, and a surprisingly good shade-grown mountain Robusta. The special blend, for those who like mild coffee, is one part Costa Rica Tournon and two parts Ethiopian Moka Limo, both Arabica. The other, slightly coarser 100-percent Arabica blend is about a quarter each Costa Rican, Moka Limo, Colombian, and Santos.

Continue east on the same street, which changes name to Via Sebino. **La Madia** (Via Sebino 2/12, corner Via Chiana, Tel: 06 841 6304, closed Sunday), another remarkable bakery and pastry shop, has been around since 1950, but, like so many prosperous shops, restyled itself and now has a studiously pseudo-rustic décor. The brick walls have niches filled with wine bottles and old tools, an antique cash register, and even a sewing machine. Nonetheless, this is a good place to have a stand-up snack—a slice of pizza, for instance, topped with just about anything you can imagine—or a perfect pastry or cookie. The coffee is Mondicaffè, and you can shoot down a good espresso made from it at the bar.

Keep walking on the same road and it will change names again, this time to Via Nemorense, where, on the north side, you'll soon see **L'Angolo dei Sapori** (Via Nemorense 45, corner Via Arbia, Tel: 06 853 57135, closed Sunday), an upmarket, chic deli with a very good choice of hams, cheeses, and wines. Across the street from the shop are the handsome, landscaped Parco Virgiliano and Villa Bianca.

On the corner of the park bounded by Via Nemorense and Via Lago di Lesina, facing Piazza Crati (a market square) is one of Rome's top ice cream shops, **Fatamorgana** (Via Lago di Lesina 9/11, Tel: 06 863 91589, www.gelateriafatamorgana.it, open daily noon to midnight). There's another Fatamorgana in the Ostiense area, but these are the original premises. Expect to find 40 ice creams and 20 refreshing sorbets every day, with new flavors each week. If the fresh chestnut ice cream is available (in fall only) don't miss it. You're more likely to find pimento, a wildly good, rich dark-chocolate ice cream with black pepper and cloves. Fatamorgana ice creams are totally natural and softer than many, and you might mistake them for *semifreddi*.

Buy a cone or *coppetta* and sit with the au pairs (called *ragazze alla pari* in Italian) in the park.

Around the corner from Fatamorgana is **MozzaRè** (Via Nemorense 76, Tel: 06 862 13453, closed Thursday afternoon and Sunday). This is the outlet for the MozzaRè mozzarella factory, which is inconveniently located on the distant edge of Rome on the appropriately named Via della Bufalotta—little buffalo street—(#663, Tel: 06 872 00066, open daily). MozzaRè mozzarella, treccia, and ricotta are always super-fresh, made daily and rushed to the shop.

Cross the street to the market square but pause first at **Arcioni** (Piazza Crati 17 and 21/25, Tel: 06 862 06616, bar closed on Monday), which is on the corner of the square and Via Nemorense. Arcioni is a *caffè*, dry goods shop, wine emporium, and also a *torrefazione*, and has been around since 1932. On certain days the scent of roasting coffee wafts out among the tables set up facing the market's colorful displays. Arcioni's top house blend is Miscela Oro 100 Arabica, and it's a strong, dark-roasted, somewhat aggressive animal. Alas, the bar blend, as is so often the case in Rome, is even more aggressive, with lots of Robusta in it, and will put hair on the tongue and lips of your average human being. In the split-level Arcioni wine store flanking the bar you'll find many fine Lazio wines. In the opposite direction, on the piazza, Arcioni has a gift boutique.

The **mercato rionale di Piazza Crati** is small but authentic, and the quality of the produce is high, because this is a neighborhood with lots of serious eaters and very few visitors or out-of-town residents. On the northern edge of the square, on the corner of Via di Priscilla, don't miss **Mercato Vinicolo Angelini** (Piazza Crati 12, Tel: 06 862 06742, closed Sunday). This traditional bottle shop has been around since 1880, and is a good example of the boxy Italian Art Nouveau usually called Liberty, with high ceilings and stained glass windows. Though there are many other wine shops in Rome with a wider choice of top wines, there are few places where you'll still find very quaffable Cesanese del Piglio DOC and Marino DOC on tap.

Kitty-corner to the wine shop is **Pizzeria La Mora** (Piazza Crati 13, Tel: 06 862 06613, closed Tuesday lunch and Monday, inexpensive to moderate), a Tuscan restaurant-pizzeria with a wood-burning oven whose scents compete with those of nearby coffee roaster Arcioni to drive the market's shoppers mad with gluttonous desire. The pizzas are perfect—crisp on the bottom and heaped with delicacies—but the house-made gnocchi and *ribollita* are hard to pass by. Save room for a *cremolato* up the street.

Detour up Via di Priscilla to **Fratelli De Angelis** (Via di Priscilla 18/20, Tel: 06 862 00724, closed Wednesday afternoon in fall and winter). Though the barmen can be crusty, the *cremolati*—mashed, frozen fresh fruit—are wonderful. This is among the only places left in town to make them. The difference between a sorbet and a *cremolato* is, the *cremolato* is not made from blended fruit with sugar and water, but rather is fresh, ripe fruit mashed and frozen, with no water, and very little sugar—none at all if the fruit is ripe enough. The coffee is better across the street at **Bar Nardecchia** (Via di Priscilla 15, Tel: 06 862 06705, closed Wednesday afternoon in fall and winter), a neighborhood *caffè* with better-than-average, house-made pastries.

Go back to Piazza Crati and pick up Via Nemorense, continuing northeast two and a half long blocks to **Pasticceria Cavalletti** (Via Nemorense 169/179/181, Tel: 06 863 24814, www.pasticceriacavalletti.it, closed Tuesday), home of the best *millefoglie*

in Rome, and possibly the best in all of Italy and the world. Celebrated pastry chef Gianni Cavaletti and his extended family supply not only neighborhood regulars, but also many restaurants and far-flung Roman diplomats, who reportedly have the treat air-freighted to them alongside the diplomatic pouch. Cavaletti's *millefoglie* is assembled from startlingly light, crisp, round layers of buttery dough, filled with barely sweetened fresh whipped cream, and then dusted with powdered sugar, like the wig of an eighteenth-century aristocrat. At Eastertide, Cavaletti makes ethereal *pizza di Civitavecchia*, which isn't a pizza in the normal sense, but rather a porous, airy, lightly sweetened angel food cake, delicately flavored with Marsala, vanilla, cocoa, and aniseed. It's heavenly.

Continue on the curving street a few more shopfronts. About 100 yards from the remarkably ugly church of Santa Emerenziana, built in 1942 of brick, you'll come across one of the city's best *pasta fresca* shops, **Laboratorio Pasta all'Uovo Gatti A. & Antonelli M.** (Via Nemorense 211, Tel: 06 862 18044, closed Thursday afternoon and Sunday). Excellent flour, good eggs, and generations of know-how ensure that the house specialties are always peerless. Gatti & Antonelli excel with agnolotti; cannelloni filled with ricotta, ground beef or mushrooms; tortellini; ravioli; and the otherwise unfindable *rotolo*, which is a roll of pasta filled with ricotta and spinach. No one in Rome makes better ribbon pastas, which include bavette, fettuccine, pappardelle, and tonnarelli.

Piazza Emerenziana is where Via Nemorense ends. If you turn back toward the center of Rome from here following Viale Eritrea, on the south side of the square, you'll curve gently toward Piazza Annibaliano, where the street's name changes to Corso Trieste. Near Piazza Istria you'll find the cult neighborhood trattoria **Da Ettore** (Corso Trieste 129, Tel: 06 855 4323, closed Sunday dinner, Monday, and August, moderate). Ettore Guerrini and his wife Maria opened for business in the mid-1950s and are still at it, flanked now by their daughter and sons. If you were casting a thoroughbred Roman restaurateur, it would be a toss-up between Il Cavaliere Gino of Da Gino, near the Italian parliament building in area 2 (see page 128), and Ettore Guerrini. Both have a charming, gentle way with guests, and both look the part, with a dishcloth at the ready, slung over forearm or shoulder. The food at Da Gino and Da Ettore is also similar: Roman classics, very well made, and remarkable for their authenticity. Don't miss the house-made lasagne or semolina gnocchi with butter and cheese, and if there's roast suckling pig on the menu, go for it. The desserts are good—luscious *tiramisù* and *crostata*—and the house wine is perfectly drinkable. There's a pleasant outdoor dining area open in warm weather.

If you'd prefer to dine somewhere slightly more up the scale but want to stay in this part of town, head to the north side of the Villa Chigi park, which is due north of Piazza Emerenziana and Via Nemorense. The area around Villa Chigi is informally known as the Quartiere Africano because many of the streets are named for African countries or cities. One block north of Viale Somalia, before you reach the busy Circonvallazione Salaria, you'll find the well-liked, upscale fish and traditional Roman-Abruzzese restaurant **Mamma Angelina** (Viale Arrigo Boito 65, Tel: 06 860 8928, closed Wednesday and August, moderate to expensive). Named for chef-proprietor Angelina Dell'Omo, this is the kind of place that concierges at mid-range hotels feel confident recommending, in part because of the solidly bourgeois décor, which looks and feels like the dining room or lobby of a three-star hotel, in part because of the quietly professional service. Yet another reason is the menu: it offers many fish dishes, and unthreatening Italian classics guaranteed to please many palates. Happily, Mamma Angelina also offers many delicate, lightened versions of Roman favorites, such as fresh *tagliolini cacio e pepe*, plus authentic *amatriciana*, tripe, and piquant chicken *alla cacciatora*. The grilled, roasted, or fried fish and seafood is remarkably fresh and flavorful, because the preparations are unfussy. The house-made desserts are lighter than what you find in many Roman trattorias, starting with the fresh apple tart, and the wine list, strong on regional bottlings, is longer and deeper, too. Expect to be surrounded by a few well-heeled Romans and, despite the unlikely location, many foreigners.

MONTE MARIO-PRISCIANO-BALDUINA

IN ROME, PILGRIMS STRIDE WITH MARTYR-LIKE JOY FROM CHURCH TO CHURCH, COVERING UNTOLD MILES, visiting untouristed, outlying parts of the city. But only determined ice cream fanatics will be willing to hike to the farther reaches of the Monte Mario district, aka Prisciano or Balduina, which is several miles north of the Vatican, past the hilltop microwave towers that are visible from anywhere in town. This is where you'll find the outwardly modest **Gelateria Quadrani** (Via Cecilio Stazio 2/Viale delle Medaglie d'Oro 419, Tel: 06 354 20407, open daily, starting mid-morning). In high season, you'll recognize the shop from a block away by the line of customers snaking out of the door and down the tree-lined, busy Viale delle Medaglie d'Oro, a main shopping street. Quadrani's classic ice creams, *semifreddi*, *granite*, and ice cream cakes are entirely handmade and natural, the ingredients the best the market can offer, and the prices as high as the market will bear. Quadrani has only been around since the early 2000s but already ranks alongside San Crispino, Gracchi, Al Settimo Gelo, and del Teatro ai Coronari. However, nowhere else will you find such simple, sublime, perfectly balanced egg-rich *crema* with lemon zest, or more chocolatey tartufo truffle chocolate ice cream chock-a-block with chocolate bits. In case you're already hobbled by gastronomic pilgrimages and feel you can't walk the distance, take a taxi or the 916 and 999 buses from Prati. They stop 50 yards uphill from Quadrani. Double back on Viale delle Medaglie d'Oro to Quadrani, buy a cone, and coast downhill back into town.

If you feel like comparing Quadrani with another very good neighborhood ice creamery, on the way downhill, detour two blocks west and stop at *gelateria* **Il Pellicano** (Via Ugo de Carolis 26/28, Tel: 06 354 50991, open starting mid-morning, one block north of Piazza Giovenale, facing the 990 bus stop). Its ice creams are also artisanal and old-fashioned, and remarkable, possibly even in the city's top 10, definitely in the top 20.

SAN GIOVANNI DI DIO–DONNA OLIMPIA

DUE SOUTH OF THE HANDSOME PARKLANDS OF VILLA DORIA PAMPHILI, EAST OF TRASTEVERE, THE Gianicolo, and Monteverde Nuovo, the slightly curving, gently inclined, tree-lined Via Federico Ozanam runs from Piazza Donna Olimpia to Piazza San Giovanni di Dio and the wide Circonvalazione Gianicolense. If you're exploring the park or Monteverde, you might want to consider detouring to Via Federico Ozanam for one of the best pizzerias in the city (open for dinner only), a very good coffee roaster, a fine pastry shop and *caffè*, and one of Rome's biggest, most popular, and least touristed open markets. For the rest of Monteverde, see area 7.

Mercato rionale di Piazza San Giovanni di Dio, where Circonvalazione Gianicolense meets Via Federico Ozanam, is a wholly ungentrified market, unchanged in appearance for the last 30 or 40 years, exception made for its ethnic food content and demographics. The square is hemmed by wonderfully hideous buildings from the 1960s and '70s, and the stands are weathered and funky. You'll see many Eastern Europeans and immigrants shopping here, cheek-by-jowl with Roman matrons and university students. The quality of the produce is very good, the prices hard to beat. A seller of salted anchovies pushes through the crowd with his cart, crying his wares, and he does so for real, not for a photo op. The mounds of vegetables and fruits are high, the voices of hawkers loud and convincing. If you want to experience a slice of working-class Rome circa 1970, this is the place. Tram #8 from Largo Argentina in the center of Rome stops on the edge of the square.

A few shopfronts away from the market, the scene changes, becoming markedly upscale. As you head down leafy Via Federico Ozanam you'll soon see **Dolci Desideri Gelateria** (#28/A), with delicious artisanal ice creams in all the traditional flavors, and **Dolci Desideri Pasticceria** (#36, Tel: 06 534 6602), with very good and sometimes very elaborate cakes, tarts, and pastries. Both are owned and operated by the same ambitious family that owns **Desideri & Caffè** (#25, Tel: 06 454 32786), the coffee shop directly across the street. It sells baked goods from

Dolci Desideri Pasticceria, serves surprisingly good Club Kavè coffee, and is the perfect place for a pick-me-up before or after visiting the market.

Between the Dolci Desideri ice creamery and the pastry shop facing the *caffè* is cult pizzeria **La Gatta Mangiona** (#30/30A/32, Tel: 06 534 6702, dinner only, closed August and Monday in low season, inexpensive to moderate). You'll recognize the yellow-and-blue sign, a line of people waiting, and, inside the brightly lit interior, the faces of delighted eaters, their mouths full of perfectly cooked pizza. The traditional, old-fashioned pizzas—*alla romana* or *margherita*, for instance—are the best of the bunch here, because the toppings don't get in the way of the amazingly light and crisp pizza dough, which has leavened for 24 hours. Even the heavier, spicy varieties with sausage meat and *peperoncino*, or buffalo-milk provola cheese and peppery speck, are easy to digest, however. Fried foods are another specialty. If you're a fan of creatively newfangled *supplì*, you'll delight in the variations of the fillings available here, from *porcini* to seafood, zucchini and zucchini flowers, to saffron and asparagus tips. The desserts are rich, from the creamy *tiramisù* to the various *semifreddi*, often served with warm chocolate sauce. There's decent Italian beer on tap, but also a surprisingly long wine list. Reserve ahead.

A few shopfronts down, next door to Dolci Desideri Pasticceria, is **Torrefazione Gasperini** (#38, Tel: 06 534 6194, closed Thursday afternoon and Sunday), a long-established coffee roaster run by a pair of certified curmudgeons. The Maragogype Arabica or Miscela Super (with Arabicas from Columbia, Santos, and Costa Rica) are remarkably good. Gasperini roasts his coffee dark, in small batches, regularly—no longer every day, but usually several times a week—and in the back of the shop you can see and smell the old roasting machine full of beans, churning like a cement mixer and chuffing like the *African Queen*.

PONTE MILVIO

THE PONTE MILVIO AREA ON CENTRAL ROME'S NORTHERN EDGE HAS A PROVINCIAL FEEL, AS IF A village of old had somehow wound up in the tentacles of a sprawling city. That's more or less what happened here. The bridge that gives the area its name joins the Flaminio and Parioli districts on the south side of the Tiber to the north side, where Piazzale di Ponte Milvio marks the junction of two ancient Roman highways. The Via Flaminia and Via Cassia consular roads meet here in a Y, cross Ponte Milvio and run straight south to Porta Flaminia and Piazza del Popolo. For nearly 2,200 years, traffic rumbled over the bridge. It no longer does. Ponte Milvio, a national monument, is fully pedestrianized, and has become a pilgrimage site for lovelorn youngsters, ever since it featured in the Italian hit novel *Ho voglia di te*, in which a young couple clamps a lock onto a railing on the bridge. Thousands of adolescents have followed suit, flocking here with locks and hearts in hand. Those who don't have a lock purchase one from the itinerant lock-peddlers with stands on the bridge, hocking their wares rain or shine. Scores of jilted lovers have gotten in on the act.

Many Romans call the bridge and area "Ponte Mollo." *Mollo* means soft or waterlogged and is a reference, it's claimed, to the rotting wooden bridge that was built here in the sixth century AD between the ruined pilings of the ancient span, which collapsed. In fact, the name Mollo is a corruption of the original, second-century BC name Molvius. Because the bridge was the main entry point into Rome for millennia, it has been the scene of famous battles, and has been rebuilt time and again. Giuseppe Garibaldi's troops, bent on freeing Rome from the papal grasp, dynamited sections of the bedraggled bridge in 1849.

The Ministry of Foreign Affairs, called La Farnesina, is on the Tiber's northern bank a quarter of a mile from the bridge, and many street names hereabouts recall its former incarnation as an aristocratic villa. The wide boulevard fronting the ministry is lined by handsome umbrella pines, and, closer to Prati, also passes by Mussolini's Foro Italico. This latter-day Fascist Forum and sports center, from the 1920s-'30s, looks startlingly like a pink Flamingo Motel decorated with outsized, camp statues, or a surreal De Chirico cityscape painted Peptobysmal pink.

Nowadays, Piazzale di Ponte Milvio is thronged at night by teenagers and night clubbers. The kiosk fronting the bridge is a cocktail bar and *caffè*. In warm weather it stays open until the early hours. There are several pizza joints, one nice old grocery store and milk bar, a could-be-anywhere *bisteccheria* steakhouse, and other anonymous hangouts. The premodern fruit-ice stand, **Grattachecca di Ponte Milvio** is near the steakhouse, on the sidewalk facing #26/27 Largo Maresciallo Diaz, which is what

THE WATERMELONS OF AUGUST

BEFORE THE DAYS OF CLIMATE CHANGE AND PAID VACATIONS, AUGUST WAS RELIABLY THE HOTTEST month in Rome. Many blue-collar Romans who could not afford a vacation sweated it out in the city. Ferragosto, the August 15th national holiday named after Augustus Caesar, was often the hottest day of all, a day for frozen coffee or fruit *granita* and *grattachecca* shaved ices dribbled with sweet syrup. Unexpectedly, given the calorie content, the favorite Ferragosto pasta was *bucatini all'amatriciana*. The requisite Ferragosto main course was chicken stewed with bell peppers—*pollo alla trasteverina*—a supreme luxury for the working class, right up to the economic boom of the 1960s.

August was and still is watermelon month in Rome: sidewalk stands run by *cocommerari* sell chilled slices of *anguria* or *cocomero*—two names for the same succulent delicacy. For years, on August 24th the annual Sagra dei cocomeri festival animated the banks of the Tiber Island and the bridges leading to it. Giant, ripe watermelons would be released into the river upsteam of the island, and Roman kids would dive in to grab them. The festival was stopped because too many youngsters drowned swimming after prize watermelons. Nowadays most Romans flee the sweltering summer city for beach or lakeside resorts, and foreign visitors have Rome to themselves. But many *cocommerari* stay on to sell sweet, chilled watermelons. Look for them on the boulevards that follow the Tiber, on Viale di Trastevere, at major Rome monuments such as the Coliseum, and along roads and highways in the city's outlying neighborhoods such as Ponte Milvio. The city's most famous *cocommeraro*, Dar Pistola, has his stand on Piazzale di Ponte Milvio facing the outdoor market and Il Gianfornaio, a bakery and *caffè*.

the southwestern edge of the square is called. Several other modish restaurants are on or near the northeastern edge of the square, including a sushi bar and a pretentious place with the predictable "creative" cooking and fish dishes certain politicos and VIPs demand.

One of Rome's most beloved fruit stands and watermelon sellers, **Cocommeraro Dar Pistola**, is here, just north of the newsstand, between the two *caffè* on the eastern side of the square, facing #s 39-43. You'll see the words in putative English "Happy Fruit by Pistola" written on the traffic-side façade of the stand. In summer, Dar Pistola stays open until 1am or 2am, hawking the ripest, sweetest watermelons in town. When it's artichoke season, Dar Pistola makes delicious fried *carciofi alla giudia*, using a portable deep fryer. See sidebar, The Watermelons of August (page 351), for more.

By day, the Ponte Milvio area is animated by shoppers, commuters, white-collar employees from the ministry, and a lively outdoor market, the **mercato rionale di Ponte Milvio**. It spreads from the east side of the square for about 100 yards along the sidewalks and median strip of Viale di Tor di Quinto. You'll find everything under the Italian sun at this market, plus plenty of exotic fruits and vegetables, and the usual sundries, cleaning products, and clothing. One stand worth seeking out is #38, **Bufala & Co.** (Tel: 339 772 5107, info@bufalaeco.it, open mornings Monday through Saturday). It's just east of the *piazzale*. The official Rome outlet for Tenuta dei Guitti, a farm in Campania, Bufala & Co. offers fresh, flavorful buffalo-milk mozzarella, treccia, and ricotta, delivered daily.

There's a *caffè*-kiosk at the market, but the best coffee served on the square is found at bakery-*caffè* **Il Gianfornaio** (Piazzale di Ponte Milvio 36, Tel: 06 333 3487, closed Sunday). Here you can sit indoors in comfortable booths, or on the outdoor terrace facing Dar Pistola, and sip an Illy espresso, or enjoy a delicious snack or light lunch. The Gianfornaio bakery is next door, on the corner of Via Flaminia Vecchia, but is also accessible from the *caffè* through a passageway. A maze of crowded, chaotic rooms, with bread, cookies, and cakes in the front, and *pizza bianca* and sandwiches in a small room in the back, the bakery throws up many a challenge to customers. Make sure to take a number when you come in. Number or not, once you have your fresh-baked *pane di Genzano* or *pane di Lariano*, your *crostata* and slices of *pizza bianca*, you'll have to fight your way to the cash register to pay.

About 100 yards east of the *piazzale* on Via Flaminia Vecchia, next to the Carabinieri (police) station, is cult pastry shop and *caffè* **Mondi** (Via Flaminia Vecchia 468, corner Via Bolsena, Tel: 06 333 6466, closed Monday). It boasts a covered terrace. Inside, the bar-top is green serpentine, the floors polished marble. Classy, conservative, and much less chaotic than Gianfornaio, Mondi is rightly celebrated for its exquisite frozen desserts, sidewalk sundaes, savory snacks, and light lunches, which are served not on paper but on fine china. Try a Mondino, which is a miniature ice cream bar hand-dipped in quality chocolate. Mondini are also presented in an edible basket of spun, caramelized nougat. The mini *tiramisù* pastry comes in a thimble-sized chocolate cup, and is designed to be popped into the mouth and enjoyed in one dazzling bite. Among the savory hot food, the *carciofi alla romana* are of the highest order. Note that at Mondi, a *genovese* is not a coffee, as it is at many other *caffè* in Rome; *genovesi* are finger sandwiches, available here with a variety of delicious fillings. If what you'd like is an espresso with a small amount of hot, frothed milk in it, ask for a *caffè macchiato caldo*—the standard Italian appellation for a *genovese*.

Even if the Ponte Milvio area had nothing else to recommend it, your detour here would be worthwhile to experience a meal at **Da Gnegno** (Via Prati della Farnesina 10, Tel: 06 333 6166, closed Sunday, inexpensive to moderate). Located next door to a garage, on a back street that curls northwest from the

square and intersects with Via della Farnesina, this archetypal Roman trattoria is named for Ennio—Gnegno in Romanaccio dialect. Ennio was the name of the original, and is also the current pater familias (and the husband of co-owner Daniela Cardinali). The same extended tribe has owned and operated the trattoria for five generations. Da Gnegno (pronounced dah nyen-yo) has a covered terrace, but the three-room interior is irresistible. You step in past an old buffet where the house white wine is dispensed on tap. In the main room stands the requisite self-service table piled with tempting appetizers—artichokes, slices of *frittata*, salads, *mozzarelline*, vegetable casseroles or grilled vegetables in olive oil, and more. On another buffet are the wonderful house-made desserts—*crostata con marmellata di visciole*, *zuppa inglese*, *torta di ricotta*. The food, ambience, and décor are reminiscent of the typical trattorias of old Rome, before the current age of gentrification and bohemian bourgeois slumming. The tablecloths are green-and-white checked, a TV set flickers, and the walls are hung with souvenirs of times gone by. Such times live on here, despite the odds. Family members weave among diners with panache and surprising joviality, dispensing good food and good cheer. The menu features traditional Roman dishes, naturally, and *the rigatoni alla carbonara* are among the best you'll find. The roast lamb, veal, or pork with roasted potatoes are exquisite. Note that lunch is served from 12:30pm, and dinner from 8pm.

If you can't get into Da Gnegno, a hundred yards away, around the corner, circling back toward Via Cassia and the north side of Piazzale di Ponte Milvio, you'll find the trendy neo-trattoria **Il Quinto Quarto** (Via della Farnesina 13, Tel: 06 333 8768, www.ilquintoquarto.it, closed Sunday and two weeks in mid-August, moderate). It has little to do with the working class, gutsy Quinto Quarto offal cuisine of the Testaccio district downstream and across the Tiber. This place styles itself an *osteria romana*, which it isn't, and attracts a predictably chic crowd, and lots of white-collars from La Farnesina. The downstairs dining room is somewhat cramped, but there's a long, narrow dining room on a covered terrace, whose white canvas sides give it a beach-bungalow feel. The chairs are of the kind once found in ice cream parlors—or public gardens—fashioned from curvy, wrought iron. There are several silly and overly ambitious dishes on the menu—fresh pasta with fresh fruit, for example, which is simply uneatable—but the *cacio e pepe* and the *carbonara* (made with very good *guanciale*) are excellent. Stick to the classic main courses and simple desserts and you'll be well served. The wine list is strong on regional bottlings.

Yet another fallback, if you can't get into either Da Gnegno or Quinto Quarto, is **Antica Trattoria Pallotta** (Piazzale di Ponte Milvio 23, Tel: 06 333 4245, closed Wednesday, inexpensive to moderate). There's a please-all menu, with a bit of everything on it, good pizza served at dinnertime, a pleasant glassed-in dining room with yellow tablecloths, and a big, ivy-covered pergola in the front yard. The place has been around since 1820, and as long as you're not expecting culinary fireworks, it's pleasant. Lunch is served starting at 12:45pm.

Directly across the square from Trattoria Pallotta is the area's best source for wine, **La Cantina XXIX** (Piazzale di Ponte Milvio 29, Tel: 06 333 3462, closed Sunday), a small shop that nonetheless has a wide range of Italian and some foreign wines. The choice of Lazio bottlings is limited. Practically next door, where Via Cassia joins the square, find **Fratelli Marcucci** (Piazzale di Ponte Milvio 26/Via Cassia 2, Tel: 06 333 3501, closed Monday morning and Sunday), a Sicilian pastry shop celebrated for its rich, creamy *pastiera napoletana* and natural, handmade ice creams, the best in the neighborhood. The fruit flavors are bright and sweet, the nut flavors—like the pastries—remarkably rich and creamy.

FLAMINIO

IF FROM PONTE MILVIO YOU DECIDE TO TAKE THE STREETCAR OR WALK THE MILE AND A HALF BACK to Porta Flaminia and Piazza del Popolo, you'll be in the Flaminio district, which abuts the tony Parioli district (which spreads on the hills due east). Stop en route at Piazzale Manila, near the Fine Arts Academy, and walk half a block toward the river. Here you'll find one of Rome's top coffee roasters, **Mister Coffee** (Via Fracassini 30, Tel: 06 320 7850, www.flaviamessina.it, closed Saturday afternoon from March to October, Sunday morning from November to April, and August). Mister should really be Madame or Signora Coffee, for the owner is Flavia Messina, an authentic coffee expert. She imports her beans and roasts them in small batches several times a week. Messina usually stocks five to eight varieties of Arabica from South America (Santos from Fazenda Exportadora de Cafè Guaxupè; Guatemala from Genuine Antigua Pastores; Costa Rica HTM from Exportadora de Cafè Tournon; Colombia Supremo 19 Medellin; and San Domingo Barahona Toral) and Africa (among them, a rather strong Ethiopian Moka Sidamo). She mixes and matches them to make blends for her regular customers. She also sells light, mild Costa Rican Caracolito—the pea-sized, round beans often used for making chocolate-coated coffee beans.

A few shopfronts west, toward the Tiber, is the upscale, handsome, traditional restaurant and pizzeria **Perilli al Flaminio** (Via Fracassini 36-40, Tel: 06 322 7591, closed Wednesday, moderate to expensive). A favorite among business people, politicians, and conservative Parioli residents, the tablecloths are white, and, like the service, starched, but the pizzas are good, and the Roman classics reliably edible. Lunch and dinner start early, by Roman standards: 12:30pm and 7:30pm, respectively.

One block north of Perilli, on a diagonal street that joins Piazzale Manila, is the casual, affordable **Pizzeria Vignola** (Via del Vignola 25/27, Tel: 06 322 7451, closed Wednesday, inexpensive to moderate). Everything is canary yellow, except, of course, the white collars of habitués. They come in for the perfect, crispy pizza baked in a wood-burning oven. The beer is on tap and the steaks or simple Roman and pan-Italian classics are good.

PIAZZA BOLOGNA

PIAZZA BOLOGNA IS A BIG TRAFFIC CIRCLE NORTHEAST OF THE SAN LORENZO NEIGHBORHOOD. THE piazza gives its name to one of Rome's typical outlying middle-class neighborhoods, built from the 1920s onward, with many buildings from the postwar era. Piazza Bologna was settled in the late 1960s by large numbers of Libyan and other North African Jews, and you'll find a smattering of ethnic bakeries, delis, and butcher shops here. There's nothing in particular to see, but if you want a taste of an authentic, absolutely untouristed part of the city, you'll be rewarded with high quality at several food-related addresses.

For one thing, the **mercato rionale di Via Catania** (between Via Pavia and Via de Mateis) is among the city's better local markets, with very good produce and a lively atmosphere. It's housed in a 1920s building that's light and airy, a typical example of Razionalista architecture. Across the street from it is **Pasta all'Uovo** (Via Catania 51), a *pasta fresca* shop, and at #77 on the same sidewalk you'll find **Favole di Pane**, a neighborhood bakery with good *crostata* and breads. The successful mini-chain of groceries, delis, and coffee roasters **Castroni** has an outlet here (Via Catania 54), and one of the extended **Volpetti** family's cousins also keeps a similar deli-style grocery shop right next door (Via Catania 58/60). Due north of the market a few hundred yards is **Salis Enoteca Romana** (Via Cremona 55, Tel: 06 442 44941, closed Sunday), an unpretentious bottle shop, in the Salis family since 1964. The selection isn't huge, and you won't find many top-flight wineries or high-priced wines, though there are some, including the inevitable imported bottles of champagne. Half a dozen Lazio wineries are usually featured.

Halfway between the Via Catania market and Piazza Bologna, on a major artery, **Limata** (Via Padova 26/28/30, Tel: 06 442 44121, closed Sunday) ranks among Rome's top *gastronomie*—it's the city's northeastern **E. Volpetti & C.**, if you will. Many regular customers will cross town to shop here, because the hams and cheeses are of the highest order, the selection of wines is good, and the cooked dishes, ready to be served at home, are remarkably delicious. They range from salads of all kinds to pickled vegetables under oil or broccoli rabe casserole ready to bake. Right next door is the good neighborhood bakery and pastry shop **L'Angolo delle Tentazioni** (Via Padova 20, Tel: 06 442 36733, closed Sunday), with all the Roman classics.

NON-TERROIR TOP OR TRENDY TABLES

AL CEPPO

VIA PANAMA 2, PARIOLI/PIAZZA UNGHERIA
TEL: 06 841 9696 ✦ WWW.RISTORANTEALCEPPO.IT
CLOSED MONDAY *and* 2 WEEKS *in* AUGUST ✦ VERY EXPENSIVE

AL PONTE DELLA RANOCCHIA

CIRCONVALLAZIONE APPIA 29, APPIO
TEL: 06 785 6712 ✦ WWW.PONTEDELLARANOCCHIA.IT
CLOSED SUNDAY ✦ EXPENSIVE

BABY

VIA ULISSE ALDOVRANDI 15, PARIOLI ✦ TEL: 06 321 6126
WWW.ALDOVRANDI.COM ✦ CLOSED MONDAY *and* 2 WEEKS *in* JANUARY ✦ EXTREMELY EXPENSIVE

GIUDA BALLERINO!

LARGO APPIO CLAUDIO 344, APPIO/TUSCOLANO/CINECITTÀ
TEL: 06 715 84807 ✦ WWW.GIUDABALLERINO.IT
DINNER ONLY *on* MONDAY, TUESDAY, *and* THURSDAY, CLOSED WEDNESDAY ✦ EXPENSIVE *to* VERY EXPENSIVE

LA PERGOLA DEL HOTEL HILTON CAVALIERI

VIA A. CADLOLO 101, MONTE MARIO ✦ TEL: 06 350 92152
WWW.CAVALIERI-HILTON.IT ✦ DINNER ONLY, CLOSED SUNDAY *and* MONDAY, AUGUST 10 *through* 25, *and* JANUARY 1 *through* 26
ASTRONOMICALLY EXPENSIVE

OSTERIA DEL GAMBERO ROSSO/CITTÀ DEL GUSTO

VIA ENRICO FERMI 161, GARBATELLA/MARCONI
TEL: 06 551 12277 ✦ CLOSED MONDAY DINNER *and* SUNDAY
MODERATE

PIAZZA CAPRERA

PIAZZA CAPRERA 5, NOMENTANA/VILLA PAGANINI
TEL: 06 853 53807 ✦ CLOSED SUNDAY, FIRST HALF *of* JANUARY *and* SECOND HALF *of* AUGUST ✦ EXPENSIVE

TRAMONTI E MUFFATI

VIA DI SANTA MARIA AUSILIATRICE 105, APPIO/TUSCOLANO/COLLI ALBANI ✦ TEL: 06 780 1342
DINNER ONLY, CLOSED SUNDAY ✦ EXPENSIVE

REGIONAL RESTAURANTS

CALABRIA

LA MIMOSA

VIA BARI 11A ✦ TEL: 06 442 91958 ✦ MODERATE
CLOSED WEDNESDAY *and* AUGUST

TUSCANY

PIZZERIA LA MORA

(see page 342)

ROME FOOD AND WINE GLOSSARY

ROMANS GENERALLY USE STANDARD ITALIAN NAMES FOR FOODSTUFFS AND DISHES; SOMEtimes, however, they also use Romanaccio dialect. The following glossary lists Roman favorites you're likely to encounter during your visit. It is not exhaustive. Note that names of dishes with an *alla romana* suffix indicate Roman classics (*fettuccine alla romana*); *alla trasteverina* indicates that the dish originated in the Trastevere neighborhood.

The standard Italian name (with plural form, where helpful) is followed by the dialect name (if commonly used), and an English translation or explanation. Where there is no standard Italian name, only the dialect name and English translation or explanation is given. Similarly, if there is no dialect name, only the Italian and English are given. Some foods have more than one name in standard Italian and dialect.

Abboccato: Wine that is slightly sweet.

Acciuga, alice, aliciotto: Anchovy. Many Roman recipes for vegetables and even meat dishes (*abbacchio in bianco alla cacciatora*) include salted anchovies. One popular fresh anchovy recipe is the Roman-Jewish *aliciotti con l'indivia*—baked anchovies with endives.

Aglio: Garlic. The Roman legions may have been fueled by garlic—the ancient expression *Ubi Roma, ibi allium* means where there are Romans there's garlic—but, contrary to common belief, contemporary Roman cooks use garlic sparingly, often hand-crushing it and barely browning it to flavor olive oil and then throwing it away. Romans eschew raw garlic, except when rubbed on *bruschetta*, or in the dressing for a salad of *puntarella* (see entry below). The favorite local variety of garlic has pink skin and is firm and full of essential oils.

Abbacchio: Suckling lamb. Favorite recipes for lamb include *abbacchio scottadito* (grilled chops), whose name derives from burn (*scottare*) and finger (*dito*); *abbacchio al forno con patate* (roasted, with garlic and rosemary, and potatoes); *abbacchio brodettato* (braised in broth with white wine, herbs, lemon juice, beaten egg yolks, and pecorino romano); *coratella con carciofi* (sautéed offal, with slivered artichoke hearts); *pajata d'abbacchio* (tiny, milk-filled lamb intestines cooked with tomato sauce and served with rigatoni, or simply grilled); *cervelli fritti* (battered, deep-fried lamb's brain, sometimes served with sliced fried artichokes); *testarelle d'abbacchio* (whole lamb's head split open, sprinkled with salt, pepper, and rosemary, and oven roasted).

Agrodolce: Sweet and sour. In Rome, that usually means the dish has been made with raisins or prunes and white wine vinegar.

Amabile: Semi-sweet wine.

Amatriciana, all'amatriciana, matriciana: The favorite red sauce of Rome, used to top bucatini or rigatoni. It's made with canned (or fresh) tomatoes, red or white wine, olive oil, chili, *guanciale* (or *pancetta*) and pecorino romano. Purists do not use either garlic or onions.

Animelle: Sweetbreads, usually of veal or lamb. In Rome, they are grilled or pan fried.

Arancini di farro: Fried dumplings or golf-ball sized rounds made of *farro* risotto, eaten as an appetizer. *Arancini* originate in Sicily, where they are a very different proposition.

Arzilla, minestra di arzilla e broccolo romano: The word *arzilla* is Romanaccio dialect for the Italian term *razza* (skate). This is skate soup with minaret broccoli and chili. Also in dialect, *arzilla* means someone who is vigorous. That's why many Romans, who eat this Canonical favorite on Fridays, consider *minestra di arzilla* a zingy, pick-me-up dish.

Asciutto: Dry wine. When applied to dry pasta, the term is *pastasciutta.*

Bocconotti di ricotta: Cinnamon-flavored ricotta fingercakes with lemon zest and a shortbread crust. *Bocconcini* are the Jewish-Roman version of the recipe, and additionally contain raisins and pine nuts.

Baccalà: Salt cod. Salt cod is very popular in Rome. The favorite way of preparing it is Roman-Jewish sweet-and-sour *baccalà in agrodolce* (with raisins, parsley, onion, garlic, white wine, white wine vinegar, sugar, plum tomatoes, apple slices, prunes, lemon zest, and pine nuts).

Broccolo romano, broccolo romanesco: Broccoli. This typically Roman broccoli (*Brassica oleracea Minaret*) has a spiraling chartreuse-hued head shaped like the top of a conch shell or minaret, with hundreds of tiny florets each reproducing the spiraling conch-shell effect. Hence the variant's qualifier: minaret.

Broccoletti, cime di rapa: Broccoli rabe. Actually a turnip, this cousin of cabbage and broccoli is officially *Brassica rapa Broccoli Raab.* It's grown for its flowering shoots that look like immature regular broccoli, but have subtler flavor and scent. In Rome broccoli rabe is usually sautéed in olive oil with garlic and hot chili pepper, though it's also boiled and dressed with raw olive oil and lemon or vinegar.

Bruschetta: Toast rubbed with raw garlic, drizzled with olive oil, and sprinkled with salt. The word is pronounced broos ketta (in Italian, ch is pronounced like a k). *Bruschetta* now comes with a wide variety of toppings.

Brutte ma buone, brutti ma buoni: Meringue drop-cookies made with crushed hazelnuts and lemon zest. The name means "ugly but good."

Cacciatora, alla cacciatora: In Rome, *cacciatora*-style preparations usually include white wine and white wine vinegar and are often further defined as *in bianco* (white, because they do not contain tomatoes). They have a sweet-and-sour piquancy. The most popular *cacciatora* dish is *abbacchio* or *agnello alla cacciatora* (lamb) and, when made by certain chefs, also contains a tiny amount of salted anchovy or anchovy paste.

Calato, calati: Literally "lowered" into a bath of liquid to be braised, usually vegetables cooked in this way. The most common recipe is for cauliflower or broccoli *calati con vino e bucce d'arancia*, i.e. braised in red wine with orange peel.

Capperi: Capers. Rome's city walls and many of its stone monuments are home to countless clinging caper shrubs, *Capparis spinosa*, and cognoscenti claim the Aurelian city walls between the Porta San Lorenzo city gate and the Ministry of Aeronautics produce the most succulent specimens. They thrive in cracks and crevices producing delicate white blossoms—when the blossoms aren't nipped in the bud. That's because capers are the immature buds of the caper bush.

Carciofo: Artichoke. Roman artichokes are large, tender, and shaped like a scaly globe. They are used in many recipes. Favorites include fried *carciofi alla giudia* and braised *carciofi alla romana* (with garlic, wild mint, parsley, and white wine). *Carciofi alla matticella* are whole baby or wild artichokes roasted in embers.

Carne secca: Also called *prosciutto di manzo* or *prosciutto ebraico*, this Roman-Jewish specialty is salted, pepper-coated breast of beef that is cured for 40 days.

Castagna: Chestnut. The ancient Romans planted two types of trees wherever they went: olives and chestnuts. Parts of Lazio are still forested with groves planted in Antiquity, though the original trees have long since died. Roman chestnuts are small, sweet, and dark brown verging on black. They're primarily used to make *castagnaccio*.

Castagnaccio: A naturally sweet, chestnut-flour tart with raisins, pine nuts, fennel seeds, or rosemary and olive oil, sold in certain Roman bakeries. *Castagnaccio salato* is the savory version of the recipe, and contains wheat flour mixed with chestnut flour, seasoned with rosemary and salt.

Ceci: Chickpeas, garbanzo beans. The essential ingredient in *pasta e ceci*, a long-cooked stew of short pasta with chickpeas, often with a pinch of salted anchovy.

Checca, alla checca: Elbow pasta with raw chopped tomatoes, basil, capers, olives, and fennel seeds, a summertime dish, usually served at room temperature.

Ciambelline: Three-inch diameter lifesaver-shaped hard cookies made for dunking into wine. *Ciambelline* contain olive oil, not butter, and are sometimes flavored with cinnamon, white wine, fennel seeds, or aniseeds.

Cicoria: Chicory. The Romans eat enormous amounts of chicory (*Chichorium intybus*), favoring three types, two of them cutting leaf chicories, the third head or sprouting chicory (*puntarella*). Chicories are not endives (*Chichorium endivia*), though many people confuse the two. They're merely the same genus (*Chicorium*). The two Italian cutting chicories are *Chicorium intybus Spadona*, alias Spadona chicory, with long, pea-green mule-ear leaves that look similar to sorrel; or *Chicorium intybus Dentarella*, alias Catalogna, Catalonia, Italian Dandelion or cutting chicory Dentarella, which looks like an outsized dandelion, with slightly serrated, dark green leaves. Both of these chicories are tangy and are boiled before being sautéed in olive oil with garlic and chili—*cicoria in padella*. See also *puntarella*.

Cipolle di Tropea: Romans prefer mild onions, favoring small to medium-sized white or red onions. The most prized local red onion is from the town of Tropea, and you will often see this fact mentioned on menus, especially in gourmet restaurants.

Cipolline in agrodolce alla romana: Sweet-and-sour pearl onions, with garlic, olive oil, vinegar, and salt.

Coda, coda alla vaccinara: Roman oxtail stew, with celery and tomatoes, seasoned with cloves.

Corallina: A long, medium-fresh *salame* with pea-sized chunks of fat, eaten primarily at Eastertide.

Concia di zucchine: Zucchini sautéed with vinegar and chili, in the style of the Roman-Jewish Ghetto.

Coppiette: Often called *coppiette secche*, this is Roman beef or horse jerky, usually found in the Jewish-Roman Ghetto, but rare nowadays because of EU health laws.

Coratella: The inner organs of milk-fed lamb or veal, often sautéed with onion or artichoke.

Cornetto (pl. cornetti): Croissant, breakfast roll. The Roman version of the croissant, called *brioche* elsewhere in Italy, was popularized during the French occupation of Rome under Napoleon. *Cornetti* come filled with jam, chocolate, or pastry cream. For a plain *cornetto* ask for *un cornetto liscio*. Breakfast rolls are also called *lieviti* (because they're leavened with *lievito*, yeast or baking powder). A *cornetteria* is a pastry shop or bar specializing in *cornetti*. Often, Roman *cornetti* are very sweet, and tend to have a tougher texture than those found in France or America. They're usually made with at least 50-percent vegetable shortening, not pure butter.

Cremolato: Crushed fresh fruit that is frozen to make a sherbet-like dessert.

Crostata alla romana: The iconic Roman jam tart with a shortbread crust and, often, a trellis of crust atop the jam, often made with sour cherries (*marmelata di visciole*).

Crostini: Mini-toasts, often spread with anchovy butter and topped with melted provolone.

Dolce (pl. dolci): Sweet. Sweet wine and sweets (desserts).

Ebraica: Jewish, often added to the name of a food or recipe to distinguish it from similar Roman non-Jewish recipes (*pizza dolce ebraica*, for instance).

Farro: Hulled wheat. In English *farro* has a confusing array of names, including emmer, einkorn, and spelt. All three are varieties of the vast class of primitive hulled wheats, the ancestor of modern wheat. Italian *farro* made up of *Triticum dicoccum* (sometimes spelled *dicoccon*) is used to make *arancini di farro* balls (see entry). That's because spelt (*Triticum spelta*), a type of hulled wheat sometimes imprecisely called *farro* instead of its precise names (*gran farro*, *scandela*, *spelta*, *spelda*, and *pire spelte*), isn't starchy enough to stick together and be rolled into balls.

Fava: Similar to, though not necessarily the same as broad beans, *favas* are a springtime treat in Rome and are eaten raw, sautéed, stewed, or in soups.

Fettuccine alla romana: The classic Sunday pasta, *fettuccine alla romana* features a startlingly rich sauce made with sausages, short ribs, ground beef, chicken livers, and tomatoes.

Finocchio, finocchiello: Fennel. Wild fennel (*Foeniculum vulgare piperitum*) is a weed in and around Rome. Its delicately liquorish-perfumed fronds, peppery seeds, and bulbs find their way into many dishes.

Fiori di zucca, zucchina: See *zucchino*.

Fritti: Romans love fried foods. A centuries-old saying claims that everything fried is delicious "even a stick." Often called *pezzetti*, most Roman *fritti* (literally fried foods) are fresh vegetables such as broccoli, sliced bell pepper, zucchini, or zucchini flowers, deep-fried in olive oil. Salt cod is also a favorite food that is fried, though usually it is called *filetti di baccalà*. When vegetables, apples and other fruit, and, sometimes, meat, are part of a *fritto misto* (mixed fry), the combination is usually called *fritto misto all'italiana*.

Frizzante: Slightly sparkling, bubbly, effervescent. Refers to wine and mineral water.

Funghi: Mushrooms. Usually *funghi* are wild mushrooms, including *porcini* and many other species. *Funghi secchi* are dry mushrooms. *Funghi sotto'olio* are preserved in olive oil.

Fusaie: *Lupinus albus* is the scientific name for the white lupin, whose pale beans are brined and eaten as a snack. Now rare, they used to be sold by dozens of street-corner stands throughout central Italy.

Galletto alla diavola: Spicy whole game hen split open and grilled flat, flavored with lemon juice, garlic, rosemary, bacon, and chili.

Gallinaccio: In Romanaccio dialect, turkey (*tacchino*) is called *gallinaccio*. The most common way to prepare turkey in Rome is *in tegame*, i.e. braised in white wine and chicken or turkey broth, with fresh herbs, and *pancetta* or *guanciale*.

Garofolato: Rump roast with cloves and bacon. *Garofolo* is Romanaccio dialect for clove, the main flavoring agent used in this long-cooked stew, which, as a leftover, is often used to dress fresh pasta.

Giugata: Fresh ewe's-milk cheese made from curds that float to the surface, are skimmed off, shaped into pats and presented on fig leaves.

Gnocchi di semolino alla romana: These are not the potato-gnocchi found in Rome and elsewhere, but rather oven-baked semolina gnocchi dressed with butter and parmigiano-reggiano.

Graté di alici: A corruption of the French word gratin, *graté* is usually a garlicky gratin of fresh anchovies.

Grattachecca: Shaved ice flavored with mint or fruit syrup and sold from a *grattachecca* sidewalk stand. The word is a conflation of "*Gratta, 'Checca*!" which means, "Shave (or grate), Francesca!" Presumably, Francesca's job was to shave the ice.

Gricia, alla gricia: Also called *amatriciana in bianco*, *gricia* (a bastardization of *grigio*, gray) is *amatriciana* without tomatoes. The ingredients are *guanciale*, chili, and pecorino romano.

Guanciale: Romans make extravagant use of cured pork jowl (*guancia* means cheek or jowl) and purists claim that without it authentic *amatriciana* and *carbonara* are impossible. *Guanciale* has a delicate, sweet taste halfway between that of bacon and lard. Roman *guanciale* is cured and aged in the same way as Roman *pancetta*, which is pork belly or unsmoked bacon. First it's brined in vats of coarse sea salt with coarsely ground black pepper and/or shredded chili. Then it's air-dried. In Rome, *guanciale* is rarely smoked, as it is in some other parts of Italy.

Involtini, involtini di manzo: Rolled beef with carrots and celery inside, often cooked in a tomato sauce or in the left-over sauce from oxtail stew. *Involtini* can also be vegetable rolls, made with bell peppers or eggplant.

Lattarini: Tiny, freshwater fingerlings that are eaten whole, usually after frying and pickling.

Lesso: The word means "boiled," and *lesso ripassato in padella* is Rome's homey, delicious boiled poultry or beef that is then sautéed with chicory and chili.

Marignani, malignani, melanzane: Eggplants. Nineteenth-century Romanaccio poet G. G. Belli first applied the term *Marignani* (sometimes deformed to *malignani*) to eggplants, which are called *melanzane* in standard Italian. Prelates of the lowest order were called Marignani, and their robes were an eggplant color, their bodies an eggplant shape. The term is still used today among Romans. Eggplants stuffed with breadcrumbs, grated cheese, and herbs (or meat) are a summer favorite, thought to have originated in the Trastevere district of Rome and therefore called *melanzane* (or *Marignani) alla trasteverina.*

Maritozzi: The classic Roman sweet, fluffy, leavened bun, split open and filled with whipped cream. Old-fashioned *maritozzi* are more dense, and flavored with raisins, pine nuts, and dry or candied fruit.

Mascarpone: This creamy, luscious northern Italian cow's milk cheese goes into several Roman desserts, notably *tiramisù.*

Mazzancolle: Large Mediterranean prawns, called *gamberi, gamberoni, scampi,* or *scamponi* elsewhere in Italy.

Misticanza: A peppery, flavorful blend of cultivated and wild arugula varieties, plus up to five different varieties each of chicory and endive, baby borage, watercress, baby lettuces, and field greens. The contents of *misticanza* vary widely. It can also be a mixture of primarily wild field greens that are cooked before being eaten (usually boiled, drained, and pan-fried with garlic and chili, like chicory).

Mosso: Slightly effervescent. Refers to wine.

Mostaccioli: Extremely hard honey candies that come in many shapes, and are also sometimes covered with chocolate.

Mozzarella: The Campania region neighboring Rome and Latium, specifically the Caserta and Salerno districts, is justly famous for its water buffalo milk mozzarella. However Rome's region turns out excellent fior di latte cow's milk mozzarella and limited quantities of water buffalo milk mozzarella from dairy farms around Frosinone, Sperlonga, and Anzio, all south of Rome. According to Italian law, the only true mozzarella is made with water buffalo milk. It has a lot more liquid and fat (8 to 9 percent compared to 3 to 4 percent) and consequently a shorter shelf life than the cow's milk product. That and the cost are why most Romans use fior di latte for cooking and buy buffalo mozzarella for eating.

Olive ascolane: Stuffed, fried olives, originally from Ascoli-Piceno.

Padellotto: *Il padellotto* is a frying pan full of hearty sautéed inner organs.

Pajata: Usually *pajata d'abbacchio*, the milk-filled intestines of suckling lamb; *pajata di vitello* (veal) is no longer available in EU countries. *Pajata* is cooked with tomato sauce and served with rigatoni, or grilled and sprinkled with salt and pepper.

Palombo: Shark. Rare now, shark used to be found on many trattoria menus, and was often sautéed with peas or *favas.*

Pancetta: In Rome *pancetta* is pork belly bacon cured with sea salt and black pepper; it is rarely herbed. *Pancetta affumicata* is smoked *pancetta*, a.k.a. bacon. It's sold in thick or thin slices, like bacon, and not in rolls, as is the case in some other parts of Italy. Some chefs prefer *pancetta* over *guanciale* for making *amatriciana* or *carbonara.*

Pancotto: Now rare, this Roman bread soup, a cousin of Tuscan *pàppa al pomodoro* and *panzanella* salad, is often made with tomatoes and spicy sautéed chicory.

Pangiallo: A dense, sticky loaf of candied fruit, dry fruit, and nuts.

Panpepato: A firm finger-cookie flavored with black pepper and sweetened with honey.

Passito: Sweet or semi-sweet wine made from dried grapes or raisins.

Pecorino romano: Aged ewe's milk cheese, used for grating, and popular in many Roman dishes.

Penne all'arrabbiata: Short pasta quills sauced with tomatoes, chili, and *pancetta.* The recipe is similar to *bucatini all'amatriciana* and probably comes from the Apennines of central Italy.

Peperonata: In Rome, a stew of red and yellow bell peppers, onions, and tomatoes, with garlic and bayleaf or chili.

Pezzetti natalizzi: Battered and deep-fried cardoons, eggplant, zucchini, artichokes, borage, parsley, nettle tips, mushrooms, cauliflower, and broccoli. Sometimes salt cod or lamb brains are added to the mixture. See *fritti.*

Picchiapò: Chunks of boiled beef that are sautéed with onions, tomatoes, and a pinch of chili.

Pizza bianca: An olive-oil based flatbread similar to focaccia but crispier, more porous, and thinner, which is usually eaten plain, and sometimes brushed with olive oil.

Pizza dolce, pizza di Civitavecchia: An airy, lightly sweetened angel food cake, flavored with Marsala, vanilla, cocoa, and aniseed.

Pizza dolce ebraica: A light, porous coffee cake with raisins, candied fruit, and dry fruit.

Pizza pasquale, torta salata: A savory bread baked at Eastertide, usually made with chunks of provolone cheese, ham, *mortadella*, and pitted olives.

Polipi in padella alla Luciana: Also spelled *alla lucana.* Baby octopus stewed in a spicy tomato sauce. The recipe probably comes from the Lucania region south of Rome. *Polipo* is the Romanaccio bastardization of *polpo*, the proper Italian word for octopus.

Pollo coi peperoni alla romana: Chicken parts Roman-style, sautéed with onions, sweet peppers, and tomatoes. Also called *pollo alla trasteverina.*

Porchetta: Spit-roasted whole pig, usually stuffed with rosemary or fennel and garlic.

Porchettato: A cooking technique similar to larding, i.e. wrapping in bacon, as if making *porchetta.* Often pork roasts, veal, game, and poultry are *porchettato.*

Puttanesca: A piquant, spicy sauce made with capers, tomatoes, olives, and anchovies, usually used to top spaghetti, and probably originally from the Naples area, but now firmly established in Rome.

Puntarella, insalata di puntarelle: Among Rome's favorite salad greens, usually dressed with garlicky anchovy dressing, *puntarella* is a type of sprouting chicory that produces tender spears.

Quadrucci: Tiny squares of fresh pasta, stirred into soup or broth.

Ricotta: Ricotta di pecora or ricotta romana is made from the whey of ewe's milk, a byproduct of pecorino romano, and is rich and flavorful. It's eaten plain, with sugar sprinkled on top, or mixed with other ingredients sweet or savory in many recipes, notably *torta di ricotta*—Roman-Jewish cheesecake.

Ripieno, ripieni: Stuffed vegetables, usually tomatoes or eggplants.

Rosato: Rosé wine.

Rucola, rughetta: Arugula (*Diplotaxis erucoides Arugula Selvatica and Eruca sativa Arugula*). A spicy, peppery tiny lettuce, Roman arugula comes in two basic types, wild (*selvatica*) and cultivated (*sativa*). Romans have always prized wild arugula (Marcus Valerius Martialis, better known as Martial, wrote of its aphrodisiac qualities when describing a contemporary first-century AD dinner). *Rucola selvatica* is almost always eaten raw, mixed with other lettuces or herbs in salads such as *misticanza.*

Rustico (pl. rustici): A rustic *calzone* or folded, filled turnover-like pizza. They're made with *pizza bianca* dough and filled with ham and provolone, pan-fried chicory with garlic and hot chili, spinach and ricotta, or sautéed artichokes. Many Romans consider *rustici* snacks, or eat them instead of a *panino* at lunch.

Salame romano: Beef salami, from the Jewish-Roman Ghetto.

Saltimbocca alla romana: Veal rolls with *guanciale*, *pancetta*, or Parma ham and fresh sage, sautéed with olive oil or butter and white wine.

Scafata: See *vignarola.*

Scrocchiarella: A crisp, thin, wavy flatbread of that name, or a "normal" pizza or *pizza bianca* that is very crisp and thin.

Secco: Dry. Refers to wine, salami, cheese, and other products.

Seppie coi carciofi: Small squid sautéed with sliced artichokes, white wine, and garlic. When squid are stuffed with breadcrumbs, beaten eggs, and garlic, they're called *seppie ripiene*, and are usually stewed with peas (*coi piselli*).

Sott'oli, sottoli: Literally "under oil," meaning mushrooms, baby artichokes, or other vegetables and, occasionally, fish or cheese, preserved in olive oil. (*Sott'aceti* are foods pickled in vinegar.)

Spinaci in padella alla trasteverina: Spinach sautéed in a frying pan (*padella*) with raisins and pine nuts, in the style of Trastevere.

Spumante: Sparkling wine.

Spuntature: Short ribs, usually of pork.

Stracciatella: Egg-drop soup.

Stracotto di manzo: Slow-cooked beef pot roast, invented or popularized by Rome's Jewish community.

Strascinato, strascinati: The technique of pan-frying an already cooked food, usually vegetables, with garlic, olive oil, and chili. The most popular such dish is *broccoletti strascinati*, pan-fried broccoli rabe, or *cicoria strascinata.*

Supplì: Fried tomato-flavored risotto rice croquettes stuffed with mozzarella (and, occasionally, other fillings, from ham to provolone). Often called *supplì al telefono*, because when you bite into them the cheese inside oozes out and forms what looks like a telephone cord. *Supplì* is an Italian bastardization of the French surprise.

Tartufo: In the rest of Italy, *tartufo* simply means truffle; in Rome it also means the chocolate-studded chocolate truffle ice cream invented by Tre Scalini on Piazza Navona and now widely imitated.

Tiramisù: The *tiramisù* that's found in Rome and all over Italy and the rest of the planet is usually flavored with coffee and powdered chocolate. Rome also makes versions with fresh strawberries (*con le fragole*) or oranges (*con le arance*). Note that Italians spell the word with an accent over the U.

Torta ebraica di ricotta: Jewish-Roman ricotta cheesecake, usually flecked with sour cherry jam or chocolate chips.

Tozzetti: Simple Roman-Jewish cookies, usually with almond shavings, similar to Tuscan *cantucci*.

Tramezzini: Triangular white bread finger sandwiches eaten as snacks and to accompany cocktails. They're filled with everything from ham and cheese to spinach and ricotta, arugula and tomatoes, or mozzarella and sautéed button mushrooms.

Trippa alla romana: Tripe cooked in tomato sauce with chili, seasoned with fresh spearmint, and then sprinkled with grated pecorino romano shortly before serving.

Uova in trippa: *Frittata* strips topped with a spicy tomato sauce, with fresh mint and pecorino romano.

Vignarola: A spring stew of fresh peas, artichokes, favas, spring onions, and, optionally, new potatoes and/or *pancetta* and/or *guanciale*. When *vignarola* contains *pancetta* and/or *guanciale* and chili it is usually called *scafata*.

Visciola, visciole: Sour cherries, nearly always transformed into jam (*marmelata*) and used to top *crostata*.

Zabaglione, zabaione: The ubiquitous sweetened egg custard, flavored with Marsala, is usually served warm in Rome, though it can also be a custard cream filling for cold desserts and pies. It was probably invented in Sicily, but has been part of the Roman repertoire for a century or more.

Zucchino/zucchina (pl. zucchini/zucchine), fiori di zucchina, fiori di zucca: Italian squash and zucchini or squash flowers/blossoms. Roman zucchini (*zucchine romanesche*) are pea green, shortish (4 to 5 inches), and fluted like marble columns, the paler the better. The large, dark-green zucchini sold in Rome's markets generally come from Southern Italy or Sicily. Zucchini wind up in many Roman dishes. When *trifolati* they are simply sautéed and served in olive oil, often with fresh mint or basil. Marinated or done in a *concia*, in the style of the Jewish Ghetto, means they have been sautéed with vinegar and chili. Zucchini or squash flowers are usually stuffed with mozzarella and salted anchovy, dipped in batter, and deep fried (*fiori di zucca fritti*). There are two types of zucchini flowers. Female flowers come attached to the zucchini fruit and are considered inferior in flavor; Romans use them in sauces. Male flowers are bigger and firmer, growing on long hairy stems that never bear fruit; they are stuffed and fried or used to top pizzas. Zucchini flowers have thicker, longer pistils than other kinds of squash flowers.

Zuppa inglese: A creamy spoon dessert, like a trifle, usually made with sponge cake or ladyfingers, Marsala, jam, and powdered chocolate.

BIZERBA
MDS

A
SI·PREGA·DI·NON·TOC
I·FIORI
GRAZI

INDEX

A

B

C

N

O

P

RESTAURANTS

SERVING REGIONAL FOOD

ABOUT THE AUTHOR

David Downie is an American author and journalist who divides his time between France and Italy. For the last 20 years he has been writing about European food, culture and travel for magazines and newspapers worldwide. His books include *Enchanted Liguria: A Celebration of the Culture, Lifestyle and Food of the Italian Riviera*; *Cooking the Roman Way: Authentic Recipes from the Home Cooks and Trattorias of Rome*; *The Irreverent Guide to Amsterdam*; and *Paris, Paris: Journey into the City of Light.* His political thriller, *Paris City of Night*, will be published in fall 2008. *Hit the Road Jacques: A Skepitcal Pilgrimage Across Burgundy* is due out in spring 2009, as is Downie's second Terroir Guide, this one to Rome. Please visit David Downie's website at www.davidddownie.com.

ABOUT THE PHOTOGRAPHER

Alison Harris has worked throughout the world shooting photos for travel books, cookbooks, advertising campaigns, book covers, and magazine stories. Her latest books, *Markets of Paris*, *The Pâtisseries of Paris*, and *Chic Shopping Paris*, are published by The Little Bookroom.